W9-ASW-092

Through the Window, Out the Door

THROUGH THE WINDOW, OUT THE DOOR

Women's Narratives of Departure,
from Austin and Cather
to Tyler, Morrison,
and Didion

Janis P. Stout

THE UNIVERSITY OF ALABAMA PRESS
Tuscaloosa and London

Copyright © 1998
The University of Alabama Press
Tuscaloosa, Alabama 34587–0380
All rights reserved
Manufactured in the United States of America

Library of Congress Cataloging-in-Publication Data

Stout, Janis P.
    Through the window, out the door : women's narratives of
  departure, from Austin and Cather to Tyler, Morrison, and Didion /
  Janis P. Stout.
        p.   cm.
    "This volume is an extension and rebuttal of earlier book : The
  journey narrative in American literature, published in 1983."
    Includes bibliographical references and index.
    ISBN 0–8173–0908–X (cloth)
    1. American fiction—Women authors—History and criticism.
  2. Women and literature—United States—History—20th century.
  3. American fiction—20th century—History and criticism.
  4. Separation (Psychology) in literature.   5. Farewells in
  literature.   6. Travel in literature.   7. Narration (Rhetoric)
  8. Home in literature.   I. Title.
  PS374.W6S78   1998
  813'.509353—dc21   97–31425

British Library Cataloguing-in-Publication Data available

For my daughters, daughters-in-law, and virtual daughters

CONTENTS

PREFACE

She came forth like a bird that got loose
suddenly from its cage.
Out of the cage came Eve,
escaping, escaping.
                    —Anne Sexton

This volume is an extension and in one sense a rebuttal of my own earlier book *The Journey Narrative in American Literature: Patterns and Departures,* published in 1983. An extension because there is obviously so much more to be said. A rebuttal because that earlier book was, as I now see it, so overwhelmingly masculine in focus. Since that time, as my interests as a reader and as a scholar have come to center more and more on the writings of women and the intellectual issues that surround them, I have seen more and more clearly both how important and how differently inflected journeys are in the lives and the narratives of women.[1] One of the chief of these differences is the insistence with which journeys are linked to home bases, to houses, in an inseparable dyad. In *Through the Window, Out the Door,* my purpose is to read the tropes of departure and journey that structure the works of a number of American women writers of the twentieth century for whom both elements in that dyad—home and venture, the private and the public—are powerfully and centrally important. In women's writings of this century, in the United States, female characters seem to be, to borrow the words of Rainer Maria Rilke, "for ever taking leave," forever manifesting "the air of somebody departing." The passage from which these words are taken is both a beautiful and a problematic one, and I want to quote it in order to make an important point. From Rilke's Eighth Duino Elegy:

Who's turned us round like this, so that we always,
do what we may, retain the attitude
of someone who's departing? Just as he,

on the last hill, that shows him all his valley
for the last time, will turn and stop and linger,
we live our lives, for ever taking leave.[2]

Just who, I want to ask, does Rilke mean by "us" and "we"? Humanity, probably. And in some translations the masculine pronoun referring to the unnamed traveler (the "he"/"him" in the third and fourth lines) is avoided, so as to support that inclusive meaning. But in the original German the pronoun is there: *er,* insistently asserting the masculinity of the traveler. Of course, one can choose to read the masculine pronoun as being "really" a neutral or inclusive one. Women have been reading masculine pronouns that way for a very long time. In that way, we, too, are or can be wayfarers, even in a poem that says *er.* But then we are not only, like the exemplary male traveler in Rilke's verses, unnamed, we are ungendered as well; in effect, written out of the equation.

But in the American literature of the twentieth century written by women, we are not the ungendered wayfarers that Rilke's poem would require. Instead, we are insistently gendered ones. That is my point, and it is a point I will be making throughout these pages. The air of departure on journeys is pervasive in the narratives of the writers I will discuss here; their narrative focus, time after time, text after text, is on the moment at which departure occurs; and that moment, that air of departure, pervades the text in an insistently gendered way. What this may mean is, of course, not only richly varied but often quite subtle. Often it entails a tension between the urge to break out, to shake the dust from one's feet, and an equally powerful homing urge, an urge to construct and maintain and to value relational ties. Often, too, it entails a gendered rereading of history and a determination to move into history—that is, an urge to move from a (relatively) private sphere of activity to a public and politically engaged one. The tension between these conflicting urges, between a centrifugal and a centripetal force underlying narrative action, is a dynamically energizing one in the texts I will examine here.

When the moment of departure from the imprisoning/comforting structure is envisioned as the moment of greatest significance, it becomes a moment of culmination. I have wondered in an earlier essay whether women writers—specifically, women poets—create images of departure because, as the heirs of a long tradition of imprisonment in houses and domestic roles, they have difficulty projecting the fulfillment of journeys.[3] That idea, however, I no longer find persuasive. True, as women, they must seal their departure from the constraints of the past (in Annis Pratt's words, "turn away from a culture hostile to their development") before they can envision the completion of their own journeys and those of their sisters.[4] The moment of departure is an essential moment of truth. But the shape and nature of the journey in women's writings are more complex than that terse summary allows. As I now read it, and will write of it here in relation to a group of five central figures and a number of contextualizing figures, departure gains its importance (indeed, its centrality) in women's writing from the resonance with which it can be used in pondering not only the imprisoning hand of the past but also a number of provocative intersections. These would include, at minimum, the intersection of gender with narrative form—that is, of feminine/feminist gender with a traditionally masculine story emphasizing heroism and conquest; the intersection of departure from past roles (temptress, wife, mother) with recognition of the distinctive resources provided by those roles; the intersection of the drive toward self-realization with the need to maintain secure relational identity; the intersection of that same drive with skepticism toward such concepts as self-realization, purpose aforethought, and individual freedom; and the intersection of the need for secure personal grounding with the urge to undertake a public role and address public issues.

Carolyn Heilbrun asked some years ago, in *Reinventing Womanhood,* what would happen to marriage if women moved out from the home "not into privacy alone but . . . into the world," and went on to comment, "No one has yet imagined it in fiction."[5] As the novels considered here demonstrate, however, women writers have imagined it with great richness.

If women writers continue to center their attention on departures rather than upon arrivals at destinations, the reason is not solely that of disability by history—that is, the impossibility, given the social constraints of the past, of projecting fully completed journeys. The moment of departure, as the moment of rupture of so many boundaries, is the node of greatest narrative energy. It generates the power Eudora Welty refers to in writing romantically (of Willa Cather) that "life is most passionate in the promise, not in the fulfillment."[6] But the reason is also, in the words of Karen Lawrence's recent and provocative theorizing of women's travel narratives, that of "a strong sense of the constraints on self-propelled movement and mistrust of the quest and its purposeful destination," a distrust of "the rhetoric of mastery, conquest, and quest" or even of the "sense of agency" itself.[7] Focus on departure implicates a women's tradition and a particular theory of knowing, as well as a particular history.

The scholarship on women's appropriation of the traditionally masculine mode of travel writing and narrative tropes of journey has reached a point of excitement and challenge. The theorizing of this transgressive body of writing, freely crossing boundaries of gender and genre, has enabled us to read individual texts and writers, as well as the conversations and sharings among them, far more creatively than we could even a decade ago. In part, that freedom and that ability to make readerly ventures have resulted from the republication of a number of texts by women travel writers of the past. Of at least equal significance in making possible our more wide-ranging readerly adventures have been the mutually enriching and mutually challenging theoretical, historical, and critical works of feminist scholars. I will not begin to mention names here, except to note that my thinking on this subject has been particularly stimulated by two important studies of the centrality of home spaces in women's writing: Judith Fryer's *Felicitous Space* and Ann Romines's *The Home Plot*. These two influential critical works exemplify much of what is best in the scholarship on women, the theorizing of difference, and the related revaluation of the central experiences of women's lives as traditionally conceived. But the importance of the home space and the home life lies not only in its celebration but also in the resistance it evokes. The insights developed by Fryer and Romines (as well as other scholars who have explored matters of gender difference) are and must be fully *there,* fully implicated in, any study of the departure from those often *in*felicitous spaces. I hope that I have made it clear how greatly I am indebted to the work of these scholars even when my own emphasis is different.

My purpose here is to engage the discourse of difference as it relates to imagery and narrative structures of journey. I use the somewhat overly poetic term *journey* in preference to the simple word *travel* because the latter, more everyday term seems to me to point toward nonfiction travel writing—an important genre in itself—as opposed to the fictive and figurative forms I am primarily dealing with. With respect to these forms, I am convinced that gender differences do exist. My approach is first to construct a historical and theoretical context relating to the journey narrative and its appropriation by women writers, especially in two texts of singular power and resonance: Sarah Orne Jewett's *The Country of the Pointed Firs* (1896) and Marilynne Robinson's *Housekeeping* (1980). Loosely approximating the temporal boundaries of the present study, these two works also define, to a great extent, the tonal range of the various engagements with the duality of home and emergence that it examines. Jewett, in her quiet fiction, provides a model for the urge toward reconciliation of outward venture with home-biding that we see in every writer considered here. Robinson, whose profoundly influential *Housekeeping* occupies a position of definitiveness in the literature of departure from home and domesticity, serves at many junctures as a kind of touchstone of more decisive departure, an eminence from which to look forward and backward so as to map a wide territory of female wayfaring.

Within the context provided by Jewett and Robinson, I examine a sequence of women writers—Mary Austin, Willa Cather, Anne Tyler, Toni Morrison, and Joan Didion—whose works are significantly occupied with homes even as they are concerned with departures and journey. These five American writers, spanning in their work a time period from 1900 to the present, demonstrate, in distinct and varying ways, a concern with reorientation from the private sphere to the public, but also a concern with maintaining, in the process, both their personal and their fictive ties to private spaces identified with home and stable relationships. Each defines a space between home and some level of wider activity, between the submerged self and the defined self, between imprisonment and freedom. The last of the five, Joan Didion, is the most fully oriented toward a public and a spatially extended narrative site; but she is also the most ironic in her assessment of what it means for a woman to be free.

I seek to explore each writer's distinctive narrative structures and images of departure, wayfaring, and nostalgia for values associated with home, and also to demonstrate the responsiveness of each to other women writers. Each chapter, then, will invoke the presence of contextualizing or resonating figures. The chapters on Austin and Cather call particular attention to their admiration for Jewett, whose fiction provided a model for their efforts to reconcile independent departure with secure at-homeness, as well as to their awareness of each other. Tyler's work is placed, at particular junctures, in contact with that of Cather and especially Eudora Welty. The chapter on Morrison invokes at some length the presence of other African-American women writers, particularly Zora Neale Hurston, Gloria Naylor, and Alice Walker. And the chapter on Didion, transgressing lines of genre, proposes commonalities with Denise Levertov and Adrienne Rich, poets who have also insistently addressed public issues and undertaken the project of fusing public and private morality. Here, in a sense, the study comes full circle, since the yoking of public and private morality was a preoccupation of Mary Austin as well.

The sequence in which these five writers are addressed, in chapters 2 through 6, is only partially chronological. It is also a charting of their orientation with respect to the private world of the traditional home-centered life, the effort of departure, and the encounters envisioned for women vis-à-vis public history and public affairs. This complex navigation is an especially tense and torturous one for Morrison, for whom imprisonment by patriarchal dominance is compounded by a history of literal enslavement, and for whom escape from and triumph over the limitations on full and heroic life that those imprisonments would affix on black women can only be shaped as an escape from history itself, even as it requires the fullest possible confrontation of that history and the making of a powerful new one. With Didion we reach the point of fullest engagement with the public, as opposed to the private, sphere—with which she insists the public or political must be linked.

It has sometimes been argued that only the members of a "striving community" (to borrow Rachel Blau DuPlessis's term)[8] have the right to talk about that community's heritage. More specifically, black scholars have sometimes argued that white women have no right to a voice in the criticism and scholarship on the writing of black women, and that those who assume such a voice are not only committing acts of cultural expropriation but courting conspicuous failure.[9] In choosing to address the work of Toni Morrison and other black women despite these cautions and my own limitation by what bell hooks calls "negative socialization," I claim authorization by Morrison herself:

> A woman wrote a book on women writers, and she has an apology in the preface in which she explains why the book doesn't include any black women writers. I think that's dishonest scholarship. I may be wrong but I think so, and I took the trouble to [say] that. I feel perfectly qualified to discuss Emily Dickinson, anybody for that matter, because I assume what Jane Austen and all those people have to say has something to do with life and being human in the world.[10]

The works of such powerful writers as Morrison contribute too much to the condition of being human in the world for literary scholars of whatever racial origin to withhold their attention.

We are all, of course, limited by our own experience and the inevitable incompleteness of our reading and study. I must leave to other scholars more knowledgeable than myself in these areas the critical reading of the richly distinctive patterns of symbolic geographic movement in other important segments of American women's writing—for example, Native American women's autobiographies and fictions and Chicana narratives, both of which are, like the writings of African-American and Asian-American women, inflected by facts of displacement and discrimination. Chicano and Chicana literature is often preoccupied with the desire for return, either to the Southwest, from which Hispanos were displaced when the area became part of the United States, or to Mexico itself, from which the Chicano or Chicana artist may feel displaced even if he or she was born in the United States. It is a cultural displacement leading to the condition of complex inner division that Gloria Anzaldúa discusses provocatively in *Borderlands/La frontera: The New Mestiza.*

The desire for a unified self entails the desire for a return to a place perceived as being one of origination. Tey Diana Rebolledo discusses women writers who, despite participating in this desire, nevertheless manifest an urge to set out for freedom by separating themselves from the constraints of rigid gender roles within Mexican-American culture as "women who wander and roam, women who walk around, women who journey: the terms imply restlessness, wickedness." These are women who "don't stay at home tending to their husbands, children, parents," women who "cross boundaries" and become "demanding, self-satisfying, and worse, perhaps . . . don't need a man." For contemporary Chicana writers, Rebolledo continues, such "mujeres andariegas" are "quite appealing; they are women who go into male spaces such as the cantina, and appropriate them." When the abused wife in Sandra Cisneros's short story "Woman Hollering Creek" leaves her husband's home to return to Mexico, she is driven by another woman, who hollers as they cross the creek. Rebolledo comments, "This hollering is no longer the rage or anguish of women suffering. It is the pure shout of triumph, of the celebration of life."[11] Culturally and literarily knowledgeable critics need to address both the outcry of the suffering Chicana woman who may have little geographic mobility and the triumphant outcry of the Chicana who finds her own celebratory voice—and they are doing so.

Such cultural inflections have all too often been ignored in treatments of the classic American journey. It has been only too easy for critics to look at the heroic panorama presented by Anglo-centered historiography, with its emphasis on the Puritans and westward expansion (even if not an overt commitment to the notion of Manifest Destiny), and to characterize that vast movement as *the* defining plot of American experience. Even so excellent a study as Joseph Urgo's recent *Willa Cather and the Myth of American Migration* falls into the language of such a totalizing vision: "The one thing that *all* Americans have in common is ancestors who, for any number of reasons, decided to detach themselves from one place and to move to another." "What *all* Americans share is not a sense of place but a sense of spatial passage." "There has *never* been an America apart from the people who arrived here from somewhere else, renamed the land, fought others for its possession and definition, and continue to arrive and to make demands." "A cultural style is manufactured by the success stories of those who move on to achieve the ends that only spatial mobility can grant *the American*."[12] In each case, the emphasis is mine, placed there because I need to ask questions. Aren't Indian peoples, many of whom aspired (and still aspire) not to move but to inhabit their own central place, Americans? The Native American worldview (to the extent that one can amalgamate many separate traditions into one) emphasizes sense of place much more than passage.[13] And what of black Americans whose ancestors never "decided to detach themselves" from Africa, but were in fact detached by force? Or the tribal groups and Hispanos who were detached and displaced by latecomers who confidently proclaimed that there was no America before their coming? What of the migrant worker whose "mobility" all too rarely leads to "success"—isn't he or she an American?

I single out Professor Urgo's rhetoric in this way only because my interest in his valuable study has placed it readily at hand. Many others have participated in the same totalizing rhetoric. I have done so myself. But my hope here is to distance myself from that rhetoric by disassembling its falsifying totality, primarily with respect to gender but also, at some points, with respect to ethnicity.

My urge to explore American women's narratives of departure is perhaps related to a yet deeper urge, well expressed by Alice Walker in lines from her poem "For My Sister Molly Who in the Fifties":

And me destined to be
Wayward[14]

Thanks are owed and heartily given to the institutions and colleagues who have generously extended their help with this project. First, for permission to quote from unpublished materials, Barbara Thompson Davis, the literary executor for Katherine Anne Porter; Jane LeCompte for the Houghton Mifflin Company, executors for the business correspondence of Ferris Greenslet; William A. Koshland for Alfred A. Knopf, Inc., executors for the business correspondence of Blanche Knopf; and officials of the following libraries: the Beinecke Rare Book and Manuscript Library, Yale University; the Harry Ransom Humanities Research Center, the University of Texas; the Houghton Library, Harvard University; the Libraries of the University of Maryland, College Park; the Pierpont Morgan Library, New York; and the School of American Research, Santa Fe. I thank the Phillips Collection, Washington, D.C., for its permission to reprint a panel from Jacob Lawrence's series of paintings, *The Migration of the Negro;* and the Minneapolis Institute of Arts for the use of Pierre Bonnard's *Dining Room in the Country.* For the use of manuscript collections, in addition to the above, I am grateful to the Alderman Library, University of Virginia; the Bailey-Howe Library, University of Vermont; and the Huntington Library, San Marino, California.

Then—and these are very special thanks—to colleagues (by which I mean both faculty colleagues and student colleagues) who have given their time in reading various parts of the manuscript and their knowledge and care in trying to help me find my way a little better: Dean Woodrow Jones, Jr., for his steadfast friendship, encouragement, and advice; David McWhirter and Larry Oliver, who read the chapter on Morrison and shared their depth of awareness and thinking about the intersections of race and gender in this troubled country of ours; Michelle Henry, who knows Morrison's work better than anyone would suppose a student possibly could and who brightened every day that included her appearance at my office door; Susan Rushing Adams, for many discussions of Willa Cather and for her insistence on the importance of windows; Mary Ann O'Farrell, for reading and helping with the preface and the postscript and simply for being the constructive presence that she is; Susan Rosowski, for advising me on locations of archival materials; Melody Graulich, for sharing insights on the connection between Cather and Mary Austin; Janet McCann, who cheered me on when I thought I had gone too far; Marian Eide, who knew a *mot juste;* Larry Mitchell, who spurred me past a failure of nerve partway through the project; Margaret Benner, for insights relating to Anne Tyler; Beth Alvarez, infallibly willing to help with knotty problems; Elsa Nettels and Mary Suzanne Schriber, who read the entire manuscript and challenged me to reach toward a higher standard at many turns; and Loren Lutes, best of husbands, who read, talked through readings, and helped me settle on a title. I especially want to thank Ann Romines and Merrill Skaggs, whose positive comments on my paper at the Seventh International Willa Cather Seminar sent me back to my chapter on Cather with renewed zest.

Portions of chapters 2 and 3 originally appeared, in different form, in *Southwestern American Literature* 21 (1996): 29–60 and are used here with the permission of the editor, Dr. Mark Busby.

A portion of chapter 3 appeared in different form in the *CEA Critic* 59 (1997): 10–22 and is used here with the permission of the editor, Bege K. Bowers.

I am grateful to the following publishers for permission to reprint lines of poetry:

One line from Emily Dickinson's poem #488, from *Complete Poems of Emily Dickinson,* ed. Thomas H. Johnson, Boston: Little, Brown, 1960; used by courtesy of Little, Brown and Company.

Lines from Emily Dickinson's poem #505 and poem #512, from *Complete Poems of Emily Dickinson,* ed. Thomas H. Johnson, copyright © 1951, 1955, 1979, 1983 by the President and Fellows of Harvard College. Reprinted by permission of the publishers and the Trustees of Amherst College from *The Poems of Emily Dickinson,* Thomas H. Johnson, ed., Cambridge, Mass.: The Belknap Press of Harvard University Press.

Lines from Langston Hughes's poem "Strange Hurt," from *Selected Poems of Langston Hughes,* copyright © 1959 by Langston Hughes. Reprinted by permission of Alfred A. Knopf, Inc.

Lines from Denise Levertov's poems "Staying Alive," from *To Stay Alive,* copyright © 1971 by Denise Levertov; "A Traveler," from *A Door in the Hive,*

Through the Window, Out the Door

Chapter 1

FINDING A WAY OUT
The Imagination of Departure

And some day when you knock and push the door,
Some sane day, not too bright and not too stormy,
I shall be gone, and you may whistle for me.
   —Edna St. Vincent Millay

I learn by going where I have to go.
   —Theodore Roethke

Muriel Rukeyser writes in her poem "The Gates. XI," "Life will come will come again / knocking and coughing and farting at your door." When it does, this coarsely bodied reality brings an invitation to come out. And sometimes, responding to that invitation, women go decisively out the door, perhaps slamming it after them as Nora does in Henrik Ibsen's *A Doll's House,* perhaps declaring with Edna St. Vincent Millay's cheeky speaker, "I shall be gone, and you may whistle for me."[1]

Departures such as these, implicating in the structure of their vision the home that is left as well as the defiance with which the move toward wider spaces is enacted, are of central and decisive import in women's writing in the twentieth century. When Margaret Atwood has Offred surrender the last vestige of control in her escape at the end of *The Handmaid's Tale,* she may invalidate the traditional—and traditionally masculine—structure of the quest, but she adopts and emphatically fulfills a female tradition that poses the moment of departure as being itself a culmination, the essential act in signaling a defection from patriarchy. The last words of Offred's story are, "And so I step up, into the darkness within; or else the light."[2] Atwood leaves her there, at the door, in the posture of departure that is so recurrent in women's writing that it sometimes seems the definitive version of women's journey narrative. But the trope of departure and journey in women's writing is often farther-reaching than that, both geographically, in its narrative playing-out, and in its implications. It pervades the language even of theory of women's writing—for example, Hélène Cixous's statement that the female writer "dislocat[es] things" and makes language "fly."[3]

Men have been, as Theodore Roethke's poem has it, learning by going where they have to go, and writing about it, for millennia. Throughout most of literary history, it has been male travelers who have undertaken heroic journeys and males who have told them or dreamed them: Abraham, Columbus, Daniel Boone; Homer, Herman Melville, Mark Twain. Meanwhile, according to traditional paradigms, women have learned by staying at home, or being induced to stay at home, or made to, and if they wrote about it their texts were, for the most part, disregarded. Waiting Penelope-like for their travelers' return, they have become themselves, through a symbolism that Karen Lawrence calls a "mapping of women as space," the land explored by free-ranging males.[4] Certainly there were those great exceptions, the Victorian lady travelers. But more often women have looked at the world through the windows of houses—openings, perhaps, of mental journeys, of visionary access to free spaces or of imagined departures, but nevertheless, however transparent, boundary surfaces.[5]

Whether in fiction, autobiographical nonfiction, or poetry, women writers have seldom, until relatively recent times, structured their narratives in the form of journeys. For this very reason, as well as because the observance or disruption of narrative convention conveys powerful social messages, when they did imagine women who (in Margaret Higonnet's words) broke out of their "virtuous domestic retirement" and undertook the "scandal" of free and public movement in pursuit of their own goals, those narratives have radiated particular significance and force.[6] The motif of the journey, particularly the act of departure, assumes a transcendent power in women's writing beyond the power it holds in male-authored texts precisely because such departures signify rupture, the breaking not only of personal and conventional walls but of whole social structures and sets of assumptions. Tragic heroines of the late nineteenth century—Edna Pontellier in Kate Chopin's *The Awakening,* Lily Bart in Edith Wharton's *The House of Mirth,* the speaker in Charlotte Perkins Gilman's "The Yellow Wallpaper"—often escape their hopeless circumstances through death or madness. My interest here is not only in more recent departures but in the (often conflicted) departures on roads of assertion and positive venture made by female characters such as

Cleófilas in Sandra Cisneros's "Woman Hollering Creek," who escape the prisons of home and restricted roles without destruction of self.[7]

Such departures gather their impact not only from the fact of women's relative confinement, lending an especially decisive import to the moment of exit, but from their inflection by women writers' relationship to traditions of the literary genres in which travel and journey have occupied male writers for centuries. The turn to narratives of active journeying centered on the act of departure is one way in which women writers in the twentieth century have written, in Rachel Blau DuPlessis's terms, "beyond the ending" of the conventional story of "romantic thralldom" concluding in the successful heroine's marriage or the unsuccessful or resistant heroine's death.[8] In making their departures, women assume the role of subjects in their own stories rather than objects sought and exchanged by men. Leaving the warehouses of domesticity in which their value is stored, they claim the right to establish their own systems of valuation.[9]

In traditional quest narratives, such a right is typically claimed and enacted only by men. Northrop Frye and Joseph Campbell, both lyricists of quest, simply assume the quester's masculinity. Part of the challenge faced by those women writers who have sought, as Dana Heller argues, to feminize the quest romance has been to free themselves of such masculine models of the form. That is a particularly pressing challenge for American women writers because, as Heller observes, American literature has been particularly obsessed with "masculine images of ritualized flight and self-exploration."[10] Claude Lévi-Strauss, on whom both Frye and Campbell heavily rely, theorized the quester's masculinity as being necessary because women serve as the objects of value for the sake of which quests are undertaken, to be (in Teresa de Lauretis's summary of his position) "exchanged and circulated among men" as the "means, objects, and signs of social communication."[11] Roland Barthes similarly theorizes male activity and roaming, female passivity and domestication: "Historically, the discourse of absence is carried on by the Woman: Woman is sedentary, Man hunts, journeys; Woman is faithful (she waits), man is fickle (he sails away, he cruises)."[12] Such theories deny female agency. The rupture made by women's departures on their own journeys and narratives of journey, then, is not only a breaking from conventionally expected roles but a fracturing of authoritative and institutionally sanctioned theories of literature and semiotics. De Lauretis forcefully argues that narrative itself has been "governed by an

Oedipal logic" that "predetermines the positions" occupied by woman and constitutes her as an "obstacle-boundary-space," thereby making even "her story" the story of "his desire."[13] One would like to regard that view as a polemical overstatement—and indeed, de Lauretis herself offers hope of change. But it is clear, at any rate, that narrative conventions and assumptions are so deeply rooted in masculine paradigms that reshaping them to serve a woman's own desire is an enormous challenge.

I do not want to oversimplify the puzzle of gendered subjecthood by exaggerating the extent to which women's experiences as well as women's narratives have been house-bound. Not only with respect to how prevalent house-bound experience has been but with regard to the nature of their affective response to it, the significance of home spaces for women and the meanings women have attached to their own roles in narrative, and as narrators, of spatial endeavors are matters of enormous complexity. To say either that women find domestic spaces more felicitous than men do or that they find houses imprisoning, as if such blanket statements applied equally well to all women and all women's writings, would be demonstrably false. Both tendencies exist, with uncounted variations in between, and both are explored in theoretical and practical feminist criticism today. Indeed, much of the unfolding of feminist criticism has involved precisely this issue of the exploration and definition of difference, as well as the earlier feminist insistence on what might be called sameness but is usually called equality. Julia Kristeva describes that earlier stage of feminism as being directed toward "insertion into history," and the later, more separatist stage as one reaffirming "the specificity of female psychology and its symbolic realizations."[14] But the feminism of difference, with its glorification of maternal *jouissance* and female bonding and its frequent validation of life activities traditionally slighted in masculine narrative, carries the danger of re-sentencing women to confinement in a separate as well as an unequal sphere. What is needed is something like Kristeva's third stage, in which women both enter history (public lives, public power, public discourse) and expand history to a plane of heterogeneity—which is the kind of having-both or opening-both that Marilynne Robinson envisions in her novel *Housekeeping*.

The meaning of home spaces for women, then, is not only the ground of a rich and far-reaching debate sociologically and psychologically, but also a matter utterly intertwined with the nature of narrative and lyric expression by women. Ann Romines's important study *The Home Plot: Women, Writing, and Domestic Ritual* has established not only the existence but the worth, in every sense, of undervalued and even underperceived narrative structures identified with houses and centered on the patterns and concerns of daily home life. Such concerns clearly seem to have been of greater moment to women and women writers than to men, and to re-valuate them as Romines and other scholars have done is an enormous gain not only in the historical accuracy of our view of our literary heritage but in what must be called its justice. But domestic plots do not constitute the only existing or valid mode in which women's imaginations have operated—nor has Romines or any other scholar that I am aware of offered them as such. Indeed, the unfolding of critical sensitivity to the home plot makes it all the clearer how much more deeply implicated are houses and homes *in women's tropes of journey* than in men's.

Karen Lawrence, who suggestively theorizes travel and travel writing as both of these intersect differences of gender, has shown that home persists, even if only as a shadowy context, a social and cultural structuring that cannot be escaped, in the travel writings of men as well. Travel writing, Lawrence argues, inherently destabilizes both the idea of domesticity and the idea of the freedom realized in geographic movement, and is thus a literature of both; it "explores not only potential freedoms but also cultural constraints" so that "home is never left behind." But just as the home itself and cultural strictures or assumptions relating to home roles are particularly present for women, so do women's writings of travel particularly implicate the home. As Lawrence seeks to demonstrate with respect to British women writers, "travel writing by women creates a permeable membrane between home and the foreign, domestic confinement and freedom on the road."[15]

Melody Graulich has similarly written of pioneer women that "like the classic hero of western literature, they head into the wilderness . . . but they do not reject their womanhood, or the home and the hearth."[16] Women's writings of journey are likely to be also narratives of home.

Nancy Miller remarks that in nineteenth-century fiction "female *Bildung* tends to get stuck in the bedroom."[17] In fiction of the turn of the century and afterward, however, narratives of women's *Bildung* incorporate acts of departure and journey with increasing frequency and tend to consider domestic (not necessarily erotic) spaces, not as the necessary end, but as a component, an option among options. Through such relocations of emphasis as this relatively greater stress on, or interrogation of, home and relatively greater emphasis on the act of departure, women writers have reconstituted one of the most traditional of narrative forms as their own, rejecting the immobility of their role in the old stories of male mobility and heroism.

It may well be that, as Domna Stanton writes, citing Barthes, "all writing, even the most intentionally subversive, is confined by the parameters of discourse at a particular moment." If so, we do indeed need to scrutinize it (as Stanton recommends with regard to the theorizing of Julia Kristeva, Hélène Cixous, and Luce Irigaray) for "the extent to which phallocentric scenes and semes are re-presented, despite the desire to subvert, eliminate, and replace them."[18] The narrative of the journey is one of those "scenes and semes." Karen Lawrence asks provocatively, "Can women writers revise the various plots of wandering (in romance, adventure, exploration, and travel narratives) without succumbing to the traditional pitfalls of these plots for a feminine protagonist?" Can women writers "repeat with a difference"? As she points out, the question arises, in part, from the embeddedness of such notions as the "typecasting" of free-footed women as "loose" women, as well as from women travel writers' "scepticism" of a (masculine) rhetoric of autonomy, defined purpose, and "mastery."[19]

Women writers such as those I take up in this study have demonstrated, I would argue, not only their desire but also their ability to subvert, if not eliminate and replace, inhospitably masculine models of literary journeying. Women writing travel, whether in realistic accounts or in the symbols and figurations of their fiction and poetry, are departing generically at the same time as they are imagining departures, at the same time as they are departing from the history and traditions that once with near absoluteness excluded them from making such departures, at the same time as they are departing from the silent role of object in order to assume the dynamic role of subject and speaker. It is scarcely surprising that, as Lawrence notes (literally, in a footnote), "the flexibility provided by the topos of travel is . . . more liberating in women's writing."[20]

One way in which women writers of the past century have subverted masculine models of the journey narrative is by reconceiving it as what might be called the home-and-journey narrative. Writers such as Sarah Orne Jewett have used such relatively plot-free narratives to establish woman-centered ideals of social life and to express their intentness on departing from the old structures—and from the old structure, the house of patriarchy. Jewett's work, especially her quietly feminized novel *The Country of the Pointed Firs* (often spoken of dismissively as a collection of sketches),[21] served as an important model for Mary Austin and Willa Cather, in particular—as did, indeed, Jewett herself, in her disciplined commitment to her writing career. In providing a paradigm of balance between departure and values usually associated with home, such as security and relational satisfaction, Jewett's work serves as an important point of departure for the study of women writers whose vision of the narrative of departure and journey is also a vision of home.

Until quite recently, the prevailing response to Jewett's work has been somewhat like that of a reviewer described by Margaret Atwood, who "talked about the 'domestic' imagery of my poems, entirely ignoring the fact that seven-eighths of the poems take place outdoors."[22] Attention to Jewett's vision of the satisfactions of the home world has tended to forestall recognition of her urge toward outdoor spaces and untrammeled movement. As Margaret Roman points out, however, her fiction includes "frequent image[s] of a woman at the window," and her "heroines are constantly trying to get out-of-doors."[23] The characteristic pattern of action in *The Country of the Pointed Firs* and the short stories that have at times been incorporated into it by later editors, including Cather,[24] is one of brief journeys centering on and returning to the comfortable familiarity of home.

Primarily, Jewett is concerned with the journeys of visitation by means of which women create a supportive network of mutual attention and response. She poises these journeys, simple and limited in scope, against a contrasting background of men's journeys, which, though spatially larger, are often personally destructive both for themselves and for the women they leave behind. Mrs. Todd, the monumentally large, self-sufficient herbalist of the coastal village of Dunnet Landing and the central presence of Jewett's late work, is one such woman. Visited by women who come to her door for herbal remedies, she in turn goes out on herb-gathering excursions and visits to neighbors and to her elderly mother, who lives on a nearby island. These spatially small, looping journeys constitute a cyclical pattern expressive of Jewett's vision of the cyclical emotional life of women, whose "feelin's comes back when you think you've done with 'em, as sure as spring comes with the year."[25] The import of Jewett's recurrent journeys, then, is one associated with individual self-definition and self-expression, as well as with the constitution of a female social network and, by implication, a feminine ideal of community.

The narrator's arrival at Dunnet Landing in the opening chapter of *Pointed Firs* quietly establishes a linkage of journey and return that is the essence of the fictional structure, since her summer's journey to the quiet village is at once a departure or withdrawal from her own home in order to complete some writing, and a return to Dunnet Landing following her brief visit the previous summer (as the brief concluding chapter is at once a departure from Dunnet Landing and a return home). After this beginning, establishing the linkage on which Jewett's cyclical pattern depends, every succeeding chapter then involves a journey, greater or lesser. These include the implied journeys of Mrs. Todd's clients, her own "slow herb-gathering progresses through woods and pastures" (6), the narrator's walks to the isolated schoolhouse where she plans to write, her visits to the homes of townspeople, the journey of Mrs. Todd's old friend who comes to visit, voyages narrated as interpolated tales, the narrator's sail to the small island where a female recluse lived and died, and two multichapter excursions taken by Mrs. Todd and the narrator together. These episodes trace not only the narrator's and Mrs. Todd's movements about Dunnet Landing and its environs but also their developing closeness.[26] The two major excursions form balancing but cumulative four-chapter units structuring the novel. The first, a visit to Mrs. Todd's elderly mother, ends approximately midway through the book; the second, attendance at the Bladen family reunion, ends in the penultimate chapter before the coda indicating departure.

In the visit to Mrs. Todd's mother, Mrs. Blackett, the two women sail out to Green Island taking along only a young boy to help carry things. Three qualities are emphasized in the telling of this excursion: the women's (especially Mrs. Todd's) independence (they do not need a man to sail their craft); the kindness and mutual caring exhibited by mother and daughter during the visit; and the importance of small matters. Conversational sharing of everyday news, so gladly received on each side, comprises the texture of a way of life and a sustaining set of relationships. The narrator finds that the walks afforded by the small island, though short, afford a view of "all the far horizons" where "nothing stopped the eye or hedged one in" (45). While there, the narrator and Mrs. Todd walk together to a hollow where pennyroyal grows—significantly, an herb used in relation to menstruation and pregnancy, matters of the female body. This excursion-within-an-excursion, then, placed at the structural center of the book, emphasizes the centrality of the female principle to life itself. The visit to Green Island is a journey at once ordinary and magical, allowing the narrator to feel that she has left the "plain every-day world" (49) behind and helping her see Dunnet Landing from a new perspective. A reunion of mother and daughter that provides exempla both of solitary freedom and of close mutuality, it anticipates the more embracing reunion shown in the corresponding sequence of chapters at the end.

Between this first major excursion (chapters 8 through 11) and the concluding reunion sequence (chapters 16 through 19) comes another voyage to an island, once the home of a woman named Joanna Todd, who had determined to live as a recluse after a disappointment in love. The narrator has learned about Shell-heap Island from a conversation between Mrs. Todd and an old friend, Mrs. Fosdick, who has come for a visit during the course of which Mrs. Todd describes a long-ago visit to the recluse. Moved by her account of the solitary woman living her stark life alone in her own way, the narrator uses a sailing excursion with one of Dunnet Landing's retired seamen as an opportunity to make her own pilgrimage to Shell-heap Island. There she visits Joanna Todd's grave, which she sees as an emblem of freedom and achievement, musing that "in the life of each of us . . . there is a place remote and islanded" (82). Clearly, one of the values affirmed by *The Country of the Pointed Firs* is the importance of finding that place and knowing it, achieving self-definition, each alone. Yet self-definition, each alone, is not the whole story. Jewett by no means advocates solitariness. Through its emphasis on acts of visiting, the Shell-heap Island sequence also affirms values of mutuality and sympathy.

In the sequence of the family reunion, Jewett offers a culminating exemplum affirming, once again, both independence and mutuality.[27] Mrs. Todd, that self-sufficient but caring and socially valued "sibyl" (8); Mrs. Blackett, who lives enisled with her reticent son William; and the narrator, who characteristically seeks out solitude for her writing, join together in an excursion to attend the annual reunion of Mrs. Blackett's family, the Bradens. Like the earlier trip to Green Island, this excursion is made without a masculine presence—and without the need of one, since Mrs. Todd proves as adequate to the handling of the horse as to the sailing of the boat. Stopping along the way for small visits, the three join a virtual procession converging, by both land and sea, on the annual celebration of kinship. Afterward, as they return to Dunnet Landing, the narrator finds that the "road was new to me, as roads always are, going back" (111)—just as she had found that the modest trip to Green Island helped her see Dunnet Landing anew. This culminating sequence is followed by a single chapter providing a lesson in loving remembrance, as the narrator makes one last visit, to the faithful widower Mr. Tilley. She then leaves for home, her journey apparently fulfilled.

The combination of sturdy independence with quiet devotion through actions centering on reunion is an idea Jewett developed in several of her short stories as well. "Martha's Lady," the story of an act of kindness that wins a simple woman's lifelong loyalty, ends in a return and a quiet festival of reunion. "Aunt Cynthy Dallett," telling of two women's visit to an elderly aunt, ends in a decision for aunt and niece to join forces in a single mutually supportive household. "A Dunnet Shepherdess" affirms a solitary woman's staunch independence and her determination, despite her love for Mrs. Todd's brother William, to remain in the isolated home where she cares for her mother. But in "William's Wedding," her mother having died, the shepherdess marries William and moves to Green Island to live with him and Mrs. Blackett. She has demonstrated her autonomy and her devotion, and now she gains a surrogate maternal attachment even as she moves (with a belatedness Jewett fully endorsed) into adult sexuality.[28] In the story's account of the quiet wedding of the two faithful lovers, both of them middle aged and confirmed loners, we again see her characteristic discovery of the momentous in the ordinary.

The trope of the great in the small is indeed the basic strategy of Jewett's handling of the journey motif. It is a strategy we see in the work of many writers of the "domestic plot," and one that would well serve Cather, in particular, as she adopted increasingly unconventional and unplotted fictional forms. Jewett offers the small and the everyday as matters of equal worth with the great and heroic. Frequently she does so by way of ennobling analogies. The simple excursion to the Braden family reunion, for example, is a "Great Expedition" in which they "might have been a company of ancient Greeks going to celebrate a victory, or to worship the god of harvests" (100). The analogy with an ancient rite culminates a series of references to Mrs. Todd as a mythic figure: a "sibyl" (8), an "oracle" (85), and a personage "lonely and solitary" with a "great determined shape" who "might have been Antigone alone on the Theban plain" (49). In "The Queen's Twin," as Mrs. Todd starts out for a visit, simply another small excursion "made afoot and between the roads, in open pasturelands" (90), she has a look "as if she were just starting on a hopeful quest" (190). She feels "one o' them travelin' fits comin' on," she and the narrator "put out across country as one puts out to sea," and when they look back from a hilltop they feel as if they had "passed the harbor bar and were comfortably in open sea at last" (194). The encroachment of "sturdy little trees" on the lonely fields of the woman they visit is as clear an illustration of "the unconquerable, immediate forces of Nature" as is a powerful thunderstorm (198–200). Again, the great in the small. Untamed nature can be seen as authentically, it seems, in the untended fields of a lonely old woman as on a great odyssey.

Within the small circuit of Dunnet Landing and its neighboring islands and backcountry, Mrs. Todd's herb-gathering walks and visits to family and friends are journeys by means of which she makes both a living and a life. Like the narrator's larger journey to Dunnet Landing and back to her home, they are journeys of self-realization and self-fulfillment. Through her participation in Mrs. Todd's compact pattern of journeying, the narrator moves from an initial determination to isolate herself for the sake of her writing to an understanding of the need for community—themes, we might note, that Jewett's masterpiece shares with Herman Melville's *Moby-Dick*, a journey narrative of a very different sort. But if Mrs. Todd's journeys constitute a network linking together an affectionate society of women, Jewett insists that they also lead back again to home, the place of quiet satisfaction.

In her women-centered innovative forms, Jewett offered readers who were able to see it a vision mediating between departure and discovery on the one hand and at-homeness on the other. Perhaps because of the gentle and understated tone of her work, as well as because of its home-centeredness, Jewett's departure both from established patterns of value and from established fictional structures has often not been recognized. One has to read closely to note the implications of the quiet fictive actions that either simply disregard or at times (as in the short stories "A Dunnet Shepherdess" and "William's Wedding") directly revise conventional plots. Clearly, her miniaturized journeys are less overtly challenging of restrictions on women's lives than are the more insistent departures of many later writers. But as critical readings have become more alert to alterity and the past dominance of masculine forms, Jewett's work and its influence on other women writers have increasingly, and appropriately, been recognized.

In association with its pervasive emphasis on departure, women's writing in the twentieth century often focuses insistently on two particular architectural features of the domestic space: doorways and windows. One suspects that such an architectural emphasis might be found in a gender-linked way throughout much of literary history.[29] I will not attempt to reach so far. But it is clear that in the modernist period, which is my primary field of reference here, when women's urge toward wider, more untrammeled spheres of experience became insistent, manifesting itself in a surge of career activities literary and otherwise, consciousness hovered at the windows and doors. We can see it doing so, with an entirely characteristic but also representative ambivalence, at powerful nodal points in Virginia Woolf's novels and essays, and we will see it doing so in the works of the writers considered at length here, particularly Willa Cather. In these important modernist and postmodernist texts and in others, women look through windows and enlarge their sense of the world. When they step out the doorway, they find themselves, like the men who have been seeking and enjoying the wide-open spaces for as long as we can imagine, able to stretch their limbs and breathe more freely.[30]

Jewett's persona in *The Country of the Pointed Firs* says as a kind of commonplace that "great prospects always give [a] sense of liberty in space and time" (45). The trope of spaciousness-as-freedom is so thoroughly embedded in the popular imagination as to seem almost a literal rather than figurative equivalency. One broadens one's horizons, dreams of a better place over the rainbow, or begs in song, "Don't fence me in." The act of leaving, of setting out to travel, is the accessing of that freedom. We can suppose that women, trapped with or within their yellowing wallpaper, have perceived that act with a particular keenness or even poignance. As Judith Fryer says in her study of the spatial imagination, women have been "conditioned not to move in space . . . but to stay fixed in their model houses." They have been "denied, in our culture, the possibility of dialectical movement between private spaces and open spaces."[31] Women's fictional journeys indicate a particular attention to the liminal (literally, threshold) moment of departure precisely because of its associations with the escape from this restriction and the attainment of freedom. In Kate Chopin's *The Awakening* (1899), Edna's movement toward "constituting herself as the subject of her own possession," and ultimately toward the desperate irony of the uninhibited swim into the ocean that will be her chosen death, turns on the moment of her "removing herself from the physical (spatial) control of her husband"—the moment when she crosses his threshold in order to inhabit her own space.[32]

By no means do women have exclusive title to such tropes. The association of freedom with spatial movement transcends gender. But freedom is perhaps not so central a value for the imaginative journeys of male writers because with men, in history as well as in imagination, the journey has also commonly borne the very different meaning of conquest. David Minter, acknowledging the centrality of geographic movement in American experience, characterizes that movement as "taking possession."[33] We see little of the act or the sense of taking possession in women's stories of journeying, perhaps because women played so marginalized a role in the historic journeys that (often) dragged them into new and unwanted spaces, while all the while the collective social voice drummed into their ears the ideology of domestic retreat. The story of the historic journey of possession, Minter continues, is one "in which women play subordinate roles and suffer . . . great loneliness."[34] The frequent and well-documented distress expressed by women of the westwardly expanding frontier of the Anglo expropriation of North America is in part their experience of the dissonance between the cultural imperative to stay within the walls of the house, making it a refuge from crass externalities, and the spousal and societal imperative to move that protected space into unfamiliar and lonely places where they lacked supportive networks among similarly enhoused sisters.[35]

A tension similar to that expressed in pioneer women's personal writings manifests itself in the pathology of agoraphobia, an anxiety disorder far more common among women than among men. A complex phenomenon, agoraphobia is analyzable not only in the behavioral and medical terms through which it is most often addressed therapeutically and in the psychoanalytic literature, but in social and cultural terms as well. Revisionist analysts Robert Seidenberg and Karen DeCrow forcefully argued over a decade ago an interpretation of the fear of open (often commercial) spaces as a response to the "historical" and continuing "intimidation and oppression of women." Pervasive cultural messages that "all women incorporate," they insisted, tend to limit women's aspirations and activities mainly to those of the home and consumerism and, through methods ranging from "unequal pay in the workplace to blame for children who turn to drugs to actual physical assault on the streets," to punish women who "travel away from" such interests. In the view of Seidenberg and DeCrow, the agoraphobic terror that contains women in their houses (or in some cases in houses plus a restricted number of other "safe" places) and also contains them in behavior patterns of dependency and incompetence is an enacted and deeply internalized "parody" or "caricature" conveying reasonable, albeit self-destructive, protest. Behavioral and pharmaceutical therapies, they argue, trivialize the pathology by not taking its causes seriously.[36]

Approaching the problem by way of a similar socioeconomic critique of nineteenth-century America's burgeoning commercial structure, Gillian Brown asserts that "agoraphobia approximates domesticity." Brown presents historical evidence that nineteenth-century physicians concerned about "the immobilizing effects of commerce" on men strove to "preserv[e] the tranquility of women and home."[37] The notorious S. Weir Mitchell, in his book *Wear and Tear; or, Hints for the Overworked* (1887), prescribed "constant bed rest and severely restricted activity" for women in order to ensure their "return to tranquil lives as wives and mothers" so that they could serve as means of combating the spread of nervous disorders and exhaustion among businessmen. The then-current idealization of an "iconography of stillness featuring invalidism, woman, and home" reinforced women's confinement in houses and house-roles and their tendency to develop the wall-clinging behaviors of the confirmed agoraphobic. The pathology of hysteria, Brown continues, "caricatures domesticity." The bizarre poses and stasis of the hysteric "elaborate the antinomy between movement and repose upheld by nineteenth-century domestic ideology." In recognition of this inhibiting pathology and its ties to the social and commercial structure of her time, Charlotte Perkins Gilman, herself a sufferer of "nervous prostration" on whom Mitchell's rest cure was imposed, "used immobility to parody and protest against domestic confinement."[38]

Such parodies and protests would naturally tend to focus on boundaries. Accordingly, in "The Yellow Wallpaper" Gilman invokes a terrifying imagery of walls, bars on windows, and wall-like hedges along which maddened women "creep." In her autobiography, in the chapter on her illness and treatment by Mitchell, Gilman reports that like the maddened women in her story she *crept:* "I would crawl into remote closets and under beds—to hide from the grinding pressure of that profound distress." The source of her distress remained to some extent a mystery, but on compelling empirical evidence ("repeated proof that the moment I left home I began to recover") she associated it with domestic life. Escape, she felt, was her only recourse. Of her first escape, a temporary one, she writes, "Feeble and hopeless I set forth armed with tonics and sedatives, to cross the continent. From the moment the wheels began to turn, the train to move, I felt better." Arriving in California, she found the Mojave Desert (very much as her friend Mary Hunter Austin would later find the nearby and similarly arid San Joaquin Valley) a "heaven."[39]

Gilman wrote "The Yellow Wallpaper," we recall, precisely to confound Weir Mitchell and his home-binding "cure." But boundaries, constraining as they are in such a story, can also be conceived as challenges to escape or as border areas, literal or figurative strips through which passage may occur, between known and unknown, familiar and unfamiliar, and by means of which change may also occur. Boundaries, then, may become permeable and as such may become spaces that deconstruct the rigid opposition of inside and outside, constrained and free. Jacqueline Rose holds out the hope that feminism may be "in a privileged position" to undermine the hold of dualistic thinking such as the pairing of "inside/outside, victim/aggressor, real event/fantasy" that locks our minds into unproductive rigidities.[40] If so, feminism may serve a redemptive process of liberation for subjectivity itself—a liberation well and aptly conveyed through metaphors of escape from spatial boundaries.[41] Images and narrative structures of journeys employed by women writers trope not only the social and political liberation of women but the freeing of consciousness and self-conception as well.

For very real and compelling reasons of history, however, such tropes have more often culminated in the moment of breaking through the boundary than they have gone beyond it. Women writers have less often than men created stories of completed—or if not completed, at any rate clearly goal-oriented and fully pursued—journeys. Adventurous quests for magical talismans such as white whales have been almost entirely products of male writers, narrating exceptionally masculine kinds of endeavor. Stories leading up to departure have often seemed, from the perspective afforded by women's history of relative restriction, dramatic enough. Women writers have often not needed or perhaps been ready to go beyond that dramatic and transformative moment by imagining the fully elaborated journeys that might ensue, but have focused on departures. In its radical openness, though, such a focus may actually imply a greater, not a lesser, degree of freedom in women's imagined journeys. To the extent that questing journeys of spatial endeavor are journeys of obsession or duty, especially what is perceived as higher duty, they might be seen as expressing a curtailment rather than an expansion of freedom. But the female departure is typically launched by a woman's own desire, in defiance of external compulsion, and to end the journey at that point is to leave the road still open for discovery.

My examination of the journey tropes of women writers, then, will begin with an assumption that these journeys convey some quality of freedom or of desire for freedom, for the emergence of selfhood, and will seek to define the nature of the freedom being sought and the degree to which it is attained or seen as being attainable. The freedom achieved by a Charlotte Douglas, in Joan Didion's *A Book of Common Prayer,* is considerably more dubious than that achieved by a Walking Woman, in Mary Austin's story of that name, even though it is Charlotte who ranges over a wider geographic space. Dubiety is the state to which the metamorphosis of modernism into postmodernism has delivered us. But in both cases, that of Austin's 1909 short story and that of Didion's 1977 novel, the initial impulse attributed to the character and the initial affect of the action communicated to readers is an impulse toward freedom.

Such an impulse breaks into actuality in moments of eruptive force. Like boiling water in a kettle, the frustration and yearning and conviction of authority on the part of women in the home builds a powerful head of steam. Adrienne Rich, in her transformative essay on Emily Dickinson, calls that force "Vesuvius at Home." Dickinson's physical escape was, of course, in the other direction, not outward from the house but inward to her own private space within it. Her upstairs bedroom, with its small writing desk, was her "freedom," a place set apart from the household activities downstairs.[42] It was there that she made her daring mental escapes. This paradox of an enclosure that is also freedom appears in Dickinson's poems in metaphors of distinctive spaces resisting ordinary enhousement. She will not, when asked, come "in" to such houses because she is enclosed in a boundary of another sort, the symbolic enclosure fastened around her like a belt in a quasi-marital act of claiming that Rich reads as "possession" by her "own power" (#273). As a possessed/possessing maker she disdains building mere houses: "We—Temples Build—I said" (#488). Within these specially set-aside spaces, however, Dickinson's anticipated escape is a bursting out, an explosive moment. Contemplating that moment, she is the volcanic "Fire" below a turf that to "General thought" seems so quiet (#1677). Though she can wish for a gentler escape in which she will be "Raised softly to the Ceilings—/And out, and easy on" (#505), she more characteristically contemplates her power as a "Loaded Gun" (#754), a "still—Volcano," a "quiet—Earthquake" (#601). Such disruptions of seeming quietness and stability occur with mysterious accessions of power such as that of the tame little boat (#30) that suddenly, and at just the moment when the tame little poem breaks into more excited rhythm, having "retrimmed its masts—redecked its sails," shoots "exultant on!" Departure comes in "moments of Escape— / When bursting all the doors— / She dances like a Bomb, abroad" (#512).[43]

One corollary of the journey initiated through such a bursting out is the possibility of expanded and more clearly understood selfhood. The restrictive precept that woman's place was in the home always carried with it (as it does today, where it still exists) an elaborate set of sometimes explicit but more often implicit or even hidden assumptions about women's natures, activities, and aspirations. To the extent that one remained within this complex web of restrictive assumptions and accepted them as one's own standards, one accepted as well a set of limitations in one's understanding of self. Breaking out of the one invited breaking out of the other, into a vastly wider arena of possible self-understanding. Again and again, then, narratives of departure involve personal growth and an expanded (the spatial metaphor again!) conception of what or who one is and might be.[44] In Cather's work, for example, especially in her earlier writings, a central subject of "the divided self" is often presented as (in Judith Fryer's words) a "conflict between woman and artist" in which narrative interest is not directed so much toward "reconciliation" as toward "creating a new context" in which the artist-self can develop.[45] To reach this new context, this new space, it is necessary to depart from the old and explore new ways. Cather serves the Vesuvian impulse, for example, in her emphasis on imagery of windows by which her characters can envision the way toward self-transformation, and doors through which they can move to set out on those ways.

The understatement with which such an impulse can be couched is illustrated by Katherine Anne Porter's "Old Mortality," where Miranda's definition of herself as a questioning and resisting daughter rather than an accepting and obeying one is conveyed in a series of graduated movements away from her family. She protests against her father's irritable refusal to discuss the harsh truth underlying family legend by loosening her hand from his grasp and stepping away. She rejects his authority by eloping from the school where he had placed her. At the end, having returned for a family funeral, she signals her determination to define her self and her life in freedom from the smothering weight of the past by sitting apart from both her father and her cousin Eva in a moving automobile, as she promises herself that she will "know the truth about what happens to me." "I can't live in their world any longer," she tells herself. Earlier, on the train, she had talked with Cousin Eva about her marriage and had evoked disapproval:

> "Shameful, shameful," cried Cousin Eva, genuinely repelled. "If you had been my child I should have brought you home and spanked you."
> Miranda laughed out. Cousin Eva seemed to believe things could be arranged like that. She was so solemn and fierce, so comic and baffled.
> "And you must know I should have just gone straight out again, through the nearest window," she taunted her. "If I went the first time, why not the second?"[46]

Why not, indeed. Having rejected the old way and now feeling only "an immense weariness" with her present situation, she has no choice but to press on. The reader knows that a decisive departure awaits only the burial she has come to witness.

Porter had experienced for herself the impossibility of living in others' worlds. Frustrated by what she perceived as her family's failure to recognize and support her potential as an artist (her father urged that if she wanted to write she could stay at home and write letters) and convinced that Texas society in general held similar views of women's potential, she left them and left the state when she began to emerge professionally. When she was preparing a review of Willa Cather's posthumous collection of essays *On Writing* for the *New York Times Book Review* in 1949, she took particular note of statements by Cather indicating her awareness, too, of the need to escape the constraining presence of the family. One of the passages Porter marked in the margin of her own copy of the essays was a comment on the difficulty of retaining an "individual soul" within a family, and the "double life" that exists "even in harmonious families," with each person "escaping, running away, trying to break the net which circumstances and his own affections have woven about him."[47] The older writer had described a situation Porter knew well. In the essay that grew out of her review, "Reflections on Willa Cather," she celebrated Cather's (and implicitly her own) departure from family and achievement of personal freedom and fulfillment, noting her refusal to be "lost among them—the longest winged one who would fly free at last."[48]

For another of those long-winged ones, Edith Wharton, liberation from the "life of constraints" imposed by the expectations of her natal family and their society meant putting distance between herself and them. She departed for Europe and refused to come back even when World War I broke out. Staying on, she threw herself into France's cause and won such a degree of freedom from New York expectations of ladylike-ness as to have, in David Minter's words, "the heady experience of making major contributions" to the war effort.[49] Wharton had been "generally uneasy in America" and was seeking a measure of amorous freedom and liberation from her marriage as well. Even so, Mary Suzanne Schriber points out, these motivations had to some measure existed in Wharton's life for a number of years. Interrogating the timing of her departure in 1912 (when Wharton signaled the ending of both her marriage and her residence in America by selling her house and moving definitively to France), Schriber identifies as the determinant factor Wharton's travel writings and the "process of self-discovery they initiated," with their emphasis on "exploration of the unknown" and their "metaphors of pilgrimage, vocation, salvation, and quest."[50] Like herself, Wharton's female characters such as Lily Bart, in *House of Mirth,* are caught between their affection or yearning for what "home" means and their need for independence. They are caught in the tension between "a fading world that offered women place—as daughters, wives, mothers, and readers—but denied them voice," and a "new order, too amorphous to provide place, yet palpable enough to call forth a voice."[51] The "place" offered by that traditional world was, of course, securely house-bound. To leave its constraining expectations, they had to leave the house itself—or else, like Undine in *The Custom of the Country,* pursue marriage in a deliberate and cynical (but nevertheless sad) enterprise of appropriation.[52]

It has been suggested by Blanche Gelfant that Wharton's escape to Europe, like that of a number of other women writers, should not be regarded as evidence of confinement but of freedom from confinement. Her point is interesting and merits careful attention. Willa Cather, Mary Austin, and Katherine Anne Porter were all, Gelfant writes, "impelled," not by what might be called a negative motivation—their powerful need to break out of societal restrictions—but by the same positive factors that lured Ernest Hemingway into a life of travel: by "a love of foreign lands, by restlessness, curiosity, need for change and adventure." These three women writers, as well as others such as Wharton and Gertrude Stein, she insists, "traveled with rhythmic regularity, alternating work with wandering; home (different homes at different times) with a world elsewhere." They had an apparent "latitude to go where they wished and as they wished."[53]

Yet the evidence indicates that for most of the women in this group the motivation and the ability to travel were more complex than Gelfant's picture of almost genderless liberty would suggest, and that their departures were not virtually routine ventures of youth into an expansive world but, indeed, gestures of extremity. Austin was able to reach Europe after years of struggle to free herself from her family's expectations as to proper womanly behavior and from her husband. She scraped together her resources and went to Italy only when she believed that she had cancer and would not long survive. Cather first went to Europe with Isabelle McClung, the young woman with whom she was in love, at least partly as an escape from her family and its traditional expectations. She later told Dorothy Canfield Fisher that the urge to escape was at the center of all her writing.[54] Porter went to Mexico and then to Europe as the farthest-flung steps in a long and often despairing process of escape from Texas and from family, including a first husband who was apparently abusive. Her retrospective accounts of that process adopt the very images of "confinement or enclosure" that Gelfant says are "inapplicable to these 'lives.' " And although it is true that she went to Mexico alone and with a journalistic assignment (though certainly not one substantial enough to maintain her by itself), she went to Europe in the company of a lover, later her husband, in a state very like that of the "somehow kept woman" that Gelfant would deny. Wharton, to be sure, had recourse to Europe as part of the context in which her family lived its life, but also as an escape from a marriage and a set of societal expectations that severely impeded her fulfillment as a writer.

Even aside from the question of where to place the emphasis in surveying the extensive travel of these women, whether on the fact that they did go places and do things or on the factors that may have impelled them to escape, it is clear that Austin, Cather, Porter, Stein, and Wharton—and we could add to the list other American women of their generation who went to Europe for their own purposes, such as Caroline Gordon, Kay Boyle, Jean Stafford, and, some decades earlier, the painter Mary Cassatt—were a very exceptional few.[55] All of these whom I have named were, for one thing, white. All had either wealth or extraordinary high-aesthetic abilities and determination or exceptional luck. Their experience was not by any means representative of American women in general. But to a very great extent it was precisely that—the experience of women in general—from which they were escaping.[56]

Probably the definitive text in which the act of departure serves as the indication and symbol of women's determination to achieve freedom is Marilynne Robinson's *Housekeeping*. This remarkable novel is like a fact of the landscape: to talk about contemporary fiction of escape from domestic constraint without taking it into account would be to misrepresent the field of discourse. Rejection of domesticity and related traditional expectations of women's lives is rendered in Robinson's novel with an absoluteness that is at once stark and richly evocative. *Housekeeping,* then, offers a model of women's fiction strikingly unlike that offered by the work of Sarah Orne Jewett. Jewett's fiction glorifies domestic relationships; its circumscribed, looping journeys constitutive of a female community circle the home, departing from it but always returning. The two novels, *Housekeeping* and *The Country of the Pointed Firs,* define two distinct clusters of women's fiction. Even so, they are clusters within a shared category. The very real ambivalence pervading Robinson's novel places it among those dualistic narratives of journey in which (as Karen Lawrence argues in *Penelope Voyages*) home is always implicated. As some readers of *Housekeeping* have argued and as I will maintain, Robinson's novel, for all its absoluteness in refusing to keep (to) the house, incorporates aspects of the home vision as well. The paradigm it offers, then, has more in common with that offered by Jewett than at first appears. It anchors, in a sense, the other end of the spectrum I am considering here.

As a first novel even now less than two decades old, *Housekeeping* has attracted a surprising volume of criticism, much of it of a very high order and often directed precisely toward the implications of the novel's development of a motif of journey narrative. My purpose here, then, is not so much to offer another reading of this powerful novel as simply to bring it into the field of discourse, to make it available as a reference point in the chapters that follow. It is a reference placed at what will usually appear some point far off toward the horizon, in that most of the writers considered here make considerably more modulated interrogations than Robinson does of traditional structures of famil(iarit)y and the need to depart on other ways. Certainly that is true of Cather, of Tyler, and even of Morrison. But my purpose is also to position *Housekeeping,* radical as is its rejection of enclosure, as a text that, like several of those I will discuss at greater length, raises the possibility of reconciliation. Despite its singular commitment to vagrancy, both in the usual and in a more radical sense of the word, we can see in *Housekeeping,* I believe, important points of contiguity with Anne Tyler's more obvious urge to keep house as well as to keep to (i.e., remain within or return to) houses, and also with Mary Austin's nostalgia for home, despite her determination to set out on trails of discovery.

The narrative outlines of *Housekeeping* are those of a move from enhousement to chosen homelessness, a life of vagrancy. Robinson's Sylvie and Ruth not only depart from the house but attempt to destroy it and elect, in its place, the radical freedom of the open road. For male characters, of course, such a story would not be so surprising. American literature is full of footloose males who "light out" for the territories and may or may not either settle down there or come back home. American history is itself full of displaced persons, whether people who have migrated to new homes by choice or those who have been driven or sold away from their homes, compelled into exile and trails of tears. But the unconventionalism of Robinson's novel lies in its following none of these lines. Here it is women who "light out," and their vagabondage is not only free but sought, chosen. Moreover, vagrancy is seen as a permanent choice, not an interim condition. It entails, as Paula Geyh points out, the even more radical choice of "a transient subjectivity."[57] Ruth and her Aunt Sylvie not only give up housekeeping and give up keeping to houses, they forego what might be called the mentality of houseness. But they do not give up the mentality of shared relationship and mutual caring. They define their being as a permanently shared, or familied, vagrancy.

The action of *Housekeeping* does not in fact proceed from security to vagrancy but from a very *insecure* at-homeness to freedom. At the start of the book, Ruth, the narrator, and her sister Lucille are already orphaned, bereft of the elderly grandmother who had cared for them since their mother's suicide and left to the reluctant watching-over of two inept and inexperienced great-aunts who hastily surrender them to their Aunt Sylvie's peculiar care as soon as she can be summoned. The aunts, Ruth says, immediately "fled."[58] The house of *Housekeeping,* then, is not the site of a stable family group and a secure life for the two girls, but only the shell of one: an important point. The fact that the house is associated, not with stable nurture, but with a series of abandonments, whether voluntary or involuntary, sets up a distinction between homes in the sense of structures of human relationships and homes in the sense of mere material structures or structures of respectability, membership in established society. It is this distinction that allows us to accept at face value Ruth's celebration of family toward the end of the book: "for families will not be broken" (194). Houses are another matter; they are part of the "architecture . . . of patriarchy," the "ideology of the patriarchal family made concrete."[59] It is only the house that Sylvie fails to "keep." Although readers may feel understandable misgivings about the quality of her child care as well, we need to recognize, as Elizabeth Meese points out, that for Ruthie at any rate Sylvie does succeed in the emotional task of mothering "in the most elemental way that others have not—she stays." Despite her overwhelming urge to be gone, she remains true to her commitment to the two girls as long as both are there to need her.[60] At the end, when she leads Ruth into a life of vagrancy, it is only the house they are leaving, not each other. Actually, they are leaving both the house and Lucille, but Lucille has already left them. The problem of Lucille remains, however, and we will return to it.

Despite a series of textual allusions to canonical narratives of heroic journey, Robinson's book locates the motivation of Sylvie's and Ruth's commitment to vagabondage not in traditional quest for some talismanic goal but very precisely in female experience, in domesticity. Her assault on basic conventions of society is direct. Sylvie has reconciled herself to surrendering her footloose life for the sake of her two nieces, but she refuses to keep house in any but her own eccentric way, which proves both startling and unacceptable to the general community. The indoor world of the house becomes unkempt, unregulated by standards of neatness, tidiness, and appropriate accumulation. Since she herself relates, as Meese comments, more to the outside world than the inside, she breaches the barrier between outside and in. Leaves litter the floor, floodwaters are celebrated, small animals and birds live in various parts of the structure while the sofa sits outside. The lines of opposition between the town of Fingerbone's demands for conformity and Sylvie's resistance to conformity could scarcely be more clearly drawn. But Lucille, who draws back her foot from the roving ways of her two kins-women, belongs to the indoor world. Embracing the demands of 1950s conventionality with a vengeance, she learns to sew, gives herself a home permanent, tries to tidy up the place, and takes refuge at last with, significantly enough, a home economics teacher. The choice is plainly defined as that between keeping house, which entails adopting a whole host of related behaviors, and freeing oneself from stereotypical femininity, that social imprisonment represented by the house itself. It is no coincidence that Ruth and Lucille, before Lucille's election of conformity, play out with their dolls "intricate, urgent dramas of entrapment and miraculous escapes" (86). The life of female normalcy they see ahead of them is one that stimulates an escape wish unless (as Lucille later does) one embraces its safety with blinders on.

As various critics have noted, Robinson highlights the choice she has posed by allusions invoking parallels between her story and those of classic American fiction. The book opens with an echo of *Moby-Dick*, phrased in a way that shows Robinson's awareness of feminist discourse about gendered voice. Rather than the imperative (imperious) "Call me Ishmael," her first-person protagonist says modestly, "My name is Ruth." Rather than Huck's raft floating toward freedom and enlightenment, a rowboat affords Sylvie and Ruth an excursion of discovery. Rather than the mentor's leaving the youth in the woods to "learn the ways of the hunt" as Sam Fathers does in Faulkner's "The Bear," Sylvie leaves her in an equally remote woods to face her loneliness and the need for a mother surrogate. There, like a Natty Bumppo, an Ike McCaslin, or even a Ralph Waldo Emerson expanding melon-like in the sun, Ruth undergoes her initiation through withdrawal to the wilderness and gains autonomous self-sufficiency, an unusual (but less and less unusual) attribute for fictive women. She becomes adequate to the life into which Sylvie leads her. The point is well emphasized by Martha Ravits: Robinson "lifts herself upon the shoulders of literary ancestors to demonstrate that the empowering attribute of self-reliance can be claimed by female as well as male protagonists."[61]

Ruthie's process of becoming, which is experienced through Sylvie's tutelage, resembles the Emersonian expansion, however, less than it does the step through the looking glass. It is a process of re-situation, a move into an-other place, that effects a reconstitution of the self. The correlation of spatial change (inside and outside, keeping house and drifting) with altered states of mind or selfhood is woven into the narrative throughout. As Ruthie's description of the women who come calling on Sylvie makes clear, it is a part of the encompassing meaning of "housekeeping." That description links these women's "notions of piety and good breeding" with their "determination" to keep Ruthie "safely within doors" (183), that is, within accepted mental constructs. The act of departure frees one not only from prescribed patterns of living but also from prescribed patterns of thinking, prescribed assumptions. It is thus an even more radical act than the choice of transience would immediately appear. It is the choice of a freed self so radical that the old self does not merely modulate but in effect dies—as, of course, the townspeople think Ruthie and Sylvie literally have.

Ruthie's recognition of the profoundly determinant import of her act of departure with Sylvie is conveyed in a (characteristically) concise statement: "It was the crossing of the bridge," she says, "that changed me finally" (215).[62] We know that Ruth will not go back, because if she did it would not be the same person who went, nor by the same bridge, and the house to which she returned would be a different (differently conceived) one.

Rather than thumbing its nose at social mores by way of endless driving, as Jack Kerouac's *On the Road* does, *Housekeeping* defies conventional norms and unsettles its readers by insouciant riding of the rails and by insisting, accurately, that Ruth and Sylvie are not the only women in America to identify themselves as railroad transients. As Ravits asserts, Robinson "steeps her novel in textual traditions that recall the very foundations of our cultural inheritance," and by shifting that literary heritage to the female perspective that has commonly been seen as lying outside it, "augments our native strain."[63] *Housekeeping* "transforms" the story of American frontiersmen into "a new one about frontiers for women."[64]

Remarkable, indeed transformative, as Robinson's novel is, then, in the clarity with which it poses issues of freedom, spatial endeavor, and the opposition between transcendence and social conformity, these issues are not in themselves peculiar, but quite traditional in American literature. What is peculiar is that it is women who pursue such endeavors and such freedom. Even so, the female transients of *Housekeeping* are only (perhaps) the most single-mindedly drawn, most startling examples of an urge and a motif that are evident in numerous texts by women authors of the twentieth century. It is the starkness with which the impulse is pursued, leading her errant heroes to a degree of freedom and a mode of life that most readers can scarcely imagine, that makes Robinson's novel so startling and so moving. It is that starkness that gives it its quality of *unheimlichkeit*—a quality we will encounter again, though in somewhat muted form, in Anne Tyler's oddities and Toni Morrison's unthinkables. But perhaps a story that radically displaces familiar structures of life so basic as the custom of dwelling in houses is inherently, as a literal translation of the word would indicate, *unheimlich*.

What, though, of Lucille? Through the person of the sister who chooses conventional enhousement—a choice the novel clearly does not endorse—the narrative is pulled back, after all, toward a quietly forlorn nostalgia for home.[65] It does not end with Sylvie and Ruth's departure, although that act is its culmination. In a summary coda we see that both sisters suffer a continuing sense of loss. Neither wishes to go back and make her choice differently, yet each feels incomplete. Lucille occasionally (so Ruth imagines) catches fantasized glimpses of her lost sister, "the haunting presence," as Geyh writes, "of the absent."[66] Robinson's lyrical prose evocatively conveys her wish and her denial, as envisioned by Ruth: "She does not watch, does not listen, does not wait, does not hope, and always for me and Sylvie" (187). But Ruth, too, feels a loss, as is evidenced by the very fact that her imagination lingers in this way over her sister, as well as by her explicit acknowledgment, "If Lucille is there, Sylvie and I have stood outside her window a thousand times" (186).[67] The ending is indeed, as Geyh puts it, "paradoxical and ambiguous." The novel offers, in Thomas Foster's words, "the possibility of women remaining transient without leaving the home, without denying their connection to alternative, feminine values."[68] It does so by positing the stability and caring of the relationship of Sylvie and Ruth. But beyond that relationship there remains a lingering wistfulness.

Even in this starkly lyrical text of departure and free vagrancy, then, there is a yearning, not toward the settled and enclosed life of convention, but toward something fuller, some undefined compromise that would afford both home and free departure. Joseph Urgo perceptively observes that in a "migratory" culture the figure of the vagrant serves as a disconcerting double, representing "the threat of destinationless migration, of futility and failure."[69] Robinson, in her definitive text, brings to its fullest and most transgressive unfolding, among the novels of linked home and journey examined here, what might be called the imagination of departure. But it does not simply express a unidirectional insistence. Hidden within the imagination of departure—rather than counterpoised with it in a yoking of equals, as in Jewett's equally paradigmatic *The Country of the Pointed Firs*—is an imagination of biding. By placing this text at the center of our discourse on women's literature and women's needs, we can better perceive the nuances and the import of others' writing of that imagination.

Chapter 2

KEEPING ONE FOOT AT HOME
Mary Austin and the "Circuit of the House"

" . . . compelled by the exigencies of the trail . . . "
    —Mary Austin

It is having a place *to come back to* that we all of
us need so badly.
    —Katherine Anne Porter

Now recognized as a pivotal figure in the literature of the West and in the
history of women's move into professionalism in the early twentieth century,
Mary Hunter Austin is also a pivotal figure in American women writers' engagement with journey narrative. Like Sarah Orne Jewett, whose work she
knew and admired, she was a writer of the home-centered journey. But she
developed that narrative pattern very much in her own way, with a spaciousness and an energy of movement distinctly different from Jewett's. Like
Jewett, she imagined journeys that stretch rather than break the tie to home;
the patterns of geographic movement in her work are most often circular or
looping rather than linear. Those looping circuits, however, are much farther-flung than Jewett's, impelled by more emphatic discontents. Among the
most outward-bound writers of the earlier half of the century, both in her
life and in her works, Austin had no truck with the angel of the house, but
in fact avowed her "antipathy to the ministering angel type of woman."[1] At
the same time, of all that group of writers early in the century who both
enacted and imagined departures from traditional feminine roles into professional and political spheres of endeavor, she is one of the most insistent on
the need for home and centering, even marital, relationships.

Austin's imagination was powerfully engaged *both* by the urgency of departure as an expression of the will to personal freedom and the liberation
of women *and* by its complement (or what might seem its opposite), the idea

of the Beloved House. Her resolution of this dilemma is, in its general out-lines, scarcely surprising: she envisioned a reconstitution of domesticity and of the public lives available to women that would afford them freedom of movement from one to the other. But in its particulars this vision was quite distinctive. Drawing on her own experiences of patriarchal repression and betrayal, both as child and as adult, she formulated and expressed in her fiction an argument that the key to women's personal fulfillment, through freedom to move out of and back into the home, was the reeducation of males. If such a reeducation could be achieved, the relations between men and women would be reconstituted and the home itself (as she was able to imagine it in her final novel, *Starry Adventure*) would become the site of re-sistance to patriarchal repression of men as well as women.

Even in the nonfictional (but not entirely non-narrative) work for which she is still best known, *The Land of Little Rain* (1903), Austin's imagination centered on movement. An imagery of trails—whether the minute, ribbon-like trails in the arid landscape followed by mice and other small creatures in their search for water, the larger trails made by humans, or the streams that constitute the "streets of the mountain"—organizes the work.[2] But if she envisioned—and experienced—the openness of the arid West as a "harbor" of freedom "healing its ailing, house-weary broods" (*Little Rain,* 11), she also envisioned houses and house-relationships that would not be weari-some, and she projected a personal yearning for sustaining love relationships and secure at-homeness in her fiction. It was in part her yearning for home that impelled her emotionally charged interest in folk cultures,[3] which she viewed as cultures firmly rooted in a home place. In her many comments on the California Paiute, for example, she especially takes notice of their vil-lages, or campoodies, and the landforms among which they live. This em-phasis on, or yearning for, home exists alongside her equal bent toward de-parture from the known. Whether as contrary visions of what it is that women want or as a warm complementarity, the two counter-urges struc-tured both Austin's own experience and her writing.

Mary Austin's life story has been called, by Melody Graulich, "a classic in the pathfinder tradition," a phrase that both distinguishes one of the pri-mary features of Austin's life and implies the close interconnection of life and work, since, as Graulich points out, her work as a whole is "filled with imagery of walking and trails," paths of movement.[4] Austin herself retrospectively defined her life as "a road mark, a pointer on the trail." What her life is a pointer to is partially clarified in her retrospective summary of her adult life as a series of "shuttlings to and fro across the continent" in a continuing desire to "escape" the "background of [her] youth" (*Earth Horizon*, 279, 131). She invokes the trail image again, in her autobiography, when speaking of her increasing activity in feminist causes after 1920, saying she "found the pointers of her own trail going in the direction of women who desired the liberation of women for its own sake" (279). This fervent feminism, regarded by T. M. Pearce as the keystone of Austin's life-work, is most clearly (though perhaps not consistently) evident in her fiction. Indeed, both Nancy Porter and Vera Norwood have proposed that it was in large part the "insistence on and assertion of a feminist perspective" in the fiction, which "rattled" male critics, that caused it to be less highly esteemed than her nature writing.[5] Recent critics recognizing Austin's creation of a distinctively female vision and voice have shown, however, that the nature writings were implicated in her feminism even as they were implicated in her sense of elation at having freed herself from her small-town origins to pursue a journey of personal and social liberation.[6]

The first great fact of Mary Austin's life was the death of her father when she was ten years old, leaving her with an unloving mother and a nostalgia for a home she never had. The second was her departure with her family, at the age of nineteen, from their home in Carlinville, Illinois, on a migration to the arid southern tip of the San Joaquin Valley in California.[7] Both of these facts are deeply implicated in everything she wrote.

As Austin indicates in her strongly autobiographical novel *A Woman of Genius* (1912), even in childhood the sight of wagon teams hitched around the town square "stirred" her (or her surrogate self, Olivia) to the "allurement of travel and adventure."[8] If she wished even then for avenues of departure, however, she also wished for the security of a cheerful home and a loving mother, but had neither. Her relationship with her mother was a deeply troubled one that never ceased to haunt her. She records in *Earth Horizon* a certainty that her mother had never wanted her and wished that she had died instead of her younger sister, Jenny, who died of diphtheria the same year as their father. At his funeral, her mother shoved Mary away from the graveside and afterward distanced or even scapegoated her even more. Needing to economize, the family soon had to move away from their pleasant rural home to a house in town that Mary acutely disliked. It is not hard to guess that this sense of never having been really at home, of never feeling secure, comfortable, and accepted in a loving environment, lay at the root of her lifelong craving for love and a home of her own. Isolated within the family by her mother's rejection and isolated from other children by her own precocious intelligence and early devotion to reading, she compensated by developing a strong sense of self, which she referred to as I-Mary.[9] It would prove a valuable resource but would issue, in her adolescent years, in what Fink calls a "withdrawn and aloof" manner that in later life became a forbidding imperiousness.

When the Hunters left Carlinville, immediately after Mary graduated from college, they were setting out to join her older brother, James, in the San Joaquin, where he was attempting to launch himself by homesteading. She would later conceive of this westward departure, a version of the classic frontier story that has often been taken to define (masculine) American tradition, as an act of escape by which she made possible her life as a free and independent woman. It was the first of many departures she would make in her life. At the time, however, going west was not so much an independent act as a passive acquiescence in a decision in which she had no part. Her mother, Susanna Hunter, was committed to an image of the older son as absolute head of the household in his father's absence, and was determined to reunite the family under his leadership. Austin later claimed not to have cared, because she expected to have to teach school until she could establish herself as a writer and could do that as well in California as anywhere else. She recalls in her autobiography that on the train going west with her mother and younger brother she became "happily absorbed" in the "vast space and silence" of the Great American Desert (*Earth Horizon,* 182). But she seems to have been, in fact, deeply shaken. If she became happily absorbed in the landscape, it was only after they had made a stop for her to recover from a nervous collapse (not her first), which her biographer attributes to "the shock of being uprooted from a familiar environment" combined with rage at her mother's having decided to make the move without consulting her wishes in the matter.[10]

Even so, this first major departure led directly to Austin's first serious writing. Once she had gotten over the shock of the seeming emptiness and deadness of the San Joaquin Valley, she began to give close attention to the hidden vitality and austere beauty of the desert setting. She found there not only a place but a self, as well as "a voice and a subject matter."[11] On the basis of a notebook she had kept while she and her family made their way by wagon and horseback from Pasadena to her brother's homestead, she wrote an essay about the journey, which was accepted and published by a journal at Blackburn College, her alma mater. Thus, travel became firmly linked, in her experience, with expanded imagination and with writing. In succeeding months she was able to roam widely—much as Willa Cather insisted that she did as well, as a child in Nebraska. Edward Beale, a rancher best remembered, perhaps, for having brought camels to the American Southwest, allowed Mary free run of his 200,000-acre ranch, with two of his employees serving as guides and instructors in local flora.[12] Exploring the arid reaches so different from the tame world she had known in Illinois, learning the terrain, and developing the skills of observation that would later characterize her essays, she laid the foundation for the book that would establish her reputation, *The Land of Little Rain.*

Austin's later departures would be made largely as journeys of separation from her mother and the traditional feminine role her mother embodied. In retrospect, she defined Carlinville as the epitome of social conformity, especially with respect to the role and status of women, a society built on a belief that "there was a human norm, and it was the average man"; any difference from that norm on the part of women constituted a "female weakness" (*Earth Horizon,* 156). She recalled being told by a Carlinville physician that "the *only* work a female should do is beside her own fireside" (152)—a message directly contrary to her own drive toward work and achievement. The sense of the blessedness of having escaped Carlinville that pervades most of what she wrote is primarily a sense of the blessedness of having eluded Carlinville's—and her mother's—ideas of what a woman should be and do.[13]

Her own ideas of what a woman should do were centered very much in her desire for significant work. Work became her means of escape, initially from her mother and older brother's domination (so total that he apparently even decreed a "right" length of time for the boiling of her breakfast egg), later from a husband and the repressive regime of conventional housekeeping, and later still from the emotional shock of an exploitative romance. Soon after arriving in California, she was able to gain work as a private teacher on a nearby ranch and move out of her mother and brothers' home. When her employers decided to move away, she faced a life crisis. Returning to the family home was unacceptable, yet she had no funds with which to make a home elsewhere, because her mother had decided to withhold her inheritance from her father on grounds that such resources should be reserved for sons. Her only recourse seemed to be marriage—an option she had already rejected, to her mother's dismay, in Illinois. In effect, her mother had maneuvered her into the very subservience to patriarchy she had long resisted. At the age of twenty-three, frustrated and needing not only a means of livelihood apart from her mother and brother but also some measure of emotional fulfillment, she made an escape of sorts by marrying Stafford Wallace Austin, a restless and apparently ineffectual man who surely had no idea what he was getting into.

Over the next several years, the couple moved about arid and mountainous south-central California as Wallace pursued shifting moneymaking schemes that he could never manage to bring off. Prefiguring incidents in Austin's second novel, *Santa Lucia,* he drifted into debt without Mary's knowledge, with the result that she was unexpectedly evicted from their lodgings while pregnant and was served with a notice of debt at her mother's home while recovering from childbirth. During these years, as she laboriously taught herself the craft of writing, she went away intermittently for stays of varying lengths in Los Angeles and San Francisco, where she became acquainted with the literary world. At one point she left to accept a teaching job sixty miles away, despite having no child care for their retarded daughter—a rehearsal, perhaps, for the move to Carmel, California, that would end her marriage. Her urge toward personal freedom in the form of freedom of movement persisted even though the circumstances of her life continued to press her toward enclosure and acceptance of traditional roles.

Austin in fact attached great importance to home and family relationships. Her futile wish that her own family relationships might provide emotional satisfaction is evident in the persistence with which, despite her bitter resentment of what she saw as her mother's blatant favoring of the older brother, she kept returning to her mother on visits or to seek approval and advice in times of difficulty. She later wrote that when her mother died she felt "too desperately displaced from the true center of her being not to feel obliged to go somewhere" (*Earth Horizon,* 274)—an interesting and surprising comment, since she generally associated obligation with enclosure, and going places with choice. Her equally persistent effort to maintain her marriage, even after it had long since proven unsatisfactory and she had begun to develop her own career, also evidenced her urge toward at-homeness and relational roles. True, she expected to maintain the marriage on her own terms, with freedom to come and go; she did not assume she should be with her husband, cooking and keeping house, continuously.[14] Still, she did keep returning to the marriage for many years, making what was in her own mind, at least, a good-faith effort to maintain it, but finding herself unable to do so because he would not accept and respect her commitment to writing. In 1906 she left her husband to make a separate life for herself as an early member of the Carmel writers' colony that included novelist Jack London, poet George Sterling, and journalist Lincoln Steffens, for whom she conceived an intense passion that would trouble much of the rest of her life. This second major departure, like the first, shaped much of her writing career.

Austin's escape from her marriage was made possible by her success in *The Land of Little Rain,* which gave her reason to believe she could support herself by writing. Once again, then, as with the essay she wrote about the cross-country journey to the homestead, writing and geographic movement (the move to Carmel) were linked. This first and artistically most successful of Austin's books can well be seen as a culminating statement of her departure from her Midwestern origins. Like *The Flock* (1906), a book of narrative essays on California sheepherding and the trails followed by the flocks, and *The Land of Journeys' Ending* (1924), her later book of essays on the Arizona–New Mexico region, *The Land of Little Rain* celebrates a landscape as different from that of Illinois as can be well imagined. Her devotion to the arid reaches of those vast areas, lovingly and expansively conveyed in closely detailed descriptions of plant life and fauna as well as the sweep of land mass and contour, is an implicit reiteration of her alienation from Middle America and all it represented. Realistically, she acknowledged in her autobiography and other works that the narrowness of Carlinville that so repelled her could be found in California towns as well. But in the geography of her imagination the West and Southwest were places of liberation, in contrast to the smothering Midwest. In this, of course, she was adopting the classic American trope of frontier freedom, but she adopted it by way of her own keenly individuated experience.

By celebrating these arid regions for what they were, visually, and for the life-forms they sustained on their own terms, rather than for their economic potential as agricultural regions (a potential that hinged, of course, upon their being changed rather than preserved), Austin distanced herself not only from the Midwest but from the expectations and goals of her mother, brothers, and husband.[15] Her ability to reach those regions and to make of them the foundation of the literary career that she equated with her very selfhood was the measure of her emancipation both from parochialism and from traditional expectations of women. In following animal trails and the "streets of the mountain," as in her decisive departure to Carmel, she followed the trail of her own individuation, a trail leading away from all that she derided as the "flock mind," including stale conventions of femininity. She was defining herself, through changes of place, as an independent woman and a writer.

A testament to Austin's close and loving observation of the landforms and life-forms of arid and semi-arid southern California and to her close and, to a notable degree, equalitarian acquaintance with the native people (Amerinds, in her later parlance), *The Land of Little Rain* is also a testament to the influence of Sarah Orne Jewett. Austin's admiration of Jewett, hinted at by brief references in *Earth Horizon* and a 1932 article called "Regionalism in American Fiction,"[16] was by no means so overt as Cather's (which will be discussed in chapter 3), nor has it been so well recognized, but it is evident in the nature of her handling of the journey motif in her fiction and is demonstrable in this first book of nonfiction. Elizabeth Ammons astutely links Austin's achievement in her nature writing with Jewett's in *The Country of the Pointed Firs* through their common emphasis on "sexually charged" geographic images of "life-giving" hollows or cavities in the earth and through their adoption of the "sketch tradition" in preference to traditional and traditionally patriarchal linear form (to which, however, Austin would periodically return).[17] Seyavi, the basket maker who serves as an exemplar of female independence in the central essay of the group, has sometimes, like Austin's "shamanistic characters" or "chiseras" in general, been seen as a descendant of Jewett's Mrs. Todd.[18] A closer parallel occurs (as Marjorie Pryse has noted) in the concluding sketch, "The Town of the Grape Vines," in a close verbal echo of Jewett's story "A White Heron," in which the child Sylvia refuses to "tell the heron's secret and give its life away." In Austin's sketch, the narrator avows, in similar terms, her refusal to betray the human wish for seclusion, saying "rather would I show you the heron's nest in the tulares" than tell the precise location of El Pueblo de Las Uvas.[19] By way of trails first

struck in the opening sentence of the opening essay and winding themselves through the book, Austin arrives, in this concluding sketch of the
little town Las Uvas, at an idyllic home whose "kindness, earthiness, ease"
are cradled in the "full-bosomed hills" of a strong female earth (*Little
Rain,* 171).

The Land of Little Rain was not the only masterwork gleaned from
Austin's early years in California. Her noted story of female freedom of
movement and oracular power "The Walking Woman" sprang from an actual encounter recorded in the notebook she kept during those years. She
mentions in *The Flock* that she had learned from the Walking Woman "when
that most wise and insane creature used to come through."[20] First published
in *Atlantic Monthly* in 1907 and then placed as the concluding story in the
1909 volume *Lost Borders,* "The Walking Woman" importantly demonstrates
the possibility of reconciling the desire for love with the desire for satisfying
work, but does so in terms that must have seemed startling to Austin's contemporary readers—and still strike one as being rather austere. The Walking
Woman—significantly, she is given no other name than this phrase that defines her freedom—goes where she pleases on "no discoverable errand,"
"steadily walking" in a "kind of muse of travel" (*Lost Borders,* 255). Her
"endless mobility" makes her, in Faith Jaycox's words, "the precise opposite
of a confined woman," gaining "heroism" through her "rejection of . . . the
'canons of gentility.' "[21] But when she tells her own story—significantly, to
another woman, the narrator, who passes it on[22]—it is not only her freedom
of movement that she emphasizes but the single episode in her life in which
she achieved perfect satisfaction by combining effectiveness in work (sheepherding) with a love relationship. The three important things in a woman's
life, the Walking Woman says, are "to work and to love and to bear children." These are the three experiences that "if you had known you would
cut out all the rest."[23] Like the schoolteacher-wife-mother of Austin's later
"Kate Bixby's Queerness" whose oddity is her determination to have both a
career and a family, the Walking Woman has had all three, and if she now
walks alone—since her husband had to go on with his flock when she could
no longer follow, due to her advanced pregnancy, and her child then died—
she seems nevertheless to be fulfilled, satisfied. Most emphatically, she is
confirmed in her identity.[24] There is no trace of the conflict and frustration
that characterize most of Austin's female characters. The calm and confident
tone of the story, and especially its celebration of the sturdy balance of the

Walking Woman's footprints, bears the stamp of Austin's glow of achievement and anticipation at the point when she had made her 1906 departure
from marriage to professionalism.

   Despite the independence and full commitment to her art signaled by
her move, Austin did not remain in Carmel for long. The restlessness and
determination already evidenced in her need to move beyond her beginnings, geographically as well as mentally, and beyond the conventions of
women's lives, continued. Convinced that she had breast cancer and wanting to see Europe before she died, she soon (in 1908) made another departure. From that time on, throughout her life, she would travel continually.
When she returned to the United States in 1910 from an extended stay in
Europe, she brought with her the experience of having marched, in London,
for suffrage. This new involvement in feminist activism, reinforcing an earlier acquaintance with Charlotte Perkins Gilman, would determine much of
the nature of the rest of her life. Rather than returning to Carmel, she went
directly to New York to prepare for the production of her play *The Arrow
Maker* and, in general, to advance her career—a concern that she, like many
other women writers, generally denied. When she later prepared an introduction to be given before one of her lectures, she wrote of herself, "She has
never been interested in building up a literary career." Her correspondence
with her publishers demonstrates, however, that she was keenly interested in
career development and publicity.[25] She would at least nominally maintain
her primary residence in New York for over a decade, but during most of that
time would continually crisscross the continent while traveling the lecture
circuit for a living. In the early 1920s her love for the Southwest became
increasingly centered on New Mexico, and in 1925 she built a house in
Santa Fe that she called Casa Querida, Beloved House.[26]
   The title of her book of essays about the landscape and ecology of New
Mexico, then, *The Land of Journeys' Ending,* is a deeply characteristic and
significant one. Austin's vision of the Southwest was shaped not only by its
landmass and climate but by her instinctive focus, developed in the course
of a lifetime of departures and journeys, on the journey aspect of southwestern history. Quite accurately, she presents the Arizona–New Mexico region
as the place where the journeys of three great peoples converge: the Pueblo,
or village-dwelling, Indians, who originally came down from the North; the

Spanish explorers and settlers who came up from Mexico; and what she calls the Nordic Americans, who came from the East. Her own life-journey converged with them there and ended in Santa Fe in 1934, two years after the publication of her autobiography, commercially the most successful work in her long career.

In naming her house Casa Querida, Beloved House, Austin expressed the powerful homing impulse that existed in uneasy partnership with her individualistic adventurism. As she viewed her life retrospectively in the autobiography, from the perspective of the house she had finally built, she may have conceived of it in terms of movement along a trail and judged that "what most women wanted" was "time and adventure" (*Earth Horizon,* 177), but she also believed that "few intellectuals of her generation [had] clung more obstinately to the idea of a home, a house, a garden" than she did (274). Mabel Dodge Luhan captured this essential duality of Austin's character and mind in commenting that she was "one of the best companions in the world in a house or on a trip."[27] Her love for the Southwest was itself dual: She saw in the desert at once a space of freedom and a place for living. Vera Norwood identifies the particular quality of her naturism as an interest in the desert as a lived-in rather than a looked-at space, and locates her esteem for Native American women in their ability to make domestic lives there that "respected the primacy of the land."[28] She attempted to make a similar domestic life for herself in Santa Fe.

The very title of her autobiography, *Earth Horizon,* indicates Austin's vision of her life in terms of a plot of departure from the hearth-and-home life prescribed for women in order to travel toward the horizon, the same image for personal growth and achievement that Zora Neale Hurston would also soon invoke in her autobiography and in *Their Eyes Were Watching God* (1937). Appropriately, for a life story centered on trails and departures, *Earth Horizon* begins with the story of a journey: her father's trip up the Mississippi to Illinois as a settler. It maintains an emphasis on westward movement as she traces her further ancestry, then narrows the focus to her female ancestors: "It is to the things that [these female ancestors] discovered in their westward trek that Mary's generation owed the success of their revolt against the traditional estimate of women." More specifically, she locates "whatever in [herself] makes her worth so much writing about" in the "saga" of these female ancestors, handed down to her in her "nurture" (14). Rachel Blau DuPlessis argues that "genius theory is a particular exaggeration of bourgeois individualism, and its evocation increases the tension between middle-class women as a special group and the dominant assumptions of their class."[29] Certainly Austin adopted such a theory in her autobiographical woman of genius, Olivia, but her emphasis here on her solidarity with her pioneering foremothers would seem to counter the idea of exceptionalism. Her most important inheritance from these women, she says, was the realization of "the predominance of happenings of the hearth, as against what happens on the battlefield and in the market-place, as the determinant of events" (*Earth Horizon*, 15). At this late point in her life, at any rate, home had come to represent for her, not the repression she rejected, and not merely the personal centering that she had always believed essential, but a positive counter to the traditionally public sites and preoccupations of masculinist culture.

Reviewing her life as a whole in *Earth Horizon* (although the book is curiously weighted toward childhood), she identifies her own sensibility as a duality: a "roving mind's eye that includes for her, in its implications, the whole American continent" (15), as well as an attraction to the hearth, the "Beloved House." Nancy Porter's comment that Austin "alternately avoided and celebrated as socially useful" the forms and ideology of "women's domestic culture"[30] is accurate but perhaps understated. The duality of her relationship to that culture was also deeply personal and central to her system of values. Sporadically throughout her fiction-writing career, but most fully in *Starry Adventure*, published only a year before *Earth Horizon*, she envisioned an ideal in which emergence is reconciled with remaining, in which the free search for self-definition and fulfillment in outward-bound endeavors is combined with a restructured equalitarian domesticity.

From the first, Austin's fiction recognized the restrictiveness of women's lives. Every one of her novels—except perhaps *The Lovely Lady* (1913)—develops a polarity between departure, with strong implications of feminist liberation, and homing, with an implied reinforcement of traditional gender roles. It is departure, however, that is emphasized. Liberation was the need she perceived as being most urgent, presumably because a domesticity of a kind she regarded as repressive was already firmly in place. Many of Austin's women characters struggle to pursue careers while also achieving lasting love relationships, a theme that is often recognized with respect to *A Woman of Genius* but in fact characterizes most of her other novels as well. In the little-read *Outland,* for example, the central female character (and the most adventurous follower of trails), Mona, is a self-supporting professional woman who has every intention of maintaining her career but also wants romance—and gets it in an ending so happy that it confirms the genre definition of the book as a fantasy. In *The Ford* (1917), an independent woman character of remarkable astuteness in business insists that women have as great a range of ambitions as men and need not marry unless they want to. She does want to marry and feels that her life is impoverished without a marital relationship, but she is happy with her business endeavors, which entail a great freedom of movement around south-central California. In these and other works Austin developed women characters who resembled an idealized self, characterized by the kind of wholeness enunciated by the Walking Woman.

The strongest of Austin's novels with respect to the right of women to pursue careers is, to be sure, *A Woman of Genius* (1912), a piece of fiction so directly related to actual life that it has been called a "dress rehearsal" for the autobiography.[31] But if we step back to the novels leading up to *A Woman of Genius*—*Isidro* (1905), *Santa Lucia* (1908), and *Outland* (1910 in its pseudonymous British edition)—we can see that the emergence of her theme of women's freedom in careers was by no means steady. The feminist theme in these early works proceeds uncertainly, in assertive leaps and stumbling backtracks.

Isidro was an encouraging start for Austin's career as a novelist in that it achieved some genuinely memorable passages and sold well. Even so, it was a false start in that the genre—a costume historical romance replete with a broadly idealized landed aristocracy, disguises, misplaced infant, miraculous reunion, capture, and rescue, with marriage at the end—was at a far remove from the studies of contemporary life and gender relations in which she would go on to achieve notable success. The gender theme vacillates as the heroine, Jacinta, first masquerades convincingly as a boy, then learns to be a lady, then resumes her masculine attire to save her beloved from a wicked Indian (a surprisingly uncharacteristic treatment of Native Americans), then resumes her ladylike role to become a wife and mother. Apparently she lives happily ever after, despite the curiously emphasized fact that she stays at home while her husband goes traveling. This concluding assurance that Jacinta is happy in stasis scarcely rings true, since she has been depicted throughout as a woman of motion and adventure who found her training in ladylike behavior a prison. We recall that when she resumed her male garb and rode off on horseback to rescue Isidro she drew "deep breaths of free-dom and relief."[32] It is this sense of relief that strikes one as carrying Austin's authentic voice, not the bliss of staying at home and minding the children.

In her second novel, *Santa Lucia,* Austin chose a contemporary setting and a mode of social realism. The romantic-sounding title is actually the name of a California town on the make. In part, but only in part, the work constitutes an argument for a woman's right to leave an unhappy marriage and home, the kind of marriage that in *Cactus Thorn* Austin would describe as one in which the woman is "a fenced and valued possession" (54). *Santa Lucia* offers three heroines and three love stories, only one of which, the most egalitarian, promises to be unambiguously happy. The most thoroughly unhappy of the three heroines, Julia, is a woman accustomed to playing the role of romantic temptress, who becomes so thwarted and miserable in her conventional marriage that she is determined to get out at any price. Her final escape, after other departures involving an amorous liaison have failed, is by way of suicide, a departure that parallels those of Edna Pontellier in Kate Chopin's *The Awakening* (1899) and Lily Bart in Edith Wharton's *The House of Mirth* (1905). In pointing out these parallels, Esther Lanigan Stine-man comments that the three works, published within a single decade, show women as assuming the authority of self-judgment rather than allowing men to judge (and potentially exile) them.[33] Even so, we can scarcely read their mode of escape as a positive model for women's lives. The story of Julia, an (over)dramatization of Austin's own escape from marriage, is indeed a strong assertion of the need for escape from domestic enclosure, but the es-cape it envisions is self-destructive.

A survivalist mode of departure from marital convention is offered in the story of the second heroine of *Santa Lucia,* the ironically named Serena, who for much of the novel longs to no avail for both satisfying work and some degree of equality in her relationship with her husband. Steered by her aunt toward the profession of teaching despite her own lack of interest (as Austin was steered by her mother), wishing to make her way in some artistic activ-ity but getting no encouragement along that line (a complaint that Austin voiced against both her mother and her husband), Serena turns to marriage in a kind of hopeful surrender. Even after her marriage, however, she con-tinues to wish for some endeavor and achievement in the larger world. In addition, she both deplores her husband's business ethics and poor financial management and resents his condescending manner toward her. Like the story of Julia, then, that of Serena launches a strong critique of marriage and restrictive assumptions about the scope of women's activities. The novel veers from its development of strong, resistant women, however, in showing that Serena not only surrenders her impulses toward departure—in part out of shock at Julia's adultery and suicide—but settles into a busy, contented domesticity and even wakes up at last to masculine superiority. In part, she is able to make this change because her husband undergoes a change of his own, a waking-up process entailing recognition of his wife's abilities and realization that society is not well served by demanding that unhappy marriages like Julia's be continued. Although it is anticipated in *Isidro,* this is the first emphatic appearance of Austin's important theme of male reeducation with regard to gender relations.

The awakening in *Santa Lucia* is a relatively modest one, with considerably greater emphasis placed on Serena's waking up to what sounds like an all-too-conventional femininity. Happily *shutting up* the blinds—that is, enclosing herself more tightly in the home, shutting off the view out the window—as Evan returns in the evening, she finds that she "understood at last his wish to be one with the current interest of his time, as the relish for life, the undaunted male attitude which begot great achievement on the West." As a result, she "felt herself shamed by its largeness forever out of the complicated futility of her moral conventions."[34] Such moments of surrender and adoption of happy home values are evidence of unresolved conflict in Austin herself, generating fictive impulses contrary to her more usual voicing of feminist ideas. Stineman points out that at the time Austin was working on *Santa Lucia* she was seeking to end her marriage, not to become resigned to it.[35] The novel is strongly autobiographical in a number of specific respects, especially its portrait of Serena's vapidly hopeful businessman husband who can't bring himself to tell his wife that she is about to be dispossessed of her basic household furniture because of his failure to repay his debts. Evan Lindley is a transparent representation of Wallace Austin, even to his involvement in water rights issues. The final resolution, however, with Serena's idealization of her husband, is evidence not of autobiographical method but of fantasy. Austin herself never surrendered her criticism of her husband's behavior.

The third of the three heroines, though she is accurately autobiographical in her outdoor interests and her vigor, also serves fantasizing or wish-fulfillment purposes for Austin both in her relationship to her parents—a doting father and a retiring mother—and in the nature of her marriage. In the story of this third heroine, surprisingly named William,[36] Austin brings the novel to a happy ending in the traditional form of a culminating marriage—but with a difference. The marriage bids fair to be one of equality from its inception. But the fact that that prospect is left as only a hope, since her story is not followed beyond the wedding ceremony, may erode the reader's confidence that even one-third of all marriages can be so fortunate. Moreover, it is a hope that at best has been dependent on luck and the processes of male career networking, since William finds her husband as a result of his being brought in, upon the recommendation of an old professional colleague, to take care of her father's medical practice when he is incapacitated. The novel finally does not offer any very satisfying resolution of the problem of the limitations on women's lives entailed by marriage.

In the story of this third heroine, a mixture of conventional femininity and a "masculine" kind of daring, *Santa Lucia* remains curiously divided against itself. William is boyish, open-faced, outdoorsy, and a youthful enthusiast of scientific pursuits. Moreover, in an act requiring physical courage and strength—certainly a departure from gender stereotype—she rescues her husband-to-be from attempted murder. Yet her story is directed into a version of the traditional marriage ending, while Serena, who raises the question of why women cannot be employed, has dropped the matter and found ways of achieving satisfaction at home, and Julia, having found no constructive way out of her marriage, has killed herself.

Santa Lucia was denied success in its own day by a moralistic outcry against the story of Julia and has been little read since, but it was a work that continued to resonate in Austin's subsequent writing. Certain elements of the novel—a character named Kate Bixby and the motif of clandestine travel to San Francisco—reappear in the short story "Kate Bixby's Queerness," which, along with *Cactus Thorn,* lay unpublished at the time of Austin's death. The stronger, convention-defying aspects of the female characters in *Santa Lucia* can well be seen, along with the writer-heroine of Austin's next novel, *Outland,* as prefigurations of Olivia Lattimore, her most emphatically departing heroine and her most fully autobiographical one, in *A Woman of Genius* (1912). The name of Julia's husband, Antrim Stairs, reappears as the pseudonym Gordon Stairs, under which *Outland* was published in England, in 1910. Austin's selection of this masculine name as her disguise for herself may well indicate her wish to identify with the "undaunted" attitude that "begot great achievements on the West," an attitude attributed, in *Santa Lucia,* to males. The value of identifying herself with such attitudes may have been felt by Austin to outweigh the cost of adopting a male persona for her temporary pen name. Her achievements as a writer had been, of course, "begot on the West," and she was no stranger to the earth-as-woman trope that the phrase implies.

In Olivia Lattimore, the "woman of genius," Austin created a heroine who, like herself, signals her departure from conventional patterns of thinking by departing geographically from the Midwest (a disguised Carlinville called "Taylorville, Ohianna"), and who wants a home and marriage but insists that marriage be based on principles of democratic equality and personal freedom. Like Austin's own, Olivia's resistance to convention and her association of mental freedom with geographical departure begin early. By adolescence she had developed "a kind of horror of the destiny of women; to defer and adjust, to maintain the attitude of acquiescence toward opinions and capabilities that had nothing more to recommend them than merely that they were a man's!" (*Genius,* 44). Olivia's demurral from conventional gender roles grows into a focus on independent work and a determined pursuit of a career as performing artist—a representation not only of Austin's writing but of her persistent interest in theater. Ultimately, in demonstration of her ability to carry out another supposedly masculine activity, Olivia also becomes her own business manager.

Olivia, like Austin, marries early, partly through the machinations of her convention-bound mother. It is a mismatch from the first. She wants adventure and personal expansion and urges her husband, Tommy, to "come away into the world," to "go out and . . . be a part of things" (131). But Tommy is as conventional as his name. He is all caution. His vision rises no higher than a secure, dull job and a snug place to live. Olivia cares about him and is committed to the marriage, but she is equally, and uncompromisingly, committed to her right to pursue self-definition through work. Like Serena of *Santa Lucia,* she wants both: "I thought that if I could only have Tommy and my work I should ask no more of destiny" (110–11). But of course she can't have both so long as she is married to a man whose ideas are limited by social convention, since conventional marriage does not afford women equal latitude for personal choice. Neither Tommy nor Olivia's brother nor even her female best friend can understand or support her artistic ambitions. After her first experience of professional theater gives her a vision of "a country of large impulses and satisfying movement"—a geographical image characteristic of Austin—there is no question but that Olivia must set out to find the way there (86). It is the road of self-realization—not so much self-discovery, the more traditional allegorical association of travel, since she has intuited the presence of this self all along, but fulfillment of what she already knows is her real identity. Until she can depart from her early conditioning and intense societal pressures toward conventionality, that self cannot emerge. Later, looking back from the vantage of her difficult success, she will regret that most of her family and friends "couldn't have walked in the way" with her, but since their attitudes are set against such an unconventional departure she has to "wal[k] in the way . . . alone" (70).

Austin's treatment of the arduousness of the serious stage performer's apprenticeship in her profession produced some of the strongest writing she had yet achieved. Clearly, her development of Olivia's emergence story is an anticipation of Cather's similar treatment of the development of the performing artist in *The Song of the Lark,* published three years later. Whether Olivia could have undertaken such an arduous professional development while also continuing the roles of wife and mother is left moot (and we are left free to doubt it) by the deaths of both Tommy and their sickly infant—a dual release much less freighted with complications and guilt than Austin's own ending of her marriage and her placement of her retarded daughter in institutional care. Olivia's departure is not merely passive, though, because she has already, even before Tommy's death, made intermittent exits (like Austin's to San Francisco and Los Angeles, as she worked toward her first book) toward the "something beyond" (*Genius,* 168). When she goes decidedly out the door of conventionality toward her career, it is because she has determined to "reach out and lay hold" of that something (168), as a fellow actress urges her.

The blossoming of Olivia's acting career is shown as being, like the blossoming of Austin's writing career, utterly dependent upon her having a high degree of mobility and control over her own movements. She learns her craft in Chicago, achieves success in New York, and travels to England for relaxation. Without the latitude to make these departures, she would not have become the strong person and the artist that she is. In England she encounters once again her one true love, a man she had met and yearned for before she married Tommy but had lost because her mother managed to separate them. She and this romantic hero, improbably named Helmeth Garrett, travel together in an ecstatic unmarried sexual relationship. Their exhilaration in the prospect of wide emotional vistas before them is conveyed by an image of a "broad window flung open" (231). But the windows of Helmeth's social vision are not so open as this image suggests. He is not prepared to make the more daring break from convention that Olivia asks of him: agreement for her to continue her profession after marriage. She refuses to marry him unless he will also marry her work, and he refuses to do so. The theme of male reeducation, then, or in this case the refusal of reeducation, becomes a crucial turning point in the story.

Olivia is not finally alone, however, even if others have refused to walk the path toward her destiny with her. Toward the conclusion of the novel she is accorded solidarity with other women, and she makes, at last, a marriage with a man who shares her professional interest—a doubly happy ending. In the most overtly exhortatory passage in the book, her actively feminist younger sister tells her that she constitutes a "forward movement" for women in herself. "Every time I see a woman step out of the ranks in some achievement of her own," she says, "I think, 'Now, Olivia will have company' " in the "conscious movement of us all toward liberty" (261).

What Austin's aspiring female characters—Olivia, Julia, Mona, and later Neith—have in common is the desire to fulfill their roles as lovers and wives on their own terms, terms that involve defining themselves as individuals through their work. They want *both* to stay within the home *and* to escape. For the most part, such dual satisfaction eludes them. When Neith, who like Olivia has refused to accept a marriage that does not encompass personal freedom and equality, finds herself alone at the end of *No. 26 Jayne Street* (1920), she feels "the future at her heart like a small gnawing worm."[37] But the solemnity of this ending does not imply that she was wrong in clinging to her principles. She may be, as Shelley Armitage writes, "living with only her principles," but Austin, I think, would not have said "only" or called the idea that marriage should be based on equality "an abstract theory."[38] In her own experience and in the convictions she enunciated, it was all too concretely real a need. The end of *A Woman of Genius* is more hopeful. Having held firm to her conviction that professional work does not leave a woman "impoverished of feminine graces," Olivia enters into a second marriage, this time with a man who, as a playwright, can also be a colleague and with whom she hopes to "solve the problem of how to keep our art and still be happy" (293). It is an ending that conveys both the duality of Austin's own hopes and, in its phrasing, the priority ordering in which she held them—with her art coming first.

Austin's emphasis toward the end of *A Woman of Genius* on feminism as a shared principle and the dignity of working toward such "Forward Movements" represents a major turn in her thinking, from solitary struggle for individual flight and self-fulfillment to active involvement in social action on behalf of all women. She spoke at a suffrage rally on October 13, 1911, joined the National American Woman Suffrage Association, and attended meetings of the Heterodoxy Club in Greenwich Village.[39] Even so, she never relinquished her hope that in her own life and in the lives of women generally, freedom to depart from conventional domesticity in order to pursue individual interests and efforts could be combined with supportive love relationships centered in homes. At times her fiction came very near to emphasizing happy wifehood above all else. The ending of *Isidro* is such a moment, as is Serena's final settling into blissful adoration of her husband in *Santa Lucia*. We see that deviation from her usual thrust, too, in the perfect (and perfectly a-careerist) sweetheart of *The Lovely Lady*, published in 1913, an astonishing swerve from *A Woman of Genius*, only a year earlier (a swerve motivated, perhaps, by Austin's strong sense of the need to produce novels close enough to reader expectations to sell). Women characters in *The Lovely Lady* seem interested only in marriage and possessions, and work is defined as "that essential essence of maleness" to which women, who are "naturally outside of it," can only "pay tribute."[40] Knowing Austin's insistence on work and career, one might well suspect parody, but the tone gives no hint of it. Her imagination centers, in this book, not on departure but on an ideal of the Wonderful House, and the division between male and female spheres of activity is restored.

Even Austin's most determinedly free heroines, however, want marriage and home—not only Olivia but Nora in *Outland* (1919 in its American edition), Neith in *No. 26 Jayne Street*, and Kate Bixby, whose mother and sisters never seem able to imagine that having achieved the status of schoolteacher, earning a salary she can share with them, she might also want love. Kate has to sever her ties with family and go into a life burdened with secrecy and the care of a dying man in order to have both a career and an affectional life, but she succeeds.[41] Such characters want to have it all, according to the terms of Walking Woman's summary of what is important: satisfying work, erotic love, and a child. The reasons why they generally cannot have it all are no great mystery: conventional attitudes that seek to confine women within domestic walls; more specifically, the attitudes held by men. As we have seen, Austin continued for many years to return, in her writing, to the pro- longed trauma of her marriage and the emotionally debilitating effort to break free of it, creating in at least two novels, *Santa Lucia* and *A Woman of Genius,* male figures recognizable as portraits of Wallace Austin.

Perhaps even more traumatic, however, was her relationship with Lincoln Steffens, the famous muckraking journalist. The story of that rela- tionship is an involved and somewhat murky one that calls for summary here because it impinged on much of her fiction from at least 1910 on, in ways directly related to the theme of house versus departure. It is doubtful, in fact, that Austin would so insistently have pursued the theme of the ne- cessity for relations between the sexes to be put on a new footing, and the related theme of the transvaluation of home in relation to public endeavor, if she had not had this shattering experience with Steffens.

As I have noted, the two became acquainted in 1906 or 1907 at Carmel, shortly after Austin had left her husband.[42] Whether their acquaintance was of an amorous nature at that time is by no means clear. In any event, she became emotionally fixated on him from that time, and the relationship was resumed in New York when she went there in late 1910 following her two years in Europe. It has sometimes been thought that she went to New York mainly in pursuit of Steffens. Most scholars have believed that whenever it was begun, she did have an affair with Steffens, and despite a recent chal- lenge to that interpretation by Karen Langlois, who interprets the episode as a case of Austin's having fantasized a romantic relationship and suffered "il- lusions of deceit," the evidence seems to me to point that way.[43] Mabel Dodge Luhan, who knew both Austin and Steffens at the time, seems to have taken it as a given that Steffens had made a romantic conquest, perhaps even in 1906.[44] Austin, at any rate, took their relationship very seriously. Fink be- lieves that Steffens, too, considered marriage. But he soon became involved with another woman—apparently without bothering to reach an under- standing with Austin first. She seems to have realized what was happening only when she chanced to encounter Steffens and the other woman looking at an apartment that she was also inspecting—in the belief that *she* would be sharing it with him!

By all accounts, the abrupt ending of the relationship was one of Austin's most shattering experiences and one that would long reverberate in her work. When she remonstrated with Steffens in letters, he showed them about among male friends, making her once again a target of ridicule, as she had been (for her appearance and certain eccentricities) among male Carmel-ites; and Austin found out. She developed an obsession with her rights in the matter (if not a "maniacal" one, as Langlois terms it) and persisted in writing to Steffens and pursuing him, trying to force him to regard the ending of the affair as being still an open question until she participated in deciding whether to end it. Mabel Luhan saw the episode as "not so much a wound to the heart as to her sense of power."[45] But the point Austin was arguing, in however extreme or even overwrought fashion, was that a romantic involvement constituted a pact or bond entered into by two people and was subject to discontinuance only by mutual agreement, not by the unilateral actions of one party. She developed this point in *A Woman of Genius, No. 26 Jayne Street, Cactus Thorn,* and even *Starry Adventure,* written over twenty years later. However obsessive personally, her argument was a rather complex one, at once "conservative" and "radical," and for that reason deserves serious examination. Women, she believed, needed stable love relationships, even marriages, homes, and families; but they had a right to control their role in these matters with the same degree of freedom accorded to men. In arguing the second part of that two-pronged proposition she departed, once again, from prevailing practices and assumptions.[46]

Probably the first portrait of Steffens that appears in Austin's work is a sociology professor named Herman in *Outland.* Given its fantasy genre, *Outland* is, in fact, surprisingly direct in its autobiographical roots, having sprung from the idyllic first year of her life at Carmel, when she and poet George Sterling spent a great deal of time together taking "long hikes over the Monterey hills, while they conjured romantic tales of forest folk and lost treasure."[47] Out of this game, and with the playful collaboration of other Carmel-ites, grew the fantasy tale of a place within the real world yet apart from it where a special race of humans live in such close harmony with the beautiful natural world that they can virtually melt into it and be seen only if they allow themselves to be. The "House People" who surround them are successfully evaded by these "Outliers," whose values and way of life are uniquely their own. It is a concept patently expressive of Austin's pride in belonging with a special subset of humanity, and the linkage of personal freedom with spatial orientation is also characteristic, despite the uniqueness of the fantasy genre among her novels. Sterling appears in a leading role among the Outliers, while Steffens, recognizable by his sociological bent and his emotional detachment, becomes the romantic interest of the narrator and central character, Mona. Austin's conclusion that his emotional nature was changed and enriched by his experience with the Carmel group could only seem, in retrospect, unduly hopeful.

Notably, when *Outland* opens Mona is feeling harried by the fact that Herman keeps pressing a marriage proposal on her despite manifesting no capacity for love. Their accidental discovery of the entrance to the world of the Outliers while walking in the woods comes at an opportune time for her. She needs an "escape" from an "inward desertness" compounded of professional anxiety and romantic (or unromantic) uncertainty, so that she can pursue the resources she intuits "somewhere within" herself as a "vast, undiscovered country full of wandering lights and crying voices, from whence the springs of great undertakings should issue"—a geographical concept comparable to the "country of large impulses" Olivia intuits and seeks in *A Woman of Genius*.[48] She needs to break out of her present situation in order to find her authentic self and restore her life to productivity. That act of breaking out is figured as a removal to an alternative place along a magical trail of departure from the known into the imagined, from the social into the natural, and from emotional frustration to emotional fulfillment. The trail, then, once again serves as Austin's central organizing image. It is established in the opening words of the book, "The trail begins at the Broken Tree with the hawk's nest" (9), and followed throughout. Mona's following of the trail is deliberate and determined; having no time to pursue it when the discovery is first made, she returns, finds the opening again, and enters Outland. Herman's discovery is accidental; he falls down a slope into Outland while looking for her. (The woman is the leader, the man stumbles behind.) After an undefined period of time spent living and moving about with the Outliers, the two return to their familiar world with a new prospect for happiness, because a "door" to emotional richness that Herman "could never swing" has been made to "swing back" (that is, swing open) and he has become capable of love (232). Their lives have been changed through an act of departure and geographic movement, very much as Austin says she herself was "altered" in the process of roving about the San Joaquin Valley (*Earth Horizon*, 198). What now makes marriage viable is a change in attitude on the part of the male.

As we have seen, similar changes in attitude on the part of men had been part of Austin's novelistic vision from the beginning. Even in *Isidro*, her first full-length fiction, the young heir beloved by Jacinta must revise his goals and his sense of what he owes the past (significantly, in the person of his father) before he can recognize his desire for marriage. He must also learn to discard his assumptions about what women can do and accept Jacinta's competence when she comes to his rescue. In other words, he must realize that the young boy called El Zarzo ("The Thorn"), her false name when disguised, and Jacinta, the lady, are in fact one person. He must learn to accept the rudiments of an androgynous ideal. In *Santa Lucia,* Evan Lindley must learn that Serena can manage household finances better than he can and does not need to be protected from the truth, so that their marriage can be one more nearly of equality and thus be tolerable to her. Even the hero of *The Lovely Lady,* whose role is to succeed in business so that he can afford a Wonderful House in which to place an ideal woman, must give up imaginings of slaying a dragon to get the princess and redefine as princess a plain girl from home who would probably kill the dragon herself (210). After the Steffens trauma, however, Austin generally pursued the theme of the male's reeducation with a greater urgency than these examples indicate. In particular, after *The Lovely Lady* she increasingly focused on the idea that a man's public principles or political ideals ought to be reflected in his personal morality. The gap between the two was the flaw she saw in Steffens. A man who passed himself off in public as a believer in democracy ought, she believed, to accept democracy—a relationship of equality—in his relations with women. Thus the theme of the reeducation of men is joined to Austin's pervasive deconstruction of the outmoded doctrine of separate spheres and her insistence on the interconnection of public and private.

What might be called the Steffens problem appears most clearly in two successive works of the 1920s, *No. 26 Jayne Street* (1920) and, after the dismal failure of that novel and a lapse of several years when Austin gave up the writing of fiction, *Cactus Thorn,* written in 1927 but not published until 1988. In *No. 26 Jayne Street,* a turgid work but one of great potential interest for its depiction of political ferment in New York during the war and its portraits of the literati, she aggressively merges love plot with political plot, the private sphere with the public. Issues such as labor agitation and America's entry into the Great War provide the backdrop for a story of a young woman's choice of a husband. Even *within* the story of that choice, public and private concerns are linked in that Neith wants a husband who will share her political freethinking and conduct his domestic relations according to principles of democratic equality, not a masculinist "autocracy of personal feeling" (290). She wants to depart from restrictive conventions but also to have a faithful husband and a supportive relationship—on her own reformist terms.

The duality of Neith's desire is expressed in the action with which the book opens, her leasing of an apartment so that she can move out of her aunts' home—an act at once of departure and of occupation. But the overriding question that emerges during the novel is whether men can be reeducated in their valuation of home and personal relations so as to see these as being of equal importance with issues of public principle. Steffens himself appears in the role of an influential journalist named Adam Frear, who possesses a "large-mindedness" that unfortunately applies only to "parties and politics," not to "men and women" (170). His personal conduct toward women is at odds with "all those principles of conduct to which he was publicly committed" (269), and he finds it irritating when the one is in any way linked to the other. But Neith sees a connection between matters of "the hearth" and such public problems as "militarism" and "Capitalism" (188). At the end, rejecting marriage to Frear on an unprincipled basis that would imply condoning his shabby behavior toward another woman, she avows her support for that woman, a noted reformer who is last seen moving "toward the door" on her way "Over There" to discover whether Frear, and by extension other men, will learn. Neith is willing to wait. But for women in general the movement is one out the door toward social reform.

Seven years later, in writing *Cactus Thorn*, Austin treated many of the same themes but in a strikingly new way, through the vehicle of the most aggressive woman character she ever created, Dulcie Adelaid. Like Kate Bixby, Dulcie makes her departure not as a rejection of the traditional relationships and values of home, but rather as a quest to redefine the terms of those relationships and to find herself and her own way. As in *A Woman of Genius,* her freedom to follow her own trail is underscored by an insistent use of railroad images in the opening and closing sequences. She moves freely and vigorously about the West along trails that others lose, and she also moves cross-country, at home with modernity. The absence of a conventional last name—she is called throughout by what are in effect two given names—is related to this freedom of movement in that it indicates she is not owned, labeled, by either her father or the husband from whom she is separated and by whom she is ultimately widowed.

Once again Austin's point is that public affairs and private relationships must be governed by consistent principles of honesty and equality. The male in question, another version of Steffens, this time called Grant Arliss, is a younger, less seasoned, and less polished Adam Frear who espouses high principles as a public figure but feels no obligation to maintain such principles in his amorous relationships. After meeting Dulcie at an isolated train station during a period of retreat to the West, he pursues a sexual relationship with her in the course of which they reach what she, at least, thinks is an agreement that their future lives are to be linked. The relationship is interrupted by the necessity for Dulcie to go nurse her (clearly unworthy) estranged husband through his final illness. Arliss, invigorated by his idyll in the West, returns to New York, where he finds it convenient to become engaged to a woman whose social standing will enhance his career. When Dulcie follows him after her husband's death and learns the truth, she kills Arliss with her dagger (her thorn) in the most violent rejection of conventionalism in all of Austin's fiction. She is last seen, at the end, riding west on that epitome of rapid movement, an express train, into the landscape that to Austin meant freedom and empowerment.

Austin's fullest development of the theme of the reeducation of men, which she saw as being essential if women were to gain full freedom to pursue their personal interests and maintain satisfying home lives on a basis of equality, came in a pair of novels published at an interval of fourteen years but conceived as the first two parts of a trilogy, *The Ford* (1917) and *Starry Adventure* (1931). *The Ford* was begun in England even before the 1910 publication of *Outland*. Austin described it to her editor as "a novel of contemporaneous Californian life . . . in which *a man* is put to the three great temptations, money, power, passion" (emphasis added).[49] When the completed work appeared in 1917, it was very different. Drawing extensively on knowledge developed during her marriage, particularly of the struggle for water rights between Los Angeles and the Inyo Valley, and on her keen understanding of a woman's desperation when she feels trapped, she developed her dual theme of departure and homing with a fullness and distinctiveness she would achieve in no other work except *Starry Adventure*. In *The Ford* she integrated a public plot with a love plot with greater success than she had in *Santa Lucia* or would in *No. 26 Jayne Street,* but also, unfortunately, with traces of the inconsistency and ambiguity that blur the thematic impact of those works and indeed all of her novels until *Cactus Thorn* and *Starry Adventure.*

Like much else of Austin's writing, *The Ford* is a book of *staying* as well as of *going.* Mobility and a fulfilled stillness are seen together, in a kind of oneness. There is a sense of movement toward a point of being "at last . . . still," as Austin once said in a poem, "Going West."[50] The essence of the vision it develops is the blessedness and fruitfulness of the land, a set of values impelling a fiction of occupation rather than of departure. The novel illustrates with great clarity the interplay of feminism and femininity, departure and homing, public endeavor and private relations, that we see, though not always so clearly, throughout Austin's career. In addition, it explores, more fully than any of her novels except *Starry Adventure,* the possibility of a change of vision on the part of men as to the relationship between home and venturing. In many ways, then, it is a considerably more interesting work than it is usually accounted.

At the center of the novel is a set of four male characters, developed with great care, all of whom learn to see the importance of women's controlling their own lives. Steven Brent, the father of central characters Anne and Kenneth, owns and operates a sheep ranch. He and the two children find that way of life "free" and "rich," but his wife, who feels cut off from the world, finds it "empty" and desperately wants a "Way Out."[51] Since the rhetoric of descriptive passages aligns the narrative voice with their valuation of the outdoor life of the ranch rather than with hers—despite the obvious fact that Austin, as narrator, could well be expected to empathize with the frustration of a woman compelled to live in what she feels to be a prison—it would be easy for the novel to condemn Mrs. Brent as a mere scold who interferes with the happiness of her family. Her behavior seems at times to invite such a judgment and leads to a series of family catastrophes. Yet she is never so labeled. Instead, the book accepts, through the attitudes of Ken and his father, the validity of her discontent and her right to want something different for her life than the rest of them wanted. Through the sad experience of his wife's frustration and discontent, Brent learns the wrongness of men's imposing their will on women. A man "*can't* make a woman's life for her," he insists (*Ford,* 154). Endorsing this realization, the novel leads the other three males—Ken, his wealthy friend Frank, and Frank's rather benighted industrialist father—along the road of recognition of women's right to make their own departures from conventional thinking.

Their progress along that road is far from steady. Frank, a potential but rejected love interest for Anne, had been certain as a boy that keeping house and having children were "what women are for" (46). Later, in young adulthood, he becomes uneasy about "what was likely to happen if somebody somewhere didn't put a firm, restraining hand on women"—they might get the idea that they were "free to do *anything!*" (194). But by the end, seeing the triumphs of the freewheeling but loving Anne—in Stineman's words a "savvy rancher who holds her own against the most notorious of rancho capitalists"[52]—Frank is brought to a state of stunned admiration shared by his father, who expects to make Anne a partner someday and vows that he would "marry her myself if I thought she'd have me!" In describing Anne's business acumen and "damned courage," he invokes a buried but significant metaphor of movement and arrival: "To think of her hitting on the one thing that you'd *have* to come to!" (426). Having grown out of her childhood intention to be just such a housewife and mother as Frank thought she should be, Anne has moved faster than Frank and has arrived before him at a mental place where he can only catch up.

Ken, at the center of the novel's perspective, is more consistent than Frank in his admiration of Anne (though he, too, occasionally falls into a regressive urge to see women dominated) and manages to generalize the object lesson she gives him, which is a lesson of both going and staying, both public influence and private fulfillment: "It wasn't in the least that a woman couldn't be both as big as Anne was, and as womanly, but that men weren't big enough to afford her both within the scope of their lives" (373). But if Anne is fully mobile, the woman Ken finally realizes that he loves, in a romantic denouement typical of Austin's efforts to write commercially viable fiction, is the traditional still point toward whom the adventuring male moves, the end of the romantic path. And precisely here Austin's vision falters. "[Ellis] saw him and stood still, waiting; the hem of her dress lay in the grasses, and the grasses stirred about her feet as though she had just risen, so blossom white and softly brown, out of the earth to be the final answer to all his indecisions. As he moved down the swale and across the Ford of Mariposa, it was, indeed, as if all the treading of the years since last he played there had been but stepping-stones of the path that led to her" (439). The passage returns woman, after all, to the status of goal and terrain of the journey rather than journeyer, the one who waits rather than the one who goes, and Austin's imagery is finally as muddled as her young men. It is unfortunate indeed that as Ken reaches Ellis, his beloved, he makes a gesture that enacts and seemingly validates his friend Frank's earlier insistence that someone "put a firm, restraining hand on women": he places "a firm proprietary hold" on her (440).

Only in its treatment of Anne, the most fully affirmed character in the novel, does *The Ford* prove adequate to the equalitarian vision it sporadically avows. Like Ellis, who serves the book's themes of fertility and occupation through her identification with the land and gardening, Anne embodies a love for the land. She regains the family ranch where she and Ken grew up, returns to live there, and occupies it to the end. But within that vision of occupying and remaining, Anne is accorded a high degree of freedom to come and go at her own volition on widely scattered journeys associated with business ventures. She is a woman who departs from convention, and her initiative impels even the love plot. If Ken makes, at the end, a patriarchal gesture of appropriation of the female, he at any rate recognizes that Anne, rather than himself, may have been the active force working toward this outcome "all the time" (439–40). The last words of the novel are, "Which proved to be the case." That is, the narrative voice confirms that the initiative has indeed been hers. All three of them have been deeply involved in the public issue of retaining water rights in the local area, and all three, through Anne's initiative, are now involved in the fulfillment of a private vision that has grown out of it. But that has been possible only because she has had the freedom to move and to act. Anne Brent joins the Walking Woman and Olivia Lattimore, of *A Woman of Genius,* in epitomizing Austin's fullest ideal for women.

Between the writing of *The Ford* and the completion of *Starry Adventure,* Austin suffered major disappointments in her career as novelist. Sales of *No. 26 Jayne Street* were disheartening, and *Cactus Thorn* was refused publication. It is perhaps surprising, then, that she would once again undertake a major work of fiction. But in these intervening years she had also settled in New Mexico, built her house, and written *The Land of Journeys' Ending.* Her imagination was once again invigorated by the West, and her sense of at-homeness in Santa Fe seems to have provided her a new degree of calm and assurance. The results were *Earth Horizon,* her autobiography, and *Starry Adventure,* her last and culminating novel. It is a novel long overdue for revaluation, a work of keen interest in relation both to what is called the new regionalism (it has been well read in that connection, and compared favorably, by Mark Schlenz, to Cather's *Death Comes for the Archbishop*) and to Austin's themes of gender liberation, departure, and homing.

Starry Adventure has sometimes been seen as merely one more stilted expression of Austin's obsession with Lincoln Steffens. Actually, however, it demonstrates a considerable flexibility in her thinking about the Steffens episode, in that the roles of male and female in the argument are reversed. Failure to perceive sexual relationships as a bond severable only by mutual decision is not simply another instance of male injustice and female need for vindication. The male hero, Gard, whose business is, significantly, the restoration of houses, becomes involved in a love affair with one of his clients, an older woman, despite the fact that he is already married to his longtime friend Jane. Though he feels a strong sense of guilt for betraying his marriage, he is relieved of narrative blame by the fact that the marriage is one in name only and has not been consummated. Instead, it is the woman he has the affair with, Eudora Ballantin (a portrait of Mabel Dodge Luhan),[53] who is guilty in that she takes their relationship lightly and pursues other romantic involvements without reaching a clear agreement with Gard that their affair is being ended. More generally, the novel represents a culmination of Austin's theme of the duality of home and outward venture, as well as her theme of the reeducation of the male. Demonstrating the pervasiveness of her conception of the creative life as one characterized both by venturousness (journeys) and by secure anchorage in a chosen home, it is pervaded by symbolism both of motion and of houses. It is both an "open-ended quest for meaning in relation to place" and an expression of Austin's "inhabitory ethic."[54]

As the title indicates, the central concern of the novel is with Gard's sense of being destined to some "starry adventure"—a phrase reminiscent of Olivia's "shining destiny" in *A Woman of Genius.* Thus, motion is central to its conception. Various metaphors of motion pervade both Gard's approaches to his life vocation and the prolonged period of confusion in which he finds himself as he gropes toward an understanding of what it is that he wants to do. During this period he is depicted in inconclusive motion, continually driving the roads of New Mexico in a truck or car, looking for things he needs or may need in his work. Equally central to the book, however, is the importance of home, both in a domestic sense and in the sense of place, a connection or communion with one's "own land."[55] As in so much of Austin's work, the two values, free range and central rootedness, are complementary. Accordingly, the central female character is introduced as a girl "poised for flight and yet still," like "an aspen, rippling alive and rooted in quietness" (78). Later she is shown to be an adventuring woman so independent that when she wants to get away to think she spends hours "off in the car" or takes lone horseback rides in "high trackless country" (408–9). Her mobility indicates her personal freedom and independence of mind. Yet her primary goal is to have a marriage of real sharing.

Resolution of Gard and Jane's complicated love story entails echoes of numerous far-reaching public events and issues, including the Great War and the resulting dispersal of families and the dynamics of ethnic relations in New Mexico. Of central importance is the arrival of each of them at an understanding of their wish (like that of Anne and Ken in *The Ford*) to inhabit their familiar place, the place where they grew up. Their marriage was entered into, in fact, as a ploy to forestall Jane's parents' wish to see her enter a marriage of social and financial advantage that would have taken her away from New Mexico to the East Coast or even Europe. At the end, their marriage consummated at last, Jane and Gard leave on a honeymoon trip around the state to conduct research toward a book on the history of houses—a deeply symbolic action, uniting motion with redundant affirmations of the importance of houses/homes and family relationships. A home-centered journey in multiple senses (they will loop back to their home, they are preparing a book about homes), it coincides with their establishment of their own union, outwardly signaled by their occupation of Gard's family home and their plans to renovate it as their own. The night before they leave, Gard is seen doing something that is always a "deep delight" to him, making a "circuit of the house," checking on its security and order (419). This "circuit of the house," a type of action often performed by women, indicates the androgynous nature of Austin's mature vision. Still wishing to pursue his "starry adventure," he muses that "so long as you kept moving" and "didn't get snagged somewhere" you could elude aging (383). But he now pursues that adventure within the context of his marriage to Jane and his link to his land. His definition of the adventure is no longer solitary.

Austin goes further yet, however, in her androgynous redefinition of the traditional male destiny, offering a striking redefinition of *masculine* destiny by analogy with pregnancy and childbirth. As the two ponder Gard's notion of being destined for a "starry adventure," Jane proposes the idea that it may not be an outward adventure but an inward one, a quiet task to be done or a change of mind. She then offers this transformative analogy: "Suppose I should be going to have a baby. . . . I wouldn't know anything about it for weeks. And then it would be only a kind of sick feeling. And no other feeling for months. . . . And what I would feel wouldn't make any difference; wouldn't stop it, or make it go faster. And when it came, no matter how glad I was to have it, it would be something terrible to go through. I might even die of it. How do you know your adventure isn't going on in you this minute?" (417). The "adventure" of gestation and birth is, of course, traditionally home-centered and contextualized by a relationship. Indeed, as Jane adds, she "might be any time" starting on that adventure, just as Gard may be sharing in it and sharing with her an adventure of the spirit and the ripening of a sense of relationship. At the end he feels himself "companioned by the adventure" (420). Austin thus provides an innovative positive answer to the question Karen Lawrence asks in *Penelope Voyages,* as to whether the woman writer can "repeat" traditionally masculine plots of "adventure, exploration, and travel" in her own way, "with a difference."[56] The vision of masculine adventure as a figurative pregnancy is indeed such a difference. Gard's reconception of the importance of home in his own life and work—that is, his recognition of the domestic sphere as one open to himself, just as rambling about the countryside or traveling abroad is an option available to his wife— is an expression of the idea Austin stated in *Earth Horizon,* the other culminating work she produced near the end of her life: that the home is a site of resistance to patriarchal values rather than enforced surrender to them. It is an idea we will encounter again in the work of Anne Tyler and of Toni Morrison.

However emphatically Austin espoused women's right to go out the door and to take the express train west with Dulcie Adelaid, she also affirmed with equal fervor the value of emotional fulfillment through relationships of heterosexual love and marriage, the traditional central relationship of women's lives. To be sure, she saw those relationships as being the site of necessary change; she insisted that they be carried on differently than in the past and be seen as a locus of real values, at least as important as the "real-world" activities of business and politics. For men this meant opening themselves to a dimension of experience they had devalued. For women it meant—despite Austin's feminism and her determination that the option of untrammeled pursuit of work in the public world would be open—a restored vision of the worth of romantic love and the home as life's emotional centers. Certainly her vision of change in love and marriage did not entail recourse to mere impulse or "free love," which in practical terms, she thought, usually meant the *male's* impulses and *his* freedom to act on those impulses unilaterally. It did mean that love and marriage were to be valued on a par with public and professional undertakings and that men (and women) were to conduct their amorous relationships on the same ethical plane of respect for commitments and for the other person's rights as the best of them might aspire to in their conduct of public affairs. She saw the sexual relation as being essentially an unwritten or even unspoken contract, and she demanded that women's contract rights be respected and men's contractual obligations honored.

Unfortunately, when Austin's imagination turned from departure and journey to houses, it also, at times, seemed to turn toward a conservative vision of women's lives at odds with the vision she more often insisted on. In part this inconsistency is inherent in her conviction that what women want is not freedom alone or erotic gratification alone or domesticity alone, but all three. In part, too, it derives from the over-fervid language and other tritenesses that she sometimes lapsed into in developing the love plots that she saw as being both commercially essential and needed for showing the constitution of the love relationship on a new basis. For the most part, however, she did not retreat to stale romances but vigorously advocated the development of a new and more moral basis for relationships between the sexes, one in which home and the larger world (larger in both a spatial and a social sense) would be linked and in which movement between the two would be as free for one sex as for the other. If her repeated return to the Steffens trauma seems compulsive, it can also be viewed as indicating her determination to draw on her own experience for the negative examples needed in a fiction dramatizing change. Steffens, in the various versions in which she drew him, represented the past system that she rejected. The fu-

ture hinged on the development of a different set of attitudes on the part of
men as well as women, and on different expectations of both men and
women in their social roles.

Austin's treatment of the theme of love and marriage, then, becomes
bound up with her treatment of women's departures and mobility (both literal and figurative), her insistence on their right to free departure and return, and her vision of a new linkage of the private and the public spheres.
Because she saw these spheres as being complementary values for men just
as they were for women, the circuit of the house projected in her fiction,
unlike Jewett's, was not developed as a women's society, but as a characteristic and important action of society in general, expressing an androgynous ideal.

Chapter 3

LOOKING OUT THE WINDOW
Willa Cather and the Vesuvian Impulse

. . . whereas house-breakers usually break into
houses, I broke out.
     —Sarah Orne Jewett

Freedom is to be found only through an open
mind and a wide and varying horizon.
     —Gertrude Atherton

Like Mary Austin's, Willa Cather's life and much of her work followed the plot of the *Bildungsroman,* the individualistic growing-up story entailing departure from home to find or make a self by journey into new terrain.[1] Although her first departure, in childhood, was an involuntary one, causing an intense feeling of displacement and loss, she would later shape her adult life as a series of volitional departures on journeys of emergence, discovery, and self-fulfillment. The energy behind these departures is what I am calling (in the terminology of Adrienne Rich's essay on Emily Dickinson, "Vesuvius at Home") a Vesuvian impulse, an impulse to break out of confinements whether physical, social, or mental. An insistently gendered vision of departure and spatial range, linked to freedom and fulfillment in work, characterizes much of Cather's writing. That expansive vision coexists, however, with an impulse of withdrawal to enclosed spaces, an urge that becomes insistent in her later work. Mediating between the two urges is the open window, a thematically laden image that recurs throughout her fiction, most powerfully in *The Song of the Lark* (1915) and *Sapphira and the Slave Girl* (1940). In that culminating last novel, the energy impelling Cather outward from Nebraska (and from her mother) ultimately impelled her back to her originary mother-place, Virginia, very much as Austin returned—but on her own terms—to the Beloved House.

Powerful continuities link the two writers. Both were members of what Nancy Porter calls the "first tide of career-minded new women to pull at the shores of middle-class convention."[2] Both speak to the intersection of gender with modernism and the emergence around 1900 of, in Elizabeth Ammons's words, "artistically ambitious women writers."[3] They met as rising professionals in New York around 1910 (if not before) and took an interest in each other's careers, Austin trying to boost Cather's books (especially *My Ántonia,* 1918) and Cather expressing to her editor at Houghton Mifflin her respect for Austin's powerful mind.[4] Yet their linkage has been known to Cather scholars as well as Austin scholars almost solely by a single incident that occurred in Santa Fe in 1926.

When Cather undertook a trip to New Mexico in 1926, by no means her first, to facilitate completion of *Death Comes for the Archbishop,* Austin offered her the use of her newly built house, Casa Querida. Austin herself was away at the time for medical reasons. Like Cather, she was traveling. The house was empty and quiet, and Cather spent several mornings writing in the wide-windowed (and therefore, to her, very appealing) library/living room. The incident, seemingly so straightforward, is paradigmatic in its fusion of journey and home. Both women were displaced, yet both were enhoused: Austin in her possession of the house she had long wished for, her own chosen home, and Cather in her use of it. Both, having gone on trips, were managing to keep one foot, after a fashion, at home. Cather, as she liked to be, was positioned near a big window, which, she noted in a letter, she had opened.[5]

Surprisingly, this peaceful incident led to conflict. After *Death Comes for the Archbishop* (published in 1927) received widespread acclaim, Austin enjoyed telling people that the famous author had written the novel, or part of it, in her house—and thereby evoked Cather's irritation and denial. She had used Austin's library, she said, only for writing some letters. Moved to rare sarcasm, she told Mabel Dodge Luhan, in a 1933 letter, that even that was done only as a gesture of politeness. But her own hand belies her. She had already inscribed a copy of the book, "For Mary Austin, in whose lovely study I wrote the last chapters of this book. She will be my sternest critic— and she has the right to be. I will always take a calling-down from my betters."[6] It is a rare instance of Cather's being, or at any rate appearing to be, the less ingenuous of the two—so rare, in fact, that one wonders why she reacted so strongly to Austin's (perhaps foolish) bragging. It is understandable, given her penchant for inviolable privacy, that she would resent being exhibited, so to speak, in absentia. Still, the reaction seems disproportionate to the offense.

But a second factor had also, prior to the writing of her 1933 letter to Luhan, provoked Cather. In her 1932 autobiography, *Earth Horizon,* and in an article in the *English Journal* published that same year, Austin had publicly berated Cather for what she considered her endorsement of French religious colonialism in a Spanish town.[7] She had thus called into question, from her own position as recognized expert on the Southwest, the slightly younger but by that time considerably more eminent writer's judgment of cultural movement (or en-placement), as her story of the use of the house had already, so Cather seems to have felt, made a spectacle and thereby called into doubt or ridicule her personal working em-placement. That is, she had impugned Cather's career standing—had questioned, we might say, how far she had come.

The incident becomes, then, paradigmatic in another way as well. As Elizabeth Ammons and Esther Stineman have astutely surmised, there existed between Cather and Austin a sporadic sense of rivalry.[8] In the incident in Santa Fe and its repercussions we see evidence of the sparring for position evoked by their sense that, as women in what was still a man's world, they were competing for limited literary turf. What I want to emphasize here, however, is not so much their rivalry as their similarities, parallels, and common interests. Among the chief of these is their shared and in many ways similar engagement with powerful complementary yearnings toward the duality that Cather refers to in *Death Comes for the Archbishop* as "the desire to go and the necessity to stay."[9]

Cather's conflicted spatial desire and necessity were rooted in her childhood displacement from verdant, hilly northwestern Virginia to the flat, untreed prairies of southern Nebraska. She later said in an interview that she was so overwhelmed she felt her "one purpose in life just then was not to cry."[10] But her long textual engagement with tropes both of departure and of homing is traceable not only to the sense of loss and homesickness produced by this removal, but also to her later wish for escape. Joseph Urgo, who emphasizes the more positive outcomes of her "migratory consciousness," sees Cather as "a comprehensive resource for the demarcation of an empire of migration in U.S. culture."[11] That view is provocative and largely accurate—certainly, for instance, the westward transferral of European religious culture in *Death Comes for the Archbishop* can be viewed in relation to an empire of migration—but it unduly minimizes her ambivalence between a sense of fulfillment, in her chosen departures, and a sense of exile from home. It also understates, in my view, the inwardness and the exceptionalism of Cather's engagement with symbolic actions of departure and journey, which was never so social or so reformist in nature as Austin's, for instance, but was more an expression of individual aspiration.[12]

Like Austin's, Cather's adult departures on her solitary journey as writer-in-the-making would be made in large part as a separation from her mother, with whom her relations seem to have been tense from early on. Virginia Cather (portrayed in the mother character in "Old Mrs. Harris") was judgmental and imperious, but she was also beautiful, warm, and gracious, very much a lady. Her vision of a woman's life was one that Cather insistently rebelled against. The importance of maternal bonding in ego development has, of course, been much theorized in recent years, and although it is still a keenly disputed subject it is clear that relations with the mother, and especially disturbances in early relations with the mother, are of far-reaching importance in women's development of a sense of self.[13] Certainly this was true in Cather's case. In a sense her relation with her mother was even more problematic than Austin's, in that it was more uncertainly mixed, a compound both of resistance and of a closeness and love that Austin could only yearn for. The conflicts of this complex relationship set up a tension that would remain with Cather throughout her life and, as *Shadows on the Rock* and *Sapphira and the Slave Girl* demonstrate, throughout her work. Even James Woodress, who insists that she had a "happy relationship with both her parents," concedes that "relations with her mother were sometimes difficult" and the two "often clashed in her youth."[14] She would retain a measure of insecurity relating to feelings of never having achieved the recognition she wanted from her mother.

After an adolescence spent largely in groping for ways to evade conventional female decorum, during which she adopted quasi-masculine modes of self-presentation in hairstyle and dress and such supposedly masculine interests as biology (all of which her mother seems to have tolerated with exemplary restraint), Cather went away to the University of Nebraska. That departure, fictionalized, is traced in "Old Mrs. Harris," where the mother appears as a blocking figure or at best an uninterested spectator, largely absorbed in her own imprisonment by sexuality, and the grandmother, representing Cather's own Grandmother Boak, takes the role of maternal advocacy and sacrifice. At the university, Cather was regarded as a rather startling personage, with her boyish clothes and mannerisms, but she soon modulated these in favor of more substantive and intellectual kinds of escape, battering against walls of politeness and deferential provincialism by adopting an aggressive "smoking pen" tone in her newspaper reviews of touring theatrical companies. After completing her degree, she found it necessary to return home for about a year, writing newspaper columns and probably helping her family during a period of economic depression but largely marking time until an opportunity for escape presented itself. It was a depressing period for her. As Marcus Klein writes, she had set her mind on professional fulfillment and was "markedly bent on escape."[15] On May 2, 1896, she told her close friend from Lincoln, Mariel Gere, that she needed to see more of the world and would be unable to do anything significant, as her parents were clearly expecting, as long as she stayed in Red Cloud.[16]

By midsummer she had made her escape, going to Pittsburgh to accept employment in the editorial offices of, ironically enough, *Home Monthly* magazine. But if she went in pursuit of a profession, she also went for the freedom to shape her own life apart from the restraint of family assumptions. Significantly, it is the urge for self-realization and achievement represented in this act of departure and its context of a rather smothering home life that is singled out by Katherine Anne Porter in her essay "Reflections on Willa Cather," where she calls her "the longest-winged one who would fly free at last"—a beautiful and accurate epithet although it conveys only one half of the polarity of Cather's sensibility, ignoring her need for secure at-homeness.[17] Certainly it was an impulse to "fly free" in a solitary mapping of the self, rather than an urge to escape repressive social conditions in order to set them on a new footing, that impelled this and subsequent departures. Years after she had achieved autonomy, Cather would write—distancing the observation by attaching it to another woman writer—that even in "harmonious families" each member is mentally "escaping, running away, trying to break the net."[18]

After a decade in Pittsburgh—first in magazine work, then in newspaper work, then in teaching, during all of which she tried sporadically to keep writing—she made another major move, leaving Isabelle McClung's home in

1906 to move to New York as a writer and editor for *McClure's Magazine*. It was while she was on assignment for *McClure's* in Boston in early 1908, verifying and polishing a biography of Mary Baker Eddy, that she met Sarah Orne Jewett. In December 1908, only a few months before her death, Jewett wrote what E. K. Brown calls "the most important letter, beyond a question, that Willa Cather ever received,"[19] advising Cather to make yet another departure—to leave her employment at *McClure's* and commit herself wholly to writing.

The importance of Cather's mentoring by Jewett has been widely noticed and documented. As Eudora Welty sees and points out in a luminous essay, she seems to have recognized in Jewett's advice a truth about her creativity that she had already apprehended for herself.[20] Even so, the older woman's advice was important in confirming that apprehension. Moreover, Cather may well have recognized in the retiring Maine writer a model both for identification with a strong sense of place (region) and for a nonconfrontational mode of independent self-definition. Jewett's assertion that she had broken out of houses (quoted in the first epigraph to this chapter) is perhaps surprising, since she is not often conceived of as having broken anything, but rather as exemplifying a sensibility of maintained and cherished continuities. But despite remaining throughout her life closely identified with family, a small circle of long-term friends, and home, Jewett managed to define herself as a professional on her own terms. The quiet balance evident in her life is manifest in her work as well. Indeed, Margaret Roman has recently argued that Jewett's handling of the duality of home and departure demonstrates a recognition of the imprisoning tendency of accepted gender roles and conventional marriage and shows that Jewett herself, as well as many of her characters, sought to get free of the "confines of the Victorian home and its garden."[21] Such a "motif of leaving society behind for the freedom of the woods," Roman says, is "prevalent" in Jewett's travel essays as well as her fiction.

Cather seems to have recognized in Jewett's gentle fiction—in its realism, its confidence in the woman's perspective and the importance of what might be called a fiction of dailiness, and its distinctive reconciliation of the impulse toward outward movement and the impulse toward homing through the pursuit of looping journeys—a prototype for her own. Her respect for Jewett's writing was public and long-lasting. Long after the older writer's death, she continued to express her confidence that Jewett's work would go on living as a model of literary excellence, even if it reached only a few discerning readers.[22] Her admiration is traceable in a close textual echo, in *A Lost Lady*, of "The White Heron"—interestingly, the same fine story that Mary Austin echoes in the final sketch of *The Land of Little Rain*. The hunter in Jewett's story who wants Sylvia to tell him the location of the heron's nest, an ornithologist who shows his interest in birds by killing them, is linked in the girl's mind with a "great red-faced boy who used to chase and frighten her." The young Ivy Peters of *A Lost Lady*, who not only kills birds but deliberately blinds one, is "well-grown" and has a red face.[23]

The yoking of spatial movement and retreat to enclosure that Cather drew in part from Jewett's characteristic mode and in part from her own impulses is, in my view, the most pervasive of the balanced or opposed dualities that Merrill Skaggs sees as characterizing her work. Ann Romines images the idea effectively in observing that her fiction "often gets its energy from the tension" between the walls of a house or room and the "human passion that batters against them—from inside or from out."[24] Romines's figure of speech is peculiarly evocative of Jewett's comment on burglars who "break in" and genteel writers who "break out." As we have seen, Cather's passion generally battered against walls from the inside.

In belated response to Jewett's advice and her own sense of weariness and divided purpose, Cather finally, in 1912, took an extended leave of absence from *McClure's* and went on an excursion to the rugged Southwest that would prove transformative. There she walked, climbed, and opened herself to a land unlike any she had known before (writing zestfully to her old friend or sweetheart Louise Pound that she had been rambling around New Mexico and Arizona).[25] After this, her life was committed entirely to writing. But geographic movement, combined with a secure, private place of residence, characterized her entire subsequent career. She traveled inordinately, making numerous trips to Europe; shuttling across the continent repeatedly on visits to Red Cloud, to Chicago, to New Mexico and Arizona, and, especially during her mother's prolonged last illness, to California; escaping northward from New York to New Hampshire, Maine, and Canada. As Cheryll Burgess points out, this "restless doubling back and forth across our vast continent" expresses the "gruelling inner pull between the opposites of East and West" that Elizabeth Shepley Sergeant observed in Cather's sensibility.[26] In part, she moved from one working place to another according to her sense of how the work was going, looking for a place where she could settle in to write. Blanche Knopf once expressed a sense of gratification or relief that, having gone away to New Hampshire, Cather sounded "happier and more content" than she had "for a long time."[27] Yet inveterately restless as she was, she felt, at the same time, a powerful homing urge.

The tension between Cather's great aspiration and restlessness and her profound homing urge is evident again and again in the patterns of her life. She became so securely settled in her home-base apartment at 5 Bank Street, which she occupied with Edith Lewis for fifteen years, that she was rendered almost physically ill by the necessity of moving out when the building was scheduled for demolition. She lamented to Mary Austin that she was now utterly without a home.[28] Unable to face serious house-hunting, she took refuge in the Grosvenor Hotel—and made it her home base for five years. To be sure, she spent relatively little time in New York during those years. Her mother had suffered a stroke while visiting in California, and Cather was continually back and forth, spending extended periods in California where her mother was being cared for as well as continuing her retreats to Grand Manan Island, where she had built a house. But she needed the security of a single established home. She was in her very essence both an incessant traveler and a homebody. Writing to Mabel Dodge Luhan to report renting a new apartment at last, she exclaimed that she simply had to have a home and familiar surroundings, and only if she did could she enjoy traveling and not feel like a vagrant.[29]

We can only suppose that the urgency of this need for a stable dwelling place grew from her childhood sense of displacement in the move to Nebraska. To some extent, her yearning for rootedness may have been associated, too, with nostalgia for the security of the conventional gender roles she had defied and abandoned. These two great counter-urges, to be footloose and to have a secure dwelling place, comprise a shaping polarity in her art as well as her life. Resembling Austin's in its oscillation between open road and home, her pervasive language of journeys also derives from the journey-of-life metaphors and the symbolic geography of the Bible, which, as the daughter of a devout Protestant family, she knew from earliest childhood, and from another virtually universal text of nineteenth-century Protestantism, *Pilgrim's Progress*.[30] Both of these wellsprings of such language, of course, permeated American literature of her time. The influence of Jewett, however, was not only a more distinctive one but arguably more significant.[31] The balance between impulses toward journey and impulses toward home-biding evident in Cather's work came in large measure, I believe, from the characteristic patterns of Jewett's works, especially Jewett's home-centered journeys, which Austin also deployed.

Cather's dual impulse, both toward and away from home, is incorporated in her fiction in complex structures of spatial movement centering on houses, often houses with large windows affording safe visual (and imaginative) outlets for the Vesuvian impulse fermenting within. As Romines points out, her "most straightforward statement" of a theory of the novel, "The Novel Démeublé," has at its center a metaphor of the house—the place from which the furniture of narrative trappings can be thrown out the window. The house is, literally and figuratively, the "locus of inspiration" from which "language can flower."[32] But it is a locus disrupted from its hereditary trappings or perhaps emptied of its accumulated impediments, its troubling associations. By envisioning her work as a disfurnishing of the house, Cather enacted what Hélène Cixous envisions as the essential business of the woman writer, "changing around the furniture . . . emptying structures, and turning propriety upside down."[33] She created both an uncluttered space and, thereby, a safe space, a space of her own.

A reading of Cather's letters (not an easy undertaking, since they are not only unpublished but widely scattered) reveals the care with which she constructed her spaces, primarily the two apartments in New York that she occupied for periods of many years, one on Bank Street, the other on Park Avenue. Her fictional interior spaces are equally important. Not that she delineates styles, furnishings, and accessories, but it is clear that the nature of the rooms inhabited by her characters matters to her. The heavy furniture to be pushed about by Marian Forrester in A Lost Lady bespeaks her husband's (and perhaps her own) intention of establishing a solid, impressive social presence. The awkward mixture inside Alexandra's house in O Pioneers! conveys her lack of social graces, her preference for the outdoors and for friends who don't care about style. The interior elegance of the Henshawes' New York apartment in My Mortal Enemy reveals the social aspirations in which they are trapped. Their social and economic decline is indexed by the deteriorating nature of their lodgings, as well as by the drivenness of their geographic movements, a process of successive dislocations in which they spend years "wandering about among the cities of the Pacific coast."[34]

Trapped in movement (insecurity, displacement) at the same time as she is trapped in stasis by her illness, Myra has dragged along the faded velvet curtains from New York. These reminders of the past are darkeners of windows, but they are also decorative devices that draw attention to windows—openings that afford visual or actual escape.

Windows are consistently a focal point of Cather's attention, signifying visual or mental passage from inside to outside (rarely the reverse except for fresh air and sunlight) and the impulse to make an actual, physical passage, a departure. The gaze out the window affords relief from claustrophobic uneasiness and expresses aspiration, the prospect of personal expansion and achievement in a wider world. Cather herself adverted to such an association of values when she described the experimental structure of *The Professor's House* as an analogue to a Dutch interior painting with an open window on one wall providing a glimpse of a spacious view. Seeing beyond the wall means imagining beyond confinement; and imagining beyond is both a satisfying state in itself and the key to going beyond. She tried to make Professor St. Peter's house "overcrowded and stuffy," she said, and then, by means of the middle section with its spacious mesa setting, "open the square window and let in the fresh air" and (a phrase often ignored when this passage is quoted) "the fine disregard of trivialities" evident in Tom Outland.[35] The window, then, provides release from conventionality ("trivialities") as well as from confinement; the two are related. It also provides there, primarily in the closing section that returns to the professor in his study, a literal opening to life itself (the outdoors, fresh air) and a figurative opening of release from the confines of the isolated self to the spaciousness of commonality with others.

We need to remember, of course, that if Cather chooses the open window, she also first chooses the room. Windows—transparent but firm surfaces, openable but also closable—serve simultaneously her preoccupation with safe enclosure and her preoccupation with expansion of the self by escape from enclosure.[36] Small rooms with expansive views were, as Cynthia Briggs reminds us, the type of structure Cather characteristically sought out as work spaces. An "insulated view of the world . . . was the crucible for her art."[37]

Nowhere is the language of windows used more expansively or integrated more fully or more subtly into a motif of departure than in *The Song of the Lark*. Thea Kronborg is not only a projection of Cather herself but also a portrait of the well-known soprano Olive Fremstad and a version of the dramatic actress in Mary Austin's *A Woman of Genius,* thus a composite representation of the woman artist.[38] And she is repeatedly, at important junctures in the novel, placed at large windows or window-like openings. Her posture at the open window helps to define her as the aspiring woman who values comfortable indoor spaces so long as they afford openings for vision and, by implication, for egress. Thea's comfortable attic room at home, a personal retreat that she has constructed with great care and one modeled on Cather's own room in Red Cloud, Nebraska, allows her to be in effect both indoors and outdoors at the same time. It is because of the window, affording her a wide, liberating view, that her low-ceilinged room can be a refuge without being an enclosure. When she drags her mattress to the window at night and lies looking out, she ranges visually and mentally far beyond the walls of the house.

Thea's imaginatively expansive gaze out the window conveys her need to escape, as Cather did herself, the limitations of her small-town home. That need and its fulfillment were central to Cather's intentions. In her preface to the 1932 edition she stated with unusual directness, "What I cared about, and still care about, was the girl's escape."[39] Thea also needs to escape her mother's limited vision of the possibilities for a woman's life. Like Olivia in *A Woman of Genius,* published the year before Cather began serious work on *The Song of the Lark,* she needs to go out the door of the natal home if she is to start down the road of defining herself as an artist. But until she can make that departure, her view out the window of her bedroom serves as a kind of release, affording her a sense of the world's spaciousness. It allows her to remain within a chosen and secure space while ranging with the eye and the mind.

The crucial first step, as is typical in the *Bildungsroman,* is the departure from home. Thea is enabled, by the bequest of her railroading friend Ray, to get to Chicago for serious training in music. She ultimately gains a freedom of movement (freedom to travel) almost as great as Cather's own. It is surely no accident that the first song she sings for Fred Ottenburg, the supportive and encouraging man she meets in Chicago, with whom she eventually makes an equalitarian marriage, is a setting of a text about heroic journey: "I prefer to steer my boat into the din of roaring breakers. Even if the journey is my last, I may find what I have never found before. Onward must I go, for I yearn for the wild sea."[40] Thea's departure from her hometown of Moonstone, Colorado, is the first in a series of moves that bring her at last to the triumphant career that is latent in her from the beginning. But she is not able to move beyond the technical proficiency she gains in Chicago until she makes another dramatic departure, like Cather's from *McClure's,* to a place unpredictable in its impact and unlike any she has known before.

The rugged Southwest, the place of transformation for both author and character, had emerged during the years leading up to Cather's writing of the novel as her emblematic landscape of freedom. In a very real sense that landscape had been the source of *O Pioneers!,* the novel in which Cather found her authentic voice after what she called the false start of *Alexander's Bridge.*[41] Elizabeth Shepley Sergeant believed the Southwest's "bold magnificence, brilliant light and physical impact" enabled her to achieve a "new artistic method" derived from the grasslands of Nebraska by "toning up her spirit."[42] The course of events seems to bear out that judgment. Cather had written a story that would become the basis of the novel in late 1911. The following spring she made her long, life-altering trip to the Southwest and within a month of that trip conceived an idea for a story to be called "The White Mulberry Tree," the story of Emil and Marie's disastrous love. The two stories came together in what she described as a "sudden inner explosion," and the book was finished by the end of the year.[43] Notably, the heroic central character, Alexandra, is characteristically seen outdoors, against the land and the sky. She prefers a life of active outdoor agricultural management, offering opportunities to move freely about the countryside, to the indoor domestic life that her brothers urge on her. Yet she enjoys, too, retreating to her snug house for days of visiting and quilting with neighbor women. She prefers, that is, to have both kinds of lives, indoor and outdoor, with liberty to pass freely from one to another. Thus, despite their great differences, Alexandra anticipates the vigorous Thea.

Cather had gotten the idea of doing a book on the Southwest, probably a group of travel essays, following her stay in 1912. She proposed such a book to Ferris Greenslet, her editor at Houghton Mifflin, in letters written between 1914 and 1916. The project could not be done from long distance, she insisted, but only from actual presence, actual travel in the area. She thought the Santa Fe Railroad might provide free travel to the farther-off places for her gathering of material. Believing that she could set a new standard for writing on the Southwest, she attempted to stake a claim on the territory by urging Greenslet not to let anyone else do such a book for Houghton Mifflin.

The unnamed other writer she had in mind would almost certainly have been Mary Austin, also published by Houghton Mifflin and edited by Greenslet. Greenslet replied, in fact, that he had only the previous week "declined a pretty good book on Arizona by a temperamental lady."[44] Austin's shadow falls across the page. But the hypothetical travel book did not materialize. Instead, Cather's interest in southwestern travel was subsumed in *The Song of the Lark,* giving the novel its central spaciousness.

In this central section of the novel, Thea withdraws from frustrations with her musical development in Chicago to the Arizona mesa country to be alone in uncluttered quiet. Spending days of solitude in the expansive high country and reaching back, by sympathetic imagination, to a time as removed from her own as Arizona is from Chicago, she is able to find (as did Cather) her authentic artistic impulse. Significantly, she does so only as a result of a dual movement—out into the wild landscape, but at the same time into a sheltering cave reminiscent of her childhood room at home. There she inhabits a space with a ceiling low enough that she can put her hands on it, like the low ceiling of her childhood room, and with one side opening, like a large window, onto a great, unrestricted vista. Again she experiences "indoors" and outdoors at once—doubly so, in that the "indoor" space is itself part of the outdoor world. Here, as elsewhere, Cather's emphasis on window imagery, unifying indoors and outdoors, reconciles the dualities of journey and home, of staying in one's familiar felicitous space while venturing forth visually and mentally on journeys of wider exploration. The spaciousness of the West and the sense it affords of connection with "The Ancient People" (Cather's title for Part IV) reenergizes Thea and gives her an enlarged perspective, a sense of "older and higher obligations" and a "desire for action" (242–43). She is "getting somewhere in [her] mind" (248). The climax of the sequence comes when, from the natural doorway of her "rock-room . . . nest in a high cliff full of sun," Thea sees an eagle that, unlike the swallows that "never dared to rise out of the shadow of the cañon walls," soars up "beyond the rim" (235, 238, 252). Recognizing in the eagle the essence of her self, she apotheosizes it in language of a pitch Cather would rarely, after this point in her career, allow herself: "O eagle of eagles! Endeavour, achievement, desire, glorious striving of human art!" (253).

At Panther Canyon, Thea has been alone but also, by the power of her intuition, allied with the self-reliant, creative women who inhabited that space long before.[45] She has also been, during a part of her stay, companioned by a supportive male with whom she shares her emotional richness and sexuality. Through this complex fusion of dual emotional impulses—toward solitary withdrawal and toward romantic companionship, the homing urge in effect folded into the journey urge—Cather readies Thea to emerge for the period of strenuous work that will define her as Kronborg, a strong woman beyond the need for the feminine first name. The next journey, one of artistic exploration and fulfillment, will carry her eastward beyond Chicago to New York and Europe. Her freedom to move among these great centers of art is a measure of her triumph. Transformation and mobility are inseparable. In the music world, of course, that linkage is a matter of simple practicality; and Cather was never a fantasist. Transformation and mobility are inseparable for the theme of emergence and self-fulfillment as well. But if Thea's departure from home (the old self) and a range of associated limitations is essential to her self-realization and success, the fact that it is from a secure sense of place, a secure sense of at-homeness, that she has emerged is also essential. Like Cather's other positively presented characters, especially her women, Thea requires both for full emotional development, a sense of secure rootedness as well as freedom of movement.

Late in the novel, after Thea is securely established as an artist, she is again shown in relation to interior spaces with windows. The scene is one in which she has been walking about her hotel room talking with her old friend Dr. Archie and they have "paused by the open window." This time it seems to serve as a window onto the past: "You tell me the old house has been pulled down, but it stands in my mind, every stick and timber. . . . That's the house I rest in when I'm tired. All the old furniture and the worn spots in the carpet—it rests my mind to go over them" (349). Being able to remember the details of home, Thea says, "saves me" by providing a counterbalance to what she "strives for," which is "so far away, so beautiful" (350). In demonstration of the restorative function she has described, we later see her after a rehearsal, enticing herself into sleep by imagining her old home in Moonstone. It is the kind of sleep from which "one awakes in shining armour" (359)—and she then sings Sieglinde so triumphantly that "the closed roads opened, the gates dropped" (363). Once again stasis and movement, home and departure, are joined. The sense of secure enclosure associated with memories of her first home is essential to Thea's power as an artist. But equally essential is her freedom to move beyond enclosure. Like many of Cather's figures, she requires a house-life with permeable boundaries.

Cather's fiction often presents itself more as a network than as a succession of discrete entities. It is a body of work crosshatched with lines of connection. With respect to *The Song of the Lark,* I have already indicated such a line to *O Pioneers!* Another extends to *Lucy Gayheart.* When Cather returned to the theme of the female artist in that novel, she retained the association of artistic and personal aspiration with windows and escape from entrapment that pervades Thea's story. Lucy is determined not to live as a "carrot" stuck in small-town domestic life.[46] Merrill Skaggs (agreeing, in essence, with the readings of Susan Rosowski and James Woodress) sums up the great differences between the two characters, however, by observing that Lucy is characterized by "rush or movement . . . that goes nowhere." She may be, as Gelfant points out, "talented enough to earn a living and independence from her family"—faculties that Cather sees as essentials of the artist's and the free woman's life—but she lacks the "high seriousness" of the innate artist.[47] These two novels of the female musician are linked, too, by Cather's strong sense of the threat of sexuality. As Elaine Apthorp argues, Cather's scrutiny of Lucy's "capacity to escape possession," conveyed in the print of her running foot, signals her wish to "secure for her an escape from the physical into the purely spiritual." Cather's wish, but not Lucy's own; hence she is satirized for "her inability to maintain clear perspective."[48]

Yet another line of connection leads from *The Song of the Lark* to *One of Ours,* where she treats the theme of departure from the village with an urgency unequaled in any of her other novels. Indeed, she once, in a letter, singled out the escape wish as the central element of the novel.[49] The escape afforded Claude, the restless central character of *One of Ours,* is the traditional masculine one of warfare and heroism. Perhaps it was the social acceptability of that escape, combined with the distancing achieved by her adoption of a male hero, that allowed Cather to develop the theme of the wish for escape with such directness and focus here.

Susan Rosowski observes incisively that Cather "used her most time-bound narratives, *The Song of the Lark* and *One of Ours,* for her most developed quest plots."[50] Claude's determination to escape is very different, of course, from Thea's; he has none of her discipline and clarity in pursuit of a goal, only a restless dissatisfaction and a vague aspiration for ennoblement of life.[51] But hidden behind Claude's story is the "untold story" of another strong woman, his "singularly unattractive" wife, Enid, who does have both determination and clarity and who, in Maureen Ryan's words, "quietly violates the norms of her time and place" by leaving home and husband in pursuit of a vision of missionary work in China.[52]

An even more interesting line of connection extends from *The Song of the Lark* to *The Professor's House,* a decade later (1925), where the language of windows again recurs significantly and where Cather again draws on her own experience of the Southwest. Here, once again, in a novel associating outward movement with public involvement and connecting the Southwest with personal freedom, Cather's path crosses Mary Austin's. Austin's fantasy novel *Outland,* which appeared in its American edition in 1919 after its pseudonymous publication in England in 1910, seems to have served Cather as a catalyst, very much as *A Woman of Genius* did when she was beginning her writing of *The Song of the Lark.* The unusual name "Outland," the name of the professor's cherished student used in the title of the central section of *The Professor's House,* is only one of a number of parallels between the two works. Both involve redemption from the crass everyday world by departure to a place occupied by pre-industrial folk whose way of life is perceived as having a kind of beatitude, the memory of which keeps the "trail" present to the inner self.

In 1915 Cather visited the cliff dwellings at Mesa Verde, Colorado, and in 1916 began a story based on that visit. As Woodress's summary of the genesis of the story emphasizes, however, she was unable to bring it to completion. She wrote to Ferris Greenslet in 1916 that she "expected to have another book ready by the next year, probably a story of the Southwest to be called 'The Blue Mesa.' This," Woodress adds, "was apparently the beginning of 'Tom Outland's Story,' which she didn't manage to finish for another six years."[53] "Didn't manage to finish": why, one wonders, didn't she? And what was it that enabled her to do so six years later? My guess is that when she read Austin's *Outland* either in 1919 or at some time soon afterward (a period during which, as her correspondence with Greenslet indicates, she was keenly aware of Austin's professional interest in her), certain elements of the book came together with the unfinished story that had been hanging suspended in her mind and she was then able to move ahead.

Austin's fantasy of escape, renewal, and refinement of values, with a sub-plot of romantic love stitched somewhat awkwardly onto it, concerns the discovery of a technically primitive but culturally rich alternative civiliza-tion by two central characters, both of whom are or have been university professors. In this basic scenario can be seen much of the general shape or tenor of the presence of the cliff-dwelling people in the central section of *The Professor's House* and their importance to the book's two central characters. The very first sentence of *Outland* presents a trail from the known to the unknown, answering Mona's felt need for escape to a more meaningful life: "Somewhere within myself I was aware of a vast, undiscovered country full of wandering lights and crying voices, from whence the springs of great un-dertakings should issue."[54] Cather's Professor St. Peter is also aware of a loss of self (a self, perhaps, whose light is "wandering" and whose voice is "cry-ing") and of a vast country of the imagination where he has spent the most important portion of his adult life—the "undiscovered" country in which the Spanish explorers about whom he has written his eight-volume master-work pursued their own "great undertakings." Mona finds such a country when she finds the elusive, well-hidden trail into the living space of the Out-liers, much as Tom Outland stumbles onto the trail to the Blue Mesa—the trail that he later shares with St. Peter. Mona and Herman have to push their way through "a thicket of wild lilac grown across the way" (*Outland*, 14) to follow the trail. Tom has to shove "through a sea of rabbit-brush" before he finds the trail, and even then he and his partner have to search several days before finding a way up to "little city of stone."[55] The landscape of Austin's *Outland*, a high "stony country" with "windy galleries and spacious caves" and "great boulders huge as houses" (*Outland*, 266–67), is suggestive of Tom Outland's mesa and the surrounding country with its "huge boulders," some "as big as haystacks" (*Professor's House*, 179). Both stories involve a hidden treasure, and both end with the discoverers being in some way transformed. If Cather's is a darker, more qualified vision, the parallels nevertheless ap-pear to be too close to be coincidental.

The darkening of the southwesterly journey in *The Professor's House*, in comparison with that in *The Song of the Lark*, is in part evidence of Cather's general sobering of vision in the mid-1920s, but it is also, perhaps, related to her choice of two males, rather than Austin's male and female, as central characters, or more specifically to her perception of differences of gender. The shift from the male-female story in *Outland* would seem to be a major one, but in fact makes less difference between the two novels than one might suppose. The relationship between Professor St. Peter and the much younger Tom Outland that Cather develops in place of the romantic subplot is, while not overtly erotic, nevertheless a very loving one. Indeed, Tom appears to have emerged as the love of St. Peter's life. Conventional heterosexual love is also an issue in the book, in that St. Peter finds himself increasingly estranged from his wife and both of them seek sporadically to renew their relationship. But the main "romantic" issue is Godfrey's need to regain a clear sense of what Tom Outland, now dead, has meant to him. In doing so, he needs to avoid becoming so preoccupied with that central relationship that he becomes isolated from the world of real, living people whom he in some sense loves. Having grown as emotionally desiccated as Austin's social scientist Herman, whose chief problem is to learn to love, St. Peter needs to regain the ability to experience spontaneous emotion. Moreover, Cather's choice of a male rather than a female central character is driven not only by the fact that the role of professor is more conventionally assigned to a male but by her need to distance herself from the painful reexaminations and revelations entailed in his characterization, which is in many ways autobiographical. Gender is of great importance to the novel, then, but not in terms of its similarity or nonsimilarity to *Outland*.

Difference of gender is extremely important, however, when we compare *The Professor's House* to *The Song of the Lark*. Unlike Thea Kronborg's withdrawal to the southwestern cliff dwellings—a sequence emphasizing her elation at the openness of spaces there, her dwelling in harmony with the place and the female predecessors whose presence she intuits, and her personal transformation as a result—Godfrey's and Tom Outland's encounters with these same spaces emphasize strenuous adventuring, destructive imposition of their will onto both place and cultural remains, and acts of appropriation. We might even compare their aggressiveness toward the setting with the masculine conquest and restlessness devoid of centering (homing) exhibited in the movements of Alexander, in Cather's first first novel, *Alexander's Bridge*.[56] St. Peter and Outland, in their different ways, seek to possess the Southwest and its heritage. Thea receives her renewing vision of art and self by opening herself to the place and its heritage. The very pots that she imagines as the emblems of a receptive art and a link with native foremothers are carried away and bestowed as keepsakes by Tom Outland.

The darkness of *The Professor's House*, related to aging and disaffection, is enacted in a drama of withdrawal to an enclosed space where the window, significantly, is not kept open. The duality of enclosure and departure here strikingly differs in tone from the relatively uncomplicated and relatively positive terms in which it is presented in those early novels that are often thought to be Cather's most characteristic—O Pioneers!, My Ántonia, The Song of the Lark—and are, as Deborah Carlin points out, the only ones "regularly taught in high schools and colleges."[57] Like Claude and that other male journeyer Jim Burden, of My Ántonia, Godfrey St. Peter has set his face toward escape and adventure (in his research on the Spanish conquistadores) as a rejection of a home life he finds stifling. Even in the novel's time present, when his situation seems to be one of house-bound stasis, he is actually, in a sense, escaping home, since the house in which he shuts himself up has been vacated by his family. Primarily because Godfrey has fallen out of love with his family, there is little of positive value associated with homes in The Professor's House. Even in his happier memories of the years when his daughters were small, he is himself situated off in his attic study, above the perils (of distraction?) posed by the "human house." We can conjecture that Cather may have been examining by way of this surrogate self an unacknowledged underside of her own complex feelings toward her family, feelings that kept her coming back in duty visits throughout her parents' lives. Godfrey's urge toward being in the house—closed in, in the familiar place, where one can be sure of oneself—is very strong, but it lacks the human warmth or gladness Cather more often associates with the home-urge.

Even so, the continuity of The Professor's House with Cather's other work is very strong, as structure and symbolism are again organized around spatial movement (or refusal to move) to or from home spaces and around mediating windows (and "windows").[58] The homing or indoor impulse, though in an attenuated and generally negative form, is counterpoised against the outward impulse toward the Southwest. The most nearly claustrophobic, in two of its three sections, of any of her fiction, with most of the first and third sections taking place within the professor's literally stuffy study, The Professor's House describes an inward-turning so profound that it entails withdrawal not just to the house but to a single out-of-the-way room. Godfrey turns his back emotionally on his family, and his actions throughout most of the book are a series of refusals enacting that estrangement. He refuses to move his study, the most personal and private of the spaces in which he lives his life, to the new house that his own efforts have made possible. Toward the end of the book he also refuses to go with his family to Europe. Given Cather's love of travel, especially European travel, and the profound significance of geographic discovery in her life, this refusal is a very significant one. Even the swimming that Godfrey engages in while they are away is actually a disguised form of retreat, in that it is not only another solitary evasion of the social world but a regression toward the private "space" of remembered childhood. This series of withdrawals culminates in his almost being smothered to death from gas fumes trapped in his closed-in study.

Balancing this pronounced inward-turning of the novel is its great movement of the imagination toward the immense spaces of the American Southwest. The West, classic American symbol of freedom and expansiveness, is invoked primarily in the long middle section of the novel, which Cather herself referred to as an open window.[59] By means of this figurative window, she affords Godfrey an outward movement into the adventurousness, discovery, and untrammeled freedom that, as Jewett observed, are inherent in images of open space. But in the time present of the novel Godfrey has lost his personal and imaginative access to those spaces, and thereby to mental and emotional vastness. His student Tom Outland is dead, and his eight-volume book on the Spanish conquistadores is completed, leaving him spent and goalless. Soured on the present, Godfrey has petulantly closed his mental and emotional window. That is precisely the problem. In his pettish alienation he refuses to recognize a second (though assuredly less dramatic or appealing than Tom) human link to the public world of humanity in general.

Complementing or even representing the figurative windows that for St. Peter are now only too tightly closed is the very literal, actual window in his attic study. By means of this small window Cather conveys the need to maintain an open commerce with the wider world. The climactic incident in which Godfrey allows the window to fall shut and almost loses his life as a consequence could scarcely be more clearly emblematic. His life becomes more and more bounded by the indoors and by his solitary brooding in his small study. Such a withdrawal, the concluding incident shows, can be a potentially fatal one if pursued to its limit. When Godfrey allows his window, that symbol of commerce with both the outdoors and the outer social world, to fall shut, thereby shutting off his access to adventure and discovery in the real world and his tie to human commonality, he almost suffocates. Literally, his withdrawal nearly proves fatal. Figuratively, the incident says that if one chooses isolation to the point of shutting out the common world, one risks the "death" of solipsism. Unlike Rosowski, who sees the final window of the novel, the symbolic extension of the literal study window, as one that opens inward to the "original self," I see the end of the book, conveying its largest meaning, as neither an endorsement nor a rejection of the private, the solitary, but an assertion of the human need for *both* inward-turning and outward-turning, a reiteration of Cather's insistence on keeping the window open to the outdoors, to the public space.[60]

If *The Professor's House,* then, is not a sign of Cather's turn from the world toward isolation, it is nevertheless a sign of her increasing *impulse toward* that turn and an overt statement of the need to resist such an impulse, a warning to herself and to others. Rather than the culmination of an inward voyage, it is an insistence on the need, by those persons like the professor and like Cather herself who are drawn to privacy, for an outward voyage. Godfrey is saved when the window is opened again, letting life rush in from the outside. The person who opens it, Augusta, the seamstress, clearly represents the commonality with which one is "outward bound." The final affirmation of the book, though it is indeed a rather subdued affirmation, is of this "outward bound" journey.

I have raised the issue of gender in relation to Cather's avoidance of the male-female love story convention in *The Professor's House* and the contrast in behavior between Tom Outland (and other males in that book) and Thea Kronborg with respect to their interaction with the southwestern setting. I now want to return to the gendering of Cather's discourse of home, departure, and journey in narratives of emergence throughout her career.

Gender is, of course, a vexed topic in Cather studies, and not solely because of recent attention to her sexuality.[61] Gender is at issue in some sense in everything she wrote, whether she chose female centers of interest or perspective or male—as she did in a perhaps surprising number of novels: *The Professor's House* and *One of Ours,* already noted, and also *Death Comes for the Archbishop, My Ántonia,* and *A Lost Lady.* An autobiographical impulse works its way through all of these texts in disguised and evasive ways, and when a female center of the narrative gaze is rendered through the perceptions of a geographically mobile male, as in *My Ántonia* and *A Lost Lady,* the opportunities for interrogation of gender are multiplied. Her fullest examinations of the urge to depart as it exists in tandem with an urge to inhabit, as both are inflected by gender, come in a darkening series of works centering (whether through a male focalizer or not) on powerful females: *O Pioneers!*, *The Song of the Lark*, *My Ántonia*, *A Lost Lady*, and *My Mortal Enemy*, where one displaced female is viewed and interpreted by another.

Alexandra, in *O Pioneers!*, is a female version and also a more powerfully motivated version of the Alexander of Cather's "first first novel," who goes here and there pursuing his profession and his amorous excitement. The paralleling of the names—Alexander, Alexandra—signals the centrality of Cather's concern with gender and departure from gendered stereotypes as she took up this second "first novel." *O Pioneers!* is a myth of emergence in which Alexandra resists assumptions about gender and becomes not only an unconventional decision maker and leader but virtually a female spirit of place, heroic in her vision for the land as well as for herself. The motif of departure and journey that we are tracing is muted here in that Alexandra remains, quite purposefully, in her place of birth; yet it is pervasively present in her firm association with the outdoors and in her freedom to go about the countryside as she wishes in making visits and conducting her (predominantly outdoor) affairs. She is not, Sharon O'Brien writes, "a conventional woman whose home is her sphere."[62] Her untrammeled outdoor movement, a transgression of the walls of spatial propriety, is importantly linked to her achievement of selfhood, which entails a necessary departure from the expected role of wife or subservient maiden sister. Alexandra, then, might be seen as an early though surely less startling precursor of Sandra Cisneros's "bad girls" who become "bad" by transgressing spatial boundaries.[63] At the same time, she is associated, both by the fact that she remains at the home farm and by her marriage at the end, with a homing urge, a love of the familiar.

Although Alexandra's transgression of gender roles is disapproved of by her surly brothers, it is vindicated by the novel, by Cather's controlling imagination, while her neighbor Marie Shabata's transgression, also outdoors, is not. Found in the orchard in sexual intimacy with Emil, Alexandra's youngest brother, she is murdered by her outraged husband. What distinguishes the two departures from convention, so that one is consigned to the right hand, in judgment, and the other to the left? Alexandra's is, in a sense, the more lastingly disruptive of the two transgressions of female propriety, defying and rejecting traditional assumptions of male dominance and male relational ties, while Marie's transgression is not only a commoner sinning but one that reinforces, only too emphatically, male dependency. But Alexandra's defiance is constructive; she builds her farm, enriches the land. By implication she constructs a society; she is a founder. Marie's transgression is evasive and destructive; she neither imagines nor instigates growth, despite her luxuriance in it. This much is obvious. More to the point, however, is the precise nature of the en-gendering of each. Marie moves toward a threatening intensification of the female, toward a virtual caricature of rampant sexuality—a role of great and immobilizing danger for the builder, the constructive artist.[64] Alexandra moves in the other direction. She "resembles Cather," Woodress notes, "in her energy, determination to succeed, and strong *masculine* personality" (emphasis added).[65] By transgressing toward androgyny, Alexandra not only assumes the persona with which Cather was herself comfortable but demonstrates female capacity for "masculine" undertakings, such as farming, financial maneuvering—or even writing. In Alexandra's story, then, movement out is implicitly linked to creative empowerment.[66]

After the more expansive and more directly autobiographical *The Song of the Lark,* with its validation of the female escape from the village, Cather returned to the Nebraska scene of *O Pioneers!* in *My Ántonia,* a work of considerably greater complexity than first appears, specifically with respect to patterns of movement. Here she first utilized an autobiographically marked male perspective, as she would again in *The Professor's House.* In the introductory frame with which the book opens, Jim Burden does not appear as a projection of Cather herself, since a presence we might call "Willa Cather" takes a role in the narrative as an "I" who meets her old friend Jim on a train passing through the tedious Midwest. The two begin to talk about Ántonia, a "Bohemian girl" who "seemed to mean to us the country, the conditions, the whole adventure of our childhood."[67] The female, that is, assumes the classic role of territory, the unconscious and unmoving land itself over which the freewheeling male travels—except insofar as the tacitly female "I" is also seen as a traveler, a rider of the rails. But "Willa Cather" quickly, after vouching for Jim's memoir of Ántonia, disappears, merging herself into the role of the professional traveler who also writes, rather than the professional writer who also travels.[68]

This was not the first time Cather had opened with a scene on a train. Among the seven *Troll Garden* stories, "Flavia and Her Artists" opens "As the train neared Tarrytown"; "The Sculptor's Funeral" opens at a railway station in Kansas where townspeople await a train; "A Death in the Desert" opens on the "derisively" named "High Line Flyer"; and the opening paragraph of "A Wagner Matinee" refers to meeting someone's train.[69] Trains, the nineteenth century's primary symbol of rapid movement, change, and the rush into the future, appear prominently, too, in *Alexander's Bridge, The Song of the Lark, One of Ours,* and others. Cather's world was a world in fast motion, though we usually think of it more as a world of still, windblown prairies. But she seldom offers positive associations with trains. The central character of "Paul's Case," a foolish enough boy but nevertheless a not unsympathetic center of consciousness, is of course killed by a train, as is Thea's friend and benefactor, in an accident modeled on an actual event that occurred when Cather was thirteen years old.[70] It is on a train that Claude gets his first inkling of trouble ahead when Enid shuts him out of their stateroom on their wedding night, and it is railroad companies that propose to "develop our West" and then create economic instability in *A Lost Lady.* In *My Ántonia* itself, the man who lures Ántonia away with false promises of marriage and then leaves her pregnant is a railroad man. It is no positive indicator, then, that Jim Burden is presented as "legal counsel for one of the great Western railroads," though the point is not belabored. It will become clear, however, that his freedom of movement over the continent in the course of his work is ultimately ironic, because it is wearisome to him. He yearns, or thinks he yearns, for Ántonia's fixity.

Like the introduction, the novel proper also opens on a train. Jim, now subsuming an array of details from Cather's own life, is riding west to Nebraska. Unlike the nine-year-old Willa who made that journey, he is an orphan. Like her, he is dispossessed of Virginia—a redundancy, perhaps, for his orphaning as it is for Cather's own displacement, since her mother was named Virginia. Ántonia, too, is on the train, just as "Willa Cather" was on the train with Jim in the introductory frame. Her family is making the last leg of their long immigrant journey from Bohemia.[71] After this one journey, however, Ántonia stays close to home throughout her life. Her single escape, the departure by train for her intended marriage, is presented—within both the male's offended view and the Widow Steavens's conventional though sympathetic one—as the straying of a fallen woman that, in Ann Fisher-Wirth's words, "serves to tie her more closely to her female biology."[72] At the end she represents, to Jim Burden at any rate, the virtues of rootedness, nurturance, and availability for return, thereby enacting the traditional female role of (at once) point of departure and goal for the male journey, the female's "mapping" as the space of his travel itself through association with "mother" earth.[73] Cather's own impulses are split in two, represented in Jim's restless movement (established in the introductory frame, evident in his determined escape from the inadequacy of the village, and emphasized in the concluding chapter) and in Ántonia's at-homeness (at the center).

Yet the story is not simply one of male adventure and female fixedness. If it were, it would scarcely move beyond stereotype. Just as Jim's mobility is modulated, even called into question, by his nostalgic turn toward home, as represented by Ántonia, so, as Janet Giltrow and David Stouck have demonstrated, is his final "optimistic" reflection on home "undercut" by the numerous references to roads and journeying that "pervade the conclusion, recalling 'the interminable journey' Jim describes in his opening sentence."[74] In addition, in the figures of the two immigrant girls, Tiny Soderball and Lena Lingard, who go off to make their fortunes half a continent away in Seattle and Alaska and San Francisco, we see that adventures and daring initiatives are the business of women as well. Cather in effect folds a new text of female spatial freedom into the traditional text of woman as stay-at-home. If she strikes a contrast between Ántonia as anchored foot of the compass and Jim as ranging foot, she also shows the need of each for the other and for complementarity. Primarily, of course, it is Jim's need for Ántonia and all she represents that is emphasized. His life is barren precisely for the lack of the qualities Ántonia represents: vigor, fertility, warmth, the stability of home. Her rich nurturance and stability at the center of the novel have led to its being interpreted over the years as a celebration of wholesome at-home virtues. Certainly Cather does celebrate Ántonia; she depicts her as a heroic figure. But that affirmation is not the totality of the book.

Ántonia has, after all, attempted to make her own departures—to her town jobs, to her proposed marriage. But she has been entrapped by her sexuality in becoming pregnant and then being abandoned by the railroad man who proposed marriage. She is entrapped, too, by her inability to devise any outlet for her energies except that of making a home apart from her birth family, in her own way. In that endeavor—and we are not to suppose it is an insignificant one—she succeeds admirably. Her children are indeed, as Lena Lingard cautiously tells Jim, "nice" (*My Ántonia,* 260), and the Cuzak farm is a wonder of vegetal and animal life, emotional warmth, stockpiles of home canning. We cannot believe that Ántonia would have preferred any other kind of life, since even when she was looking forward to the marriage that never occurred she was troubled by the thought of having to live in a city. Even so, Cather shows us, in indirect ways running as an undercurrent to her overt celebration of all that Ántonia represents, that the role of a mother-woman and effective head of a farm household is a hard one. When Jim returns to drink once more from the spring of Ántonia's vitality, he finds a "grizzled," "battered," and nearly toothless, shapeless woman (261–62, 264), continuously overworked and hard used by time. This fact qualifies—for the reader, though apparently not for Jim—the affirmation of homing.

It is easy enough for him to say that Ántonia's losses don't matter; he has not been the one to suffer them. And plainly there is an advantage to him in her lifelong immobility. He has a household to which he can return at will to indulge in nostalgia and reawaken the illusion of boyhood, without risk of being caught in the wrong story, the domestic plot.[75] As Romines points out, he guards against that risk by insisting on sleeping out in the barn with the boys, away from the house. But for Ántonia, who was once such a bright, alert, and winning child, life might have been more fulfilling if it had included more of the change and personal unfolding associated with movement. Clearly, she does not intend her younger daughters to be so submerged in the role of the mother-woman. She tells them a different story, one centered on female departure and self-definition. It can only have been through her telling that the independent businesswoman Frances Harling has "come down as a heroine in the family legend," and she sounds pleased when she reports that the children of another of the immigrant hired girls will have "a grand chance" (My Ántonia, 256). Frances is Ántonia's "window," affording her a vision of more expansive opportunities than she has had herself.

This is not to deny that the primary values of Cather's best-loved novel are the values of home and stability. They are. And the sunny, fulfilled tone of this home-affirming book, in its concluding chapters of return and affirmation, is more emphatic, more "compellingly" and "mysteriously beautiful"[76] than the discontents of a book like The Professor's House, which presents homing more nearly as suffocation. Even so, secondary values also present in the book call these primary values into question in relatively subtle or disguised ways. It is this balance of values, this willingness to entertain tensions within the celebration, that make My Ántonia so much more satisfying and mature a book than Cather's later, almost naively univocal celebration of home, *Shadows on the Rock,* which can so illuminatingly be paired with it.

I want to defer consideration of that important and under-read work, however, in order to pursue another pairing with *My Ántonia, A Lost Lady,* published five years afterward, in 1923. Cather herself called attention to the pairing, telling her editor that the original of Ántonia had done housework for the original of Marian Forrester.[77] *A Lost Lady* can well be seen as a grittily realistic redaction of the sunnier work. Woodress has called it "not at all a serene novel, though it is a polished work of art."[78] That lack of serenity, evident also in *My Mortal Enemy,* three years later, may have resulted from Cather's interrogating not only marriage and the dangerous myth of romantic love but also the possibility that she herself had given up too much in exchanging the inheritance of daughterhood for her independence from the constraints of home and its conventional roles. She deflects the question from its actual terms in her own experience by invoking the terms of the traditional romantic love story that she (but not Isabelle McClung, whose marriage in 1916 had precipitated an emotional crisis of the first order for Cather) had long since forsaken.

Like Ántonia, Marian Forrester in *A Lost Lady* is presented to the reader through the perceptions of an idealizing male, this time much younger than herself, whose vision of the charming Mrs. Forrester is inadequate both to her frustration and to her real vitality, which he attempts to restrict and control as he presumptuously attempts to decide what is best for her. Marian Forrester at first seems to live out a fairy-tale story of marriage to a protective hero. During the years of her husband's vitality and prosperity she happily, it seems, plays the role of trophy wife in a male-driven drama with the house as stage. Even when she is loved and treasured, however, such a woman is still an exhibited object. It "gratified" the Captain to hear business friends "admire his fine stock, grazing in the meadows," and it also "gratified" him to see how those same men admired his wife (5). Cather places these parallel phrases in successive sentences, as if to point out the comparability of attitude. An object lacks mobility, lacks self-determination. Mrs. Forrester's seeming freedom of movement is actually not her own at all, but is controlled by her husband, a boon that can be purchased or withheld—or lost—according to his ability and disposition.

When Captain Forrester suffers financial reverse, illness, and finally death, she finds her life reduced to drudgery and the house itself a trap from which she can no longer afford to escape for sparkling winter seasons of parties in Denver. Ironically, the house that now imprisons her is the only property she owns, and with the slump in property values due to a widespread economic depression in the once booming West, it is no longer worth enough to buy her liberty. Until this point, Mrs. Forrester's seeming freedom of spatial movement has been both the expression of her zest for living and the relief that allowed her to love her secure and gracious home. Each made the other possible. We have seen her strolling out to distribute cookies to picnicking boys, running across a pasture, popping in on friends in town, riding in a sleigh, dancing. But when the circumstances of her life change, narrowly restricting her movements, we see her only moving heavily and restlessly about the house, scrubbing floors, carrying water, and making pastry. Her story has become that of a woman trapped in the feminine roles she had earlier enjoyed using to advantage.

Niel, the imperceptive narrator, fails to realize how cramped her life has become even when he sees her struggling with heavy work. Seeing only that she is no longer as pleasant to look at as she used to be, he chooses to look away. When she mentions that she comes down to the grove in the afternoons to "get where I can't see the house," he blandly turns the conversation to other matters. But if Niel's vision of her defeat is inadequate, so is his appreciation of her victory at the end. Hearing that she has been seen in South America and that she is still beautiful and laughing, he feels glad that she is once more being cared for by a man of wealth. He has no more idea of the ingenuity that must have been required for her to make her departure and secure her present situation than he had of her desperation. Nor does the reader, in any clear sense; that aspect of the story, lying outside Niel's perspective, is silenced. But it is clear that even if her triumph is a hollow one in its reliance on traditional feminine wiles of self-presentation (the only skills she knows), she has at any rate made good her escape.[79]

In *A Lost Lady* Cather gives us, as she said she intended, the sense of a woman's charm, but she gives us as well a tacit indictment of a social system based on exploiting that charm and caging it up in houses. It is her most unqualified endorsement of the adult impulse to escape from domesticity. If Marian Forrester is in fact lost, as the title indicates, it is only because her social conditioning has deprived her of horizons equal to her vitality. Or if it is only in Niel's view that she is lost—that is, not in fact lost at all—the reason is that his idea of her was inadequate from the start. Whichever way we read the title phrase, Cather undercuts Niel's narrative vision by providing the context of a broader and better-informed view. She shows the alert reader how limited Marian Forrester's options were, how like a pet or valuable possession she was treated, and how enslaving the housework is when one can't afford hired help and vacations.[80] It is not that homes are not desirable. Part of the ache of the novel is that the real value of home has been, for a woman like Marian Forrester, so demeaned. "That's what I'm struggling for," she says at one point, "to get out of this hole" (107).

Offering another of those pairings that are so illuminating in Cather's oeuvre, *My Mortal Enemy* again shows Cather's recognition of the urgency of the escape wish, both for the young person and for the mature woman desperate to escape the marital home. The vision of *My Mortal Enemy,* however, is even darker than that of *A Lost Lady,* as it develops a theme of the distortion both of the homing urge and of the urge to freedom of movement. In the earlier part of the novel, before she is immobilized by poverty and illness, Myra Henshawe is seen continually in motion, both the motion of escape and the motion of excitement or social flitting. The statue of Diana "stepp[ing] out freely and fearlessly into the grey air" (21) outside her New York apartment is Myra's very image. But her freedom of movement proves illusory, collapsing into a frenetic drivenness that is itself a virtual imprisonment.

The most decisive departure of the book, Myra's escape from her uncle's home in a "runaway marriage" (3), has occurred long in the fictive time past. A believer in the all-sufficiency of romantic love, Myra had so longed to make her escape from what she perceived as an oppressive home that she "used to lie on the floor all night and listen to the express trains go by" (71). It is one of Cather's sly ironies that the then up-and-coming young man Myra forsakes a fortune to marry, who later proves unable to prosper in business, works for a railroad. In escaping her uncle's house she moves, not into endless enchantment and freedom, but into frustration. Elopement does not, after all, mean escape from the constraints of home but, in this world of limited options for women, departure from one home in order to establish another.[81] But home, especially without the realistic advantage of money to prop up romance, is too small an arena for Myra's imperious energies. She is trapped with a philandering husband whose income is never adequate to the level of social interaction she demands, neither of them able to escape the other.

In the brutally rendered world of this terse novel, without money one has little freedom, though one may have a kind of mobility: an insecure and steadily downward mobility that Cather declines to present consolingly. Near the end, Myra complains that "by the time you've learned the short cuts, your feet puff up so that you can't take the road at all" (54). She dies facing the Pacific, the vaster route of escape she can never take, fully recognizing the mockery of her life and how sadly the one value for which she gave all else, romantic love, has proven to be as destructive as the hatefulest enemy.[82] Both *My Mortal Enemy* and *A Lost Lady* resonate retrospectively with the far more affirming *My Ántonia* and prospectively with *Shadows on the Rock.*

Clearly, the only female departure that Cather fully endorses, in the sense of envisioning it as being both entirely compelling and likely to lead to victory, is the emergence of self-fulfillment in work, not marriage. This is the kind of freedom of movement seen in Alexandra, who does not marry until after she has achieved heroic stature, and in Thea Kronborg, who may be lonely and implacable at times but would not—we are certain of this— exchange her life as an artist for a life of conventional domesticity. The fact that departure to self-fulfillment is denied Ántonia, who remains Cather's single most luminous female character, might seem to call her endorsement of the emergence narrative into question. Ántonia has fulfilled herself by location, rather than movement. But the circumstances of her life have taken their toll, and the point is made with considerable emphasis that even though she lives in a house-bound world, where the family of many girls as well as boys in which she is the central principle can be called by a myopic idealist "Cuzak's Boys," she is determined to give her daughters a chance at another kind of life.

It is this kind of departure, bringing the chance at that other life, that Cather shows as the central, fully validated act in what is probably her finest short work, "Old Mrs. Harris," published in 1932 as one of the three stories making up *Obscure Destinies.* Here she returns to the mode of indirect autobiography that she had used so successfully before, and to the form of the *Bildungsroman,* to show once again the impelling need for escape from the constraints of home and small town. Escape is the key to personal development for the talented female. While emphasizing the difficulty of escape, Cather also shows its success through the effort of the old grandmother, who manages to find a way for Vickie to go away to college, that classic (at the time, classically male) route to self-realization. Emergence requires that one "follow the long road that leads through things unguessed at and unforeseeable" (one recalls Thea's beckoning road with open gates), and Grandma Harris's determination will enable Vickie to follow a more adventurous and fulfilling road than she followed herself.[83] Certainly it is a road seen as an escape from the dreary cycle of pregnancies that constitutes the life of Vickie's (Cather's) mother. A beautiful and important work, "Old Mrs. Harris" focuses Cather's vision of female emergence on the single autobiographical moment she views as being the key to it all, her own departure for the University of Nebraska. It also reaches forward to *Sapphira and the Slave Girl,* Cather's last novel and one in which motifs of emergence are interrogated in relation to Cather's feelings toward her mother and her Grandmother Boak more openly than in any previous work.

Despite her endorsement of departure in "Old Mrs. Harris" and her portrayal of the life of the home as a kind of life sentence to servitude, the general movement of Cather's imagination during this later period in her career is one of retirement or withdrawal inside protective walls. After the troubled reclusiveness of *The Professor's House* in 1925, a sequence of major works recapitulating or revising earlier concerns—*Death Comes for the Archbishop* in 1927, a return to the Southwest; *Shadows on the Rock* in 1931, a return to housewifery; and then *Sapphira,* a return to home and mother—shifts her imaginative balance in a progressive closing in or battening down. These late works have a tone of emotional retreat expressed largely through their patterns of spatial movement and spatial constraint as these relate to the characters' concerns and aspirations. The commonly expressed view that Cather's later novels, especially *Shadows on the Rock,* showed a turn to conservatism is essentially correct. More precisely, her late novels demonstrate a turn to caution or even defensiveness, a walling up of the self inside thick fortifications both tangible and emotional. We encounter, as readers, increasing difficulties in reconciling the openness of her texts with the conscious conservatism of her principles.[84]

In *Death Comes for the Archbishop,* Cather returned once again to the arid Southwest, the region that had opened up her own life course and provided a profound and liberating openness in *The Song of the Lark* and *The Professor's House.* Locating her narrative almost entirely in New Mexico and in the past, the point in the mid-nineteenth century when by the Treaty of Guadalupe Hidalgo, 1848, Mexico ceded vast stretches of its territory to the United States under force of arms, she addresses the ethnic diversity of the area in a way she had scarcely touched on in the earlier works. Her interest in the Anasazi cliff dwellings, some of which she visited in 1912 and 1915, is of course well known, but her interest in Indian life was by no means confined to the ancient peoples. Letters to Elizabeth Shepley Sergeant indicate that she also visited, in 1912, Hopi villages, Acoma, and Isleta (one of the Rio Grande pueblos). Letters to Mabel Dodge Luhan mention visits to a number of important Indian sites in the 1920s, including the pueblos of Laguna and again Acoma (which figures prominently in *Death Comes for the Archbishop*), the city of Gallup (which she thought hellish), and the Canyon de Chelly, the historic and sacred center of the Navajo people. She considered herself enough of an insider to sneer at outsiders she referred to, borrowing the designation of a program of organized tours operated by the Fred Harvey company, as "Indian Detourists."[85] Her interest, however, does not seem to have extended to the history of white America's dealings with Indian peoples. She seems unaware, or at any rate does not acknowledge, that the territorial government of Arizona, the state where her redemptive experience of place and cultural heritage occurred in 1912, had officially endorsed a policy of extermination.[86] As she prepared for the writing of *Archbishop* during the mid-1920s, her research focused on Bishop Lamy and his efforts of clerical reform and the development of his diocese. That focus eventuated in the Eurocentric tone of the work complained of by Austin.

The opening scene of the novel, after an expository prelude, is one of spatial immensity in which the newly appointed bishop, Father Latour, is engaged in a journey of search. Throughout the book we then see Latour and his friend Father Vaillant making, as Fryer observes, "endless journeys across this vast and strange diocese" and in fact beyond it: through the immense New Mexico landscape, to Mexico and back, to Baltimore and to Europe and back, to Colorado. Clearly, Woodress is correct in seeing *Archbishop* as being "based on the journey motif."[87] It is probably Cather's most wide-ranging book, spatially. Yet, in a sense, the novel finally forsakes its apparent mood of vastness and spatial as well as spiritual openness, turning instead toward enclosures at the end (a kind of mirror reversal of the movement of *The Professor's House,* which finally rejects its prevalent mood of stuffiness or withdrawal). The movement of values in *Archbishop* is toward the indoors, toward sheltered stasis. Instead of the open-sided caves of *The Song of the Lark* and *The Professor's House,* resembling comfortable rooms with large windows transformed into outdoor spaces and providing what Gaston Bachelard refers to as "intimate immensity,"[88] Latour comes to a closed-in, dank, and disturbing cave with cracks and holes opening toward ever lower and more threatening depths, along with a visually impeded opening to the outdoors. He is eager to press on from this cave of bottomless ambiguity toward constructed houses.

Fryer comments that "shelters are frail" in the world of this novel.[89] That is generally true. The Navajo hogan that Latour finds "favourable for reflection" is explicitly termed "frail"; letting in both light and wind, it is one of Cather's recurrent unions of indoors and outdoors. But Latour's place of greatest comfort, his *most* felicitous space, is the study of his thick-walled house, not at all frail or a blending of outdoors and indoors, and his life's goal is the building of a stone edifice. As archbishop, he literally turns the rocks of the vast New Mexico outdoors into stone walls, the walls of a cathedral constructed, significantly, along very traditional European lines. And Cather, clearly enough, affirms this act of authoritarian spiritual colonialism as a good and virtuous deed—the affirmation that drew Mary Austin's objection in *Earth Horizon.*[90]

If the end of *The Professor's House* emphasizes the need for renewing, on even a modest scale, St. Peter's earlier openness to discovery and companionship, the end of *Death Comes for the Archbishop* validates a rigid certainty imposed on a space of religious and cultural uncertainty. The great sense of movement in the work derives from its evocation of the spacious Southwest, the sense of cultural movement and borders, and the energy with which Latour and Vaillant pursue their mission. That energy is expended, however, in the service of institutionalized order, not liberty. The reader's task in this novel is by no means an easy one. Like the cave where Latour takes refuge with his guide Jacinto, the text comprises layer beneath layer of ambiguity. Latour himself chooses to retire to a country villa in the New World rather than the Old. He seems to recognize, near the end of his life, a movement of his own sensibility away from the European traditionalism he had thought he most valued toward the intense light and free movement of winds in New Mexico, a quality in the landscape "soft and wild and free" that "picked the lock, slid the bolts, and released the prisoned spirit of man into the wind" (*Archbishop,* 273). Escape or liberation is powerfully implied in this image of the opening door. Yet Latour feels a "great content" at being once again in his old room with "thick, wavy white walls that muted sound, that shut out the world" (271). The book ends, as its title indicates, not with a departure or with a symbolic adjuration to keep the windows open, but with the arch-bishop's death and his funeral observances. Cather said that she imagined Latour's death as his and Death's riding off together.[91] That would indeed be a movement of freedom fulfilling his urge for release into the wind and the morning. Still, death necessarily means cessation of movement. At the end, Latour's body lies before the altar in his cathedral, preparatory to entomb-ment—the ending of all journeys. The book enshrines his wide-ranging journey to stasis.

In a sense, then, *Archbishop* represents an even more decisive turning point in Cather's career than *The Professor's House.* Beginning here, her nar-ratives not only become even more emphatically discontinuous than they had been before (Cather herself invoked the term "narrative" when readers found *Archbishop* not novelistic), but turn toward certainty, toward the past, toward return, and toward private as well as public order. Here and in her other late works she turns away from discovery of the "physical world" toward, as Rosowski notes, orientation by means of stable spiritual sym-bols.[92] She turns, as well, from outdoor expanses toward insulated indoor spaces.

That turning is yet more pronounced in *Shadows on the Rock,* where Latour's beloved thick-walled indoor retreat becomes a virtual fortress of do-mesticity, which Cather offers as the very emblem of good in the world and a sufficiency unto itself. Although the beginning of the book emphasizes how dependent this fortress-like space is on journeys across great distances (both the ships' journeys from France and the explorers' journeys into the forest), by the end it is Cécile's wish *not* to go on journeys, her preference for being at home, indoors, that matters. The emphasis is on "stability" or on "perma-nence and security," symbolized by the rock.[93] Restlessness, a quality recog-nized or even affirmed in earlier works, is now identified as a "dark spirit of discontent." It is the disagreeable and rather sinister bishop, not young Cécile or her father, Euclide Auclair, who has "restless" eyes.[94] Cécile suc-cessfully evades the plot of male restlessness that threatens the story she is writing, as her mother's amanuensis, in her life, but does so not by invoking an alternative story of emergence and exploration but by stepping into the old plot of female stasis. The firm anchorage of Ántonia's life-giving housewifery is fortified inside stone walls devoid of the riot of vegetal life with which she was surrounded.

Cather treats the rocky land-monument on which Quebec is established very differently than she does the rocky landscape of her Southwest in *The Professor's House*. There, and even more so in *The Song of the Lark,* the massive rocks that make up the mountains and cliffs are humanized, made comfortable. Her emphasis is on ancient peoples' ability to make dwellings within and among the rocky cliffs and on the openness of their cave-chambers, affording great expansive vistas. In *Shadows* the emphasis is on immobility and protection. The vista of the river offered both at the beginning and at the end of the book is scarcely an opening of vision or a beckoning to adventure, but is valued primarily as an avenue for the importation of commodities needed to sustain domestic life in this fortress town. Not exploration but the dignity or even imputed sanctity of such housekeeping skills as cooking and maintaining order is primarily valued and affirmed. It is a dramatic change from Marian Forrester's need to get where she "can't see the house."

Pierre Charron, Euclide's friend who becomes Cécile's husband, quotes as a kind of axiom, "Religion for the fireside, freedom for the woods" (*Shadows*, 175). In earlier novels, Cather's expansive young women had been able to choose both—if for "religion" we substitute a related but secular term such as inner fulfillment. Here, the choice for Cécile and for her father is one or the other, and it is never a contest: they choose the fireside and religion. Indeed, the book's choice of fireside and religion as centers of value is so emphatic that some twenty-two saints and religious figures are mentioned, some at length. Central among these is Jeanne Le Ber, a "reclusive mystic" whose impulse toward isolation, the impulse that is rejected in *The Professor's House,* is not only embraced but idealized. Skaggs calls Jeanne the "bad daughter" who defies her parents and breaks their heart,[95] but in my reading the book presents her religious commitment as a transcendent kind of goodness they simply are unable to understand. Moreover, her retreat to the enclosed space of the religious cell is paralleled by Cécile's clearly affirmed retreat from the larger world. As Jeanne finds in her cell a paradise, so Cécile finds a kind of paradise within the home.

Cécile lives inside "layers and layers of shelter," a "climate within a climate" (*Shadows,* 158, 198). To be sure, she also goes sledding in winter. But when she "stays out of doors and away from the house as much as possible" late in the book, it is not because of a spirit of adventure, like Thea, and certainly not because she can't face the house, like Marian Forrester, but because she is distressed by her father's notion of leaving Quebec (228). During this period she voices her single rebellious wish to wander, but this too is in a sense a wish to stay home, to go deeper into Canada, rather than to leave as her father hopes. She stays away from home to avoid confronting his wish to leave home—that is, her home. Auclair himself, wishing to go back to France with the count whom he has long served, thinks of the St. Lawrence River as an "avenue of escape" on which men could "travel, taste the sun and open air, feel freedom, join their fellows, reach the open sea" (7)—a sequence that seems to imply a desire for the venturous life. The language here is the most explicitly open and journey-affirming in the novel. But its apparent celebration of voyaging is really a celebration of homing. Auclair feels this beckoning only because he wants to escape from the New World back to the Old, to *his* home. He and Cécile merely have different definitions of home.

The redefinition of home serves, of course, a pattern of movement of another kind, the movement and gradual revision of culture. Cécile embodies a new spirit of Canadian identity. In this capacity, she accommodates her parents' old-world traditionalism to the needs of the founding of a new culture. Indeed, the glimpses Cather affords of wide-ranging travel, both on the ocean and upriver into the (to Europeans) trackless inland spaces, are all given with reference to this cultural movement, not an individual freedom of movement. On the individual level, Cécile is absorbed into the home-centered role of mother, her wish to travel Canada's rivers unfulfilled, just as Pierre Charron is seemingly absorbed into the role of householder in the conservative society of the aristocratic Upper Town, within the town on the rock that is the center of political power, as opposed to his previous life of free-ranging travel in the emblematic backcountry of freedom.[96]

In *The Song of the Lark,* Thea's beloved room has a large window letting her sense the vitality of the outside world, and her regenerative cave on the mesa is like a windowed room, isolated and enclosing yet open. Retreat is combined with expansive vista. In *Shadows,* the architectural emphasis is not on the windows in the walls, but on the walls themselves, especially their thickness. The buildings of Quebec are "heavy" (6). Houses have "double walls, with sawdust and ashes filling in the space between the two frames, making a protection nearly four feet thick" (9). Reinforcing them is the "perpendicular wall" (156) of the cliff, surmounted by the Count's massive chateau. Granted, Cécile and her father enjoy keeping their doors and windows open in the spring, but the reader is reminded, in the Count's deathbed dream of a "terrible man" lurking outside, that there is danger at doors and windows (244).

The language of image and symbolic motion in the novel indicates that for Cather, at this period of her life, as well as for her characters, the danger at the windows and doors outweighed the promise of freedom and imaginative expansion. She wrote *Shadows on the Rock* at a time when she had come through a series of family crises. It served as a reassurance for her; it supplied a need. Rosowski calls this the need for stability. Skaggs sees it as the need to re-create herself as the ideally domestic daughter her parents had not had, thus effacing her guilt for having, to whatever extent, disappointed them. (Cécile's "shingled head" makes it clear that she does indeed represent a young Willa.) I would define the function that the book served Cather at the time primarily as one of protection. It allowed her to indulge a wish that she had earlier rejected as destructive, the wish to retreat from the world, to seal oneself up so tightly that danger could not come in, that one could not be disappointed. But the price she paid for such protection was the curtailment of her own urge to freedom and adventure, as well as the lessening of that urge in her work. The atmosphere of *Shadows*, for all its overt celebration of how housekeeping maintains a culture, is one of fear and retreat, one that might even be called agoraphobic. It is a dramatic and unrewarding turn from the simultaneous security and openness of her earlier work.

In *Sapphira and the Slave Girl*, despite its being on the surface as darkly troubled as any other book she wrote, departure and journeying are fully and beautifully reconciled to the sustaining value of at-homeness, and the liminal image of the window—the image at the center of Cather's novel of personal starting-out, *The Song of the Lark*—is the means of that reconciliation. Cather returns in this work to her personal roots in Virginia to explore the conflicts and cruelties of the social order within which her parents had grown up and from which, some seventeen years after the Civil War, they departed for the Midwest. She brings to fullness her persistent theme of displacement and the hope for restoration—evident in *My Ántonia*, in *My Mortal Enemy*, in many aspects of *Death Comes for the Archbishop* including, as

Ann Fisher-Wirth points out,[97] the story of the Navajo's exile to the Bosque Redondo and their return to the Canyon de Chelly, in Euclid Auclair's sense of displacement from France in *Shadows on the Rock,* and elsewhere.

We might see this return to the place of origin as a symbolic return to and reconciliation with her mother, Mary Virginia (Jennie) Cather.[98] Yet the peculiar positioning of the actual grandmother and mother in the characters in which they are represented gives one pause: the order of generations is reversed. In Rachel Blake, Cather's Grandmother Boak (her mother's mother) becomes the daughter, rather than the mother, of Sapphira, who represents (in part) Cather's own mother. The inversion may indicate Cather's relative repositioning of the two with respect to her sense of emotional closeness, distancing the mother and, in generational terms, moving the grandmother closer. Even so, a symbolic reconciliation with Virginia Cather is served, in that she is represented in the novel not only by the "bad mother," Sapphira, but also by a "good mother," properly placed in the narrative as the daughter of Mrs. Blake, who enters the novel in its closing, avowedly autobiographical scene.

Much of the world of *Sapphira* is tightly constrained, a world of exile for Sapphira herself (forever displaced from the higher-toned Loudoun County), for the elderly slave Jezebel (who still remembers her African home), and for other central characters as well.[99] The aging Sapphira occupies her house as a force of domineering control, restricting the freedom not only of those who are literally enslaved to her but also of her emotionally enslaved husband. She also to some degree restricts the freedom of her widowed daughter, Rachel, usually referred to in the novel as Mrs. Blake, who had once made good her escape from her mother but been forced back by economic necessity. As the book progresses and Sapphira's health deteriorates, she becomes completely immobile, not only strongholded in her house but restricted to it by dropsical lameness. The book would seem, by this account, to express not only a condemnation of home, through depiction as a place of sickness and imprisonment, but a sense of sharply restricted possibility. In fact, however, it resoundingly affirms both liberation by escape and also return and the restoration of emotional ties to home.

The imprisoning nature of Sapphira's house and household is a localized image of the central fact of the book: slavery. If Sapphira is trapped in the house by illness in her latter days, her slaves are trapped on the property throughout their lives by their legal status. For the young and graceful slave

Nancy, toward whom Sapphira has conceived a hatred based on unreasoning jealousy, home is worse than a prison, it is a place of torment and sexual peril. Spinning out vindictive plots in a sinisterly spider-like manner, Sapphira brings onto the place a young and disreputable nephew in the full knowledge that he is likely to conceive an expropriative passion for the attractive mulatto girl.[100] When nature and the slaveholder's tradition of sexual dominance seem likely to take just the course Sapphira had expected, at which point Nancy laments to Mrs. Blake that she is "most drove out-a my mind" and would rather "drown myself before he got at me than after," Rachel arranges to have Nancy spirited away across the Potomac and by underground railway to Canada. As Fryer puts it, "escape from confinement, made possible through the bonding of women, is literally the story" of the novel. It might well, in fact, be called the "story" of all of Cather's work—as she once acknowledged, in a letter to Dorothy Canfield Fisher[101]—and it is a story that embraces men as well as women: Sapphira's husband, the miller, ponders that "a man's got to be stronger'n a bull to get out of the place he was born in" (*Sapphira*, 130).

The act of escape is more dramatic, however, more historically validated, and more urgent in its motivation here than in any of Cather's other books. (It is also more multiply crossed by historical complexities, which will be taken up in chapter 5, where additional readings of the novel are proposed.) Even so, dramatized and historicized as it is, the escape from slavery is only an intensification of the more general motif of women's need for liberation from a bondage of sorts in the home, the locus of a great and inhibiting complex of traditional societal expectations. Buried in the silences that are always a part of Cather's *demeublé* fictive structures is an implied parallel between Nancy's plight, at once constrained and sexually vulnerable, and that of women in general. Cather does not elaborate that implication, but it is there, as is the idea that it is women themselves who must take the initiative if they are to break out of such constraint. It would seem that in the situation thus constructed, Cather's impulse would for once be unidirectional, away from the home. Nancy could become a kind of Sylvie or Ruth (of *Housekeeping*), shaking the dust of subservient domesticity off her feet and turning with glee to the adventurous life on the road to Canada. But Cather's imagination does not run to vagrancy. Once again she circles back to the central, stable refuge—but a refuge with a view.

Rachel Blake, the initiator of Nancy's movement toward freedom, is

shown throughout as a woman whose degree of freedom from house-con-
straint is exceptional. Indeed, Cather characteristically conceives of spatial
freedom in terms of exceptionalism.[102] Although Mrs. Blake's range is limited
by the paucity of her resources, she is able to move freely about the community on errands of benevolence. Accordingly, her house, like other indoor
spaces favored by Cather, affords a vision of outdoor freedom through its
large window. It is through the same window, but looking in rather than out,
that a family friend watches one of Mrs. Blake's daughters, ill with diphtheria, exercise the freedom of following her own impulse to drink when she is
thirsty, despite a male physician's instructions that she have nothing to eat
or drink. Cather attributes to this moment not only the power of restoration—the child lives while the other daughter, unable to obtain for herself
the fluid she needs, dies—but even a Communion-like quality. The child is
healed by communion with her own deepest instincts, her selfhood. Notably, that freedom of intuition occurs beside a wide, liminal window, but *inside* Rachel Blake's house, not outside it. If Rachel embodies free movement
about the neighboring area and free *mental* movement to values that reject
slavery, she also serves as another of Cather's women who affirm the power
of the home and their maternal, communal roles. Like Jewett's strong Mrs.
Todd, Mrs. Blake goes about visiting, nursing, advising, but always comes
back to her house, which she occupies with contentedness.

But *Sapphira* is a novel of return to the home place in a more dramatic
way. In the final episode of the novel, Nancy returns after an absence of
twenty-five years. Rather than the house where she was once persecuted, she
returns to the home of an idealized Cather family including a child named
Willa, the grandchild of Rachel Blake. Here Nancy is reunited with her
mother in a satisfyingly emotional scene presided over by Mrs. Blake, her
deliverer, still at hand and still bringing order to the lives of others. The setting for this reunion is another of Cather's wide-windowed rooms, a third-
floor bedroom where the ill child has been brought so that she can watch
the road for the coach that will bring Nancy. In contrast to the claustrophobic atmosphere of the mill house where Sapphira held sway, the atmosphere
as they await Nancy's arrival is one of liveliness and movement on both sides
of the window, with "as much restlessness inside the house as there was outside in the wind and clouds and trees" (281). When the coach approaches,
Willa's mother (there is no need to write it as "Willa," since autobiography
and fiction have merged) carries her to the window so that she can see the

arrival, while Nancy's mother remains in the bedroom so that the child can also witness the moment of restoration. It is a child's dream, or at any rate the dream that a novelist might well be expected to attribute to her child self: to be in on everything, to witness life's most powerful moments so that she can later (as the book proves) witness to them. Even as a child, then, and even on a day when she is most confined in the house, she has access to outdoor vision and to the freedom that vision affords.

If Cather is present in that room in the form of her imagined child-self, now fully empowered with the memory-materials of her future artistic vocation and fully, satisfyingly mothered, she is also present, I believe, in the figure of Nancy herself. Like Nancy, Cather had to get away from a confinement that threatened her very life, her sense of herself as an artist. But she, too, needed to return and did return repeatedly, both in life and in her fictions. Ann Romines reminds us that Nancy, like Cather, embodies a reconciliation of the necessity for escape and an "affinity for home ritual."[103] But the primary reason for identifying Cather with her character Nancy is the transformation that escape has wrought in Nancy's speech. Before being liberated from Sapphira's house and from her enslavement, Nancy spoke in dialect: "I'd go anywheres to git away from him. I'd sooner go down to Georgia an' pick cotton, 'deed I would." She returns speaking a language of almost "too precise . . . distinctness" (218, 284). Her escape to a place far from home, from which she had the freedom to return without being trapped, has not only given her good, tasteful clothes, a husband of her own choosing, and personal dignity—in short, the freedom to become herself; it has given her literate language.

Denise Levertov invites us to "imagine" a house with permeable walls, "a house without doors, / open to sun or snowdrifts."[104] Levertov's imagined house reconciling indoors and outdoors, and by extension insiders and outsiders, is an ideal shared by Mary Austin and Willa Cather, and also, as we shall see, by Anne Tyler. It is an ideal brought to radical realization, of sorts, by Marilynne Robinson, who imagines an en-housed woods: Sylvie (her name, from the Latin *sylva,* means "woods") keeps a house where dry leaves accumulate in corners and birds and small mammals are welcomed in. A strong continuum, in fact, runs from Sarah Orne Jewett through Austin,

Cather, and Tyler to Robinson. All five are concerned with the realities of women's lives and the importance of their achieving freedom of personal direction, which means freedom to choose when to stay and when to go.

As we have seen, both Mary Austin and Willa Cather affirm the traditional relational roles of women but redefine these roles to include, sometimes in displaced or indirect ways, the departures, outdoor intervals, and journeys by which an expanded self is found and realized. In this way, but only in this way, do they affirm the value and felicity of home and the fulfillment gained through nurturing roles. Both adopt Jewett's structure of looping, home-centered journeys, developing it in complex structures of plot and image with longer trajectories of departure, while still making the dual affirmation of journey and at-homeness. Their projects differed, however, in very important ways. Austin's vision was ultimately a more social, reformist one than Cather's, which always centered on the individual and on individual fulfillment. Austin's involved a vision of change for men as well as for women, primarily with respect to marriage. It was insistently heterosexual, invoking again and again the traditional love-story plot. Perhaps because her own foregrounded heterosexuality gave her a position of greater social security, she was able to be more assertive, more direct or even at times startling, in challenging the repressive conventions of patriarchy, while Cather, ambiguously or homosexually gendered, developed a fictive rhetoric of evasion and indirection.

Manifesting, in her living and in her fiction, both a desire for stable enclosure in residences and relationships and a determination to go beyond the house and its traditional roles, Cather was in a sense the more unconventional of the two in her homing urge. She defined the home role in her own way, which never had anything to do with heterosexual domesticity. She did not openly challenge the stable patriarchal social order in marches, protests, and public pronouncements as Austin did, nor is she often thought of as an aggressive careerist. Yet that label fits her quite as well as it does the more strident Austin. Susan Rosowski writes that Jewett had provided Cather "a model of a successful woman writer."[105] That model, Jewett recognized in a letter to Annie Fields dated July 5, 1889, required the writer to adopt at times a kind of ruthlessness (she called it "cold selfishness") for the sake of her work.[106] It might require her, too, to leave other commitments in order to focus on her writing, as she advised Cather to do in 1908 and as Cather in fact did four years later. Like Austin (who may also have benefited from the example of Jewett), Cather lived a pattern of determined departure from home and the maternal model, seizure of opportunities, and, as her correspondence with Ferris Greenslet makes clear, self-promotion. It is not coincidental, I believe, that both writers, both of them determined career-builders, were also restless travelers.

In Cather's most successful and still best-loved books, *My Ántonia* and *O Pioneers!*, she managed to create fictional structures that accommodate mutually questioning readings, affirming feminine home-values of nurturance and caring while at the same time showing the erosion that such roles cause and the strength and achievement that a woman like Alexandra may gain in unconventional, outdoor ways. At the end of *O Pioneers!* Alexandra has both, marriage and the kind of achievement usually thought of (by her brothers, for example) as masculine.[107] Traditional readings of Cather, however, have scarcely risked underestimating her home-urge. More often they have scanted her resistance to domestic confinement by way of such characterizations as that of Marian Forrester, with her defiant restlessness and her wish to get to where she can't see the house, and Sapphira, who becomes an embodiment of domestic enslavement. If Cather found it personally imperative to get away from home to pursue satisfying work after what might be conceived as a masculine model, and if she recognized married women's dissatisfaction within the prison of the house, she nevertheless wished, and repeatedly attempted, to reconcile the two, home and the urge to departure. In her final completed novel she held the impulses of escape and of return, of caring and of defiance, in a fine and ambiguous balance.

Chapter 4

ESCAPING THE HOUSE
Anne Tyler's Fictions of (Leaving) Home

Always in his mind each member of these social
units is escaping, running away, trying to break
the net which circumstances and his own
affections have woven about him. One realizes
that human relationships are the tragic necessity
of human life.
— Willa Cather

How I have loved this house in the morning
before we are all awake and tangled together like
badly cast fishing lines.
— Katherine Anne Porter

Like Willa Cather, Anne Tyler writes a fiction of both biding and departure,
but with signal differences both in her relative valuation of these terms, less
as complementarities than as competing alternatives, and in her siting of
them within conventional marriage and child-rearing. Whereas Cather generally defines the self as an entity to be gained or at least sighted somewhere
beyond the familiar space, from which it returns to an indoor repose affording the visual sense of expansiveness (the view from the window), Tyler
identifies the self with its home, specifically with a house. Nevertheless, she
insists on the necessity of departure, if that house is the original, natal
home, because the self, whether male or female, cannot reach maturity
otherwise. In addition to this essential primary departure, she examines the
need of many adults, especially women, to make secondary departures from
their marital homes. These two basic types of departure, recurrent throughout Tyler's work, can be seen as analogous to those Annis Pratt terms the
"social quest," usually associated with the *Bildungsroman*, and the "spiritual

quest" or "journey of rebirth," whose heroes are usually middle aged or older.[1]

Because she so clearly sees and delineates the cramping nature of both kinds of homes, there are few writers who recur with greater insistence than Tyler to the act of departure. The need to depart is locked, however, in persistent conflict with the urge to inhabit, or more precisely the urge to retreat to the house and remain there. Together, the two needs, inseparably linked to the problem of selfhood for both women and men, occupy the center of her abundant fiction, giving rise to plot structures of back-and-forth movement. Her novels may seem, then, compulsively repetitive in their fixation on plots that develop what John Updike refers to as the "fundamental American tension . . . between stasis and movement, between home and escape."[2] But these reiterations are importantly nuanced. Moving from relatively simple treatments, in her early novels, of the theme of youthful departure from the small-town home (in North Carolina, where she in fact grew up) to increasingly complex treatments of adult conflict and redefinition of self, Tyler's work darkens and becomes more and more strongly inflected by issues of gender, age, and social class. In her most recent books she has also shown a strong interest in discovering, through her plots of departure and return, the significant hidden within the ordinary, the interesting in the apparently uninteresting: a tall novelistic order.

My interest here is in part to trace the shape of Tyler's career with respect to the emergence of these patterns and inflections. For that reason, I will engage her novels, for the most part, sequentially.[3] First, however, I want to examine a work that I believe offers, in many ways, a key to understanding Tyler's work as a whole, *Celestial Navigation* (1974).

Tyler has often been described as being not only focused on "the home world"—Paula Geyh, for example, groups her among writers who draw upon "the traditional themes and domestic settings from earlier 'sentimental' women's fiction" in contrast to writers such as Marilynne Robinson who "validat[e] the figure of a female wanderer"[4]—but focused actually on agoraphobia, a fear of open public spaces. Joseph Voelker, in his very useful study, develops this view with particular insistence, seeing agoraphobia as the central concern of her fiction.[5]

Certainly agoraphobes are a recurrent character type in Tyler's novels. Their sheer number, clearly a statistical improbability, indicates how fundamental is her concern with issues relating to the tension between indoors and outdoors, being at home versus being lost, remaining versus uprooting. In my view, however, agoraphobia is, in itself, less pervasive in her work than it has generally been accounted. Even Jeremy Pauling of *Celestial Navigation,* the most conspicuous of her agoraphobes, is a character whose withdrawal is explained largely by his fixation on his art and whose single most dramatic act is a departure. Interestingly, in the full range of her characters who retreat to enclosure in the home, Tyler disrupts the actual clinical occurrence of agoraphobic anxiety by gender. In reality, such a disorder occurs far more often among women than among men. In her novels, however, a dread of open or commercial spaces, binding sufferers to home and familiar routine, more often afflicts males. Moreover, she assigns to the severely agoraphobic Jeremy a set of traits often regarded as feminine, including a feminized body shape. Tyler's fiction of the contrary yearning for and fear of outward venture, then, holds special meaning for women even when her anxiously withdrawing figures are male. With respect to the urge to retreat fearfully to the house, as in other ways that we will note, Tyler blurs what are usually emphatic gender distinctions and moves toward androgyny.

Another way in which *Celestial Navigation* can be seen as a key text in Tyler's oeuvre is its focus on Jeremy's house. Houses are a central presence in her fiction. It seems significant, then, that Tyler's favorite book as a child, which she recalls receiving for her fourth birthday, was *The Little House,* by Virginia Lee Burton.[6] A picture book with simple text, *The Little House* asserts visually the centrality of the house in human affairs. From the cover design, repeated on the title page, to the decorative flyleaves at the end, the illustrations (most of them full-page) on twenty-one of the forty pages place the house itself either at the center or, when it is being moved by truck to escape urbanization, at the focal point of action. The designs of eleven of the remaining nineteen pages either carry over from pictures focusing on the house or otherwise direct the eye across the binding to the adjoining scenes where the house is at the center.[7] Tyler's comments on the book, however, emphasize not the position of the house but transitions surrounding it: the vision it offers of "how the years flowed by and people altered and nothing could ever stay the same." In much the same way, her novels center on houses but emphasize movement away from them and back, as well as the individual and social alterations that result.

Tyler in fact glorifies neither home-biding nor the freedom of the open road. As Barbara Harrell Carson writes, she sees "non-dualistically" and undermines simple dualities.[8] Resisting unqualified adoption of the familiar symbolic structuration that associates departure with the pursuit of freedom and houses with "archetypal enclosures,"[9] she refrains from associating staying at home with stultification, or personal growth solely or necessarily with going away. Thus she does not advance a fictive pattern such as Mary Robertson sees in Robinson's *Housekeeping,* which in its choice of "the equivalent of Huck Finn's 'lighting out for the territory' . . . perpetuates the old either-or dilemma for those stifled by family closeness," but moves toward resolutions that are not "either totally within the family or totally outside it."[10] For that reason, departures do not generally appear as culminations in Tyler's narrative structures, but tend to occur toward the beginning and to introduce periods of struggle or uncertainty. In this respect, however, *Celestial Navigation* is an exception.

The house in which Jeremy has grown up and which he still fearfully inhabits is a dark, shabby lair into which it has been all too easy for him, like his mother before him, to retreat. Within its walls, he is shut off from other people and from any wide range of experience. Like other houses in Tyler's novels, it accumulates objects, making life cluttered and crowded. Such clutter complicates the process of breaking away to freedom and gets between people, barring rather than enhancing relationship.[11] But Jeremy's house offers positive resources as well. If it "crowds" him in much the way of his mother and now his common-law wife, Mary, reinforcing his weaknesses, it also affords him needed safety and comfort. Since it is spacious, it accommodates other people in the form of roomers who both provide him a living and keep him from being totally isolated. (Roomers, not boarders, though they have sometimes been called that; neither he nor his mother would have been up to providing meals.) Though Jeremy does not go out into the world, his lodgers to some measure bring the world in and keep it with him.

The windows of Jeremy's house, especially the window in his third-floor studio, function much like the windows in Willa Cather's novels, affording him the presence of the world visually and enriching his art with its sense of motion and variety. After watching from the studio window as his agent, Brian, departs following a routine visit, Jeremy begins a statue of Brian "rounding the corner—a man half running, glad to be gone" (*Celestial Navigation,* 162). Jeremy has recognized in himself, perhaps, and expressed in his creation a corresponding urge to escape the house and achieve freedom.

Or more precisely, he has recognized a wish that he could be the kind of man who could do so. The statue, though, is an ambiguous image. Undoubtedly it is, as Frank Shelton calls it, "a sculpture of a man fleeing all entanglements"[12] and thus much in the mode of the *pater absconditus*. But for Jeremy, running across the street and around a corner as he sees his agent doing would be an act of involvement rather than detachment, a venture into the public world from his position of excessive privacy.

Jeremy's sporadic fantasy life, represented obliquely in his statue of Brian, is far removed from his actual mode of living. He daydreams of rescuing Mary from tasks too difficult for her, going on a pilgrimage that will redeem all his shortcomings, or driving off to some far place and living in a "small, bare, whitewashed cubicle" (*Celestial Navigation*, 225, 152–53). But these notions are empty fantasies. He has certainly never driven a car, and to leave the house would be to leave his identity; he would no longer be Jeremy Pauling, but would need, he ponders, a new name. In that event, emergence might not, after all, mean the achievement of identity, but rather its effacement. Tyler problematizes the linkage of the two. Jeremy's task is to find a way of allaying the dissatisfaction that prompts these fantasies so that he can respect himself and pursue his life freed of self-destructive shame and unrealistic desires. He does so when he makes what is for him a heroic excursion to go see Mary and the children, after she has left him. This is the culminating incident of the novel.

Mary, too, is a person of anxieties related to houses and family structures. Having impulsively left her natal home to marry and then just as impulsively having left her marital home to go off with another man, taking along the little girl she has no way to support when the inevitable happens, she has chosen Jeremy as a refuge and an anchor to counteract her destructive urge to "break loose, to go to foreign places, to try some adventure" (56–57). Like Elizabeth Abbott in *The Clock Winder* and Duncan Peck in *Searching for Caleb,* the novels that preceded and followed *Celestial Navigation,* and anticipating the more extreme Morgan Gower of *Morgan's Passing,* six years later, Mary has felt a stubborn longing to escape the narrowness of a single identity by living multiple lives. But having tried adventurism and having experienced the insecurity of the world, especially for a woman with a child and no job skills, she has found that above all she wants a house from which "it would never even occur to [her] to run away again" (66). She has learned that "moving on" hurts, and she attempts to insulate herself from the possibility of incurring such hurts again by bearing child after child, multiplying her living anchors to home. Even six anchors, however, are not enough. When Jeremy, oppressed by the complications that love for Mary has brought him, by the sense that his identity is draining away, and by her increasingly quasi-maternal treatment, evades legalizing their relationship, the old impulsiveness returns and Mary takes her brood to live in a kind of seaside shack belonging to Brian—whose own freedom, caught in Jeremy's statue of his hurrying stride, will apparently now be compromised.

Jeremy's brave excursion by bus and on foot to see his family, made in defiance of his profound agoraphobia, succeeds in proving to himself and to Mary that he is not so helpless as they have both supposed. He weatherstrips the decrepit shack with rolled newspapers and takes over, despite his ineptitude and terror, her chore of rowing out to dry the sails on Brian's boat. What he doesn't do is say to her clearly that he wants her back. And for all her competence and venturesomeness, neither does she express honestly her feeling of hurt that he has let her go. Having demonstrated his ability to rise above his limitations, Jeremy is still himself, still tethered to his identity and his house as firmly as the boat on which he now sails around and around in circles is tethered to its anchor. At the end of the book he is back at home, more timid than ever before, a shuffling, prematurely old man.

Tyler never lets us doubt that this failure is sad; the happier ending, at least in conventional terms, would have been for Jeremy to make good his emergence and reestablish his place in his family. Even so, she provides an alternative interpretation. To the understanding awareness of Miss Vinton, Jeremy's longtime lodger, he is a hero. Miss Vinton knows what an effort his excursion cost him, and knows, too, that however infirm he may appear, he "sail[s] by celestial navigation" on adventures of his own—the adventures of his art, the making of "great towering beautiful sculptures" (130, 247). His failure at the level of daily life and relationships is in that way entirely sublimated. Despite his house-bound life, he has paradoxically, through his art, escaped the house.

We can see in Tyler's parable, I think, a fear of being dehumanized by the distant star of art and the withdrawal it invites or perhaps necessitates. Such a withdrawal, especially for a woman deeply involved as a wife and mother, as Tyler has been, naturally poses itself as an urge to escape from the duties and encumbrances of the family, which it is more emotionally acceptable to cast as the duties and encumbrances of the house. To admit such an urge is traditionally to admit failure in one's relational obligations, failure as a woman. Thus the story must be displaced. It is displaced, indeed, to the point of being extreme, even bizarre. There is an improbable ease in the way that Jeremy, having satisfied his own (and his creator's?) demand for evidence of humanity by making his heroic excursion, relinquishes his relationships and turns entirely to his art. That commitment, however, is also presented as being heroic. Accordingly, it is characterized by Miss Vinton in terms of a journey: "He *lives* at a distance. He makes pictures the way other men make maps—setting down the few fixed points that he knows, hoping they will guide him as he goes floating through this unfamiliar planet. He keeps his eyes on the horizon while his hands work blind" (129).

In reality, of course, the artist, or at any rate Tyler the artist, cannot make so absolute a choice. She must choose both: to go on being herself, which for her as for Jeremy means being active in her art and the discipline it entails, and also to go on being a person with relational ties. In her more realistic novels the answers are not so absolute as they are in this parable of the march to the radically different drummer. More often her fulfilled characters *both* escape the house and fully, humanly inhabit it. Paradoxically, for all that he is shut in the house, Jeremy is not a part of it in its fullest sense. He is within but not of the human dwelling.

We can also see in Tyler's parable, especially when read as a parable of Tyler herself in her relation to her parental as well as her elective home, an echo of Eudora Welty, the writer she has named as her favorite and whose role as exemplar is pervasively evident in her work.[13] Welty's autobiographical book about the making of the artist, *One Writer's Beginnings,* begins with what Ann Romines has called a "luminous paragraph" giving a "concise domestic idyll" in which the child Eudora laboriously buttons her shoes with a buttonhook while listening to a whistled or hummed duet between her father, upstairs shaving, and her mother, downstairs cooking breakfast.[14] Romines's beautifully inflected reading of this opening paragraph shows how it captures both the felicitous domestic space to which Welty would remain attached throughout her life and also her pursuit of the "wanderer's task" of preparing the shoes in which to leave it. Through the practice of her art, Welty departed from the home place even as she proclaimed, both in her personal life and in her fiction, her allegiance to it. Tyler has enacted much the same memorializing of home and family combined with departure by the (often isolating) road of art. Like Welty, she has opened herself to accusations of debilitating nostalgia in her depiction of familial structures and traditional culture. But a careful reading of both shows that the vision of the staying/departing, remembering/creating artist is actually quite astringent.

Jeremy Pauling provides what might be called a test case for addressing the difficult question of whether Tyler can better be seen as a writer of escape from the house or as indeed (as she has so often been described) a writer of household enclosure, a shaper of the home plot whose house-centered interest in family relationships situates her at a far remove from a fiction of release, exploration, or postmodern free play. Jeremy would seem to be a powerful statement of home-biding. Yet even the significance of this most house-centered of her characters is ambiguous—or better, dual. In that respect, too, *Celestial Navigation* is a key text.

Central as houses and the shaping experiences that go on there are in Tyler's fiction, their value is uncertain. Her characters often need to leave home in order to enlarge their lives and their sense of who they are or can be, but even more importantly, they need to leave in order to gain perspective on home itself, so that they can transform it or occupy it anew, in their own way but (unlike Jeremy, perhaps, whose art entails different standards) in a way that is caring and nurturing for the people with whom they share it.[15] It is for this reason that Tyler's fiction characteristically embraces returns as well as departures, remaining focused on homes and domestic relationships even beyond the escapes. The lure of freedom is very great in her work and, for women as well as for men, is generally linked with departure. But her view of freedom, like her view of the house, is qualified and often distrustful. Her recurrent bête noire is that epitome of spurious freedom, the deserting father, represented most notably in Dr. Hawkes of *If Morning Ever Comes,* Beck Tull of *Dinner at the Homesick Restaurant,* and the otherwise likable Morgan Gower of *Morgan's Passing.* When freedom-intoxicated males light out for territories afar, she shows by adopting the point of view of those left behind (much as Toni Morrison does in *Song of Solomon*) the negative results of their ducking out on responsibilities.

Tyler's vision of the fully human life is one grounded in a central place, the home, and central relationships. It is a principle (even a fixation) that reflects, perhaps, nostalgia for her early years spent in Quaker communes, with their strong sense of community.[16] Even so, she is not so wholehearted an affirmer of home values as critical comments and even her own statements sometimes seem to indicate. She validates a compromise. Her fictional world is also a world of the escape wish. Whether it is one in which imprisoned women (and men) *make good* their escapes is less clear. Her novels do not, in a bottom-line sort of way, follow that trajectory. Many writers of what has been called, by one of Tyler's critics, the "runaway housewife novel" render the act of escape as being more decisive and rewarding than she does.[17] Jane Smiley's *A Thousand Acres,* for example, which seems to have exerted a strong pull on Tyler's imagination during the writing of *Ladder of Years* (1995), shows the housewife's departure not merely as a wish but as a startling and irreversible act that entails sweeping change in her life and goals. Robinson's Ruth and Sylvie, in *Housekeeping,* make a departure with absolutely unsettling implications. None of Tyler's characters makes that kind of absolute departure. Her interrogation of the need to depart from traditional structures of home and famil(iarit)y is considerably more modulated, even uncertain. Her trajectories are plural; they loop, falter, and double on themselves.

Tyler's concern with the fundamental tension between homing and escape is one she shares with Welty, whose work also offers both an apotheosis of domestic ritual and the counter-pull exerted by departure and mobility. Welty's dual interest in the "home plot" and in possible alternatives for women's lives, sometimes exemplified by "exuberant wanderers" who "disentangl[e] themselves from domestic ritual" in order to redefine their lives, is perceptively elucidated by Romines, who demonstrates that her range of female characters includes not only women who find their primary meaning in domestic ritual but women for whom its "immobility" is "galling" and who thereby constitute a threat to the social order, as Welty represents it in her preferred small-town settings.[18] Such women include the committed artist-figure Miss Eckhart of "June Recital" and other stories; Virgie Rainey, who at the end of the final story of *The Golden Apples* (1949) is "poised to depart"; and Laurel McKelva Hand of *The Optimist's Daughter* (1972), who in leaving her home of origin at the end of the novel "disentangle[s]" herself from domestic ritual and turns her face toward open possibilities in a larger world. Even more emphatically committed to the "setting aside of home, ritual, and custom" in favor of "the possibilities of travel" are the stories in Welty's last collection, *The Bride of Innisfallen* (1955), a volume described by Welty, interestingly enough, as a book entirely of travel in Europe but which actually includes four stories set in the South. Among these is "The Burning," a startling story involving "abrogation of housekeeping." What Romines recognizes in this large body of work, most commonly seen as a celebration of domestic life and kinship or "staying put," is an impulse toward disentanglement and "boundless possibility," the lure that Welty herself refers to in *Losing Battles* (1970) as "the road up ahead." Romines has heard both Welty's tribute to home and her embedded question of whether women can find lives outside domesticity, and has recognized as the "most positively powerful women in Welty's work" those whose lives "aspire to both."[19]

In this respect as in others, including her frequent recourse to the *démeublé* mode, Welty is the heir of Willa Cather, whom she has read judiciously and with admiration. In somewhat the same way as Cather, Welty holds remaining and departing, or the possible results of departing, in ambiguous balance. Her women characters ponder, from the vantage of their homes, alternative possibilities. Anne Tyler, then, in maintaining a similar, acutely realized ambivalence both about going and about staying, can well be seen as the heir of both Cather and Welty.[20] Family structures may occupy the center of her fiction—and in the most literal sorts of ways, not only as "structures" of relationship but as literal structures, houses. But she affirms these structures only by way of questioning them. She shows the need for houses to have open doors and windows, permeable walls. The goal is the emergence of the self, a process that requires departure from the primary home and the role of child and may, especially for women, require departure from the secondary, or marital, home, but at the same time, a process that for most people requires firm siting, thus a sense of home. Tyler's characteristic affirmation, then, is not of home as a given but (to borrow a phrase from James Fenimore Cooper) of home as found, a redefined or reconstituted home, a home chosen on one's own terms.

This overriding impulse to occupy the home anew, on altered terms, is one that tends to distinguish the female's departure from the male's in Tyler's work. Several of her males, however, are feminized as "motherly men" (as she labels Ezra Tull in *Dinner at the Homesick Restaurant*) who share the woman's urge for (enlightened) enhousement. Her novelistic project, then, is by no means absolute in its differentiation according to gender. This is not to say that gender is not an issue in her work; it will be a shaping concern in the remainder of this chapter as I trace the sequence and progression of departure and return in her novels.

Tyler's first three novels—*If Morning Ever Comes* (1964), *The Tin Can Tree* (1965), and *A Slipping-Down Life* (1970), all set in small-town North Carolina, are occupied with the need to leave the primary home in order to achieve adulthood. It is not clear whether the reiterated concern, in three consecutive novels, with difficulties relating to parental love and departure from the parental home emerged from some personal anxiety, but certainly it indicates that at this stage of her life Tyler recognized emergence as a key to individual identity. I want to examine *If Morning Ever Comes,* the novel that inaugurated Tyler's unusually productive career, in some detail, not only because I believe it tends to be unduly dismissed by critics intent on praising her more elaborate later novels, but because it initiates several patterns related to emergence that characterize her work as a whole. These patterns include concern with family and with contrasts between family customs and an uncomprehending outer world, a theme that might well occupy a young adult (only twenty-three when the novel was published) recently emerged from an upbringing far from typical.[21] This first novel also establishes Tyler's interest in themes of loneliness or isolation *within* the family; the domestication of oddity; the *pater absconditus;* and, most important for my purposes here, patterns of departure and return and a merging of the spatial and the temporal.[22] That she has found it rewarding to continue, over an extended period, to develop themes and concerns evident in such early work is remarkable. Her technique and the complexity of her understanding have evolved and grown, but her central concerns have remained relatively constant.

The opening words of *If Morning Ever Comes,* "When Ben Joe Hawkes left home," are ironic in that Ben Joe, a rather amorphous character Tyler later dismissed as "bland," has in fact had trouble doing so. Twenty-five years old and three years out of college, he is still emotionally a child despite having left his hometown of Sandhill to start law school at Columbia. The main action of the novel will be his effort to make a belated crossing of the threshold (a figurative threshold closely linked to the literal one of the house in which he grew up) into adulthood. In the opening scene, in cold New York

City, he cocoons himself in a "quilt from home" and wistfully sniffs the "warm and comforting" smell of other families' cooking (*If Morning*, 2–7). On the flimsy excuse of needing to check up on how his mother, grandmother, and six sisters are coping with his absence (quite well, it turns out), he decides to catch the next train home to Sandhill.

Ben Joe's homesickness is compounded by anxiety about adult masculinity. As the lone male in a family of females, he has needed a stronger role model than his father, now six years dead, provided him. In classic *pater absconditus* style, Dr. Hawkes had left his wife and children to take up residence with a younger woman, with whom he later had a son. Though he subsequently moved back home, on the night he died he had returned to Lily Belle's house. Yet there is some evidence that he intended to come home that night. Ben Joe is confused. What did his father really want? Whom did he really love? Or did he even know that himself? Ben Joe also bears a burden of guilt for having intercepted a letter Lily Belle sent his father while he was back with the family. Perhaps the letter would have helped his father make a clear decision—something men are supposed to be able to do. Or perhaps it would even have saved his life, by enabling him to decide sooner to go back to Lily Belle, thereby relieving tension and forestalling his heart attack. This heritage of uncertainty and personal guilt still causes Ben Joe to dream about his father and to deny that he does so. The entire family, in fact, denies, refusing to confront the circumstances of the death and their feelings about it. As a result of all this confusion about his father, Ben Joe is also confused about his own proper role. He alternates between, on the one hand, expecting his all-female family to understand and care for him in a prolonged childhood and, on the other, asserting quasi-patriarchal dominance, imagining that as the only male he "headed up" the family and they should "just let *me* take care of them"—though in fact they organize their own lives and don't need to be taken care of (5, 145).

For a while after his father's death Ben Joe "took to riding trains" (102)—that classic symbol of mobility and change—in a fruitless peregrination expressive of his uncertainty. The present, more purposeful train trip brings him several potentially enlightening encounters. He sees black families in which masculine and feminine roles are comfortably, if somewhat reductively, mingled.[23] He has a dream about denying that he dreams about his father—alerting him to the need to resolve his oedipal anxiety. He experiences fleeting delusions of an interchange of motion and stasis, as if the "rushing" train were "standing still" and his house were in motion like a train (28)—alerting him, perhaps, to the threat of immobility and to the linkage of spatial and temporal change. He also meets a curious exemplar of himself as he may become, a very old man who had left Sandhill sixty-six years ago and now, coming home to die, is "astonished" to see that the place has changed. "Been traveling too long for *my* preference," Mr. Dower says, and it is clear that his remark does not refer to the train ride alone. Ben Joe challenges the old man's claim to have left permanently. Since he is now coming back, he can't have left permanently, can he? But Mr. Dower insists that he can, because "what I left ain't here to come back to." Ben Joe, too, had thought he was making a permanent departure when he went away to law school; he "left planning not to return." But, as he complains, he "just can't seem to *get* anywhere. Nowhere permanent" (43). It is his task now to get beyond that state of indeterminacy.

Ben Joe's family epitomizes a society of restless centrifugal impulses barely contained by the loyalties and the practicalities of home. They all suffer from insomnia and seem to spend their nights pattering about, "out wandering around somewhere beyond his jurisdiction" (223). His oldest sister, Joanne, has just "r[u]n away from her husband" in Kansas and come home, bringing her toddler-age child (19)—only the most recent in her long history of abortive escapes. Though Joanne, with a smile that "could make everything seem safe and in its right place" (28), represents to Ben Joe the reassurance he associates with home, she had actually been gone for seven years, partly because of her mother and grandmother's squabbling over who was at fault for her father's leaving them, and even before that had once run away with a traveling salesman. As her husband cheerfully acknowledges when he comes to take her back to Kansas, she has always been "one of those gals that flits around a lot" (235). Clearly, that is still true; she has already, to Ben Joe's dismay, started going out on dates, another sign of her arrested maturation.[24] Insecure because of the family past, Joanne has been so fearful that, like her mother, she would alienate her husband through failure to express her love ("history repeating itself"—a recurrent fear in Tyler's work), that she kept reassuring him of what he never doubted and it "got so I couldn't bear my own self" so "I left" (239, 74): the first of Tyler's recurrent presentations of departure as escape from oneself. Like Ben Joe, she is doomed to repeat adolescent patterns until she can get beyond them by making a fully deliberate departure from home.

Having left her adult home to return to her childhood, or primary, home, Joanne, like the old man on the train, realizes that "it's not the same place I'm coming back to, really" (74). But even though Ben Joe has now heard that lesson twice, he resists it, claiming that "of course it's the same place" (75). He wants home to be always there and always reliably the same. Joanne, too, has difficulty with that lesson, in that she is unable to generalize it to include her marital home. She hesitates to return with her husband because she has "never . . . believed in going backwards instead of forwards" (246)—a claim belied, of course, by her presence in Sandhill.

The pattern of dislocation extends also to Ben Joe's wan girlfriend, Shelley, who has been "wandering around" for some years, during which her parents and sister, victims of mobility, were killed in a car wreck. She has now returned to the family home, which seems to have been sitting there empty, waiting for her, but she feels unsettled, like a "homebody" left "straphanging in empty space." What she really wants is to move from her primary home to a secure adult home with a man who will "stay, and think about me sometimes, and let me have a kitchen with pots and pans" (104, 100, 206). It is so blatantly conventional a domestic vision that it conspicuously weakens the novel, but it does at any rate seem to offer Ben Joe a needed model of adulthood. He proposes marriage two pages later.

The novel ends in a tidy balancing of the beginning, with Ben Joe on the train again, this time heading back north with Shelley. Besides the object lessons in transience that Ben Joe has received during his stay at home, he has taken steps to resolve his anxieties. He has opened himself to memories of his father and discussed them, for the first time, with Joanne, and he has even gone to see Lily Belle to admit his guilt about the letter and ask her forgiveness. In the process he has noted her sturdy acceptance of uncertainty about the past. He has had a dream-vision of people "shuffl[ing] around helter-skelter," getting into different houses and yet going comfortably to sleep there, and has received that humorous vision gratefully, with (almost) a smile (217). He has confided to Shelley his feeling that when he leaves Sandhill again he will miss it again, but now he realizes that what he misses is not the place itself or even his family but (anticipating *Dinner at the Homesick Restaurant*) a wished-for idealization of both (199–201). He may be doomed to homesickness, but at least he will be better able to understand its nature—an essential step toward growing beyond it.

All these lessons come together as Ben Joe prepares to leave. Listening to Joanne's worries that going home with her husband might mean "going backwards," he reminds her that (as both Mr. Dower and she herself have said of Sandhill) "sometimes it's not the same place when a person goes back to it." His echoed message, it seems, opens a door for Joanne. She reacts as if applying this idea to her marital home is "a brand-new idea that would have to be given time to soak in" and sounds "relieved." But Ben Joe is relieved as well, because this time, hearing himself say these words, he has realized that it may also be "not the same person" who goes there (248). If so, going back may be going forward.

The Ben Joe Hawkes who rides the train back to New York in the closing scene, with Shelley by his side, is indeed not the same person who rode it before. He is now able to achieve at least tentative resolution of his problem of beset masculinity, in a series of swift changes in attitude justifying Stella Nesanovich's calling the trip as a whole a "metaphor for his psychological journey from adolescence to adulthood."[25] Not yet entirely free of patriarchal illusions, he sets himself the task of "keeping guard" over Shelley very much as he had previously imagined he was taking care of his mother and sisters. He drifts into a vision of his wife and an imagined son "still and obedient." But he clings to that vision for only a moment before correcting himself and letting it go "dancing . . . off again" because he "knew he had to" (266). Old habits are hard to break; the old impulses still come; but now he reminds himself to relinquish them. He is learning that masculine fulfillment doesn't have to mean possession and control. Although his "re-evaluation of himself as well as his family"[26]—a task Tyler regularly assigns her characters—is by no means complete, he at least realizes now that his problem is not just to understand his home and his sisters, but also to understand himself. It is with this realization that he releases his determination to keep his eyes "fastened" protectively on Shelley and drops off to sleep beside her, while the train goes "rattling along its tracks" (266) in a classic road-of-life image.

Alice Hall Petry, reading the ending as a parable of a "match made in patriarchal heaven," points out not only Ben Joe's none-too-subtle traces of patriarchalism but also his bride's "gender-specific helplessness and sweetness," labeling her one of Tyler's "female characters . . . troubled by their gender-based roles" but "unable or unwilling to change them." Petry regards the conductor's terse statement on the last page, "Won't have to change," as an indication that the two will persist in their repressive traditionalism.[27] But it is *after* that statement (which the conductor had made going the other way as well) that Ben Joe has his vision of wife and son, resists holding them "suspended . . . still and obedient," and lets them dance on. His vision does change. It is also after the conductor speaks that he thinks what a mystery are not only his sisters and the "house he was born in" and his not-yet-wife and hypothetical son but "even Ben Joe Hawkes" (266). That is, he recognizes his need for self-reassessment and self-knowledge, a need that may go on forever. That recognition is apparently the final task he needs to accomplish just now; he relaxes into sleep, accepting the kind of uncertainty that had earlier caused him anxiety. This ending seems to me less closed, less repressive and tradition-bound, than Petry reads it.

It is also important to note that Ben Joe's behavior while at home has scarcely been masculinist, at least not in every respect. He has been willing to go visiting with his grandmother, has shown a fine ability to banter with his ten-year-old sister in ways that please her, has asked his sister's advice on a financial matter, and has held and rocked his infant niece. He has renewed, then, not his falsely patriarchal self but an androgynous self. Thus the conductor's reassuring message of not having to change may mean simply that Ben Joe and Shelley are on the right road.

In *The Tin Can Tree,* published just one year after *If Morning Ever Comes,* and again in her third novel, *A Slipping-Down Life,* five years later, Tyler told essentially the same story of the disrupted move out of the primary, or natal, home. There is great variety in the characters and incidents of these early works, but the basic structure is essentially the same: entrapment at the point of departure. In both, as in *If Morning Ever Comes,* the physical domestic structure, the house, plays a central role.

In *The Tin Can Tree,* opening references to what are normally images of stasis—a death and burial, a house—evoke, instead, uncertainties of change and movement which yield to an elaborate pattern of goings and comings. What all this motion portends is never clear. James Green, perhaps the central character of a rather large cast, is a bachelor who as a child had been "forever running away" until his parents "locked doors and tied knots" to keep him home (123, 236). Despite having now moved away, he remains stalled in uncertainty, unable to propose to Joan, the woman he wants to marry, because his unhappy childhood home has, in a sense, come with him—in the person of a hypochondriac brother, Ansel, who spends most of his days reclining on a sofa beside a "big front window" (18, 13). Ansel is not exactly an agoraphobic figure, since he occasionally takes a notion to "star[t] walking" and goes off (158), but is certainly an inert one whom James cannot imagine imposing on a wife. But Joan, too, has left home without really leaving. Having moved in with her aunt and uncle at the other end of the odd tripartite house where James lives, she is also caught in indeterminacy, like a long-term houseguest. Despairing of James's love, she takes her two suitcases and starts back home by bus, but gets off at an intermediate stop and comes back. Only Ansel has even realized she left.[28] Meanwhile, ten-year-old Simon, whose little sister's funeral opens the book, goes off feeling unloved, pursuing Ansel's idle stories of a hometown that never was, where all the boys wore rings in their ears like pirates. All of these characters are casting about for change, but are caught between nostalgia for a nonexistent past perfection and a desire to establish themselves in a new grounding of personal adequacy and worthiness to be loved.

The ending of this modest novel is as indeterminate as that of *If Morning Ever Comes,* but again implies a hope for change. Simon has been fetched back home. Ansel summons the energy to give up his reclining space on the sofa so others can sit down and makes the uncharacteristic gesture of getting up to open the door for Joan when she comes back from her abortive return home and no one else hears her knock. If his behavior signals change, it may be that James will be enabled to move beyond his prolonged emotional stasis. Bereaved by the death of a child, all the major characters have been forced to deal with questions of mutual responsibility and the brevity of life, and as a result they have experienced the "conflict between individual freedom and duty to others"—or perhaps love of others—that is one of Tyler's persistent themes.[29]

The ending of *A Slipping-Down Life,* Tyler's first novel to include departures from both a primary and an elective home, gives more positive indications of movement toward adult self-sufficiency. Evie Decker, almost as inert a character as Ansel Green, has left home to marry a feckless rock star after signaling her lack of selfhood by carving his name into her forehead with scissors. Her dreary marriage has led, however, only to a continued miring in dissatisfaction and emotional numbness. Realizing at last that her husband is an emotional as well as commercial deadbeat and that she needs to prepare for the child she is expecting, she discovers that she does, after all, have the ability to exert initiative and fend for herself. She gets a job and leaves him. Despite the fact that this second departure entails a return to her father's house, it does not mark a surrender (as Joan's return home presumably would have in *Tin Can Tree*), since his parental authority, such as it was, has been removed by his death and Evie is now making her own decisions, shaping her own life. As Nesanovich points out, she "uses work," a job at the public library, "to break free of her confinement"[30]—an important component of Tyler's later, more complexly gendered novels. Both work and maternal or quasi-maternal relations will remain powerful driving forces.

Work as an impetus to departure and change is particularly emphasized in the novels of what might be called Tyler's early mid-career, three of which center on women's lives: *The Clock Winder* (1972), where Elizabeth Abbott moves from job to job after leaving her parents' home; *Searching for Caleb* (1975), where Justine Peck takes the initiative in reconciling restlessness with home-yearning by finding appropriate jobs for herself and her husband; and *Earthly Possessions* (1977), where Charlotte Emory's growth in independence and personal fulfillment is signaled by her new ownership of her work as a photographer. For the women characters in all of these novels, work—or what might even be called careers (of unconventional kinds, to be sure)—is linked with self-definition and also with patterns of departure and journey. Tyler's males also, of course, typically define themselves and gain freedom through their work. The point is that it is not a rigidly gendered association; it does not follow the stereotypical linking of men with work and women with home. In this respect as in others, Tyler's fiction moves toward androgyny.

In *The Clock Winder,* the novel in which Tyler may be said to have come into her own, gender emerges as a central theme of her fiction. At the opening of the book, Elizabeth Abbott has left her natal home in North Carolina, where, as the unbelieving daughter of a Baptist minister, she clearly could "never be herself." In the course of following her impulses and rambling from one job to another in a search for viable self-definition, she has wound up in Baltimore. (In its geographic movement the novel enacts Tyler's own personal and professional change of venue. From this point on, her work, as well as her life, would be sited in Baltimore.) Chancing upon the widowed and somewhat helpless Mrs. Emerson, she is hired as general factotum. Mrs. Emerson, a conspicuously feminine, well-groomed matron securely ensconced in a big old house,[31] continually tries to maneuver Elizabeth into adopting more feminine ways by making "suggestions" on her appearance and attempting to shift her duties to those of maid and cook, jobs Elizabeth will have none of. She prefers the designation handyman (not "handy-woman," as she has sometimes been called), with occasional duties as chauffeur. Her attire runs to blue jeans and moccasins, her fingernails are stubby, she can't walk in high heels, and she adopts an offhand, decidedly unco-quettish manner toward men. Her masculinized self-presentation is, in short, another of Tyler's moves toward androgyny. With her bluntness and good humor, Elizabeth is one of Tyler's most refreshing characters, like a fresh breeze bearing the fragrance of wood chips from the carving she does as a hobby.

With *The Clock Winder,* social class, too, begins to play a stronger role in Tyler's fiction. As in the later *Searching for Caleb, Morgan's Passing,* and *The Accidental Tourist,* downward mobility is associated with liberation.[32] When Peter, the youngest of Mrs. Emerson's sons, whose distinctly lower-class wife seems to have left him, laments that you "shouldn't hope for anything from someone that much different from your family," Elizabeth, seeing the vitality underneath the girl's unpolished demeanor, replies, "You should if your family doesn't *have* it" (294). She is in that position herself, supplying the vigor and resourcefulness and instinctive good cheer the Emersons lack. She seems, indeed, to supply these qualities genetically; her toddler son, already competent, is seen happily rescuing his fearful grandmother and uncle from a cicada. At the end, living in the big Emerson house, Elizabeth (now called by the comfortably androgynous name Gillespie, picked up from Mrs. Emerson's garbled pronunciation following a stroke) is enmeshed in Emersonian habits, fears, and emotional demands, but she manages to maintain her quirky selfhood and seems to have created a new, freer life for the family.

Tyler has expressed surprise that readers generally take the concluding picture of Elizabeth ensconced in the Emerson household—keeping all the human clocks harmoniously ticking, offhandedly suckling her young, and allaying fears of seventeen-year locusts—to be a happy ending. True, the once footloose is now house-settled and all but smothered by the needy adults who bask in her care, piling their problems at her feet just as she had earlier complained they were trying to do. Yet she appears to have actualized her potential as a self-reliant person, free of the need either to rebel or to surrender. Her active life is at any rate far preferable to the depression and inactivity into which she sank during a retreat to her parents' home. The ending leaves one expecting that, as Elizabeth says after being shot in the shoulder, "of course" she will be all right. Certainly she is a happy presence for the Emersons. In the final action of the book, when seventeen-year locusts—an intrinsic symbol of self-definition by emergence—are terrorizing the more timid members of the family, Peter makes a departure that promises to be successful because Elizabeth has had a hand in it. Toddler George watches him go "absently, as if, every day of his life, he saw people arriving and leaving and getting sidetracked from their travels" (295). Like his mother, he can accommodate change, and he has a secure home base from which to do so. By Tyler's usual standards, that is a happy state of affairs.

In her characterization of Elizabeth Abbott, Tyler comes very near to the kind of celebration of the female transient or wanderer that Robinson makes in *Housekeeping*. Perhaps that is why she is dubious that Elizabeth's enhousement is a happy ending. The wonderful Muriel, of *The Accidental Tourist,* and Daphne, a lively and perceptive minor character in *Saint Maybe,* are similar figures in terms of their variety of jobs and their free spirits, but not so geographically mobile. Also similar to Elizabeth, in her cheery unconventionalism and her negotiation between values of staying and going, is Justine Peck of *Searching for Caleb,* published three years later. *Searching for Caleb* is similar in many ways to *The Clock Winder.* The large Peck family resembles the Emersons, extended to multiple generations, just as the large but somewhat run-down Emerson house is elaborated to three large houses of a family compound, also less prosperous than it used to be. Even so, it is not repetitious, but rings several interesting variations on Tyler's theme of stasis versus mobility, including an interrogation of whether familial resemblances constitute a kind of biological determinism.

The impulse to ramble and the urge to remain are assigned to two distinct types within the Peck family. Those identified with stasis, the prevalent type, are models of decorum and conservative business mentality who keep very much to themselves. A great gulf, it seems, is fixed between them and the non-Peckian world. But in each generation a Peck turns up who "sets out on his own" like an "*explorer*" (*Caleb,* 117; Tyler's emphasis). The presence of two distinct types is accounted for by Justin Peck's having married twice, back in the 1880s. Caleb, the son of the first wife, takes after his mother's family and proves to be the most spectacular of the family explorers. Even as a child he would stray off on his tricycle following, as he does throughout his life, any "distant music" (52–53). His half-brother Daniel, who resembles *his* mother, becomes, most emphatically, one of the keep-to-themselves

Pecks, but marries an outgoing young woman named Margaret Rose, lovingly called Maggie Rose by Caleb, who feels a natural and perhaps amorous sympathy with her. In 1911, after being continually squelched in her spontaneity by Daniel, Margaret Rose moves out, leaving her six children behind to be raised by their Peck grandmother. Soon Caleb also disappears, taking only his violin.

All of this has occurred long in the novelistic past. The novel opens on a train, with the now aged Daniel and his granddaughter Justine traveling to New York in search of clues to Caleb's whereabouts. Still a stay-at-home Peck at heart, Daniel laments the evils of mobility as they go. But Justine, who is characteristically seen in motion throughout the novel, loves "the sensation of speed" and the sound of the wheels, hinting that "something unexpected might happen at any minute" (8). As a child, she had been more like her grandfather, one of the home-centered Pecks. Living away from Baltimore because of her father's job, she, like her Peck mother, had wanted above all else to get back to the family compound, and once they moved back she could scarcely be compelled to leave the house. In her teens, however, she fell in love with her explorer-type Peck cousin Duncan, who had estranged himself from the family by moving away to a rented room with only (like Caleb) a single possession, his toolbox. Misinterpreting her father's telephoned advice "you've got to get out of there" (111), by which he actually meant she needed to get away from a potential Peck husband as well as from the family compound, she married Duncan and moved with him to the first in their series of homes, thereby unifying the two Peck counter-strains. It is a delightfully comic (perhaps sadly comic) conception.

Duncan drifts from job to job in a steadily descending spiral, carrying them into identification with lower social strata. Like Elizabeth in *The Clock Winder,* who enjoys wearing an old chauffeur cap and acting the part, he likes to try out different lives—an impulse Tyler has avowed of herself ("I write because I want more than one life; I insist on a wider selection")[33] and one she would bring to fullness in *Morgan's Passing* in motifs of theater and disguise. At first Justine is insecure with all this moving; she still thinks of herself as a home-centered person. When she learns fortune-telling and lays out her own fortune, only to find "journeys, upheavals, surprises, new people, luck, crowds, hasty decisions, and unexpected arrivals," she decides it must not be valid to try to read one's own cards (146). But after she comes to identify with her "runaway grandmother," Margaret Rose (149), thus in her own mind validating mobility by linking it with the family, she falls cheerfully into the pattern of frequent moves and goes "rattling down the highway . . . bright and reckless" on a "wild, careening journey through life," shedding such encumbrances as furniture as she goes (147, 152). Her ability to transform herself from one type to the other—indeed, in the end to assume leadership in mobility—is an affirmation of open possibility in defiance of such imprisoning forces as biological determinism and family tradition.

For Justine, the point of the search for Caleb with her grandfather has always been "the trips themselves," more than any anticipation of actually finding him. When the search is turned over to a private detective upon Daniel's ninety-third birthday, she becomes unhappy and wishes they could all "just get in the car and drive, or catch a train somewhere" (225–27, 262). Caleb is indeed found. Unfortunately, Daniel's letter of greeting is sadly judgmental, reinforcing rather than bridging the estrangement, and he dies waiting for a reply. It is left to Justine to bring resolution to the search by catching a plane to New Orleans, confronting Caleb in a nursing home for the indigent, and bringing him back. But the return does not work out well. Caleb, having gone "far afield" (307–8), has led a marvelous, improbable life as a blues musician in Louisiana. Now, though he is happy to be out of the nursing home, he has no desire to return to the family. Justine begins to doubt that he is really her uncle at all, really a Peck. When authorities in Louisiana start checking on him, he disappears again rather than risk being returned to the care center. He may be confused about the extent to which he is still part of the family, but at least he knows what he wants, the freedom of the road.

Duncan and Justine, it seems, are not so well off. They have failed to replace their grandfather's secure Peck-ness with Caleb, and Duncan has again lost his job. Lacking a boldness equal to his restlessness, he is content to drink bourbon and play solitaire as he waits for something to turn up. They drift perilously near moving back to the family compound for survival—a return that Tyler clearly sees as a defeat. In this extremity Justine emerges into full adventurous selfhood, becoming, as one reviewer said, "her own woman at last."[34] After gaining enlightenment from two sources, she saves herself and Duncan by initiating change.

The first source of enlightenment is a bread-and-butter note from Caleb, postmarked Wyoming, which demonstrates, in its quintessential Peck-ish style, that however far one goes one still carries one's family identity. After grasping this point (as indicated by her sharp laugh), Justine takes up a deck of cards, the second source of enlightenment, and once again lays out her own fortune. Now she sees not only journeys but a card meaning "journeys beyond other journeys" (323). At once she goes out and arranges for Duncan to go to work as maintenance man for a traveling carnival, for which she, of course, will serve as fortune-teller. "Runaways from respectability," as Susan Gilbert incisively calls them,[35] they will live in a small trailer, a merger of at-homeness with mobility. The ending finds them on another moving day, Duncan driving a truck loaded with their (now fewer) possessions and happily trying to catch up with Justine, who, driving their car, is "by now only a puff of smoke in the distance" (328).

Justine is Tyler's strongest tribute to female departure and journey. Bolder than her merely restless husband, she manages to step outside the patterns of a lifetime to redefine not only herself but the course of both their lives. The neighbors they leave behind may think Duncan is the one "carting [her] off every which way" (326), but in fact he has only (in quasi-feminine style) accepted her lead. It is Justine's initiative that determines their escape and the reconciliation of her own counter-impulses toward both home and adventure. Interestingly, not only does her boldness make her Tyler's closest approximation to Robinson's Sylvie, but she has also, like Sylvie, long since given up respectable housekeeping and conventional cooking. In a way, she has even, in the style of *Housekeeping,* brought the outside in: "tangles of plant vines" grow up *inside* Justine's window (262). Like Sylvie and Ruth, she realizes that loving relationships are not dependent on fixed structures and conventional lives. But unlike them, she keeps her ties to extended family and a home of sorts. She and Duncan will have both at once, freedom of movement and their own home. It is the kind of happy compromise toward which Tyler's fictions often move, a mediation of her frequently noted "contrary urges to settle and to roam."[36]

Justine is, in my view, the single most triumphant female character in Tyler's work, in that she is most closely associated with purposeful departure and journey motifs and most fully in charge of her life. Later female characters who might be seen as Justine-figures include the previously mentioned Daphne and Muriel, the problematic Charlotte Emory of *Earthly Possessions,* and even the dotty and irritating Maggie of *Breathing Lessons,* despite the fact that both have drawn the ire of feminists through their seeming inability to imagine lives apart from the conventional roles of wife, house-keeper, and mother. Maggie, with her sliding-down panty hose (noted for the *third* time on only the forty-eighth page) and her acting out of such trite and belittling stereotypes as the "woman driver," is indeed irritating and hard to accept. It is scarcely surprising that she has been seen as a caricature or virtual buffoon. With both Maggie and Charlotte, however, I believe that Tyler is working in ways that call into question the dichotomies of conventional and liberated, constrained and free, and is thus unsettling the conventional structures she seems to endorse.

From a feminist perspective, Tyler is a problematic figure. She speaks at times from the perspective of those (numerous enough) women of late-twentieth-century America who mistrust feminism's disruption of domesticity. Alice Hall Petry castigates her for having created a "gallery of women who never seem to have heard of the feminist movement" and quotes her as saying in an interview, apropos of liberated women, that she personally had really never felt "imprisoned."[37] The statement has an oddly combative or defensive ring to it and simply evades the issue of group imprisonment (the constraints on women's lives in general imposed by traditional social structures) and the degree to which Tyler or any other woman shares those constraints simply by the fact of sex. Perhaps, by some quirk or feat unknown to sociologists, Tyler really has lived a life of perfect freedom, so far as gender is concerned, but it seems unlikely. Nor does it seem likely, given the keenness of novelistic observation evident in her work, that she has simply failed to notice. Yet many of her female characters—no more politically aware than they are usually career-minded—are surprisingly contented with, or at least resigned to, staying at home.

Charlotte Emory is not one of them, but is a woman whose desire for personal freedom is conveyed by her desire for travel. It is frequently objected that though she is initially offered as a woman wanting to escape from domesticity, Charlotte is denied volition by having her escape turned into a kidnapping. Worse, she surrenders even this limited impulse toward autonomy by abjectly returning to an exploitative husband. Such a reading perhaps reflects the present conflict within feminist criticism between political feminism, seeking to develop a firm self with equality and autonomy, and the feminism of difference, seeking to disperse the core of the self in merging and a distinctly female *jouissance* expressed by "writing the body."[38]

Tyler's characterization of Charlotte Emory cannot, of course, be fully identified with either; it belongs in the realm of realistic fiction with its depiction of mixed human natures. It can be validated in feminist terms, if at all, only through an extension of difference to include the possibility that some women do find their primary fulfillment in traditional relational patterns. Those who object to Charlotte are really objecting to the logical implications of the discourse of difference.

Charlotte's escape wish is established unambiguously at the outset, in one of Tyler's characteristically important openings. *If Morning Ever Comes* opens with the words "When Ben Joe Hawkes left home." *The Tin Can Tree* opens, "After the funeral James came straight home, to look after his brother." *A Slipping-Down Life* opens with the statement that Evie is "not musical," a reference to one of her many lacks. *Searching for Caleb* opens with a train trip in the first chapter and a moving day in the second. *Celestial Navigation* opens with the statement that Jeremy never left home. All of these openings serve as strong pointers to the main burden of the book, either directly (*Searching for Caleb* is indeed insistent on motion) or ironically (Ben Joe has not really left home, Evie develops abilities). In *Earthly Possessions* the opening words point directly to Charlotte's decision to escape the house: "The marriage wasn't going well and I decided to leave my husband" (5). She immediately takes steps to do so, going to the bank to withdraw cash.[39]

Charlotte's need to make a departure is more deep-seated than the opening indicates. Still living in the house where she grew up, even though she has long been married, she has never achieved even the primary separation that is needed in order to establish adult identity. Essentially, then, she enacts both of Tyler's typical departures at once; she leaves her parental home in leaving her marital home. By the end of the second chapter (even-numbered chapters being given to retrospection) we learn that even as a child Charlotte feared that she would "never, ever manage to escape to the outside world" (17). Looking back, she admires the woman next door, who became her mother-in-law, who was "so much braver, freer, stronger than I had turned out to be" (156).[40] Charlotte's quest throughout the book is to become, or to demonstrate that she too has become, brave, strong, and, most important, free. Her strength is in fact demonstrated by a great many things: her juggling of roles and duties, her resistance to easy capitulation to her minister husband's religious views, her nursing of her dying mother, her accommodation of the various waifs Saul brings home. Her bravery is demonstrated by her coolness while being held at gunpoint after being taken hostage during a robbery at the bank and when eventually walking away from the kidnapper despite the very real threat that he may shoot her in the back. But freedom is more difficult to achieve, and remains ambiguous. This is the source of feminist critics' objections.

Being taken hostage by the young bank robber, Jake, is only the last in a series of kidnappings to which Charlotte has been subjected in her generally passive and manipulated life. As a child she was literally kidnapped by a refugee woman who had lost her own child. On that occasion she went along quietly, even cooperatively, in part because the strange woman said she loved to travel, and Charlotte, at the age of seven, already found that appealing (37). Indeed, it was her restoration to her parents that she perceived as the real kidnapping, as if they were "stealing" her away from where she belonged (43). Later she was figuratively kidnapped by her father, who insisted she learn to help in his photography studio. When she thought she had made good her escape from that by going away to college, she was "kidnapped" back by his death, since her grossly obese mother could not possibly manage alone. She has a pattern, then, of being made to follow roads not of her own choosing.

After drifting into marriage, Charlotte realizes that she should have refused, since she had "never planned to take a second person on this trip" (77). In words reminiscent of Olivia's in Mary Austin's *A Woman of Genius,* she urges Saul to "set out and seek your fortune . . . take off tomorrow, travel anywhere." But he decides he has been called to preach in a local church, a commitment that means in effect holding her hostage at home, "keeping me here forever," she laments, "all the long, slow days of my life" (76, 96). Although she has come to picture herself in the guise of the remembered refugee woman, "walking down a dusty road that I have been walking for months . . . casting off encumbrances . . . stripping for the journey" (40–41), she in fact accretes possessions. Her life becomes one of persisting, with occasional ineffectual rebellions, in patterns she sees no way out of. As long as her mother lives, she cannot bring herself to abandon her; and afterward not only husband and children but other family members, the management of the house, and even the dog require her to stay at home in what she perceives as a stultifying existence.

Being taken hostage by Jake, then, is only partly an imposed act, since he is merely forcing her to do what she already wanted and meant to do on her own. It is in effect an amalgam of kidnapping and voluntary departure. As they head south in a stolen car, the passenger-side door chained shut to keep her in, their relationship gradually becomes rather amicable and Jake begins to ask her advice in dealing with his pregnant girlfriend. Relationships, it appears, will ensnare her wherever she goes; they are part of who she is (a lesson that will also be learned by the even more problematic Delia of *Ladder of Years*). As Charlotte and Jake share their feelings—both are claustrophobic, both feel frustrated and disapproved of by their families, both yearn to escape—he hits on a piece of wisdom that proves transformative: "I really believe that any time you see someone running, it's their old, faulty self they're running from" (175). For Charlotte his words are like a lightbulb coming on. At their next stop, despite Jake's determination to keep her as a mother-figure and intermediary, she walks away to catch a bus home.

The resolution of this story of withdrawal and return is finally ambiguous, reflecting an uncertainty about escape that would characterize, perhaps even more emphatically, the seldom-praised *Morgan's Passing,* published three years later. Charlotte's return to her dour husband and her old life of housekeeping and clutter (she has only made a start at the kind of jettisoning Justine accomplishes) has been seen as "little more than another manifestation of her capacity to be passive."[41] I take it more positively. She has wanted all her life to establish her identity. Building on Jake's groping message, she is now prepared to find that identity at home—but on her own terms. Linda Wagner-Martin correctly observes that in walking away from Jake she "relies for the first time on her sense of what she wants to happen" and at the end is "now living the way she wants to live."[42] That way of living may be identified with home, but she has discovered it—her self has emerged—by traveling. She gains a new sense of accomplishment in her photography business, now referring to "my camera" rather than, as before, her father's camera, and when Saul offers to do some traveling she says she doesn't "see the need." In a merging of the spatial with the temporal, she now sees their life as a whole in terms of motion, as a traveling in time: "We have been traveling for years, traveled all our lives, we are traveling still. We couldn't stay in one place if we tried" (222). With her new understanding has come assertive leadership:

when she tells Saul to go to sleep, he does. It is an ending expressive of satisfaction and of ripeness, one that brings repose without entrapment. But a departure and flight were necessary to achieve it.

Tyler's most complex and expansive works, and the ones that have seemed to most readers her finest achievements, are two novels of the early to mid-1980s, *Dinner at the Homesick Restaurant* (1982) and *The Accidental Tourist* (1985). Both are centrally concerned with a theme she would take up again in *Breathing Lessons,* the countering of misery, as well as the idea that we have seen to some degree in all her novels, the urge toward freedom from the accumulated habits and resentments associated with houses.

Members of the Tull family in *Dinner at the Homesick Restaurant* demonstrate the truth of Jake's observation in *Earthly Possessions* that people who run away are running from themselves. As one of the minor characters puts it, "You could say that what I'm leaving behind is my own poor view of me, right?" (*Homesick,* 273).[43] More specifically, what the Tulls are running away from is the burden of their family history, caught in the family home like stale air. But the multiplicity of departures, the Tulls' relative ordinariness among Tyler's generally odd cast of characters, and the book's focus on life-stage experiences such as the growing up of children, aging, and the death of parents, all sustain a sense that the pattern of departure, return, and remaining they enact is not peculiar to themselves, but universal.

The departure of furthest-reaching impact, shaping the lives of Cody, Ezra, and Jenny, is that of their father, Beck Tull, who ducks out on his responsibilities when Cody, the oldest, is fourteen, thereby dooming them to a troubled and unhappy childhood. Pearl, their mother, left behind to bring up three children alone, is an abider, a person true to her obligations, but she feels trapped and shows her resentment in abuse both verbal and physical, so well particularized in Tyler's clear prose that it is painful to read and all too believable. On one appalling occasion she calls the children "parasites" and screams that she wishes they would "all die, and let me go free" (59). Jenny, the youngest, suggests to her brothers that they run away from home, but as Cody points out, they "don't have anyplace to run to" (56). At least until they grow up, they are as trapped as their mother.

In adulthood, the legacy of childhood anxieties is evident in their varied strategies of escape and in their repeated returns, or in Ezra's case, remaining. Cody, tormented by the lifelong suspicion that it was some transgression or inadequacy of his own that alienated their father, has grown up ironically reenacting those very failures in an endless circle of demonstration and guilt. His adult life of incessant mobility, an implicit rejection of all that home meant to him, repeats their father's on-the-road job-centeredness. It is an unwitting attempt to earn the absent father's approval by achieving success in the only kind of endeavor he had seemed to understand. When Cody marries (having deliberately stolen Ezra's fiancée for reasons of a deep-seated rivalry and the need to prove himself as bad as he fears he is), he is so determined to keep his wife and child with him as he moves from consulting job to consulting job that they never really have a home at all. Alienated by this possessiveness, his wife leaves him at one point but gets only as far as the bus station. Their son, Luke, fares better, hitchhiking to his uncle Ezra's restaurant and the nearby family home, which to him seems a haven. Ezra, the opposite of Cody in many respects, never really leaves home at all except for an abortive induction into the army during the Korean War era. He reacts to the family instability by clinging to home and mother (rather than, like Cody, unconsciously emulating the father) and by trying to achieve a perfected transformation of the home experience through his nurturing Homesick Restaurant.

Jenny, the youngest of the three, reacts to their father's desertion and their mother's abuse by adopting a series of complex coping strategies, neither Cody's constant motion nor Ezra's stasis. Compulsively perfectionist at school, she tries to achieve female perfection in her own body through anorexia and neatness. Just as she tries to avoid bodily accretion, so she attempts to evade emotional baggage, distancing herself by conspicuous achievement in college, by reducing her visits home to an absolute minimum, and by choosing a suitor whose notion of a proposal sounds like a business letter. She marries impulsively and divorces, marries again and divorces. But none of these attempted evasions of the past succeeds as a real escape. When she breaks down from stress and overwork during her medical internship, while also single parenting, she fulfills her own worst fear by repeating the past, acting out toward her own child her mother's abusive behaviors. Predictably, the childhood home that she has left has stayed with her. After her recovery, "carr[ying] herself as gently as a cup of liquid" (239), she copes with anxiety by adopting a totally different persona, as a slightly unkempt, frazzled joker, thereby protecting herself from the threat of taking things seriously. Her final escape, then, is another kind of denial, a denial of identity. Marrying for a third time, she decides that she has permanently settled in, since, having taken on her husband's already traumatized children, she cannot possibly traumatize them further by leaving again. Even so, she makes a figurative escape from that house as well, both by maintaining emotional distance and by abandoning housekeeping—not an unusual adjustment among Tyler's women.

Pearl Tull, the mother, is ultimately a more sympathetic character than the scenes of her abusive tantrums would indicate. Proving herself once again a forgiving author, Tyler reconciles the reader to Pearl by showing both her mellowing with time and her regrets. Even so, her death proves liberating in that it frees Cody, Ezra, and Jenny to enact a rite of return and forgiveness in a funeral meal at Ezra's Homesick Restaurant—a demonstration of homesickness but, like Joan's in *The Tin Can Tree,* "not for any home [they'd] ever had" (*Tin Can Tree,* 130). Even their long-absent father returns and gains a measure of forgiveness.[44] Relieving Cody of the imagined guilt of having caused him to leave them in their mother's "clutches," Beck confesses that he simply wasn't up to staying the course in the face of his own weaknesses and the general "grayness of things"; Pearl, he thought, was (340–41). Her dissatisfaction with his failures, he says, "wore me out." The novel ends with Cody's memory of an emblematic moment not long before his father's departure, when he had shot an arrow from his new archery set but it had not yet reached its accidental but significant target, his mother's shoulder. His memory of that moment of happiness before the fateful wounding, with its "little brown airplane, almost motionless, droning through the sunshine like a bumblebee," replicates, in a beautiful structural parallel, his mother's dying memory of her own perfect moment, before her fateful marriage, which also included a single buzzing insect, "a bottle fly . . . in the grass" (343, 314). Since these moments of beatitude, they have all in some way wounded each other. No one has been omitted from the circle of pain. Now the score is even, and Cody, it seems, is freed to make good at last his escape from the old "house" of the family, even as together they constitute a true family, wounded but recovering.[45]

Three years after *Dinner at the Homesick Restaurant,* moving from triumph to triumph, Tyler published what has been her most popular novel, and the only one thus far made into a film, *The Accidental Tourist.*[46] Here the desire to stay and the urge to go are so closely intertwined that they not only became contending impulses within a single character but, in a brilliant feat of compression, are fused in the image of Macon Lowry's travel guides for people who prefer not to leave home. The conventional story line, following a plot of masculine choice between two women representing opposed kinds of life, is saved from triteness by a surprising and particularly amusing set of minor characters and incidents. At the same time, the book continues the shading toward darkness evident in *Homesick Restaurant,* as Tyler's generally sunshiny palette is considerably darkened by an eruption of senseless violence, in the killing of Macon and Sarah's young son and the resulting pall of grief that hangs over the novel. In Susan Gilbert's words, both the novel and the movie made from it are "imbued with the sense of peril."[47]

Despite the spotlight on travel both in the title *The Accidental Tourist* and in the opening paragraph, Tyler actually emphasizes agoraphobic clinging to home more emphatically than in any other of her novels since *Celestial Navigation,* eight years before. The book opens with Macon and Sarah driving home from an unsuccessful, grief-haunted vacation. In a few short pages, the scene conveys a vivid sense of car travel: the strain of driving in bad weather, the impact of intense emotional exchanges on one's control of the wheel (when Sarah abruptly says she wants a divorce), the possibility of using the need to watch the road as an avoidance tactic, the combination of fast movement with almost claustrophobic enclosure when the windows are up and visibility is poor.[48] The fact that it is toward rather than away from home that they are traveling is significant, setting up an ambiguous elision of enhousement and motion that is developed throughout the book. As they move down the road following her announcement, Sarah acknowledges Macon's preference for being at home, saying she will move out and let him keep the house since he "never did like moving" (5).

After she leaves, Macon embeds himself in the house, devising cocoon-like arrangements for reducing his activities and schemes for avoiding basic errands. Finally he impairs even his capacity for mobility by breaking his leg, a self-wounding that conveniently serves his urge to retreat to his grandparents' house, where he grew up and where his two brothers have already taken refuge in the care of their sister, Rose. Together the four Lowrys play card games that mystify outsiders and keep house according to such arcane schemes as the alphabetizing of groceries, using these private customs to build walls between themselves and the rest of the world. Macon's retreat to "the house . . . of the grandfather" has been characterized in Lacanian terms

by Anne Ricketson Zahlan as a return to a parodic version of "Freud's association of parental authority and the super-ego," the "domain of the law"
from which he will have to free himself.[49] Both Macon and Sarah will later
return to their own house in an attempted reconciliation; through most
of the book, Macon is nothing if not uncertain about what he wants to do.
The vacillation evident in this back-and-forth movement is paralleled by his
sister, a confirmed spinster who surprisingly marries Macon's publisher and
moves away, then leaves her marital home (in that image of transience, an
apartment) and returns with her new husband trailing behind.

Houses appear to triumph. Yet the force of inertia cannot withstand the
energy of Muriel Pritchett, a quirky yet competent woman Macon meets
when he has to board his dog during a business trip. Muriel has successfully
executed an adult departure, having left her husband and, in the process,
what Rose Quiello calls "confinement in conventional scripts."[50] Predictably,
she yearns to travel. She exemplifies the zest for going and discovering that
we see in Justine, Charlotte, and later Maggie. When Macon takes her on her
first flight, she exclaims, "We'll have to take just lots of trips!" (199). Indeed,
it is her determination to travel to Paris that leads to Macon's choice of her
over Sarah at the end. Sarah also follows Macon to Paris, to care for him
when he develops back spasms, but her presence brings a return to the stale
patterns of the past rather than the release from them that Muriel offers.
Whereas Muriel energizes Macon, Sarah further immobilizes him, dosing
him with sleeping pills. His choice of Muriel is a choice of life.

Both women are in fact identified with houses, Sarah with her upper-
middle-class marital home, Muriel with the ramshackle structure she inhabits in a deteriorated part of Baltimore that proves vitalizing when Macon
goes looking for her and moves in. Like Jenny's in *Homesick Restaurant* and
Justine's in *Searching for Caleb,* Muriel's style of housekeeping is in itself an
escape. Her cooking and cleaning are erratic; her walls, in effect, permeable.
Acquaintances drop in at all hours, trailing complications and dripping snow
on the floor in an urbanized (and of course far less radical) version of Sylvie's
fusion of indoors and outdoors in *Housekeeping.* Her house is messy but liberating, in contrast to Sarah's, which is tasteful but imprisoning. Macon's
choice between the two women is also, then, a choice of which house to escape and which one, meaning which life, to occupy, with a third possibility
being permanent retreat to the (grand)parental home. That Muriel's house
is distinctly lower class in its ambience and surroundings is no deterrent.

For the first time in his life he has a sense of volition, of "tak[ing] steps" rather than simply accepting whatever has "befallen him" (339). His choice, then, is not only happily made but entirely free from regret for the comforts he is giving up. Even so, it is not unambiguous, not a clean break. In real life, he realizes, things "weren't so clean-cut" as in movies, where people "walked out and never returned" (294). Initially he thinks of this muddied state as merely the necessity of tying up awkward loose ends. But at the end of the book, as he tells Sarah that he is leaving her (balancing her similar declaration to him at the beginning),[51] he realizes that his life will always be in some ways tied to hers, "no matter what separate paths they chose to travel" (340). It is one of Tyler's central and governing principles that lives get intertwined and relationships are both more important than any relocations people may make and more inescapable than houses.

Discussions of *The Accidental Tourist* often invoke that prototype of male wandering, the *Odyssey*.[52] Like Odysseus, Macon spends a period of time roaming before settling down with his faithful woman, but the parallel becomes more problematic the more one examines it. The gendering of the *Odyssey* is overridden by Tyler's urge toward androgyny, Macon is not *kept* from home as Odysseus is, and if it is Sarah, his legal wife, who represents the faithful Penelope, having remained (so she says) chaste during their separation, it was she, after all, who first left—scarcely the act of a Penelope. Furthermore, Sarah is the only approximation of a sorceress who gives out potions, and the sleeping pills she administers to ease Macon's back pain are neither a very close approximation of the classical prototype nor a parodic inversion. There is no parallel at all to Odysseus's boasting. Finally, it seems to me, the *Odyssey* is simply not a very useful starting point, either as a prototype or as target of parody. Moreover, invoking it gives rise to a false assumption that this modern (non)Odysseus returns home. But he doesn't. In Anne Jones's words, he and other Tyler characters "travel from homes where everything stays the same to homes that admit change, variety, and surprise." As Lin Humphrey observes, "change wins out over stasis."[53] That is a very different outcome from Odysseus's homecoming, and for Macon a happier one.

Tyler's novels following the triumphs of *Dinner at the Homesick Restaurant* and *The Accidental Tourist—Breathing Lessons* (1988), *Saint Maybe* (1991),

and *Ladder of Years* (1995)—have seemed to most critics to represent decline. Although Karen Levenback considers *Breathing Lessons* "perhaps Tyler's most accomplished novel to date," and Linda Wagner-Martin praises the
"narrative brilliance" of *Saint Maybe,* such praise has been a minority report.[54] The central characters of all three have been seen as losers who fail
to take initiative in shaping their lives. In all of these works Tyler to some
extent repeats long-established patterns and motifs. *Ladder of Years* is indeed, in my view, pointlessly repetitive. In *Saint Maybe,* however, she addresses issues of gender in especially thoughtful ways, with the result that
the novel becomes surprisingly linked to the important earlier work *Celestial
Navigation.* And in all three of these late works she sets herself, and I believe
successfully negotiates, the challenge of finding significance in the ordinary,
even what appears at first glance the uninteresting, an endeavor that Voelker
sees as one of the most pervasive traces in Tyler's work of the "decidedly
fortunate influence" of Eudora Welty. It was Welty, he insists, who made Tyler aware that "the familiar, the ordinary, was a rich field for cultivation."[55]

The characterization of Maggie Moran in *Breathing Lessons* is anchored in
an unblinking view of the weight of social and economic circumstance bearing on people (especially women) of the lower middle class, living in an
unstable world and confronting the inescapable evidence of their own aging
and mortality. By launching the novel with Maggie and her husband Ira's
journey to the funeral of a man the same age as themselves, she confronts
them with issues generally recognized as being of universal and ultimate
concern, even while the details of their trip and their conversation as they go
reveal that their life-journeys are inescapably "unadventurous."[56] The reader
is challenged to accept that unadventurousness, to accept the grittiness of the
Morans' lives, to pity Maggie for her awareness of her inability to work things
out for those she loves, and at the same time to develop admiration for her.

Several qualities in Maggie evoke such admiration. One is her lovingness;
she actively cares about her family members and even about strangers who
dial the wrong number and blurt out their distress. Another is her social
openness, her relative freedom from preconceptions about people like the
elderly black man with whom she strikes up an acquaintance. Primarily,
though, it is Maggie's association with journeying (in strong contrast to Ira's
sister, one of the most severely afflicted of Tyler's agoraphobes) that constructs her as an estimable person. However overwhelming the discourage-
ments in her life, not the least being her daughter's asking her when it was

that she "decided to settle for being ordinary" (30), she remains a person in motion, with an adventurous spirit, always "adjusting to new developments" (184). Besides the trip to and from her friend's husband's funeral, with a detour to visit her former daughter-in-law, she is retrospectively seen making secret trips to check on her only grandchild and prospectively seen on a trip to take her daughter off to college, to launch her in her own independence. She is not too deadened by Ira's incommunicativeness and faultfinding to get out of the car at one point and walk away, planning how she will start life on her own (as Delia does in *Ladder of Years*); nor is she too wrapped up in her anger to drop it when he comes back and says lightly, "Hey, babe . . . care to accompany me to a funeral?" (46).

Critics who have seen Ira as nothing but a wet blanket seem to have missed such turns of phrase. True, Maggie's readiness to get back into the car with him can be seen, like Charlotte Emory's return home, as evidence that she is little more than a doormat. Her self-confidence has sagged by then, as she thinks that after all there is "no such thing on this earth as real change" and people are all "just spinning here . . . revolving like those rides at Kiddie Land where everyone is pinned to his place by centrifugal force" (46). But her choice to rejoin her husband on the road can also be read as a recognition that she has shared a lot with Ira (whose dissatisfaction and in-expressiveness mask his own wish for escape and adventure, manifested in his preferred reading material). She is glad to have him along to harmonize as she sings, while they drive and she ponders how it feels to grow old, "But I ain't going down that long old lonesome road all by myself" (180).[57]

Maggie is not without an inkling of the larger resonances of ordinary experiences: "Wouldn't it be wonderful," she thinks when her son's wife leaves him, taking along only her natural-fiber clothes, "to save only what was first-class and genuine and pure, and walk out on everything else!" (277). But she does not live a life of such absolute renunciations. Her identity is one of plugging away in the life she has. That does not mean that her spirit makes, or at least envisions, no departures. If the novel ends with Maggie still at home and Ira still playing solitaire, it also leaves her feeling "a sort of inner buoyancy" and a keen anticipation of the next day's trip (327). She has preserved what is for Tyler a highly symbolic zest for travel even as she juggles her responsibilities as a caring adult. As Margaret Morganroth Gullette observes, in Tyler's fictional world "whether [characters] like travel or can't bear it matters."[58] By juxtaposing Maggie's anticipation of tomorrow's trip with her question to Ira, "What are we two going to live for, all the rest of our lives?" (326), Tyler again employs, though in a less assured manner than in *Earthly Possessions* or *The Accidental Tourist*, the road-of-life metaphor, using a linear space to represent linear time. Macon, in *Accidental Tourist*, thinks to himself, "The real adventure is the flow of time" (342)—a flow that, as Frank Shelton comments, "involves change, openness to life."[59] Maggie, like Charlotte or Muriel or in the end even Macon, shows such an openness.

In *Saint Maybe*, Tyler continued to ponder the dark question of what can make life worth living. It is her one book in which escape from an overwhelming domesticity is scarcely even conceivable. Ian Bedloe is so mired in stasis and borne down by overwhelming responsibilities that he never even moves out of his primary home, but gives up college in order to stay and care for the three orphaned children of his elder brother's widow, two from her previous marriage and a third of doubtful paternity. Despite the possibility that none of the children is any blood relation, Ian feels responsible for them by reason of guilt, since it was his act of blurting out, in a moment of anger, the charge that Lucy was with another man that led to his brother's apparent suicide and thereby the later suicide of Lucy as well.[60] It is a mistake, however, to read Ian as being motivated solely by the determination to expiate his guilt. There is also the practical matter of what will happen to the children otherwise, since Lucy had no known relatives and Ian's arthritic mother is not up to caring for them. Moreover, he has already proven to be an unusually effective baby-sitter with the three children, communicating with the two older ones easily and inspiring the baby to feats of arm-waving, whoops, and smiles. The scenes in which he holds and rocks the baby, as well as later scenes in which he steers the three of them through the various trials of childhood and adolescence, show him as a deeply and readily "maternal" man, reminiscent of the baby-rocking Ben Joe Hawkes in Tyler's first novel, the emotionally disturbed Andrew Emerson in *The Clock Winder*, who is shown near the end happily holding Elizabeth's baby even though he had earlier shot Elizabeth in the shoulder, and the explicitly "maternal" Ezra Tull, who also never leaves his parental home.[61]

Ian's androgynous role subjects him to many of the pressures and fantasies usually associated with women who feel bound by domestic and child-rearing responsibilities. We know by his momentarily picturing himself driving off in a car and abandoning the children that he shares, to some degree, the feelings of the ultimately suicidal Lucy, who says she is "about to lose my mind cooped up all day" and "going stir-crazy" from "cabin fever" (27, 62). Surrendering to her escape wish and the despair arising from her inability to conceive of managing her life without a man, Lucy enacts a version of the role more commonly played by the deserting father. Apparently it is a more appalling role when played by a mother, since her neglect of the children and her suicide bear strongly Gothic trappings. Ian, on the other hand, reacts to his impulses toward escape by reminding himself of the children's needs and carrying out the practical aspects of caregiving. To be sure, he has the advantages of extended family and his odd church, and these are shown to be significant resources. At one time he weakens to the point of hiring a private detective to search out any surviving relatives Lucy may have had (allowing the private detective of *Searching for Caleb* to make a return appearance), but quickly realizes that he could not give them up in such a way. His unbidden fantasy of driving off and leaving them is not so much repressed as smothered by an immediate rush of love: "such a sense of loss that it made his breath catch" (210).

One of the most fully house-bound and duty-bound of any of Tyler's central characters, male or female, Ian achieves self-definition within the structure of the family and within the family structure, the house, much as Charlotte Emory does in *Earthly Possessions* but without the intervening journey that affords her a measure of detachment and re-vision. But by the end of the novel the house(hold) that Ian inhabits is a radically transformed one, not only with respect to the changes that have occurred over time and Ian's unusual shuffling of life-stage patterns, but in the composition of the extended "family" securely anchored there. The older daughter, Agatha, has a successful medical career; the younger one, Daphne, is a promiscuous job-hopper; and the son is an educational computer game developer. Ian himself finally marries an exotic-looking woman who operates a clutter-reduction business, and he is liked and visited by the shifting ranks of international graduate students who live down the street, as well as by members of his church. No one in the group is Ian's blood relative except his elderly father and the baby born just at the end. Conservative as Tyler is usually considered, she has departed from convention to the point of endorsing the kind of redefinition of family often derided in today's popular media as a "politically correct" delusion. With truly existential irony, she has shown Ian's stay-at-home, duty-bound life to have brought him a full measure of freedom after all.

Fetching home, at the end of the novel, the cradle he has made for his infant son, Ian experiences a lurch of temporal displacement. His present situation and his situation at the age of fifteen, over a quarter century ago, suddenly slide together in his mind. It is a moment that validates an earlier insight voiced by the oldest of the three now-grown children—an insight that comes, in one form or another, to many of Tyler's most fully affirmed characters, hinging on the idea of space-time equivalence: "Living in a family is like taking a long, long trip." The view of that trip that Agatha expresses is, for most people's lives, entirely valid: "After you've traveled awhile at close quarters . . . you just have to get away from them. You have to leave home." But that is not the only possible view; some people experience the trip differently. Daphne, the daughter still closest to Ian, replies, "Well, I guess I must not have traveled with them long enough then" (312–13). Ian, too, travels without leaving. In this way, and also in his pronounced androgyny, Ian is another Jeremy Pauling.

In the totality of her fiction as well as book by book, Anne Tyler achieves a compelling exploration of the pursuit and the achievement of self-definition by characters who are, for the most part, relatively powerless in a social or economic sense. However striking their oddities, they represent people of ordinary means. She achieves, as well, a realistically and sympathetically evoked sense of the constraints felt by women whose lives are identified primarily with home and family. Through characters such as Charlotte Emory of *Earthly Possessions,* Emily Meredith of *Morgan's Passing,* and Mrs. Bedloe of *Saint Maybe,* she demonstrates the truth of Justine's uncle's comment, in *Searching for Caleb,* that "women's lives are right dull" (221). Such lives promote the wish for escape, for some kind of departure. Frequently this means a literal, physical setting forth on journeys of exploration, whether geographically extensive or only emblematic in scope. Her fictional world is crowded with women who wish to, and often do, escape the house. After Delia, for example, walks away from her family, in *Ladder of Years,* she finds a job managing the household of a man whose wife had longed to escape— and had finally done so. Charlotte Emory returns to the house she was born in, which has become her marital home; Maggie Moran returns with Ira to anticipate another trip tomorrow. Both enunciate a vision that defines home as being itself a kind of journey. Narratively, on their own terms, they have not merely stayed behind, because they have not (as Karen Lawrence says of Penelope, "with time on her hands, her hands at the loom") told only the "one story" of the household and stasis. Instead, they have "semanticize[d] . . . centrifugal impulses" by their "use of the figure of movement."[62]

Is the figure of the emblematic journey, applied to an essentially domestic pattern of life, merely sleight of hand on Tyler's part? Certainly there is an ambiguity about it that is troubling as well as rich. Some of her characters, female as well as male, go further and make good their literal escapes. The free-spirited Muriel Pritchett of *The Accidental Tourist* left home and husband to make her own life and her own living, and she makes a defiant trip to Paris when Macon refuses to take her. Macon escapes both a repressive marriage and regressive urges. Ben Joe of *If Morning Ever Comes* escapes his fixation on his parental home, and James Green of *The Tin Can Tree*, having already escaped home and the parents who sought to imprison him there, manages to escape his anxiety about them. Ian's adopted daughters in *Saint Maybe* go their own ways, both very much in control of their lives, even though for one this means living a continent's width away as a conspicuous achiever in a traditionally male profession and for the other it means job-hopping on impulse while staying close to home. Among the more ambiguous escapes is that of Elizabeth Abbott of *The Clock Winder,* who escapes her restrictive parental home and her own fear of involvement, but does not escape enhousement, though she does move into a role in which her spontaneity and practical capabilities bloom. Achieving a new identity of mingled domesticity and leadership, she is given a new, androgynous name. Like Charlotte of *Earthly Possessions,* she has been enabled by her journey to develop control of her own life, though, to be sure, a life enmeshed in what she once sought to escape. Several of Tyler's women make figurative escapes from the house by redefining housekeeping, thus freeing themselves from preconceived notions. Emily Meredith of *Morgan's Passing* takes up exercise walking to satisfy her restlessness and hears her shoes thump out "gone, gone, gone" as she goes along, while "songs about leaving, about women who packed up and left" ring in her head (211).

What Emily hears as she goes is her own desire for escape, not a message of the larger political and historic conditions that have led to that desire.

Such larger messages are all but absent from Tyler's fictional milieu. Emily deals only with her own dissatisfaction, alone. If it is unclear whether in the end she achieves any degree of liberty that we can call by that name; she does at any rate move to a different space, one of her own choosing. Moreover, she continues to escape in a figurative way by moving into alternate lives through her puppetry.[63] She shares with Jeremy Pauling the escape vehicle of transcendence through art.

In a paradoxical sense, it is finally Jeremy, the most house-bound of all Tyler's characters, who most fully escapes the house. Jeremy remains her most teasing and resonant figure. Not only does his pathological agoraphobia place him at a conspicuous extreme of her concern with what Cather calls, in *Death Comes for the Archbishop,* "the desire to go and the necessity to stay"; not only do his appearance and manner clearly evoke the androgyny that is so thematically important to Tyler; but he is very clearly a representation of Tyler herself, the artist-woman, the artist-mother, grappling with her counter-impulses toward both isolation and family involvement. As Doris Betts points out, Jeremy's "development from collage to sculpture seems to parallel Tyler's literary progress from story to more and more complex novel." That Tyler saw her writing as a defense against dereliction and, at the same time, as a substitute for it, was clear in an interview published three years after *Celestial Navigation:* "Probably I would be schizophrenic—and six times divorced—if I weren't writing. I would decide that I want to run off and join the circus and I would go. I hate to travel, but writing a novel is like taking a long trip."[64] Jeremy learns that he can, after all, summon the strength to make a journey out. Having learned that, and having made one brave journey, he returns to the confines of his house and to the creation of "towering, beautiful" works that constitute his private escape. But he is reminded, too, by his caring friend Miss Vinton, of the need to make himself go out into the public world, even if his journeys are only to the corner grocery.

When readers have remarked on the oddity of her characters, Tyler has responded that she believes the most ordinary people turn out to be odd if examined closely enough. By the same token, she seems to believe in the persistence of the ordinary, and of ordinary human needs, despite oddity and change. Hers is a remarkably tolerant fiction. She recognizes and accepts the urge to depart—from the home, from the ordinary—but does not insist on it. Her characters walk out, gain perspective, return on a new footing, find freedom in persistence; and the ordinary continues in altered forms. It is perhaps this willingness to accept the persistence of the customary that has led to Tyler's being read as a conservative domestic novelist. I see her, instead, as a novelist attempting to navigate between conservatism and departure, concerned with trying to find ways of accommodating the departures of social change to the persistent needs of human beings. As a reviewer once noted, she is concerned with "an existential examination of the nature of freedom"; with, in Anne Goodwin Jones's words, the choices that determine "personal psychic growth."[65] Her eagerness to look for the odd hidden in the ordinary implies an openness to resistance and innovation. If she is devoted to a fiction of the house, she does not demand that all houses look alike. Some may be, like Duncan and Justine's in *Searching for Caleb,* circus trailers.[66] Even so, the centrality of that structure, the house, implies the persistence of social structures, as well. Individuals may make their departures on whim or on principle at a moment's notice, but the remodeling of the house is a slow process and one that, in its merger of continuity and change, Tyler seems to enjoy.

Tyler's novels are shaped by a revisionary rather than revolutionary vision; they seldom follow what Elaine Showalter calls "transgressive plots." Both in her sympathetic exposition of the counter-weight of home nurturance and in her persistent acknowledgement of the negative weight of fear, she manifests a sense of limitation by the social order, a sense that Karen Lawrence associates with "constraints on self-propelled movement."[67] Most of her central characters sooner or later *want* to leave, to escape. Many of them do make departures of at least a provisional nature, leaving the house for a time and, upon reflection, returning—but often on revised terms. If Tyler's women, in enacting these returns to their marital homes, are at some level simply "seduced into consenting to femininity,"[68] as Teresa de Lauretis puts it, that at any rate is not the full range of possible interpretations she offers—though she does, with Elizabeth in *The Clock Winder* and Charlotte Emory in *Earthly Possessions,* recognize such a possibility. Rather, she offers such returns after escape as realizations that home and family do, after all, offer important satisfactions both of nurturance and of opportunities for nurturing, and she holds out the possibility that males as well as females will be able to make their homes function that way.

She does not claim it always works. Still, her insistent foregrounding of home, often in the form of a nostalgia for a home that never was, conveys a precautionary message of the needfulness of home, a modernist vision of "the necessity, if one doesn't have a home, to make one up."[69] It is a delicate balance, and one that never reaches equilibrium. Her characters are ambivalent about departing from their familiar worlds, especially if departure means abandonment of their relational roles. In this, Tyler is perhaps not so different from Robinson as she may seem. Robinson may imagine a female self unlimited and radically free, but she does not imagine a female self unconcerned with what is for Tyler a central concern, "the trait of lovingness."[70] The crux of Robinson's vision of escape in *Housekeeping* is precisely that: that it is possible for a woman to escape the house without betraying the relationships that matter the most, that one can go on the road without ceasing to be a loving person. Robinson submits that loving can go on outside of houses. In the classic gesture of the radical, she decries material possession, severing nurturance from real estate, commitment from the economic legalities and appurtenances of the unitary family—which is where Tyler sees lovingness, imperfect as it is, as usually occurring.

Chapter 5

ESCAPING HISTORY
Toni Morrison and the Migration Blues

How they led
Armies
Headragged Generals
Across mined
Fields
            —Alice Walker

In the northbound journeys of the African-American hegira, an extension of the African diaspora, a great many women like the masculinely named Joe in Langston Hughes's poem "West Texas," overworked in cotton fields or exploited in other ways, decided to "pack up" and "go" even if they had nothing to pack up[1]—women in head rags leading or accompanying their people through the virtual minefields of the long trek. This historic epic, the Great Migration, resonates through Toni Morrison's works in recurrent narratives of departure and journey that take on redoubled weightiness and meaning because of their embeddedness in history. The departure of women from confinement in domestic roles (and women writers from imaginative confinement in plots of what Rachel Blau DuPlessis calls "romantic thralldom") can regularly be seen as an escape from a virtual enslavement. But the distinctive versions of departure projected by African-American women writers convey not only this escape from the figurative slavery of the gendered past into the emancipation of defiant authenticity and self-definition, but escape from a past of literal slavery and its long and melancholy heritage.

Grace Epstein writes in an essay on dream flight in Morrison's work that the business of the woman writer is "escaping from the confines of cultural narratives that, in accordance with the hierarchical and privileged designs of patriarchy, constrain her and her reality too tightly." Such designs are even more constraining when they intersect the designs of racial exploitation. The complexity and varying en-valuation that we have seen in Marilynne Robinson's, Anne Tyler's, and others' visions of the escape from the house are compounded, and their dramatic impact intensified, when black women writers combine that plot of escape with the plot of departure from the imprisoning heritage of slavery. In doing so, however, they negotiate between seemingly conflicting goals, both in the sense of their "double marginalization"[2] and with respect to their sense of history itself. On the one hand, their goal is the recovery of history; they undertake to recover, bring to light, and confront an authentic but stolen or suppressed history that has allowed the racist and classist hegemonic order to construct and believe in an Edenic myth of America which elides much of black experience.[3] On the other, these writers undertake to disrupt and escape history—that is, to disrupt that myth and to escape the lengthy after-effects of past injustice. In the act of discovering or imagining and writing their own versions of history, they escape the oppressive heritage of history—both "history" in the sense of past events and "history" in the sense of hegemonic interpretations of the past.[4] Toni Morrison's work, a preeminent example of such writing, is firmly situated in historically authentic experience, interpreted, reported, and re-membered by an assertively racial consciousness resistant to, and triumphant over, past erasures and apologetics. In Farah Jasmine Griffin's words, her work as a whole "attests to the dispossession, displacement, and mobility that characterize black life in the Americas."[5]

The extent to which Morrison's confrontation of and escape from racist history and her re-memory of racial history overlap a confrontation of gendered, sexist history is a disputed ground. Eve Lennox Birch links the two by viewing them analogically, arguing that Morrison's "informing impulse," like that of "feminists who demand a rewriting of history from which they had been written out," is the recuperation, re-personing, and revaluing of history. Similarly, Sally Keenan more directly links the enterprise of "contestation" of the ways the African-American past has been "erased by or subsumed within the historical discourse of the hegemonic culture" with the "feminist enterprise of recovering women's lost or unrecorded history."[6] Morrison has insisted that she writes "without gender focus," at any rate in her mature work. Yet her novelistic vision is repeatedly—and not alone in the early novels, where she admits to being "preoccupied" with the humanity of female characters[7]—drawn to women who, in their suffering as well as their strength, are validated both as transcendent individuals and as what DuPlessis calls, with specific reference to Alice Walker's *Meridian,* "representative[s] of a striving community."[8] Morrison herself has spoken of the need for "remembering the horror . . . in a manner in which it can be digested, in a manner in which the memory is not destructive."[9] That, as I see it, is the complex task she has undertaken: to escape the destructive oppressiveness of history and of historical narrative, and to do so by confronting a truer history, re-narrated from a previously suppressed perspective.

The motive force, then, of such works as *Beloved* and *Jazz,* the two novels that will be the particular focus of this chapter, is complex indeed: an escape from a racial and racist history, but also a confrontation and reconstruction of that history; a confrontation and vindication of women's experience within a racially inflected culture and history; and also a definition of individual selfhood and transcendence as a function of a gender-inclusive community. Both of these powerful and lyrical works envision a mutuality of male and female.[10] While according her women heroes dignity and authority, Morrison does not pit them in opposition to male heroism, but especially in these later novels she reconceives both in partnership. The partnership of male and female within a sharing community both enriches and problematizes the theme of the emergence of the self. As in the work of Tyler, we must ask ourselves if the self, especially the female self, can be realized *only* within the context of male-female partnership in family or if that partnership is seen as being an enhancement of an emergence that can be fulfilled in solitary departure.

Surprisingly, Morrison once told an interviewer that the action in *Song of Solomon* involves a journey because it is a book "driven by men" and the "rhythm of *their* lives is outward, adventuresome" (emphasis added). Milkman, she continued, "need[ed] to go somewhere."[11] She has expressed pleasure in the idea of black male mobility: "The fact that they would split in a minute just delights me."[12] The implication would seem to be that women's lives are not outward or adventuresome, that they do not have such a need. Yet Sula, in Morrison's second novel, counters that idea, and Morrison herself came from a heritage of female departure. Her maternal grandmother "left her home in the South with seven children and thirty dollars" in order to escape the exploitative and threatening heritage of racial history.[13] In doing so she enacted the imperative need, expressed by Langston Hughes, to take a "one-way ticket" north. She enacted the African-American need to get anywhere that, in Hughes's words, is "not Dixie."[14]

On this point, as in so many instances, I trust the tale more than the teller. It seems evident, especially when one considers the testimony of *Beloved,* that Morrison does see women's lives, as well as men's, as being open to the need for departure and travel, perhaps for purposes of adventure or outward expansion but often for the fundamental purpose of escape, the enactment of a heroism of a different kind. Morrison's work shares with that of (for example) Zora Neale Hurston, Paule Marshall, Gloria Naylor, and Alice Walker an informed grounding in black oral tradition, a tradition in which escape from oppression is a major structuring action. Houston Baker writes, "Departure is a well-rehearsed configuration in a literature that commences with fugitives."[15] In sorrow songs, or spirituals, and in traditional tales such as those of physical flight back to Africa from which Morrison drew *Song of Solomon,*[16] the recurrent motif of escape is not only deeply impelled but an evidence of transcendent power. Written or dictated slave narratives, as well, which Morrison terms a "nineteenth-century publication boom," establish a resonant context for subsequent literary narrative.[17] Melvin Dixon links the slave narrative with slave songs as "the beginning of tradition in Afro-American literary history," and Birch calls slave narratives the "building bricks" of African-American literature. She sees such narratives as demonstrating qualities of "resourcefulness, intelligence, love and endurance" that still characterize African-American women's writing.[18] Shaping that tradition is a symbolic geography in which the route of pilgrimage to freedom and achievement of full selfhood moves through emblematic places of captivity, trial, and deliverance, with the pilgrim's achievement of selfhood often being signaled (as it is in *Beloved*) by the assumption of a new name.

Dixon has described this powerfully symbolic geography, which appropriates the biblical story of the children of Israel as an expressive form in which to articulate actualities of experience, as one centering on wilderness, the uncultivated and often dangerous space lying outside the domesticated plantation and offering escaping slaves both a refuge and an ordeal to be traversed in order to reach "free" territory. The fugitive becomes a "pilgrim" bound to Canaan who has to "walk that lonesome valley" or wilderness in order to reach the "mountaintop" of what Dixon calls "personal triumph and witness."[19] We see such a wilderness, for example, in the escape sequence recounted by Nanny, Janie's grandmother in Hurston's *Their Eyes Were Watching God* (1937), who describes how she hid in the swamp "full uh moccasins and other bitin' snakes" with her week-old baby because she was "more skeered uh whut was behind me."[20] From the early songs and narratives to novels such as *Their Eyes Were Watching God,* Naylor's *The Women of Brewster Place* (1982) and *Mama Day* (1988), Walker's *The Color Purple* (1982), Marshall's *Praisesong for the Widow* (1983), and Morrison's *Beloved* (1987), all of which incorporate telling and singing out the news, witness has been a significant component of the literature of liberation.

Such sources as sorrow songs and slave narratives resonate in a very literal way in the poem by Langston Hughes mentioned at the beginning of this chapter, as well as in other works informed by the tradition. They resonate more figuratively, as well, in numerous works in which the modern-day social conditions that are the heritage of slavery are presented as being themselves a kind of enslavement. When such works are those of women writers, patterns of geographic movement—their directionality, their linearity or circuitousness, their purposes or seeming randomness, their completion or interruption—take on a multilayered signification, in effect an elaborate signifying.[21] The departures and journeys of characters in such works, as well as textual metaphors of journey and escape, have reference to present and past curtailments of freedom and to the need for personal and collective advance. They have reference to genetic origin, or race, and to social class, moral and spiritual wounding or liberation, and certainly gender, as all of these experiences and concepts intersect with color and thus with a complex and painful history. It is by no means incidental that Hurston, whose personal story was one of northward migration, return to the South, and remembering through both her folklore research and her writing of fiction, named her autobiography by the traces of her movement: *Dust Tracks on a Road.*

In her 1990 polemic *Playing in the Dark,* Morrison takes Willa Cather's *Sapphira and the Slave Girl,* a text long neglected even by Cather scholars, as a major point of reference. It is a useful point of reference here as well, not only because of the issues Morrison raises but because, as Morrison's atten-

tion to the book indicates, Cather's concerns in this late work, the ambiguities of good mother/bad mother and of South and North, are resonant ones
for her.

The story of Nancy, the "slave girl" who returns at the end of Cather's
novel after a long and transformative sojourn in Canada, is the occasion by
which *Sapphira* raises, though only partially addresses, a complex set of maternal and quasi-maternal problematics. These include Nancy's relation to
her mother, Till; Till's relation to her mother, who died by fire in a horrible
accident Till witnessed; Till's relation to her mistress, Sapphira, toward
whom she feels an overriding loyalty; Rachel Blake's relation to her mother,
Sapphira, whom she has defied in arranging Nancy's escape; the child
Willa's relation to the understanding mother who appears in the final pages
of the novel; and the black mother and daughter's relation to the white
mother and daughter in whose home their reunion takes place and for whose
benefit it is in some ways staged. Standing outside the text is yet another
maternal problematic being addressed, the adult Willa Cather's actual relation to her actual mother, Mary Virginia Cather (called Jennie), whose middle name importantly resonates the name of the mother place. By returning to Virginia as she did in 1913 and 1938 and in the writing of *Sapphira*
(which she had spoken of to the Knopfs at least by 1931), Cather was returning to her mother(place), the idyllic locale of the mother she had known
in early childhood. This set of fictional mother-child relationships, shading
into actual ones, all of them loving but in various ways impacted and
blocked, becomes the nexus of dynamics of race, history, class, and political conviction (Rachel's abolitionism). Cather uses this nexus of conflicts to
project not only her personal ambiguities but the interpenetration of public
and private relationships and moralities. Nancy's journey to freedom in Canada and her return visit to Virginia, the mother place, constitute a portion of
Cather's own life story and those of the persons, both real and fictional, with
whose lives hers is entwined. Nancy's journey is emblematic, too, of a vast
public action whose implications are still with us. This dramatic departure
and return in *Sapphira and the Slave Girl* is an instance, then, in which the
stale motto "the personal is the political" is brought to life.

Both Morrison's provocatively transgressive reading of the novel as a
"work full of violence and evasion" and Elizabeth Ammons's reading of it in
Conflicting Stories emphasize its political dimension, specifically its inscription of white privilege. Racial privilege is evident not only in the obvious

power of the slaveholder, but in Rachel Blake's ability to arrange the escape and even in the very fact of her intellectual and moral sensitivity, since, in Ammons's words, black people in the novel seem to have "no political or philosophical objections to slavery."[22] Sycophancy toward whiteness is evident, Morrison argues, in Till's "complicity" with Sapphira and in the appropriation of Till and Nancy, at the moment of reunion, "for the pleasure of a (white) child."[23] As these critical responses make clear, Cather's text occupies a disputed ground either of commonality or of conflict with the texts of black women writers such as, in Cather's own time, Hurston and Nella Larsen and, in ours, Morrison, Walker, and Naylor, all of whom have engaged in similar discourses of liberation and empowerment in strongly gendered terms.

Like the journeys of other fugitives from slavery, that taken by Nancy is both an escape and a quest: an escape from sexual persecution as well as from servitude, though very specifically not from the female role of housekeeper, and a quest for her full humanity. In Nancy's story, however, the escape/quest is also an errand, since she goes not only fearfully but reluctantly, carrying out arrangements made by the determined (even as she is merciful) Mrs. Blake. All of these modes—escape, errand, quest—demand attention as we respond to the story and its idyllic and heroic ending. That Cather signifies the fulfillment of the quest in the clear and polished speech that Nancy has developed during her years in Canada, in contrast to her regionally and racially marked dialect in the earlier part of the novel, is in part the evidence of her own discomfort with dialectical speech, a function perhaps of her aesthetic affiliation with highly literate language but certainly a function of her race and class as well. But it is also, in terms of Cather's intention at any rate, a tribute to Nancy's achievement.

In writing this novel about a fugitive slave—in some ways, as Morrison says, a "classic fugitive slave narrative" that also "describes and inscribes its narrative's own fugitive flight from itself"[24]—Cather invokes the tradition of the slave narrative genre and casts it in a distinctively female mode, primarily by combining it with the autobiographically motivated issue of maternal closeness and distance. To regard her feminizing of the genre as an innovation, however, would not be strictly accurate. Mary Helen Washington points out that some 12 percent of all known slave narratives were those of women, despite the fact that the narratives of men have been better known and have been taken as being representative of the genre as a whole (as their treatment by Robert Stepto in his study of African-American narrative demonstrates).[25] The direction of movement in *Sapphira,* of course, appropriates that of slave narratives both male and female, in that it is northering, specifically escape to Canada, that promises freedom.

This directionality has been firmly established in African-American traditions and texts for over a century and a half, so firmly established indeed that it has sometimes been used ironically.[26] Inherited from spirituals and blues and from slave narratives, it has persisted in fiction of the Great Migration from rural South to urban North of the early 1900s and since. Farah Jasmine Griffin has explored in some detail, in her study of migration narratives, the " 'push' factors that contributed to migration" out of the South, such as economic deprivation, educational deprivation, and violence (lynching). For women, these "push" factors included an additional element: sexual violence and exploitation—the threat and the reality both of rape and exploitation by white men and of domineering and abuse by black men.[27] Griffin points out that among twentieth-century migration narratives a unidirectional valuation of northerly movement as the way to (putative) freedom is adopted by Jean Toomer in *Cane,* by Richard Wright in *Uncle Tom's Children* and *Twelve Million Black Voices* as well as other works, and by painter Jacob Lawrence in his multi-panel narrative sequence *The Migration of the Negro* (1940–41).[28] We see that valuation, too, in the hopefulness and anticipation of Nella Larsen's Helga Crane, in *Quicksand* (1928), as she rides a train "rushing north," away from the manipulative system of self-abasement she experienced at southern Naxos College.[29] When the direction is reversed, when Helga, disappointed and denied both in the North and in Europe, returns south after marrying a preacher she scarcely knows, she falls again into bondage, though of a different and more inescapable (biological) kind—repeated pregnancy.

Directionality in the abundant and varied tradition of African-American literature is not, however, so simple as a mere rejection of the South in favor of the North. In the folktales of literal flight drawn on by Morrison in *Song of Solomon* and Naylor in *Mama Day,* the direction of liberation and restoration to power and autonomous (but also communal) selfhood is eastward, toward Africa. It is "in Africa" rather than in heaven that Janie and Tea Cake's friend Lias, in *Their Eyes Were Watching God,* promises to meet them "if Ah never see you no mo' on earth" (148). "Southern" may be, as Griffin proposes, "a metaphor for all sites where black people are dispossessed, disenfranchised, and brutalized," but the "South" left by African Americans "running from want and violence" to New York in Morrison's *Jazz* encompasses East St. Louis (where race riots orphan and dislocate the girl Dorcas) and such other northerly places as "Springfield Ohio, Springfield Indiana, Greensburg Indiana, Wilmington Delaware," where "whites had foamed all over the lanes and yards of home."[30] Even when the literal direction is changed, though, it is still departure from what is represented by the South, the hell of Sterling A. Brown's bitterly humorous poem "Slim in Hell": "De place was Dixie / Dat I took for Hell," Slim laments, to which St. Peter replies, "Where'n hell dja think Hell *was,* / Anyhow?"[31]

Still, despite the South's unquestioned role as the site of servitude and its legacies, a southerly direction and southward movement may at times be associated with nostalgia or return to an authenticating past. South carries such troubling connotations, for example, in Morrison's *Beloved* and *Song of Solomon*—troubling, because the nostalgia it evokes can never be separated from its evil. In works of the greatest complexity, the South becomes the locus of an all too real ambiguity. The return to the South may be, for the woman writer, a return to the site of black women's lives and creativity, as it is for Alice Walker in her memories of her mother's gardening, but it is also a return to the site of the foremother's captivity and brutalization. This compounding of comforting associations of home with threatening ones recalls the similar ambiguity we have seen in the work of Mary Austin and others, but here it is exacerbated by overwhelming historical fact.

Such an ambiguity in the meaning of southerly direction and southward movement contributes to the richness of Hurston's *Their Eyes Were Watching God,* perhaps the single most important work in the black tradition that contextualizes Toni Morrison's work. A novel of gender liberation and achievement of female selfhood as well as of racial liberation and validation, Hurston's powerful work is structured by paradox, not only directionally but in other respects as well. The most powerful paradox is the fact that Janie's achievement of freedom comes as a result of a journey south, rather than north, a journey that, like Nancy's escape to Canada in *Sapphira and the Slave Girl,* is at once a heroic quest and an errand. That is, Janie's geographic movement is controlled largely by the will of another. This may mean, as Mary Helen Washington states, that the "questing hero as woman" was a problem Hurston "could not solve"; she had to make Janie dependent on a male guide.[32] But it seems to me that she did solve the problem, by extending Janie's *Bildungsroman* not just to the threshold of adulthood but to the free space of fulfilled widowhood. By the time she completes her journey, returning alone and insouciantly to Eatonville, Hurston's questing hero(ine) is fully independent and fully competent.

Beginning her life in West Florida under the domination of her grandmother, Nanny, who conceives of her care for the girl as the provision of a "highway through de wilderness," Janie expresses her urge for freedom by "gaz[ing] up and down the road" (*Their Eyes,* 15, 11). Her idea of the road is considerably different from her grandmother's. While Nanny thinks in terms of the narrowness of the road and the dangers alongside (her daughter "got lost offa de highway"), for Janie it is the inviting length of the road that is important, the distance it can take a person. Her marriage to old Mr. Killicks at Nanny's insistence does not take her far down that road, since his sixty acres are located literally within walking distance of Nanny's home and he desires to squelch rather than nurture her aspirations. On the other hand, since his sixty acres are conveniently located "right on de big road" (22) and his domineering behavior galvanizes Janie's determination to strike out for the horizon, that first marriage does lead indirectly to her ultimate achievement of greater freedom. When Joe Starks comes down the road speaking for "far horizon . . . change and chance" (28), Janie heads east and south with him to Eatonville (Hurston's actual birthplace near Orlando, founded in 1886). When she takes up with Tea Cake, after Starks's death, they go about a hundred miles farther south to an area of rich black farmland near Lake Okeechobee: the area Tea Cake refers to as being "on de muck." There Janie enjoys the greatest personal freedom she has ever known, though not the greatest she will know.

This seeming inversion of the directional assignments of freedom and servitude, release coming through southerly rather than northerly movement, is based on two factors. First, as Hurston explains in her autobiography, the "lake country" of Florida was an area of comparative wildness and freedom from the South's plantation system. As the stronghold of Indians who in the latter 1700s waged a "last great struggle" (culminating in the Seminole War in the 1830s) against white planters whose own stronghold lay farther north, it remained a site receptive to black fugitives willing to join with still resistant tribes. White settlement, mostly spreading down from the north, arrived later there than in other parts of the South.[33] Thus, southward movement in this case was, comparatively speaking, a move away from the center of (white) political power in the South, which meant a move away from the historic center of repression. A second factor, though, that makes Janie and Tea Cake's southward movement one toward freedom is that in going "on de muck" they join a community which they experience as liberating in its friendliness and mutual encouragement. As DuPlessis summarizes the action of the novel, Janie "breaks out of the narrow definitions of womanhood understandably bequeathed by the rigid and fearful ex-slave, her grandmother," and breaks out of her first two husbands' authoritarian view of marriage to a "growing identification with folk life." Similarly, Washington celebrates Hurston's structuring of a narrative journey "not away from, but deeper and deeper into blackness, the descent into the Everglades with its rich black soil, wild cane, and communal life representing immersion into black traditions." Janie moves, Jerome Thornton puts it, "from conventional materialism back to her black heritage."[34]

In addition to north and south, upward and downward directions are also important in *Their Eyes Were Watching God,* as they were in the traditional slave narrative (Stepto identifies Frederick Douglass's *Narrative* as "the paradigmatic narrative of ascent")[35] and as they are in Morrison's work. Accordingly, Janie's grandmother establishes in her narrative of hardship and escape to the wilderness an emblematic pattern of high and low ground. The low, swampy places where she and her baby were threatened by poisonous snakes yield, in her vision, to the "high ground" she wants to seize for her daughter and then for Janie (*Their Eyes,* 15–16). Later, Janie and Tea Cake's ordeal in the flood recalls Nanny's ordeal in the swamp, as they search for *literal* high ground. Before the hurricane comes, however, their experience illustrates, as Dixon says, the paradox that "the lowlands can be high ground,"[36] as the low-lying Everglades farmland affords them a peak of self-fulfillment through chosen work and friendship. In another sense, however, it constitutes a low in Janie's experience of black society, since it forces her to realize the fact of color-based prejudice among her own people. Her final climbing of the stairs toward her upstairs bedroom, at the end of the novel, derives much of its significance from this carefully prepared pattern of low and high.

Like Hurston, later writers Alice Walker, Toni Morrison, and Gloria Naylor also free their narratives of departure and journey from a rigid geographical symbolism in which only upward and northerly movements can indicate release and transcendence. They, too, affirm their southern heritage, much as Hurston affirmed it in her fiction and in her return to the South to study folk materials and later to spend her hard-pressed last years. The value of a sense of at-homeness, of being rooted in one's native place, is affirmed by all of these writers, even when that native place is redolent of historic oppression. In Walker's *Meridian,* return to the South brings liberating fulfillment to the confused civil rights worker who reaches a moral and per-sonal "elevation" by going "*down* among the people," a kind of submersion that also entails an inward descent to fundamental selfhood.[37] In Naylor's *Mama Day,* a daughter of the South who had gone to New York in pursuit of a liberated life returns south to discover the fullest affirmation of love and release from corrosive self-doubt and envy of whites. Similarly, Milkman Dead in Morrison's *Song of Solomon* travels from Michigan to Pennsylvania and on southward to Virginia in order to achieve an understanding of his familial and cultural heritage and a complex personal freedom. The South, for him, is a "site of history and redemption" where he can "begin to piece together the fragments" of the heritage that makes sense of his life.[38] Even so, the play of movement in these novels gains its significance and its complex-ity from this grounding in and play against a well-established association of north with freedom.

In *Their Eyes Were Watching God,* Janie's movement from her grand-mother's house through her two successive marriages and then to a freely loving relationship with Tea Cake and community with other farm workers is also a liberation from silencing. That liberation is confirmed when she returns to Eatonville and, in the frame story that demonstrates her empow-erment as a speaker, narrates her experiences to her friend Pheoby. Her grandmother had also been a powerful speaker, but because of her condi-tioning by slavery could only speak a language of fear and caution. Explicitly invoking a metaphor of confinement in describing the hardships that have conditioned her life—she speaks of "de hold-backs of slavery"—Nanny ex-plains that since she was born in those circumstances she couldn't "fulfill [her] dreams of whut a woman oughta be and to do" (15). Although she wishes that Janie could fulfill such dreams, fear causes her to arrange a mar-riage to a propertied older man, the only way she knows to spare her grand-daughter the hardships she has suffered herself. Janie's progression from that imprisoning marriage to the marriage with Starks that is seemingly liberat-ing but actually imprisoning in a different way (she is bound by a role that will enhance her husband's status) subjects her to explicit silencing. After

Joe's repeated insistence that she has no business speaking out and, being a woman, no ability to think, she finally "pressed her teeth together and learned to hush" (67). But when she manages to follow the road that beckons to her—that is, to live her life as she wants to live it and to experience a loving sexual relationship—she achieves freedom both from the history of slavery that has controlled her by way of her grandmother's fears and from an imprisoning and silencing system of gender relations. She can now dress as she chooses, let her long hair hang freely, and—the culminating freedom—tell her own story with her own interpretations. Like Cather's Nancy in *Sapphira and the Slave Girl,* published three years after *Their Eyes Were Watching God,* but in an idiom of her own that does not require the white validation Cather would feel impelled to give Nancy's speech, Janie has achieved both authority and capability. Fifty years after Janie, Morrison's Sethe, in *Beloved,* would also achieve freedom from the haunting past of slavery only after she had managed, at last, to speak of it, speaking to the very bodied medium of that haunting.

In discussing Hurston's novel, Elizabeth Meese refers to speech as "one of the highest forms of achievement and artistry in the folk community." The fact that that self-authenticating power had been denied Janie, most obviously by her second husband, signals the status of *Their Eyes Were Watching God* as a narrative of the departure from the home of gender discrimination and constraint as well as of the history of racial discrimination, from slavery both literal and figurative. In addition to a freed speech, Meese argues, Janie achieves a "new epistemology" grounded in direct experience, the theory of knowledge she enunciates aphoristically as "Yuh got tuh *go* there tuh *know* there" (*Their Eyes,* 183). "Having gone there," Meese adds, "you are changed, and the story you have to tell is a different story."[39] The reader, of course, "goes there" by reading Hurston, as Pheoby "goes" by listening to Janie. In a sense, then, this "new epistemology" is undermined by Hurston's own text. But in the sense that Janie fulfills it, it serves to constitute her as the knower and the validated speaker.

Janie's struggle, survival, and claiming of the right and power to tell her story define her long journey as a heroic quest. Culminating an image pattern that pervades the novel, she has "done been tuh de horizon and back," and at the end she is able to tell herself with satisfaction that she could now pull in her horizon "like a great fish-net" with "so much of life in its meshes!" (*Their Eyes,* 182, 184). Similarly, Hurston says in her own person at the end of *Dust Tracks on a Road* that "already I have touched the four corners of the horizon" (255). But the horizon remains largely empty of specificity, except as it is associated with wishes and "dreams mocked to death by Time" at the beginning of the novel. The fact that Janie's experience is so often subjected to male dominance (willingly so, when she submits to Tea Cake's intermittently impulsive and dominant behaviors) demonstrates, like Nancy Till's inability to will, let alone to direct, her own escape in *Sapphira and the Slave Girl,* the difficulty of reconceiving the traditionally masculine quest as a woman's venture. Janie assures Pheoby, before she leaves with Tea Cake, that she "jus' loves dis freedom" (*Their Eyes,* 89)—a condition necessary to full heroism. But after her journey toward the horizon ceases being an escape, she leaves its direction largely to him. We see something of the same problem or conundrum in Alice Walker's *The Color Purple,* where escape is clearly motivated and happily accomplished, but the nature of the questing journey, whether it is Shug's or Celie's or Nellie's, is either unclear or scarcely credible, a quasi-fairytale of (compelling) wish fulfillment.

It is within this rich tradition of (to borrow Walker's term) womanist and African-American aspiration and heroism, as well as within the context of her own earlier works, that I wish to read Morrison's *Beloved* and *Jazz,* works in which the heroic quest is both fulfilled and believable. The stature of both novels is derived in part from the fullness of their humanity, but in large part, too, from their appropriation of magical realism, a merger of the fantastic with the realistic linked to their secure grounding in history. In both of these novels the sense of the past is importantly dual: history is both to be escaped and to be recovered and reclaimed.

In *Playing in the Dark,* Morrison lists "some topics that need critical investigation" by literary scholars. Among these she calls for analysis of the "manipulation" by whites of the "Africanist narrative . . . of being bound and/or rejected" as a "means of meditation—both safe and risky—on one's own humanity." In effect, she calls for an analysis of narrative in the Africanist tradition that will demonstrate how that narrative unites concern with the private or individual with concern with the public or communal, so that address of "one's own humanity" becomes an opportunity for address of "ethics, social and universal codes of behavior, and assertions about and definitions of civilization and reason." Morrison concludes, "Criticism of this type will show how that narrative is used in the construction of a history and a context for whites by positing history-lessness and context-lessness for blacks."[40] That is, her thesis throughout this group of polemical essays is that just as whites have visualized their "white"-ness largely by contrast to blackness or darkness, so have whites been enabled to define themselves as free and possessed of a glorious history only by dwelling on a definition of African Americans as bound and lacking a worthwhile history.

The challenge to black writers in our time who, drawing on the rich but heretofore generally unrecognized heritage of African-American literary tradition, have wished to create lyric and narrative works addressing both the personal and the public, has been to refuse to allow this construction by whites of a state of "history-lessness and context-lessness." The task of these writers has been to escape the "history" constructed by whites and disseminated in generations of textbooks that in effect robbed black people of their own history, both in the sense of a factual knowledge of the past and in the sense of interpretive voice, the subjectified telling of that past. The task of African-American writers has also been to address the past, that is, events that actually occurred, so as to constitute that previously silenced historic voice, the voice of scholars and writers interpreting events from their own, rather than an imposed, perspective. Morrison's fiction has accomplished such a dual task of re-historicizing the experience of African people and their descendants on the North American continent. She has constructed a new vision of the past of her people, a retelling that does not elide but rather foregrounds those elements obscured by Europhile telling of history. Such an accomplishment of the informed imagination entails both the act of telling/writing and the act of escaping the heritage of deprivation and affront imposed by the formerly (and to a great extent, still) hegemonic history.

Morrison shows her readers that until blacks escape the white-constructed history of servitude and its heritage of denial of black selfhood (in Craig Hansen Werner's words, denial of "the reality of [African Americans'] experience"),[41] they are trapped in its falsifying terms and doomed to disintegration, just as the text of the long-standard Dick and Jane reader, posed at the beginning of *The Bluest Eye,* disintegrates into jibberish. The Dick and Jane reader assumed a familial situation alien (in more ways than just in its illustrations of white family members) to the experience of black children to whom it was assigned. Moreover, through its repeated imperatives—

"See Jane," "See the cat," "Come and play," "Come play," "See Mother,"
"Laugh, Mother, laugh," "See Father," "Smile, Father, smile," "See the dog,"
"Run, dog," "Play, Jane"—it demanded imaginative conformity with such a
vision. The text not only imposed desires and aspirations impossible to attain but in effect denied an alternative identity. Figuratively, the Dick and
Jane reader forced black-eyed children to wish for blue eyes—that is, for that
which was as contrary to social fact as blue eyes would be contrary to nature. Those unable to achieve the impossibility demanded by the reader simply did not exist in its universe.

Like the black children who had to attempt to learn to read by means of
a text irrelevant to their experience, which held up for their assent a version of life bearing no resemblance to their marginalized and radically exploited experience of America, so black people in general have been expected to "read" their lives through a version of history that belies or ignores
their ancestral experience. In Adrienne Rich's words with reference to another marginalized and exploited group, they have had to read from "a book
of myths / in which / [their] names do not appear."[42] Just as black schoolchildren learning to read from a Dick and Jane reader were expected to be-
have as if the goals and ideals they found there were plausible for their
lives—an attempt and an expectation that Morrison says destroys them, as
Pecola's sanity is destroyed by the wish for and the delusion of blue eyes—so
have black Americans been expected to conduct their economic and social
lives in accordance with the standards of the group writing the history, while
living with the bitter heritage of the actual but unacknowledged history (that
which was experienced, that which occurred) belied by the official (expur-
gated, white-idealizing) version, the history told in books. The result of so
extreme a dissonance between theory and actuality, between the accepted
version and the lived experience belied by that version, is the profound and
widespread anomie with which we are all now familiar.

In *The Bluest Eye*, Morrison brilliantly conveys that discordance and the
complex process of its far-reaching effects through the device of the deteriorating Dick and Jane text, set in apposition to Pecola's personal deterioration.
The novel opens with a straight transcription of the vapid reader itself, followed by the same text run together without punctuation or capitalization,
then the same text without spaces between words: a vomit of letters. Periodically throughout the book, fragments of the opening Dick and Jane text
return with distorted repetitions or curtailments. These misshapen frag-

ments of the text according to which American experience was read by schoolchildren comment with bitterest irony on the novelistic text proper. The deterioration of the Dick and Jane text represents and expresses the destructive process instilled in the rationality and selfhood of the reading black child. By extension, it represents or conveys the destructive process instilled in African Americans generally and in their sense of self-esteem and community by the imposition of an alien version of history within which they have been expected to live and interpret their lives. Caught between a frustrated wish to emulate the white culture that oppresses her (the wish for blue eyes) and a futile wish to escape that oppression, Pecola stands with "elbows bent, hands on shoulders, [flailing] her arms like a bird in an eternal, grotesquely futile effort to fly"—a negative anticipation of Morrison's positive use of the story of flying Africans in *Song of Solomon*.[43] The causes impelling her flight firmly established, Pecola is seen in a thwarted enactment of the "leap from land into sky" that Dixon calls the "principal movement in Morrison's fiction."[44]

In succeeding novels, when Morrison returns to the motif of flight or an impulse toward flight, that aspiration is not always so frustrated as Pecola's. In her second novel, *Sula,* she creates a sequence of black women poised between a yearning for escape and a shaping rootedness: Helene, who has shaped her life by her determination to go north so as to get "as far away" from New Orleans "as possible"; Helene's daughter, Nel, who tries to define herself by the fact of a journey back south, thinking she had "gone on a real trip, and now she was different"; and Nel's friend Sula, who, when Nel chooses the conventionalism of marriage, turns a departing back.[45] Sula stays gone for ten years, her life during that time summarized as a list of place-names: "Nashville, Detroit, New Orleans, New York, Philadelphia, Macon and San Diego" (*Sula,* 104). Her return is heralded by a plague of robins, emblematic, perhaps, of her impulse—and ability—to fly.[46] Unlike Nel, who only thought her traveling had transformed her, Sula finds in her freedom of movement the freedom of selfhood: "Girl, I got my mind. And what goes on in it. Which is to say, I got me" (123). In Morrison's own words, Sula is "sort of an outlaw . . . available to her own imagination."[47]

The structure of *Sula* ultimately devolves as much on houses as on departures and journeys, specifically Nel's conventional home and the unconventional, multigenerational structure where the freer-spirited Sula lived as a child, into which she withdraws after her return, and where she finally dies.[48] Even so, despite her lapse into stasis in her grandmother's boarded-up room after her friendship with Nel is disrupted by a combination of her own sexual rapacity (she initiates a sexual relationship with Nel's husband) and Nel's conventional possessiveness of her husband, Sula continues throughout her life, for good or ill, to depart from convention. In contrast, Nel, who once saw the central act of her life as a journey, has settled into convention-ality and timidness. Only after Sula's death does Nel realize that the man over whom she broke off their friendship was of far less importance to her life than Sula had been. Her realization is validated, but its futility, in that it is belated, is imaged as a circular motion, going nowhere.

Just as *Sula,* with its pattern of at least a partly fulfilled flight, reverses the frustration of the urge to fly in *The Bluest Eye,* so *Song of Solomon* reverses the attitude toward return to the South conveyed in *Sula.* After her escape from New Orleans to the North, Helene made only one trip back and found it a humiliating re-immersion in overt racial prejudice.[49] But Milkman Dead finds enlightenment and restoration in returning to his southern roots.

The earlier novels' embedded motif of an urge to fly blossoms in *The Song of Solomon* into a central myth of achieved escape by flight, as Morrison draws on and brings into twentieth-century life the traditional story of slaves who rose from their work in the field and flew away back to Africa—the same powerful myth that Naylor draws on in *Mama Day.* Before his journey south, Milkman "thinks constantly of escape, of slamming the door of his father's house and never returning, of flying away."[50] The frustration of that escape wish by his overpowering urge to achieve the wealth and social prominence that his father values is conveyed in an image of a beautiful white peacock that cannot fly because it is weighed down by the "shit" of vain plumage.[51] Returning to the past of his family origins in Shalimar, Vir-ginia, stripped of the accoutrements of his false (white-centered) self-es-teem, he becomes capable of wonderment. Learning of his descent from a slave believed to have flown away back to Africa, he exclaims in amazement, "He could fly! You hear me? My great-granddaddy could fly! Goddam!" (331). The song he hears being sung by the children of Shalimar (a corrup-tion of "Shalleemone," or "Solomon"), which includes a reference to Jay or Jake, his grandfather, ends,

Solomon done fly, Solomon done gone
Solomon cut across the sky, Solomon gone home.

Milkman, too, has gone home, and if it is not clear, at the end, that he can literally fly, he can at least trust himself to the air and to the "killing arms of his brother" (341).

It is tempting and easy to read Milkman's story as one of redemption and enablement through identification with the heroic male ancestor. And indeed the voice of the novel (an elusive voice, to be sure) does rejoice with him in his elation at discovering that his great-grandfather "could fly!" One hears, behind the narrative voice, Morrison's personal voice avowing her delight in masculine spatial transcendence, the fact that they would "split in a minute." But again the tale exceeds the teller's avowal, just as Milkman, at the end, in fact *excels* his great-grandfather—precisely because he has learned a different story in addition to the story of male flight. Michael Awkward astutely points out that Milkman's "monomythic quest" is interrupted by another story, that of Hagar's self-deprecation and death, which "expose[s] phallocentric myth's failure to inscribe usefully transcendent possibilities for the female." Milkman must learn, and Awkward insists that the critical reader must also learn, not only the "joy of knowledge-informed male flight" but also the "immeasurable pain of desertion felt by females" such as Hagar and also Milkman's great-grandmother, left behind with her many children when her husband, in effect a spectacular *pater absconditus,* takes to the air.[52] Milkman reaches a more fully human transcendence than his great-grandfather because of his awakening to a literally fuller humanity—one that regards desire and liberation from a female as well as a male perspective. Like Paul D in *Beloved,* he moves toward androgyny and dares to fly toward, rather than away from, human arms.

Song of Solomon is considered by many of Morrison's readers her finest work. It was *Beloved,* however, that earned her the Pulitzer Prize and resulted in the award of the Nobel Prize. Reviewers summoned up their greatest superlatives in describing the book, calling it compelling, majestic, a triumph, searing, shatteringly eloquent, richly mythical, stunning, extraordinary. In my own reading and that of many others who have found themselves returning to the book again and again, it is all of that. But why? In essence, I believe, because *Beloved* is a novel so deeply engaged with African-American history that it both escapes the inadequate representations that have belied and in great measure eradicated that history (often by minimizing its horrors) and, at the same time, brings to life the authentically lived past that constitutes the basis for a new and more adequate representation. The heroic departure and journey seen in the story of Sethe's and Paul D's escapes from slavery in the South to triumphant new life in the (however flawed) borderline North is also the journey from an inadequate to a restored history situated, as Sally Keenan notes, within the larger context of the African diaspora.[53] *Beloved* resonantly evokes the past and restores it (re-members it, puts it back together) to present meaning, and even to present livingness, since, as Morrison writes, "nothing ever dies."[54]

Morrison, like Hurston, succeeds in delineating a female questing hero by aligning her portraiture with the structure of an extended *Bildungsroman*. She also solves the "problem" that Washington identifies (of shaping a "questing hero as woman") by placing her in partnership with a male questing hero. Not only does Paul D achieve freedom and a full, self-defining (though still societally limited) selfhood, but he achieves a fully humanized identity by defining himself, in part, in feminine terms.[55] Sethe's long journey, completed both with the help of and despite the opposition of Paul D, is complex in that it involves a quest for freedom and selfhood that is grounded in historic fact and in a richly historic imagination. Her quest is crossed by issues of race, by a conflicted sense of nostalgia for the place escaped, and by issues of gender and of gendered human sharing. Indeed, it directly engages, at various points, the difficult intersection of race with gender that is sometimes so confounding in feminist discourse.[56]

Sethe departs on that quest from a state of literal enslavement so constituted that she had no knowledge of the world outside the farm that bounded her permissible life and no right to exert even her own mothering. The condition at which she arrives, seemingly in completion of the quest but actually in completion of only the most literally geographical portion of it, is a state of insecure freedom haunted by the specter of return and the long aftermath of that social and historic condition. Morrison based her character on a factual predecessor, Margaret Garner, a fugitive in Cincinnati in 1851 who, in an act that has been called an "emancipatory assault,"[57] killed her child with a butcher knife and tried to kill her other children (and herself) in order to prevent their recapture into slavery. Similarly, in an act of horrifying love, Sethe beheads the baby to whom she had struggled so hard to bring her milk. The murder of her child was, in her compelling belief, the only way to protect her from having to experience slavery, a state that Sethe implicitly defines as being worse than death. The return of the spirit of the murdered infant to haunt Sethe and the house where she lives is not only a representation of her sense of guilt for having killed her baby but a figurative statement of the haunting of black lives in general by the past, that is, by slavery's long (and indeed still persisting) after-effects. When Paul D exorcises the ghost, its power reasserts itself in intensified form in the fully bodied return of Beloved, the young woman who emerges from water (at once death, the subconscious, and amniotic fluid) to reclaim her own infancy and forestalled maturation even as she recalls (because Sethe's past is inseparable from the group past) the collective memory of the Middle Passage.[58] The presence of Beloved, who finally becomes a kind of vampire, is a sign that the past is completely taking over Sethe's present life. Trudier Harris reads the destructive fixation of Sethe and Beloved on each other during the latter quarter of the novel as a parodic reinscription of slavery, in that they seek to own each other. "Human freedom," she adds, "is not about ownership or possession."[59] Re-memory does not have to mean letting oneself be devoured by the past.

In moving from the South to the North and from slavery to a limited and haunted freedom, Sethe moves, too, from warmth to cold, from a desire to express her sexuality in love to a fear of expressing it. The directional symbolism is ambiguous. In a brilliantly conceived and realized way that is fully convincing psychologically, the devouring presence of the past prevents her from conquering her fear of loving and thus fulfilling this aspect of her quest. Her release from the dead past (from the vampire that Beloved has become) is accomplished by her own and Paul D's victory over that compellingly motivated fear of sexual love, figured in his case by an image of his heart, his capacity for love, as a box whose lid is rusted shut. But it is only because Paul D has been able to persevere in his own quest and because he is able to achieve a fully human, feminized self—he is shown at the end caring for Sethe in much the same way as Baby Suggs once cared for her—that the two are together able to complete the journey and make Number 124 Bluestone Road, for the first time, really a home, still full of memories (revalued memories, re-memories) but no longer haunted. The novel's pervasive language of departure and journey, roads and wayfaring, maps, in effect, these undertakings and Paul D's and Sethe's achievement.

It is not, however, a unidirectional map. The South from which Sethe and Paul D have escaped, and from which Baby Suggs, Sethe's saintlike mother-in-law, was redeemed by her son's laborious purchase and the resettlement efforts of emancipationists, is presented as a surprisingly ambiguous region. Harboring atrocities at every turn, it nevertheless harbored, as well, a home that was in some sense a "sweet" one. In memory, its natural presence seems one of verdant fertility: vegetal abundance, big shade trees, richly brooding nights. Sweet Home, the farm in Kentucky from which Baby Suggs was redeemed and where Paul D and Sethe (and their friends) later suffered atrocities until she escaped and he was sold, was for a time an enclave where male slaves were treated like men and female slaves could bring flowers into the house to cheer their work. In comparison to conditions experienced by slaves at other farms and plantations, the life it afforded was idyllic. But the point is that even this best the South could offer—a best for which Sethe and Paul sometimes become nostalgic—was a prison, since the slaves who lived there were forbidden to venture beyond its bounds. If they did they were liable to brutalizing treatment. The participation of Sweet Home in an evil system meant that it could not in fact be "sweet." The name is inescapably ironic. Denver catches this truth when she says (though for her own reasons), "Look like if it was so sweet you would have stayed" (*Beloved,* 13). Its sweetness was deceptive. Mr. Garner, the benevolent master there, might have called the Pauls and Sixo men, but that was only his "naming" (125). They could not name themselves men, nor could they hope that any white man outside Sweet Home would do so.[60] Moreover, the sweetness Sweet Home afforded was not only delusive but fragile, since it was solely dependent on the life and impulse of a single man. When Mr. Garner died, the sweet prison became, with the advent of a different master, not merely a prison but a hell.

The imprisonment suffered at Sweet Home by all its black people is made real and tangible (rendered in what T. S. Eliot called an "objective correlative") in the experience of Paul D, who, after killing the abusive master to whom he was sold, is sent to prison and locked in a subterranean box. The chain with which Paul D and the other prisoners are fastened together is a tangible sign of his linkage to a shared heritage and a shared dehumanization. From that very literal prison, a descent into an all too convincing approximation of hell, he and the forty-five other black prisoners to whom he is chained escape by "wad[ing]" and "scrambl[ing]" out during a flood. Water delivers him, just as it harbors and ultimately delivers the ghost of Beloved, the embodiment of both a personal and a collective past. Just as his escape from being buried alive (a narrative passage of the most acutely realized horror) could have been accomplished in no other way except through the instinctive, seemingly miraculous cooperation of the entire group, so his and Sethe's achievement of full selfhood can be achieved only within and with the help of a community possessing a shared history of suffering, departure, journey, and reconstruction.

Like Paul D's chain, Sethe's suppurating scars, swollen feet, and laden uterus are tangible signs that when she goes "running off" from the horror that Sweet Home has become she carries the past, both personal and collective, with her. Taking along the burden of a past that they must later confront and try to understand despite their desire to escape it, both are impelled to departure by the affront of their incarceration and by very specific atrocities. In Paul D's case, these include such physical punishment as the wearing of an iron bit, the spectacle of systematic rape of his fellow prisoners by the prison guards, and burial alive in snake-infested ground (78, 107–10).[61] In Sethe's case they range from the general—"dogs, perhaps; guns probably," the implements of enforcement that were part of the shared experience of fugitives—to the separate and peculiar: her savage beating and such degradation as the repugnant "mossy teeth" of Schoolteacher's white nephews who, in a shocking parody of both sexual congress and infantile dependence, sucked her milk-filled breasts in a perverted kind of rape, a rape of her maternity itself.

After his escape, Paul D defines himself by his movement, calling himself "a walking man" who has been "all around this place. Upstate, downstate, east, west; I been in territory ain't got no name, never staying nowhere long" (46). The ability to move represents his unfamiliar freedom. At the same time, it represents his inability to remain in one place for long, his fearful reluctance to settle and to form emotional ties. With admirable aesthetic tact, the book elides particularities of Paul D's journey not only because they would detract from the focus on his and Sethe's mutuality and the surrealistic conflict that occurs when he finds her, but because we are to read his journey, not as peculiar to himself, but as the epitome of many like it, both when he escapes and when he continues to drift. He represents what Stepto calls the "archetypal . . . weary traveler" of the slave narrative.[62] Morrison explicitly takes in, beyond the wandering figure of Paul D, a vast social movement in continuation of the African diaspora:

> The War had been over four or five years then, but nobody white or black seemed to know it. Odd clusters and strays of Negroes wandered the back roads and cowpaths from Schenectady to Jackson. Dazed but insistent, they searched each other out for word of a cousin, an aunt, a friend who once said, "Call on me. Anytime you get near Chicago, just call on me." Some of them were running from family that could not support them, some to family; some were running from dead crops, dead kin, life threats, and took-over land. Boys younger than Buglar and Howard; configurations and blends of families of women and children, while elsewhere, solitary, hunted and hunting for, were men, men, men. Forbidden public transportation, chased by debt and filthy "talking sheets," they followed secondary routes, scanned the horizon for signs and counted heavily on each other. Silent, except for social courtesies, when they met one another they neither described nor asked about the sorrow that drove them from one place to another. (*Beloved,* 52–53)

Howard and Buglar, Sethe's sons, are in fact scarcely seen in the novel except in the act of running away from the haunting presence of the past, manifest both in the infant ghost and in their fear that Sethe might kill them as she did Beloved. They are only two small side effects of the great hegira of escape, drivenness, search for human connection, and volitional expression of the freedom to go: all combined. Their departure is a reenactment of their family's, and many other black families', history of geographic scattering. Baby Suggs's husband had also "run," and two sons had "cut" (142–43). It is against this vast spectacle of dislocation and search that we read Sethe and Paul D's story of the road and of finding one another and making "a life" (46).

Just as Paul D is impelled into escape and transience by the abuses he experienced in Georgia, so is he unhoused by the power of Beloved's return from the other side. She is the ultimately unknowable embodiment of a past that has already gone on haunting him in other ways, anytime his energies were not totally taken up with the essentials of living. But it is only the story of Sethe's killing of her baby that sends him once again into real transience. By this time he is tired of being a fugitive; he wants to make "an exit that is not an escape" (164). Nevertheless, the knowledge of how Sethe violated her motherhood in order to fulfill it—that is, to fulfill her determination to nurture her children by keeping them away from slavery—is a shock that drives him into drunkenness and living on the street, sleeping where he can.[63]

Streets and roads carry a varied freight of associations in this novel. In addition to dislocation and transience, they convey certainly the traditional meaning of the road of life, the cumulative course of experience in both the social and the personal sense. It is this sense that is uppermost when Stamp Paid, a kind of folk saint who ferries slaves across the Ohio River to free soil and then helps arrange for their care, stops one day in his tracks and turns to "look back down the road he was travelling," seeing behind him not only an actual road but the road of his whole life and the road of history. One thing that road has taught him is amazement at the perfidy of whites: "He turned to look back," that is, at the actual road he has just walked, "and said, to its frozen mud and the river beyond, 'What *are* these people? You tell me, Jesus. What *are* they?' " (180). At other points the road and the town street serve, more specifically, as a means and medium of solidarity. The escaping and emancipated slaves' journey is a cooperative one. "Nobody could make it alone . . . you could be lost forever, if there wasn't nobody to show you the way" (137). Stamp Paid's ferrying, his back-and-forth journeys across the Ohio River, are a part of that showing.

A series of meetings in streets also provides the way back to healing and community. Stamp Paid meets with Baby Suggs in the street and tries to hearten her. Paul D, Denver, and Sethe go to the carnival, and their shadows on the road form the shape of their potential for familial solidarity—a potential that is disrupted by Denver's insecurity and Beloved's demanding presence, but one that is ultimately fulfilled. Stamp Paid meets Paul D on the street when he is far gone in drink and takes steps to find him a place to stay, a place in the community, and help in getting past his shock at Sethe's deed—a meeting that proves redemptive. Denver, so traumatized by her family past and by the hostility of whites in the outer world that she has not ventured into the street in years, finally, when Sethe is near destruction by the ghost of her past, becomes sufficiently galvanized by concern for her mother (and by simple hunger) that she forces herself out into the public way to find help.[64] That venture, too, proves redemptive, as Denver emerges into adult competence and begins to build herself a life.

In the culminating sequence of the novel, the street again serves as the avenue of redemption through community as neighbor women gather in Bluestone Road in front of 124 to drive out the ghost with whom Sethe has locked herself up. These women, coming belatedly to save one of their own, serve as a chorus of prayerful communal support when she emerges to attack a representative of white society who happens to pass in the street at the same time. Ironically, it is Bodwin, the Quaker emancipationist who has helped Sethe and many others. Seeing him approach, she relives the approach of Schoolteacher years before, when he came to take her and her children back to slavery. This time, however, she directs her mistaken attack at the astonished embodiment of her oppression, rather than at her own child, now grown to an ominously pregnant maturity. With this direct enactment of her rage, the vampiric ghost of the past retreats. Finally, it is by way of this same Bluestone Road that Paul D returns to care for Sethe in ways that very specifically parallel Baby Suggs's care when she first arrived at 124, at the completion of the first phase of her quest.

Beloved's presence in the narrative also, of course, follows the structure of a journey. She walks "out of the water" and waits beside the road (50). Quizzed about her origins, she insists (in the childish idiom that reflects her incomplete maturation process) that she had walked "a long, long, long, long way" (65). It was indeed a long, long way: all the way, we are to believe, from "crawling-already" infancy to early adulthood, and all the way, in recapitulation, from Africa through the Middle Passage. That larger, historic journey is hauntingly if confusingly summarized in one of the two short chapters near the end of the book whose style moves well beyond narrative prose into a new expressive territory for which we have no name. Like many other women writers of the departure from confining roles and the journey to assertive selfhood—writers such as Sandra Cisneros and Gloria Anzaldúa—Morrison transgresses generic boundaries as she envisions the breaking of social boundaries.

It is out of and against all this—the long heritage of capture, the Middle Passage, group persistence through and beyond death, the journeys of fugitives and lost emancipated slaves like Paul D, Sixo's woman who escapes with his seed growing inside her, Baby Suggs's husband and sons, and the thousands of nameless others gathered into the epic story—that Sethe's heroic journey moves as the central action of the novel. Told intermittently, as she can bring herself to look back at that time, Sethe's story is one of heroic perseverance and strength as, despite a brutal beating that has laid open her back in a pattern as intricate as a tree and despite her late pregnancy and badly swollen feet, she keeps going. We see her "walking through the dark woods to get to her children who are far away" (77–78) and being assisted in her escape and the birth of Denver by a repressed and abused white girl who is herself a wanderer. Black and white, the oppressed achieve heroism through movement. The road of Sethe's life includes a wagon ride down Bluestone Road to prison after her murder of the baby, but it also includes the road back from prison and the long road she has walked to work as a cook for years since then, the same road that she follows around "one more curve" to lock herself up with her memories (199) and her fixation on her own guilt and the impossible need to make amends. It is little wonder that she and her two daughters—the one real, the other a spirit presence that we scarcely know whether to read as physically real or not—take delight in ice skating together: it is an act of free, gliding movement, driven by no one and nothing, aimed toward nothing—movement for its own sake—in which they are answerable to no one when they fall (174–75).

At the end, when Paul D returns to 124 to care for Sethe after both have reached what seems to be the end of their roads, he returns in much the same way as he first came north: through flowers. Escaping from prison and from the South, he had "raced from dogwood to blossoming peach," the "traveling companion" of spring as it "sauntered north" (112). Returning to Sethe's house, he is "amazed by the riot of late-summer flowers . . . sweet william, morning glory, chrysanthemums" (271). The road to the freedom of what will be a real home of mutuality is, like his first road to freedom, a way of beauty. Bathing Sethe just as Baby Suggs bathed her when she arrived filthy from her journey of escape, Paul D wants only to "put his story next to hers" (273). If they have not achieved what Stepto designates as the highest point in the ascending quest from South to North, literacy, they have at any rate achieved the freedom and the confidence to tell their own stories. And in Denver's expectation of attending Oberlin College, that achievement as well—the woman writer's achievement, perhaps, of textual telling of the story—is promised.

To the extent that Morrison herself, then, is identified with Denver through this last implied promise that Denver will achieve literary speech, she is positioned (as Cather is positioned in *Sapphira*) as the daughter of the good mother/bad mother, who might be defined as one who keeps her child free by keeping her away from the South. Morrison has said that her own mother "never once went back South to visit because her experience of it had been so bad" but "talked about it as though it were heaven, absolute heaven"[65]—or in other words, as if it were a very Sweet Home.

In *Jazz*, published five years after *Beloved*, Morrison again juxtaposes the story of a woman's departure and long journey against that of a man, and juxtaposes both against a great historic spectacle of movement, this time the Great Migration of rural African Americans to cities in the North in the early decades of the twentieth century. Once again the contextualizing presence of the historic past adds resonance to the story of individuals, and once again the past figures as the ongoing presence of the dead, again a murdered beloved, in a way that must be both encountered and ultimately escaped. That is not to say, however, that *Jazz* is merely a replication of its celebrated predecessor.[66] It is in fact a very different book, in a very different linguistic medium, one that invites analogy with jazz idioms and forms—an analogy securely grounded in an extensive theorizing of the linkage of jazz idiom and tradition with both African-American literature and postmodern fiction. For Houston Baker the quality that validates this analogy is movement. The blues as a form, he writes, exists in a "ceaseless flux." The blues artist is "always at this intersection, this crossing, codifying force, providing resonance for experience's multiplicities," because "singer and song never arrest transience."[67] Baker is speaking, of course, of "transience" with respect to musical idiom and structure. But transience is associated with the subject matter of blues lyrics as well. "Leaving/travel/journey" is commonly identified as one of the "pervasive themes" of the blues. Steven Tracy comments that the "frequent repetition among blues singers of 'I'm going away, babe' in some form suggests a pervasive need for escape or for finding something better."[68]

Morrison's interest in music is well established. She has often commented on the musical nature of her home life as she grew up, and has characterized jazz as "one of the most vital artistic forms in the world, having an "incredible kind of improvisation, a freedom in which a great deal of risk is involved."[69] Improvisatory freedom is indeed at the essence of *Jazz*, both thematically—in its concern with the achievement of the freedom both to draw on and to depart from the past, history—and stylistically. Verbal motifs and images "stated" in the opening return again and again, always with variation, as Morrison shows her virtuosity in playing changes. The call-and-response structure characteristic of the blues and gospel roots of jazz also provides a useful vehicle for conceptualizing the relationship between individual and community, as important a concern here in the story of Joe and Violet Trace's migration to New York and the evolution of their sense of belonging as it is in *Beloved*. Craig Hansen Werner proposes, in *Playing the Changes: From Afro-Modernism to the Jazz Impulse,* that the "jazz impulse (grounded in blues and gospel) engages basic (post)modernist concerns including the difficulty of defining, or even experiencing, the self; the fragmentation of public discourse; and the problematic meaning of tradition."[70] Morrison engages such problematics in *Jazz*. Like the blues artist Baker speaks of, she finds a structural and emotional "equivalence" for the "ceaseless flux" of African-American life in the 1920s—a time that she says her parents always spoke of in "gleaming terms of excitement and attraction."[71] In so doing, she places what Baker calls the "multiplicities" of the jazz form and also of 1920s Harlem at the center, rather than the periphery, of twentieth-century American experience itself.

In much the same way as the past plays, with changes, through the present of the novel, so does the South play in the characters' experience of the North. Morrison makes of South and North a kind of trope of past and present. At the center of the pattern is Violet and Joe's journey from the South of their birth and early marriage to New York City, where they establish themselves economically and emotionally, where in essence they become "themselves: their stronger, riskier selves" (*Jazz*, 33). The year of their journey is 1906, when the great migration from the South is "a steady stream."[72] Like others in that "wave of black people running from want and violence," they go primarily for economic reasons. But they go, too, because they have caught a vision of equality that cannot be realized in the South. Learning that "Booker T. was sitting down to eat a chicken sandwich in the President's house," they first decide (as an act of faith in the future) to "buy . . . a piece of land," from which they are dispossessed by legal maneuvering implicitly designed to keep property ownership a prerogative of whites (107, 126). As a result of that dispossession they redefine their vision of equality as the freedom to move rather than the freedom to settle, and decide to take the train north. The exhilaration they experience as they move beyond the reach of Jim Crow laws, beyond the imposition of a "green-as-poison curtain separating the colored people" from the whites on the train, and as they near the

"During the World War there was a great migration north by Southern Negroes," Panel No. 1 of *The Migration of the Negro* by Jacob Lawrence, tempera on masonite (courtesy of The Phillips Collection, Washington, D.C.)

jazz-rhythmed city of what they believe to be beckoning possibility, is expressed in the laughter and dancing with which they enter New York. Unable to sit still any longer, they stand in the aisle and "train-danc[e] on into the City" (31, 36).

The energy and sense of massive movement of this moment in the text catches very much the affective sense expressed visually in several panels of Jacob Lawrence's *Migration of the Negro* series. In the first panel, captioned "During the World War there was a great migration north by Southern Negroes" (shown here), we see in a stylized, impressionistic way the eager press of crowds getting off the train at a composite station indicating Chicago, New York, and St. Louis—two of these being, of course, cities important in *Jazz*.[73] Nine additional panels directly involve the railroads by which migrants came north, notably No. 23, "And the migration spread," and No. 45, "They arrived in Pittsburgh, one of the great industrial centers of the North, in large numbers," where facial expressions and gestures convey the kind of excitement Joe and Violet express by dancing in the aisle.

The arrival in the northern city is a defining moment in a major episode of U.S. social history. Morrison captures, in the prose within which the fig-ures of Joe and Violet move, very much the same sense of great numbers that is captured visually by Lawrence:

> Some were slow about it and traveled from Georgia to Illinois, to the City, back to Georgia, out to San Diego and finally, shaking their heads, surrendered themselves to the City. Others knew right away that it was for them, this City and no other. They came on a whim because there it was and why not? They came after much planning, many letters written to and from, to make sure and know how and how much and where. They came for a visit and forgot to go back to tall cotton or short. Discharged with or without honor, fired with or without severance, dispossessed with or without notice, they hung around for a while and then could not imagine themselves anywhere else. Others came because a relative or hometown buddy said, Man, you best see this place be-fore you die; or, We got room now, so pack your suitcase and don't bring no high-top shoes.
>
> However they came, when or why, the minute the leather of their soles hit the pavement—there was no turning around. (*Jazz*, 32)

The passage could be from a history text, if history were written lyrically and if the Great Migration were traditionally presented more as celebration and less as social problem—a problem, that is, primarily from the vantage of those who didn't want the dark-skinned newcomers.

But if Morrison's treatment of the Great Migration can be compared to Jacob Lawrence's painterly treatment of the same epically historic phenome-non, it can be compared even more directly, in its pervasive sense of the ambiguity of geographic movement and in its incorporation of jazz idiom both stylistically and as a subject, with Albert Murray's recuperative *South to a Very Old Place* (1971). Murray's virtuosic book is one of the chief of those blues songs on which Morrison is riffing in *Jazz*.[74] She takes up, for one thing, Murray's complex shaping trope of home and departure, nostalgia and antipathy—the necessity for the black intellectual to leave home on a northward journey of emergence but the necessity, too, for that black intel-lectual/ writer not only to remain committed to the (racial) cause but to go on remembering. Her engagement with this idea of the conflicted meaning of the return South is, in part, biographically impelled, as her comment about her mother's never returning south despite speaking of it in terms of heaven would indicate. As Albert Murray puts it, returning south is return-ing to a place where the nostalgia for home and people who call you "homes" and a condition that can only be summed up as downhome-ness can never be separated from racial fear and disgust: "*Yes, homecoming is also to a place of very old fears.*"[75]

In a move that Morrison takes up both in her review of Murray's book and in *Jazz*, Murray evokes Harlem by way of music and connects both with his sense of the South as a troublingly ambiguous home:

> *Sometimes, of course, all you need to do is hear pianos and trumpets and trombones talking, in any part of town or anywhere else for that matter. Or sometimes it will be pianos and saxophones talking and bass fiddles walking; and you are all the way back even before you have time to realize how far away you are supposed to have gone, even before you become aware of even the slightest impulse to remember how much of it you thought perhaps you had long since forgotten.*
>
> *Sometimes it can be downhome church organs secularized to Kansas City four-four in a neighborhood cocktail lounge. It can be a Count Basie sonata suggesting blue steel locomotives on northbound railroad tracks (as "Dogging Around" did that summer after college). It can be any number of ensemble riffs and solo licks that also go with barbershops and shoeshine parlors; with cigar smoke and the smell and taste of seal-fresh whiskey; with baseball scores and barbecue pits and beer-seasoned chicken-shack tables; with skillets of sizzling mullets or bream . . .*
>
> *So naturally it can also be Lenox Avenue storefront churches, whether somewhat sedate or downright sanctified.*[76]

I have quoted at such length in order to demonstrate Morrison's closeness to this other black writer/intellectual for whom she has expressed her admiration. Even the specific elements of this passage are present in *Jazz*: the train, the sense of music in the air of Harlem, the barbershops (or beauty shops), the fried fish, the storefront churches. More, even, than specifics such as these, *Jazz* employs the same kind of riffing style, including not only the rhythm and suppleness of phrasing but the repeated jazz-motif-like return of elements such as, in *South to a Very Old Place*, references to baseball. And this style, I believe, characterizes the novel to much the same effect as in Murray's book: as a dialogical metaphor with an overtly political tenor. Murray calls for a political leader for whom the "dynamics inherent in the blues idiom" will be not only a language but a methodological model, a schooling in the ability to "confront the facts of life."[77] His book both advocates and enacts attentiveness to that model—for instance, when he says of the Second Memphis Confrontation that brought Martin Luther King, Jr., to the Lorraine Motel, "any American crossroads-store power technician could tell you what the name of the game is and whose ball and bat it is going to be played with,"[78] a passage that takes up his baseball motif for another riff. Morrison similarly, I believe, both plays and comments on the blues for purposes that are ultimately historical and political.

When Violet and Joe come to New York, they find a place to live in the Tenderloin district, the West Side between 20th Street and about 65th, which was indeed in 1906, the year of their arrival, the primary concentration of blacks in the city. There, *Harper's Weekly* reported in 1900, "negroes" were "a terror to white neighbors and landlords alike." Especially the Irish, *Harper's* said, had an "antipathy to the negroes."[79] The move to Harlem began by 1914, twelve years before the Traces are found there in the opening time-present of the novel. Like Joe's and Violet's, the motive of most denizens of the Tenderloin who went to Harlem was the desire for better housing at rents reflecting the surplus created during early-century overbuilding (still, though, rents higher than those charged whites).[80] By moving, then, the Traces improve their situation a second time, going to Harlem just at the time when its "star was rising," when Harlem was becoming the "Negro capital of the world," a "high-spirited and engaging" place of recognized significance, both real and symbolic.[81] Once again, as it had at their moment of entry, the city beckons to them with a promise of personal opportunity.

Even here, however, in this place where jazz (black) music pours into the streets, where the rhythm of that music and of life itself sets people to dancing their way in on the train and "command[ing] the center of the sidewalk; whistl[ing] softly in unlit doors" (*Jazz,* 50), the troubles of the past cannot be escaped, any more than the blues origins of jazz (and before the blues, the sorrow song, or spiritual) are eradicated as the form evolves. (Langston Hughes writes in *Black Magic,* "Behind jazz is always the blues.")[82] True to the view of human experience delineated in her earlier books, Morrison shows that the past lives on in the present. History, in the sense of the past itself, is never escaped, though the long heritage of a history of exploitation and the distortions of a selective official history, in the sense of majority-consensus reportage of the past, may be. The sorrow songs come back in the narrator's "memory" of "the voices of the women in houses nearby" back in rural Virginia, those voices "singing 'Go down, go down, way down in Egypt land' " and, in improvisational jazz form, "answering each other from yard to yard with a verse or its variation" (226). The blues come back in the narrator's final singing of her own blues. Pondering Violet and Joe's reconciliation to their past and to each other, which is also a reconciliation to the future, she realizes that she, too, ought to go through the window, out the door: "I ought to get out of this place. Avoid the window; leave the hole I cut through the door to get in lives instead of having one of my own" (220). Observing the Traces holding hands in the public street, she envies them "their public love," having "only known it in secret, shared it in secret and longed, aw longed to show it. . . . *I have watched your face for a long time now, and missed your eyes when you went away from me. Talking to you and hearing you answer—that's the kick*" (229). Her italicized words that she cannot say "out loud" might well be a song lyric. Here and elsewhere, the title *Jazz* comes to refer to what the novel is stylistically, as well as to the distinctive musicality of its milieu.

People cannot escape who they are, and who they are is the cumulative store of what they have not only experienced but also inherited. Part of that past, for Joe and Violet, is Dorcas, the girl he loved and then killed, to whom he had been able to pour out his loneliness for a mother in a way that he never had to Violet. We are not allowed to suppose that his killing of her is ever shrugged out of his or Violet's awareness. They are not, but very well could be, haunted by "a young ghost with a bad skin" (223) just as Sethe and all her family at 124 Bluestone Road were haunted by the ghost of the killed baby and finally by its grown-up incarnation. They are spared that haunting through the initiative and the resulting presence in their lives of another young girl, Felice, who was herself so haunted by the memory of her dead friend that she sought out Joe and Violet in time, before their prolonged period of grief and despondency caused some irreparable rift between them, and mediated a breakthrough toward reconciliation. As a result of her mediation, they turn toward each other in an ongoing effort of mutual exorcism and solace.

In a larger sense, though, the past that holds the potential for haunting Joe and Violet and the many thousands like them who went north during the Great Migration is the South itself. The attitude felt toward the South by migrant blacks in the North, Houston Baker writes, is a "sharp dilemma."[83] As in Morrison's previous novels in which blacks displaced from the South feel a troubled nostalgia for their life there, the Traces cherish memories of soft nights, big trees, and (because Joe was a hunter) abundant game. Joe recalls "fields and woods and secret lonely valleys"; Violet speaks of how they "ate good down home" (107, 81). But if "down home" was a place of natural plenty, it was also the site of social deprivation. As the descendants of former slaves, they were denied that plenty that the South afforded, instead being compelled to work inordinately for scant return and to suffer the effects of ancestral despair.

That despair has, in a very direct way, orphaned them both, driving them into unspeakable or at any rate long unspoken preoccupation with the knowledge of their motherlessness. Violet's mother drowned herself in despair at her inability to provide adequately for her children. Joe's abandoned him soon after his birth and chose to live namelessly (called only "Wild") in the woods, refusing to confront human society. The loss of her mother and the realization of her mother's suicidal despair drives Violet into refusal of mothering (she has abortions) and a consequent fixation on the wish for a child after it is too late, after menopause. The same loss drives Joe, during his adolescence, into an unsuccessful search for his wild mother, leaving him with a need, long years afterward, to tell his loss to someone who will listen. Until they break free at the end, that someone could not be Violet, since the two of them have long since been driven into inability to tell or to listen by the many bitter memories that weigh them down. Their past, centering on the loss of their mothers (loss of origins, the true past), haunts them long after they think they have put these old losses behind them by migrating. Violet carries away someone's baby for a few moments of holding, lies down in the street in disheartenment, buys herself a doll to sleep with. Joe renews his search for his mother in the form of a search for the young girl to whom he can sing his blues. That young girl, Dorcas, herself orphaned in the East St. Louis riots, accepts his story of loss along with his body and his weekly gifts until she can no longer bear his lugubriousness, then breaks off their peculiar liaison, triggering his act of jealous murder. Joe's responsibility for her death is never questioned—certainly he does not question it himself—despite the fact that the killing need not, perhaps, be regarded as murder in a technical sense, since it was her refusal of medical attention for the gunshot wound that caused her to bleed to death. She need not have died. Her own despair and disheartenment, then, also contribute to the event. As in *Beloved,* the past keeps coming back in different forms, like changes on core material in jazz.

The ambiguity of Joe's and Violet's feelings toward the South, the place of deprivation and hardship toward which they feel a nostalgic longing to return, is epitomized in the loosely (but resonantly) interpolated story of

Golden Gray, a racially mixed young man related neither to Violet nor to Joe but involved in the families of both. Golden Gray, the offspring of a privileged white girl and a poor black youth of whom she became enamored, returns south in a quest for his father much as Milkman Dead, in *Song of Solomon,* goes south in quest of his (plural) fathers. How Golden Gray's mother and father met and mated is never fully explained and remains scarcely credible, a part of the mysterious chasm of sexually charged race relations underlying southern society. Raised by his mother in Baltimore in the guise of an adopted orphan or foundling, with the help of a black servant who was in fact Violet's grandmother, he never even suspects his black blood until she, True Belle, tells him. Certainly his "radiantly golden" skin and "floppy yellow curls" were too decidedly different from her dark coloration for him to suspect any kinship with her. When he learns the secret of his birth, he is at first appalled. But his second thought is outrage at his father's abandonment. Following directions provided by True Belle, he heads south with horse and carriage to find his father and denounce him—a search that becomes a quest to reclaim the father and, in the process, his own "authenticity," his blackness (139, 160).

Before he can complete the quest for the father, Golden Gray must confront black maternity, in the form of a full-term pregnant black girl who proceeds to give birth to Joe in his presence. The birth scene of this fairytale-like sequence, then, brings together figures representing various components of black America's complex social heritage: the fugitive lurking at the margins of a repressive system (the unspeaking girl, Wild); the mulatto of no defined place (Golden Gray); the black deprived of his past (the infant Joe); and the sturdily independent freeman who lives close to the land (Hunter's Hunter, who will become Joe's foster father). In effect, Morrison has incorporated another characteristic feature of blues, the use of personification and personally casted story lines to explore social issues and the experience of racial struggle.[84] Represented by none, in this story of Reconstruction America, but lurking behind all of them, is the institution of slavery itself. To reclaim his personal heritage, Golden Gray has had to confront this fact of his group heritage.

In the South, where Joe and Violet saw that the price paid to whites for their cotton was two dollars a bale more than that paid blacks, where black women sometimes earned ten cents a day and black men a quarter, they had no hope of escaping grinding poverty. In the North, though things are hard, they can nevertheless find ways of making a place for themselves. They obtain decent housing and enjoy the life of the streets in a section shared with thousands of other African Americans. At the same time, they are pulled away from each other both by the weight of the unconfronted past and by the daily necessity of moving around the city on the separate routes by which they make their living, Violet dressing hair in people's homes because she isn't licensed and can't work in a shop, Joe working as a bellhop or selling cosmetics. At home, in the South, they had shared a small number of fixed places, the most important of which was the tree beside a cotton field where they met. They had had roots and therefore a sense of home in that "very old place," despite its very old hostilities. Here their separate movements both express and contribute to their sense of separateness and of rootlessness.

Jazz, like *Beloved,* gives a great deal of charged attention to streets, roads, and movement. The Traces' name itself is an old word for a trail or road made by the passing (the traces) of people, animals, or vehicles. The name carries, then, both the idea of their migrancy and the idea of the lingering of traces of the past. But the dirt roads of their rural southern home have led to the railroad of departure and then the paved streets of New York. City streets lead to chance encounters that may be either revitalizing or devastating. Streets may bring people together in community or may expose them to gazes of ridicule or hostility—the kind that "fix you" on a Prufrockian "pin," like the gazes of those who point at Violet to accuse her of baby-snatching (21) or the gaze of the narrator at the opening, as she hisses "Sth, I know that woman." The city streets lead with a seemingly "insidious intent" to the overwhelming act of murder or provide a way out of loneliness and depression by leading one (as they do Violet) to a place where one can drink a cup of tea and confide one's troubles. Or, as they lead the young Felice near the end of the book, to a place where one can cry over a friend's having preferred death to friendship and yet be invited back to supper with catfish and music and a little dancing.

The city streets, then, are as indeterminate a symbolic presence as the migration road that carries the Traces and thousands like them out of a hateful victimization but lands them in a state of permanent nostalgia. They are part of the promise held out by New York: "Steel cars sped down the streets and if you saved up, they said, you could get you one and drive as long as there was road" (106). In the spring, especially, "people notice one another in the road" and it becomes clear that "citylife is streetlife" (117, 119). But precisely because the streets do draw people out of their homes into a flowing pattern where they have chance encounters, they destabilize life. For people already dislocated, that destabilization can be a major threat. The narrator comments (in a variant of the literal and figurative musical idiom that pervades the novel) that Joe is "bound to the track" that "pulls him like a needle through the groove of a Bluebird record. Round and round about the town. That's the way the City spins you. Makes you do what it wants, go where the laid-out roads say to. All the while letting you think you're free" (120). A sexually unhappy man is a man on the streets, prowling: Violet admits that she "didn't give Joe much reason to stay out of the street" (83). And when Violet falls into confusion and despair she first sits down in the middle of the street and then, feeling herself breaking apart, watches that other self people refer to by the joking name Violent "walking round town, up and down the streets wearing my skin" (95).

Expressive of the city's stony and impersonal surfaces (in contrast to the thick grass and shady bowers Joe remembers in the South), the streets are "slick and black" (181), icy like death yet open to the distances like freedom: always a plurality of possibilities. Accordingly, Violet's alter-ego parrot that said "Love you," which she put out in the cold to die when she could no longer love herself, just might (so the narrator speculates) "manage somehow to fly away on wings that had not soared for six years" (93). That doesn't happen. The parrot does not survive its encounter with the unfamiliar element of northern winter. But Violet, faring better than either her winged or her Violent other self, does survive. The end of the novel finds Violet and Joe reconciled and moving freely, and together, about their chosen place, the jazz-paced city. They "walk down 125th Street and across Seventh Avenue" and "saunter over to the Corner and join the crowd listening to the men with the long-distance eyes," men for whom they share a liking (223).

The important thing, Joe thinks, indeed "the best thing, the only thing," is to "find the trail and stick to it" (130). At the time he thinks this, when he is still fixated on his young girlfriend and victim, he despairs of ever doing so. Needing to find the trail (the trace) is equivalent to needing to find himself, and to do that he needs to relocate the trail of the past, the pattern connecting it to the present. He visualizes the course of his life as a path or road choked with growth, hard to find, but once found, leading from one event to another in a kind of inevitability. Before leaving Virginia he had "tracked" his mother one last time in the free indeterminacy of the woods, and in that instance the trail "led me right to her." He realizes that that trail and his process of tracking are linked with the city streets and his tracking of Dorcas after she has broken off their affair: "I tracked Dorcas from borough to borough. I didn't even have to work at it. Didn't even have to think. Something else takes over when the track begins to talk to you, give out its signs so strong you hardly have to look" (130). The continuum of country trail and city street, of hunting and searching and a search that ends in the shooting of female game, an act Hunter's Hunter had always condemned, are expressive of his sense of a continuum in his life, the persistence of the South and his early experience there into his present existence. It was the rejection by his mother and the uncertainty of his attempts to find her that led to his outdoor life and his fall from a tree practically onto Violet; that in turn led him to the city; in the city his trail through the streets as a seller of cosmetics leads him to the apartment where a customer is having a party and he speaks to Dorcas; and the sense of rejection and loneliness from his mother's abandonment, carried with him through this long trail of his life, leads him to pour himself out in bedded talk to the young girl who had also lost her mother as well as father and who feels, for a time, a corresponding need to share her secret unhappiness. The novelistic structure becomes an elaborate set of changes signifying on the core material of maternal loss, displacement from the South (home), search for home (mother), and, at the end, the achievement of community.

Pondering Joe's "running through the streets in bad weather," the indeterminate, im-personalized but highly personal narrator says that all that time she/he had "thought he was looking for her," Dorcas, not "Wild's . . . home in the rock" (221). But the narrator's comment is disingenuous, because he/she has long since led the reader to realize that the search for the mother has taken Joe along the same road as the search for someone he could tell about his mother, and that same trail has led him guiltily away from Violet. When Dorcas breaks off their relationship in order to pursue younger adventures and adventurers, the trail that had led him to her leads him on to murder her. The trail may be inevitable, but it leads to self-destruction: "But if the trail speaks, no matter what's in the way, you can find yourself in a crowded room aiming a bullet at her heart, never mind it's the heart you can't live without" (130).

The last part of the novel, then, shows Joe learning to live without that (aspect of his) heart, Violet learning to live without her longtime wish for a child, and the two together learning to live *with* the griefs of their linked past. The key to their doing so is the visit paid by Felice, who comes to their apartment ostensibly to try to find the ring Dorcas had borrowed from her the night of the shooting, but mainly to tell Joe that he should stop his obsessive weeping for the dead girl because she wasn't worth it. In the process, she weeps out her own grief for her friend and her friend's desertion of her—she sings a variant of Joe's and Violet's blues—and becomes the mediator who helps them begin their process of reconciliation. The language of the novel becomes, in these last few pages, a blues-y song of praise and celebration: praise of Felice's ability (reminiscent of Denver's at the end of *Beloved*) to move freely and self-confidently through the streets between home and public spaces, "nobody's alibi or hammer or toy" (222); celebration of Joe and Violet's reconciliation and their freedom to saunter about the city or, when they choose, "stay home figuring things out, telling each other those little personal stories they like to hear again and again" and "whisper[ing] to each other under the covers" (223, 228), much as Paul D and Sethe are freed to tell each other their stories at the end of *Beloved*. Even as the narrator sings her/his final sorrow song, the style becomes ecstatically lyrical, constituting Joe and Violet and Felice as the nucleus of a sense of community that draws together the countless and varied newcomers and old-timers of the big city—implicitly, the nucleus of the community that is Harlem. Their "breathing and murmuring" and the click of their heels on the sidewalks become a jazz rhythm, like the "sound of snapping fingers under the sycamores lining the streets" (226): the very pace of life.

It is ironic, perhaps, that after polemically exposing the shortcomings of Cather's dual vision of the home place and the return home in *Sapphira and the Slave Girl,* Morrison essentially replicates that vision here, in her mingled tribute both to the road of departure and journey and to the solace of quilt-enwrapped homing. As she hovers meditatively, in the person of the androgynous narrator, over the three characters grouped in mutual need and mutual regeneration at the end, she envisions a perfect place "already made for me." That perfect place is Wild's home in the sheltering hollow of the rock, out in the free, woodsy outdoors, "both snug and wide open. With a doorway never needing to be closed" (221). Morrison's felicitous place of intimate immensity is a replication of Cather's ideal of the open enclosure, the place at once indoors and safe, outdoors and free. Like Cather's in *Sapphira,* it is a place in the mother-region, the South. As Cather turns back to Virginia, the name of the mother, so Morrison echoes the mother-talk she has recalled from her own childhood: "she talked about it as though it were heaven, absolute heaven."

Melvin Dixon, in his valuable study of geography and identity in African-American literature, has identified in Morrison's work (specifically in *Sula*) a "complex figuration of land and identity."[85] In her fiction of African Americans who find ways of living authentically and freely despite the weight of a dehumanizing past, Morrison has claimed for herself and for her people that myth of geographically constituted transcendence so often conceived as a Eurocentric myth that simply ignores the different experience of America of African Americans, Native Americans, and Mexican Americans. She has sung that myth, that sorrow song, in a jazzy new idiom, as richly idiosyncratic and as richly embedded in a racially defined tradition as jazz itself. In *Playing in the Dark,* Morrison defines the writer's calling this way: "Responding to culture—clarifying, explicating, valorizing, translating, transforming, criticizing—is what artists everywhere do."[86] Especially in *Jazz* and *Beloved,* she has fulfilled this definition by envisioning and valorizing re-memoried structures of spatial movement and new habitation.

Chapter 6

MOVING INTO THE POLITICAL
Joan Didion and the Imagination of Engagement

The past is a country from which we have all
emigrated.
        —Salman Rushdie

Nothing
will do but
to taste the bitter
taste. No life
other, apart from.
        —Denise Levertov

I'll chance
the pilgrim sandals
        —Denise Levertov

We live in an age of migrancy and displacement. The word *diaspora,* which once had a single, specific referent, may now, in the last years of the turbulent twentieth century, refer to any number of mass movements of peoples who have been forced into migration by political upheaval, economic pressure, repression, or terrorism. Untold thousands have experienced a "migrancy" of a different kind as their homes have in effect shifted under their feet in the breakup of nations. In the United States, the age of migrancy has been largely a matter of economic displacement, some of it voluntary, in the form of moves made for reasons of restlessness or hope for betterment, but much of it involuntary, from causes ranging from relatively benign corporate transfers to plant closings to entrapment in patterns of migrant agricultural labor. At the same time, an insistent striving for release from the gender constraints that were resumed with a vengeance after World War II has led increasing numbers of women to go out the door of domesticity into lives of enlarged public involvement and interaction, ostensible freedom of choice, and mobility. If one believes in human equality, the result can only be seen as positive, but it has undeniably entailed pervasive cultural uprooting. Among the ways in which that uprooting is manifest are the loosening if not severing of multigenerational family ties and a weakened sense of identity through association with place.

No American writer has been more attuned to the rootlessness of the mid- to late-twentieth century than Joan Didion, whose departure from the house of domesticity has taken her further into the realm of the political than any other writer considered here. Didion's journalism and fiction alike chronicle a society of estrangement. Writing always as a moralist, albeit a relentlessly ironic one with a self-confessed "predilection for the extreme,"[1] she has observed what sometimes strikes her as a culture of "children who have moved around a lot" and has attributed its anomie to a failure of traditional moral instruction: "At some point between 1945 and 1967 we had somehow neglected to tell these children the rules of the game we happened to be playing. Maybe we had stopped believing in the rules ourselves, maybe we were having a failure of nerve about the game" (*Slouching,* 123). Such comments have understandably led to Didion's being labeled a moral and political conservative. Reviewers have placed her "among the most fundamentally conservative writers in America" and have seen her "essentially conservative nature" manifested in traces of class elitism in her work.[2] Accordingly, she is also generally regarded as a non- or even anti-feminist. In part, at least, this judgment is based on the strength of her mocking tone in the essay "The Women's Movement" (*White Album,* 109–18). But as Salman Rushdie, probably the most famous of contemporary international and intranational migrants, has said, our identities as citizens of this disrupted late-1990s culture are "at once plural and partial."[3] That description applies quite well to Didion. Labels such as "conservative," whether applied to her fiction or to her nonfiction, are indeed partial if not misleading. At minimum, they are inadequate for understanding her considerable body of work.

My purpose here is to show that the prevalence and general import of restless movement in Didion's writing not only continues the patterns in women's writing that I have been tracing—both personal escape and escape from the personal—but extends it. Moving, in her novels, from what has been called an "internalized quest" in *Run River* to the explicitly geographical search of *Democracy,* and moving in her nonfiction from localized (and always precisely located) observation to ever more far-flung sites of interest, she represents the farthest reach of that outbound trajectory curving from home to whatever distance it is that represents free movement and engagement with public, as opposed to domestic, issues.[4] In Didion's writing, unlike that of Cather, Tyler, and even Morrison—but not unlike Austin—the movement out the door into the public space becomes a movement into the political, or what might more properly be called the politicized historical. In making this assertion, I am aware that Didion herself has stated she "never had faith that the answers to human problems lay in anything that could be called political."[5] Perhaps she meant by that the political process, narrowly construed. I do call her concerns political, in a broader sense perhaps but nevertheless a very literal one.

Clearly, Didion's outward impetus to the public, the political, seems to carry with it an inevitable recoil, an urge to retreat to a quieter, more private, and morally more pristine world. It is that, I believe, which accounts for the reactionary tone occasionally heard in her anxious and weary voice. Like all of the writers we have examined, she recognizes the need for a full, rather than a partial, life and defines such a life as one involving anchorage to some known and secure place, even as it involves freedom to ramble in the outer spaces beyond the door. For Didion, that freedom to ramble has meant navigating public spaces and engaging public issues. But like the departures and journeys navigated by Austin, Cather, Tyler, Morrison, and indeed Robinson, her movement is dual, reflecting a deep-seated ambivalence. The tether by which a satisfactory anchorage might be maintained would have to be a very long one indeed to accommodate her peripatetic engagement with public issues, but she regards with alarm the possibility of its breaking.

In her personal life, Didion is firmly anchored—so firmly, in fact, that for years she returned to her girlhood bedroom in her parents' home in Sacramento to complete her books. Descended from longtime Californians, including a member of the illfated Donner-Reed party who (fortunately) left it before it became wintered in and resorted to eating its dead, she habitually traces her somewhat unusual ethical sense to early teaching of a kind she believes is peculiar to the California of westward pioneers. She sees things, she has said, as being "right or wrong, in a very rigid way," but does not expect to impose those perceptions on others, because she also believes, in what she regards as a true western spirit, that ethical judgments are "strictly *laissez-faire*."[6] California as a kind of metaphor, what Michiko Kakutani has referred to as a heritage of "an almost palpable notion" of Manifest Destiny or movement toward opportunity and the cessation of movement at "the end of America,"[7] is at the essence of Didion's sensibility. Various critics have noted the presence of that sadly voracious mind-set even when her journalistic or novelistic vision is directed elsewhere. Her personal vision emerges from, and returns to, the historical.

Something of the same is true, of course, but with a considerable difference of degree, even in the work of Willa Cather and Anne Tyler, seemingly the least politically engaged of the five writers examined here. In their novels as well, the movement out the door and then back again is one whose implications are to some degree generalized. Blanche Gelfant, while acknowledging that Cather's *One of Ours* "creates a continuum between personal desire and public life," finds that her work "usually ignores or satirizes historic events shaping the world of its characters."[8] But we might remind ourselves that Cather not only addressed the impact and import of the Great War in *One of Ours,* but touched on issues of business ethics in *A Lost Lady,* what we might call business satisfactions or dissatisfactions in *My Mortal Enemy* and *My Ántonia,* and, in a curiously filtered way, the historic issue of slavery in *Sapphira and the Slave Girl.* To the extent that she took note of public issues, not only in her fiction but in journalism, essays, and letters, her approach was that of the moralist.[9] She was interested in how public events affected individual lives and conduct. This element looms fairly large, in fact, in the view of Sharon O'Brien, who writes that Cather "was consciously collapsing the traditional nineteenth-century distinction between 'public' and 'private,' male and female space."[10] Tyler's fictions are similarly centered on the private life. Yet in the very insistence with which she returns to themes of domestic life and the contrary impulse toward freer range, she, too, implies a generalizing of her vision. This, she seems to say, is the commonality of life, the reality that makes up the life of a public, a people. Wars, economic systems or disruptions, and social upheavals go on far in the background of her books, felt as they impinge on the life of the home.

It is with the more outspoken Mary Austin, among this group, that Didion can best be linked. The linear progression of this study from most centered on home issues to most directed toward public issues, then, is really a circling pattern. Austin is, to be sure, in some ways the most insistently home-centered of the five, the one nearest the end of the spectrum anchored by Jewett. Always grieved by her inability to achieve a satisfying home life, always wishing for the security of a "beloved house," she directed much of her energy toward reform of the domestic life to make it more fulfilling for women. Yet Austin also wrote on a wide range of social and political issues (water rights in the West, Native American landholdings and autonomy, women's issues), and directly, rather than indirectly like Cather, addressed the question of the interrelation of private and public morality—a question that has continued, as we near the century's end, to vex the repose of public-minded feminists. Writing to a production editor at Houghton Mifflin in 1920, Austin described the "real moral interest" of her novel *No. 26 Jayne Street* as "the question whether there can be any genuine democratic reform while the private lives of the reformers deny the democratic principle."[11]

A similar yoking of theoretical and practical political issues with the domestic lives of families, and specifically of women, has engaged Joan Didion throughout her career. Like Mary Austin three-quarters of a century and more ago, she has insisted on bringing public issues and rhetoric to bear on private relationships, and has persisted, equally, in bringing a private, family persona into her engagement with public issues. One might well argue that this stance in itself qualifies her as in some sense a feminist. Teresa de Lauretis writes, "To feminism, the personal is epistemologically the political, and its epistemology *is* its politics." Issues such as "lesbianism, contraception, abortion, incest, sexual harassment, rape, prostitution, and pornography" are not "merely social . . . or merely sexual" but both "political and epistemological."[12] De Lauretis's words echo, among others, those of Adrienne Rich, who envisions the presence of the political in that seemingly most private of situations, a scene of sexual betrayal:

The phone rings unanswered
in a man's bedroom
she hears him telling someone else
Never mind. She'll get tired—
hears him telling her story to her sister

who becomes her enemy
and will in her own time
light her own way to sorrow

ignorant of the fact this way of grief
is shared, unnecessary
and political[13]

Notoriously feminist and nonconservative as she is, Rich is nevertheless notably at one with Didion on precisely this point: the movement between private and public concerns—more specifically, between private and public morality, implying a linkage of the two. Singular as Didion may at times appear, she is scarcely a lone voice crying in the wilderness. The content of her retrograde nostalgia for a firm center and her derision of the new, especially when the new lends itself to being called trendy, may set her apart from many of the women writers of her time, but the structure of her thought and sensibility is, in this particular respect, one that is widely shared. Women writers of the post-1950s era, but not in the novel alone, have signally and increasingly set about the work that Mikhail Bakhtin calls, in *The Dialogic Imagination,* the "major task of the modern historical novel": to "overcome" the duality of the personal and the historical, to "find an historical aspect of private life, and also to represent history in its domestic light."[14] Moreover, as a novelist as well as a journalist/essayist, Didion responds directly to the events and public tensions she witnesses. In flight from a stultifying 1950s idealization of the domestic life, she follows the arc of departure farther than any other novelist addressed here except perhaps (in a very different way) Robinson, and to a point further within the political than any except perhaps Austin, with whom, in her confrontational style and her understanding of the pervasiveness of politics, she has her strongest affinity.

Despite obvious differences including but by no means limited to genre, Didion has strong affinities among her own contemporaries with Denise Levertov and, as I have already indicated, Adrienne Rich. I want to turn aside briefly to propose Rich and Levertov, two of the strongest voices in the mid- to late-century literature of feminist departure to the political and linkage of public and private dimensions, as contextualizing figures for Didion's work. The parallels that their poetry offers to her writing, both fiction and nonfiction, are apt and illuminating. Both have made "that inductive leap from the personal to the political" (*White Album,* 114) that Didion mocks in "The Women's Movement" while making it herself on almost every page. Both Rich and Levertov, whose evolution has followed an especially similar path to Didion's, are concerned, as de Lauretis observes, to show that "nothing—not the most hidden aspects of the psychic life of the individual—exists apart from the pressures of a historical era."[15] Both, as well, have associated their political and public-private themes with recurrent motifs of geographic movement, so that the move from the private to the public is as firmly linked to literal spatial movement in their work as it is in Didion's.[16]

Rich's poetry, once she moved beyond the tight formalism of her earliest work, is shot through with an insistence that private griefs have political ramifications. Often (as in "Translations," from which I quoted above) this insistence is stated explicitly, but sometimes it is implicit in her structured movement between the two. In "A Woman Dead in Her Forties," for example, she writes about love and also about war; in "For Ethel Rosenberg," about a woman and about political reaction. Again and again she moves back and forth between such pairings, implying by the juxtaposition that there exists a connection. In "When We Dead Awaken," the "lovely landscape of southern Ohio / betrayed by strip mining" is juxtaposed with the "thick gold band on the adulterer's finger" (151). In "Snapshots of a Daughter-in-Law," the punishments envisioned for a woman who dares to "smash" the "mold" of domesticity include such hyperbolically public ones as "tear gas, attrition shelling" (38). What happens in one realm affects the other; corruption in one reflects or even produces corruption in the other. "Poetry," she insists, "never stood a chance / of standing outside history" ("North American Time," 325).

Even in her first volume, *A Change of World* (1951), when she was writing the tightly formal and apolitical verse that she later associated with the sway of powerful males in her life, Rich poised female figures at windows and doors. In the noted "Snapshots of a Daughter-in-Law" from her third volume (1963), the "unlocked door" is ironically "that cage of cages" (37), its seeming openness mocked by unseen barriers more absolute than any tangible bars. The central female figure is caught and immobilized between persistence in conventional life patterns and departure toward a longed-for freedom. Similarly, the woman in "The Trees" sits writing letters beside an open door while resolutely ignoring the fact that her house plants are "disengag[ing]" themselves from their containers and "moving out into the forest" (60–61), achieving a freedom that she herself does not dare face.

Increasingly, however, Rich's hesitation at the windows and doors fell away, and her poetry took on a wide-ranging spaciousness and recurrent imagery of motion. The rupture of domestic imprisonment is famously envisioned in "Snapshots" in the image of a helicopter "poised, still coming, / her fine blades making the air wince"; but when Rich invokes that image again in "In the Woods" she makes it a presence rather than a visionary anticipation, referring to her soul as "my helicopter" (57)—that is, designating her essence as one of movement and maneuverability. In "Shooting Script," invoking a different form of transportation, she admits that she was a long time "simply learning to handle the skiff; I had no / special training and my own training was against me" (145). By 1969 she has made her departure. In *Leaflets* (a title implying public communication, perhaps a broadside distributed on the street) she urges her readers, "Don't look for me in the room I've left; / the photograph shows just a white rocking-chair, still rocking" ("Ghazals: Homage to Ghalib," 105).

With *Diving into the Wreck* (1973), Rich began, as de Lauretis says, to "break with" archetypes in favor of "prototypes."[17] Prototypes are models, action plans. More and more insistently, she addressed such public issues as the Vietnam War and protest marches, while she also became more directly personal, pondering, for example, the reorientation of her life toward the love of women. To a world of "gunning down the babies at My Lai" and "computing body counts"—an act she defines as "masturbating" (a presumably private act, in dual senses) "in the factory / of facts" ("The Phenomenology of Anger," 166)—she counterposes an ideal that consistently entails escape from society's structures to move freely in outdoor spaces. She defines her ideal of self as keeping her "mind / with the wild geese" ("From an Old House in America," 217) or "run[ning] wild" like daylilies that have " 'escaped' . . . from dooryard to meadow to roadside" ("Culture and Anarchy," 275). This ideal self is seen as a skier "walking, skis and poles shouldered, toward the mountain / free-swinging in worn boots . . . dressed for cold and speed" ("Transit," 283) or as a girl or young woman "winged for flying" ("Education of a Novelist," 316). But when she turns her eye toward the past, in "In the Wake of Home," she can only brood over a politically torn world in which movement has not always been free: a "continent" of "diasporas unrecorded / undocumented refugees / underground railroads trails of tears" (323).[18]

Denise Levertov has also mourned that world of many "trails of tears." As her work evolved from intensely private or subjective, spiritual, or naturalist concerns to directly political ones, she became, as the title of her own first book of essays puts it, "the poet in the world." Having grown up in a family atmosphere steeped in religious mysticism, Levertov has throughout her career written a poetry of luminous concern with the dailiness of life from a pointedly female perspective. The justly praised "Matins," for example, from her relatively early volume *The Jacob's Ladder* (1958), moves from the morning's act of "rising from the toilet seat" to hairbrushing, to preparation of the "sacred grains" of breakfast, to sending her son off to school. Such "quotidian moments" are vehicles for "the numinous."[19] Sandra Gilbert has written that in "confronting the apparent ordinariness of the world," Levertov is "continually surprised by joy."[20] Household dailiness also serves her as a medium of solidarity among women:

> Yes, in strange kitchens
> I know where to find the forks,
> and among another woman's perfume bottles
> I can find the one that suits me.[21]

Such solidarity holds the potential of serving as a basis for political coalition, and in a series of volumes in the 1960s and 1970s Levertov used it in precisely that way. Even in the 1950s she was involved in the antinuclear peace movement, and in her mid-career work she became even more insistently public and political in her concerns than Rich. As she came to perceive the war in Vietnam as essentially evil and again became active in public protest, she directed her sense of female solidarity toward a poetry of empathy for Vietnamese victims of the war. She became a poet of purposeful confrontation.

When critics have responded negatively to Levertov's politicizing of the lyrical impulse she earlier voiced so well, she has insisted that political poetry, even of a "hortatory" nature, has "a long and illustrious history" and that "political verses attain to . . . the condition of poetry" by the "same means as any other kind: good faith, passionate conviction and, in equal measure, the precise operations of the creative imagination."[22] Her praise of Pablo Neruda and Muriel Rukeyser, also poets on the Left, singles out the fact that they have "consistently fused lyricism and overt social and political concern." That fusion, she believes, is the primary strength of both. Her praise for them emphasizes, too, precisely the fact that they *went,* that they sited themselves as poets of conscience in places of political turmoil and repression where they hoped to make a difference.[23]

Geographic siting and movement, *going,* are inseparable from Levertov's assumption of the role of poet of conscience. She has been, throughout her career, "constant in pilgrimage," continually "wayfaring."[24] Less systematically, perhaps, than Rich, but always resolutely, she has moved from positioning herself almost exclusively in private spaces—in her kitchen, her bathroom, at a window inside her house—to positioning herself in a lecture hall, in public streets (either in actuality or in the imagination), in a Puerto Rican prison, in Vietnam. Subsequent to her most intensely political phase, during the Vietnam War, when she went to Hanoi and met with American prisoners of war as well as North Vietnamese officials, she turned her attention back toward the private, the personal—but never exclusively so. Her poetry has continued to move between the two, the personal world of "Milk to be boiled / egg to be poached / pot to be scoured" and the world of far-flung public issues ("A Visit," *Life in the Forest,* 37). Her own presence in the expansive body of her work is that of a woman moving about the world, with business in a great many places. Her act of traveling to Hanoi in defiance of political prohibition, in 1972, an act of resistance *by* travel, has remained at the essence of her public and political address.

Levertov and Rich epitomize the woman writer as social critic and social activist. Their poetry and polemics manifest with clarity and directness the political engagement which in Didion's work is often obscured by heavy irony. Significantly, both associate their engagement in social issues with changes of place, movement away from the familiar domestic space to the unfamiliar, the outdoor, the far-flung. Both, too, insistently link these poles of their existence and their poetry. They insist that private morality be consistent with public principle.

It is interesting to note how closely Didion's career as journalist/essayist/novelist overlaps the careers of Levertov and Rich, and how all three track major public events. Eleven years younger than Levertov and five years younger than Rich, Didion was born in 1934 and entered the publishing world (going to work for *Vogue*) in the mid-1950s, by which time both poets had published their first books (Rich's second appeared in 1955, Levertov's second in 1957) and were working to break out of the tight traditional forms that characterized their early work. Didion's first book, *Run River,* a novel of restless marriages and uneasy social relationships, appeared in 1963—the year in which the Civil Rights Act was being drafted, George Wallace stood in a "school house door" in Alabama, a federal antipoverty program was being planned, President Kennedy was assassinated, and Rich published *Snapshots of a Daughter-in-Law,* with its powerful images of female discontent.[25]

Levertov's *O Taste and See* appeared the following year. There, although she continued her mode of celebrating "the mystery of the living thing, of the thing's vital energy,"[26] she also took note of sexual and racial injustice (in "Hypocrite Women" and "A March," with its epigraph from James Baldwin). Levertov's first Vietnam protest poems appeared in 1967, in *The Sorrow Dance,* where she also treated domestic unrest, the race riots in Detroit. Didion's highly praised first volume of nonfiction, *Slouching Towards Bethlehem* (gathered from pieces published earlier in the *Saturday Evening Post* and other magazines), appeared the following year, 1968. She would later single out that year as the essence of the period, a time when private illness was a function of public events: "An attack of vertigo and nausea does not now seem to me an inappropriate response to the summer of 1968" (*White Album,* 15). In 1968, military spending was soaring because of Vietnam, universities appeared to be coming apart, Martin Luther King, Jr., was assassinated,[27] and Adrienne Rich was becoming involved in radical politics in New York. All three of these intensely private women were confronting a world in disorder and responding by directing their attention beyond the window, taking steps out the door, into the streets.

Didion did not address the divisive issues of the war, protests, and civil disobedience as directly as Levertov and Rich did. Largely fixated on the California scene, "where we run out of continent" (*Slouching,* 172) and apparently out of hope as well, and where she had returned in 1964 after almost a decade in New York, she instead addressed, from an oddly dual stance, at once conservative in its moral nostalgia and unconventional in its positioning within dissenting circles, what might be called the generalized private life, the social disruptions attendant upon these public and political events. From a dramatic and rhetorical stance in the San Bernardino Valley, "haunted by the Mojave just beyond the mountains"—Mary Austin country—she observed that the "Golden Dream" had failed and asked "at just what pass the trail had been lost" (3, 31). There could be little doubt that California and its history were serving as a synecdoche for American culture in general. Michelle Loris is correct in observing that the California setting of much of Didion's work "at once embodies America's frontier myth of itself as a new Eden and exposes that story as fraudulent."[28]

Throughout the turbulent 1960s and 1970s, when she was publishing her first five books and beginning to attract critical attention as an important literary voice, Didion, like Rich and Levertov, cast herself as a public moralist and, in necessary conjunction, an inveterate traveler, a watcher of events in far-flung places. That is to say, despite her curiously brittle disparagement of women's urge to gain "their 'freedom' " (*White Album,* 113), she presented herself as a person of apparently unlimited freedom of movement. In her career as journalist, she has not only slouched figuratively toward Bethlehem but moved about investigatively or contemplatively among Las Vegas, Los Angeles, San Francisco, Miami, Honolulu, El Salvador, Bogotá, and Amman. As the quasi-fictional actor-observer "Joan Didion" in her 1984 novel *Democracy,* she turns up in Hawaii, London, Singapore, and Malaysia. Whether in fiction or in reportage, she has variously exposed drifting and drug abuse among the young, political manipulation among dissident groups, callow image-building among establishment politicians, and massive victimization in wars. The terms in which she protests against the atrocities she witnesses are not the direct and impassioned ones of Rich and Levertov, but a more indirect rhetoric of sharp-edged irony and dark existentialism that exposes and demonizes these atrocities. Her protest or outrage, if it is that—her commentary, at any rate—is couched in a dry, often sardonic tone which she refuses to modulate into the strong tonic chord of direct statement. But it is still an atomizing that exposes and, by exposing, denounces.

Didion's implied social or moral criticism emerges in many indirect ways, among them the shape of spatial movement within the world of her discourse. Restlessness, both observed and imagined, conveys a lack of stable values and the ennui that comes with absence of purpose: she is distressed by "the loss of an intact historical world."[29] In *Play It As It Lays,* for example, the pervasive anxiety and directionlessness of Maria's life are spatially represented in her relentless driving of the Los Angeles freeway system, motion whose only aim is motion. As I have noted elsewhere, driving the complicated interchanges allows her to focus her full attention on the road and forget the disorders of her life.[30] Didion would subsequently begin her essay "Pacific Distances" with this same feature, at once real and metaphoric, of life in Los Angeles: "A good part of any day in Los Angeles is spent driving, alone, through streets devoid of meaning to the driver, which is one reason the place exhilarates some people, and floods others with an amorphous unease" (*After Henry,* 110). That she did not exempt herself from such social patterns is evident at many points—in the insistence with which she points out her own anxieties and "uneasy devices" ("We are here on this island in the middle of the Pacific in lieu of filing for divorce" [*White Album,*

133]), in her understanding that "one runs away to find oneself" (*Slouching*, 148). Against the "absence of narrative" (that is, an absence of coherence or sense of causation and result) that she sees in such compulsive random movement, she juxtaposes a diverse set of public phenomena: nuclear anxiety, the impermanence and social disjunctions she sees as characterizing Hawaii, the lives of refugees from Vietnam at a processing center in Hong Kong. The element shared by these phenomena, disparate as they are, is a radical destabilization. Instability is typically more alarming to Didion than enclosure or stasis. "She knows," Thomas Mallon writes, that one "travels at one's peril any real distance from home and the past."[31] Even so, it is evident, both from her various acknowledgments of the potential oppressiveness of home and from her presentation of herself as a person who cares about and participates in public issues, that like an Edith Wharton or a Willa Cather, but at farther-flung distances and in a far more confrontational style, she moves insistently beyond domesticity. Her self-presentation is a performative argument of departure.

Didion's writing, then, is not unidirectional. It is not writing either of departure or of domestication but rather of movement between public and private, home and political arena, in which the two are drawn together. In Chris Anderson's words, she "sees her personal experience as an index to larger issues and social problems," and her "characteristic strategy" is to "reflect on contemporary life from the standpoint of her own experience or to engage in autobiographical narrative which ultimately leads to commentary on the social problems of the time." Her work in the vein of investigative journalism, then, is more accurately regarded, Anderson perceptively argues, as "an important hybrid" of journalism and that more personal form, the essay.[32] At times, conveying only a frustrated *wish* to move from the personal to the political, not its achievement, she wearily pronounces Levertov's kind of activism futile: "If I could believe that going to a barricade would affect man's fate in the slightest I would go to that barricade, and quite often I wish that I could, but it would be less than honest to say that I expect to happen upon such a happy ending" (*White Album*, 206). At times this impulse is activated in moments of intensely dual experience, the political and the personal fused within a single work or a single character. Accordingly, in *A Book of Common Prayer*, Charlotte Douglas resists her husband's urging that she leave Boca Grande, explaining that she has "*walked away from places all my life and I'm not going to walk away from here.*"[33] Charlotte's decision is a knowing confrontation of a doom at once political and deeply private. She chooses, in effect, to go to the barricades despite a lack of belief in the efficacy of what she does.

Often, however, the movement between private and public in Didion's work is less a fusion than an alternation. In *After Henry,* a collection of pieces first published in the *New York Times* and the *New York Review of Books,* Didion sites herself retrospectively, in the first sentence of the first essay, in a domestic space and situation: "living in a borrowed house" and having "a new baby" (15). But in a later essay in the same concise volume, "Shooters Inc.," she strikes a decidedly mobile and public stance in which she "happened to be in Amman" and happened to be talking with "officials at the American embassy there" (88). In "Girl of the Golden West," also in *After Henry,* she uses a family document, the diary of one of her ancestors, in conjunction with excerpts from the diaries of other overland emigrants to California as a leitmotiv in attempting to understand the mental processes of Patricia Hearst, then uses that psychological study as a tool for understanding the culture Hearst seems to epitomize. The movement here is from history, in the sense of the past, to the personal (Hearst's psyche), to the historical in the sense of the historicized general—social experience in time.

Didion's freedom to move about the world epitomizes her personal freedom as a woman able to move among roles—wife, mother, journalist, novelist. Seeing actor John Wayne as a latter-day icon representing a conception of America as "a place where a *man* could move freely" (*Slouching,* 31, emphasis added), she appropriates that masculine and classically western dream for herself. In "John Wayne: A Love Song" and elsewhere, particularly in her earlier essays, she distances herself, by her detached or even mocking tone, from conventional wives, identifying instead with "those who live outside rather than in." She is a person on airplanes, in airport waiting rooms, in bars near train stations. Contemplating her own experience as a writer, she finds it a blur of uncertainty and movement: "waiting for a train? missing one? 1960? 1961? why Wilmington?" (*Slouching,* 35, 63, 131). In *Miami,* perhaps the hardest-hitting of her investigative political writings, Didion's geographic mobility is both foregrounded and viewed as essential to the enterprise of knowing and telling. She begins her effort to know the social world of Miami directly by spotlighting her own act of flying there and her sense of "heightened wariness" in making the trip.[34] Her personal feelings are insistently implicated in her political judgment (an-

202 Moving into the Political

other linkage of private and public), and both emotion and judgment are triggered by travel to the disputed territory. Her freedom of inquiry as the analyst on location is linked to her impunity in defying cautionary spatial prohibitions (as Levertov did in traveling to North Vietnam) and going "without incident to all of the places I had been told not to go" (39).

Repeatedly, however, Didion mentions that she has brought along on her public journeyings (movements about public spaces, carried out for the purpose of addressing public issues) those essential emblems of her private roles and traditional femininity, her husband and her daughter. Even as she engages in public rhetoric, then, she presents herself in her capacity of involvement in private relationships. In one of the segments of "In the Islands" she is seen "spend[ing], my husband and I and the baby, a restorative week in paradise." Domesticity is inserted into the act of journey even in the structuring of the sentence. In another segment of the same essay she is at the Royal Hawaiian with only the daughter, age four (*White Album,* 135, 140). In "In Hollywood" she displays herself and her husband "fly[ing] to Tucson with our daughter for a few days of meetings on a script" (*White Album,* 160). In "On the Road" (a title whose echo of Jack Kerouac can scarcely have been accidental) she takes along her daughter to "divert" her on a book publicity tour: to divert, to turn her aside (in the radical meaning of the word) from the public(ity) to the familial. For a while she and the daughter fall into "illusions of mobility" and want to "stay on the road forever," but at the end they abruptly and with intense relief reject that illusion to "hea[d] home" (*White Album,* 174–78). At the end of "On the Mall," Didion is seen "flying back across the Pacific" regretfully lugging a toaster, that emblem of domestication, bought on impulse in Hawaii (*White Album,* 185).

The tone in such passages, like that of her more overt ironies, is hard to assess. As I have indicated, she would seem to be characteristically more worried about instability than about the doom more commonly feared by women writers who take departure as a central act: immobility. She suffers meaningless motion as an "amorphous unease" (*After Henry,* 110). Even so, she insistently chooses the role of traveler, and at times she does acknowledge a dread of immobilization in the home. Despite her ridicule, in "The Women's Movement," of "idle ladies" and the feminist "invention of women as a 'class'" (*White Album,* 110), she also sees that domesticity can be an "entrapment in the mechanics of living," and she frets over women's adoption of the "nothin'-says-lovin'-like-something-from-the-oven" mentality (*Slouching,* 212, 113). She speaks of "the burden of 'home' " (note the evasive punctuation) and recognizes both the desire to "get away from ourselves" and the possibility that "the way to do that" is to go somewhere else, to "drive" (*Slouching,* 165, 214). Avowedly committed to "the exploration of moral distinctions and ambiguities" (*White Album,* 113), she draws back from full engagement as determinedly as from full retreat. She locates herself "at once 'outside' and 'in' the social environments and situations" she writes about.[35] In short, she sees double.

Didion's most searching use of geographic movement as a narrative signifier conveying this double vision occurs in *A Book of Common Prayer* and *Democracy.* In both, with a less brittle and ultimately more searching import than in the earlier *Play It As It Lays,* she employs the compulsive mobility of twentieth-century life as a measure of social and moral instability. Freedom of movement is reinterpreted as the curse of movement—an inability to remain still, to come to rest, to be anchored. Even so, it is because they do possess a considerable freedom of movement that the central female characters in both of these novels, Charlotte Douglas in *A Book of Common Prayer* and Inez Victor in *Democracy,* are able to escape personal prisons of inauthenticity in order to achieve what must finally be called redemption. Much as in the nonfiction *Miami* and *Salvador,* which offer illuminating linkages, movement is seen as essential if anything approaching public truth is to be served, and especially essential for women if they are to escape the ennui and exploitation entailed in the debasement of traditional roles apparently endemic in contemporary American experience.[36] Seeing double, then, takes on double meanings: the seeing of both public and private dimensions, located in far-flung places and at home; and the seeing of those dimensions in both positive and negative ways. Ambivalently, Didion wishes that women's traditional roles of wife and mother could be viable and satisfying; she believes that they ought to be. But since they are not, she envisions radical departures from these roles.

A Book of Common Prayer chronicles the peculiar doom of Charlotte Douglas, the distraught wife of a prominent left-of-liberal attorney and the mother of a terrorist daughter who has gone into hiding, as seen through the eyes of a woman who at first seems very different from Charlotte but at last comes to seem, in many ways, her double. Stunned by the seemingly impossible fact that her idealized daughter Marin has participated in violent acts of radical protest and disappeared into hiding, Charlotte is torn between two men. Her first husband, and Marin's father, Warren Bogart, is a savagely egotistical, domineering, and sociopathic representative of an obscurely reactionary southern culture. Her present husband, Leonard Douglas, is equally egotistical though less blatantly so; equally domineering, but in manipulative rather than abusive ways; equally sociopathic in that his behind-the-scenes pursuit of international political causes in the name of some species of liberalism amounts to little more than a refined form of gunrunning. Unable to rid herself of an obscure and intensely sexual bondage to Warren, and apparently preferring his directness, however brutal, to Leonard's patronizing of her and his overly rationalistic deviousness, she leaves Leonard in order to join the cancer-ridden Warren in an orgiastic flight from death.

When Charlotte left Warren, years before, she left unannounced. This time she forces herself to tell Leonard first—a moral rise toward owning her actions. When Warren's abuses and affronts to social decency prove too much for her to tolerate, she flies to New Orleans, where she gives birth to a child, Leonard's, conceived during her nightmarish months with him in an apparent attempt to replace Marin. The child is born with hopeless physical defects.

Refusing to abandon the infant despite Leonard's urging that she do so, Charlotte takes her dying baby daughter with her on the first in a series of flights about the Caribbean that finally lead her, after the baby's death, to Boca Grande, a "thinly disguised amalgamation," in Lynne Hanley's words, of Nicaragua and El Salvador.[37] There she stubbornly remains, refusing to run away again even after she realizes that the place is so politically unstable that a coup is imminent, and so politically corrupt that the coup will have no significance except a temporary rearrangement of the players in the power game. Her own likely death, if she insists on remaining through the upheaval, can also be expected to have no significance except in the most existentially symbolic sense.

Didion's long attention to the machinations hidden behind political gesture and to the disorders attendant upon the breakup of social structures— even those which so deserved breaking up that the process could only seem inevitable—issues here in a work of perverse tragedy and an ultimately spiritual obscurity. Celebrated for its technical brilliance and compulsively taut style, *A Book of Common Prayer* is at once a novel of great singularity and a re-echoing of the preoccupation with the torturous "desire to go and necessity to stay" that we have seen in Cather, Tyler, and others. As even the superficial summary I have given here reveals, the novel is vertiginously absorbed in questions of the mutual impingement of private and public distresses. Hanley, commenting that it is a novel in which "war at home and war abroad intersect," offers an insightful analysis that makes it clear how precisely the work fulfills Bakhtin's important and historically astute call for a literature overcoming the duality of personal and political. The fictional Boca Grande, Hanley writes, is not only a version of actual Central American trouble spots, but also the "historical correlative of the war zone the American home has become," as "sexual relations between men and women . . . mirror" the obsessive political conflict in the tiny dictatorship. Charlotte Douglas is "the common target of sexual and international masculine enemies."[38]

As I have indicated, there are strong connections between Didion's fiction and her nonfiction. Obvious similarities in details of setting, atmosphere, and event between *A Book of Common Prayer* and *Salvador,* published six years later, underscore the documentary sense of the novel, despite its air of strangeness or surrealism. These parallels between the imaginary dictatorship propped up by U.S. dollars and the real one include an absence of tourists, the existence of a useless superhighway paid for by the United States, overbuilding of facilities such as hotels because of a baseless optimism about possibilities of "development," the fact that the "leading natural cause of death is gastrointestinal infection,"[39] and colored lights weirdly strung about the city. Citing the United States Government Printing Office *Area Handbook for El Salvador,* Didion explains that these surrealistic strings of lights put up in the fictional Boca Grande as an insane "specific against typhoid"—one of the details most likely to be remembered by the casual reader—are based on an equally fanciful attempt by the dictator of El Salvador from 1931 to 1944, General Maximiliano Hernández Martínez, to halt a smallpox epidemic by "stringing the city with a web of colored lights" (*Salvador,* 54). Moving back and forth between fact and fiction, she blurs the line between them. Charlotte Douglas's death at the hands of police recalls with great poignance, though actually with less vividness than in Didion's nonfiction account of what she saw there, the numerous political deaths in El Salvador—deaths so numerous, indeed, that they would seem wildly improbable if she did not cite factual documentation. Both books, then, the fictional as well as the nonfictional, bring to light the political instability and corruption of Central America and the role of the United States in either tolerating or actually fomenting an inhumanity that appalls her.

The central female "characters" of the two books, the traveler Charlotte Douglas in the novel and the journalist Didion in *Salvador,* are also, like Charlotte and Grace Strasser-Mendana, the narrator of *A Book of Common Prayer,* more similar than they at first appear. Didion does not come to El Salvador precisely as a tourist, as Charlotte at least nominally comes to Boca Grande, but her stay is even briefer, a mere two weeks. Knowing that, one can barely resist agreeing with reviewers who complained that the book lacked credibility because no one can gain any useful insight into so tangled a situation in a mere two weeks. But perhaps that is precisely the point: that the essence of the situation in El Salvador, its cheapening of human life, is so blatant that it *can* be adequately sized up by an observant person in two weeks. Sharon Felton, writing in refutation of the complaints of glibness directed at *Salvador,* asks rhetorically "how many mutilated corpses . . . one needs to see in order to be convinced of the abuse." Denise Levertov, we might note, also addressed the turmoil in El Salvador at about the same time as Didion and in much the same way, by graphic recording of physical atrocities.[40]

Didion does not pretend to analyze the causes of the situation in El Salvador or to formulate a plan for rectifying it—indeed, she goes far, as Mary Louise Pratt points out, toward rendering even the observer's viewing of events "destabilized" and anything that might be called truth "inaccessible"—but undertakes only to expose its brutality and the all-too-evident speciousness of the Reagan administration's pretenses of enlightened democratization there, even as she exposes the speciousness of the imperial stance.[41] In the novel, where she does not so drastically reduce to essences, the roles of visiting outsider and of narrator are split, so that the outsider (though she scarcely seems to be an observant one), Charlotte, becomes the foil for the reflections of a more knowledgeable insider, Grace. Charlotte has another label, however. According to her visa, she is not only a "TURISTA" and by nationality "NORTEAMERICANA," she is by "Occupation" a "MADRE" (*Common Prayer,* 15 and again 43). Like Grace, who is a member by marriage of the wealthy ruling family of Boca Grande, Charlotte becomes embroiled in political events (in history), despite her seeming "innocence of history and politics."[42] Like Charlotte, by "occupation" a mother whose mothering is disrupted, Grace is troubled by her relationship with her child. Like both of them, Didion, in *Salvador,* is both a person of conspicuous involvement in politics/history and a person defined (in part) by her role as wife: she emphasizes that she is accompanied in El Salvador by her husband. All three, then, are women of both private and public concerns. All three, most emphatically, are travelers—between roles as well as between places.

The figure of woman as traveler is established in the novel at the outset. The book opens with a terse one-sentence paragraph, "I will be her witness." The motif of travel is then immediately established when the reader is *addressed as* a traveler: in direct second-person address, the narrator, Grace, points out that the Spanish phrase meaning "I will be her witness," *seré su testiga,* "will not appear in your travelers' phrasebook because it is not a useful phrase for the prudent traveler" (*Common Prayer,* 3). Charlotte is then quickly introduced (the novel's staccato, sometimes stammering rhythm is also established at the outset), though not yet by name, as being, like the reader, a traveler: she "left one man, she left a second man, she traveled again with the first" and at last "came to Boca Grande, a tourist, *Una turista.* So she said. In fact she came here less a tourist than a sojourner but she did not make that distinction" (3). A few lines later Grace is a "prudent traveler" originally from the United States. "We" are all, then, linked. We, characters and reader, share an understanding, whatever it may be, of travel, and two of "us"—the reader and Grace, though not Charlotte—share the quality of prudence. It is a useful rhetorical ploy, casting the reader in a role of cautious (prudent) weigher and balancer, even as Grace will cautiously observe, analyze, and attempt to explain Charlotte's behavior. "We" readers share with her this detached approach. At the end, then, when it becomes clear that Grace has not been able to maintain such a detachment, that in fact she maintains the detached tone as a protective device against what is actually an intense emotional involvement, the reader's defenses, too, are overturned; we, too, identify, to some unwilling extent, with Charlotte. We see that we, too, are at risk of being destroyed by "history."

This bold strategy of reader involvement is of absolutely central importance if Didion's story of this conspicuously odd "Norteamericana" is to be taken—as I believe it should—as in some way representing the lives of women in general. Grace, the voice of a person maintaining the kind of reasonable and detached stance that the reader would like to maintain toward this troubled, eccentric "turista," is, despite her apparent status of insider, in fact like Charlotte, "*de afuera,*" a stranger. She, too, like Charlotte, lives in "tropics" of "fever and disquiet" (82)—literal ones. She, too, it seems, understands despair. And if we are initially inclined to view Charlotte's recurring dreams of "sexual surrender and infant death" (much like Maria Wyeth's dreams of sexual surrender and infant death in *Play It As It Lays*) as peculiar aberrations indicating profound neurosis, we are quickly assured that these are in fact "commonplaces of the female obsessional life," that indeed "we all have the same dreams" (53).

Charlotte, it seems, would echo an aunt of Grace's who advised her, at the time of her marriage to Edgar Strasser-Mendana, that if she were to survive life in the tropics she should assume that marriage was itself a source of "fever and disquiet." At the time the novel opens, when Charlotte has come to Boca Grande, she has experienced two marriages of "fever and disquiet" and has fled both. Whether for that or for some more obscure reason, she suffers from longtime severe depressions during which she manages to function, if at all, only by the determined following of a scripted routine and the maintenance of a brittle cheer the falsity of which was recognized even by her child. She thinks of this depression as "separateness" and has no idea that, as Grace tells us, it is also shared, "usual," among women (111). Finding in marriage either the cause of her gloom or at any rate an unavailing counterbalance to it, she attempts to center her life in her role as mother. She becomes indeed, as the Boca Grande authorities lamely say, in an ironic variant of the traditionally formulaic "housewife," a professional mother.

It is impossible, however, to live as a professional mother. Marin, her daughter, in becoming a radical terrorist (a fictionalized version of the Patricia Hearst story from real-life news), has been "lost" to "history." It is a curiously ambiguous phrase that may mean either lost from the private world to the public, *to* history, the times in which they live, and very specifically lost by her family to the interfering news media and governmental agencies; or lost so far as history can tell, lost from the public record-keeping of people and events, the public telephone directory, so to speak; or bereft of history, lost in unprecedented acts sustained by no historic decorum. The second child, the infant that Charlotte bears in New Orleans, born hydrocephalic and lacking viable liver function, is lost to "complications"—in effect, to mortality itself. The infant dies in Charlotte's arms as she walks and sings to it in a Mérida parking lot, a random way station on her flight from her entire life, while the taxi waits. It is one of the most harrowing scenes in all of modern fiction.

The story of Charlotte's failure to achieve satisfaction as either wife or mother would seem, in its particulars, unusual, even bizarre, but when those particulars are generalized as "history" and "complications" they become, like the obsessive dreams "we" share and the status of traveler "we" share, the common human lot, or at any rate the common female lot. None of us, the narrative insistence on generalization implies, can define ourselves satisfactorily as private persons. All of us must flee to "history," to the public. And there we must not only carry our private roles with us, but wake up—as Charlotte does, too late—to the nature of the corrupt world around us. We must, like Grace Strasser-Mendana, becomes witnesses.

What does that mean? At the end of *A Book of Common Prayer*, Grace says that she has not been the witness she wanted to be. The most obvious meaning of that sentence is that she has not been a detached or what is commonly called an objective witness. At the outset she defines herself as a rationalist, a scientist who believes that if the human vagaries she designates as (in quotation marks) "personality" can be excluded from one's field of study—as she believes that they are from her scientific field, biochemistry—one can get "demonstrable answers" (4). Her narrative style throughout is designed to transfer, as nearly as possible, the supposed methodological certainties of scientific investigation to her study of Charlotte Douglas. That study is, as she says in her opening sentence, an act of witnessing—that is, in one sense, of observing. In her observance and description of Charlotte, she limits herself to a strict empiricism. Scrupulously distinguishing (except in Section II, where much of the narration becomes less clearly that of Grace) between what she has observed herself and what she has heard or what she guesses, she reports observed fact. She strives for certainty. But toward the end of the book, as she comes to care about Charlotte and to identify with her, she increasingly admits into her narrative phrases conveying heightened and compressed emotional engagement and statements of a more speculative kind—for the most part, inferences derived by cross-checking among statements made by others who know Charlotte and by Charlotte herself. She finds that on occasion she "liked Charlotte very much" for her values and her honesty: "No irony. However cheap" (234).

Grace becomes, then, a participant rather than merely an observer of

Charlotte's story. She tries to get Charlotte to leave the country to safety, she contacts Leonard Douglas seeking his help in persuading her to do so, she travels to Buffalo to see Marin despite the fact that she is succumbing to cancer, and, once there, persists in pressing their tense conversation to the point that Marin will recognize her love for her mother. No longer detached, Grace abandons her faith in the empirical method: "The wind is up and I will die and rather soon and all I know empirically is *I am told*" (280). Without the shield of her former (unfounded) certainty and artificial detachment, she is compelled to recognize that her field of observation has been characterized all along by uncertainty—much like the opacity of the field of observation that Didion encounters in El Salvador. At the end Grace is left with inconclusive scraps rather than data:

> I am told, and so she said.
> I heard later.
> According to her passport. It was reported.
> Apparently. (280)

Recognizing the inadequacy of these scraps to construct the kind of explanation she hoped to provide for the behavior of this peculiar woman, she admits the failure (by her own standards) of her witnessing: "I have not been the witness I wanted to be" (280). She has instead become another kind of witness (still in the sense of see-r, witnesser) and a better kind, a witness who can imagine an event she had no way of observing: Charlotte's walk to the place where she was arrested, fully expecting that that would happen and that she would die. Paradoxically, this view of Charlotte, produced by the informed and sympathetic imagination rather than by detached actual observation (eye-witnessing), is a fuller certainty than the empirical truth Grace had intended to pursue.

We might extend our interrogation of Grace as witness to ask how effective she is as a political witness. Clearly, her position with respect to the events of the novel reflects that fusion of the private and the public which we see elsewhere in Didion's work. The narrative she constructs by observation, by hearsay, and by sympathetic imaginative engagement is primarily a story of personal relationships—Charlotte's unusual ties with and estrangements from two husbands and two daughters. But it is also a story of public, political events. Leonard is a fund-raiser for insurgent groups around the world, Marin steps into public scrutiny as a revolutionary terrorist, Grace is at the perimeter of power struggles in Boca Grande that, while petty and repetitive enough, have attracted the attention and interference of some unknown additional power, and Charlotte steps into the nexus of all these matters when she strays into the unstable little country. (I do see Charlotte's arrival in Boca Grande as a straying, or more precisely a stepping aside to wait—for Marin, for her own self-possession—and not as an effort to "begin again," as Jennifer Brady views it.)[43] As a political witness, Grace has wanted, very consciously, to be savvy, informed, above the action and immune to surprises. But she has been surprised when the October Violence that proves fatal for Charlotte exceeds predictability. She does not know who the outside power is.[44] She is not the expert, unbothered witness of events, never under any illusions, never caring much, that she hoped to be.

But if Grace is less knowledgeable than she hoped, she is also more engaged than she once hoped to be. She has become a witness in an altogether different sense, that of an advocate or spokesperson, a witness *for* rather than *of*. It is this kind of witnessing that is not useful for the "prudent traveler," for the reason that it is dangerous. In speaking for Charlotte in this sense, she constitutes her as a kind of existential secular saint. At the same time, Charlotte becomes a kind of daughter to her. That quality of their relationship is pointed out when Grace goes to catch her plane to leave the country on the night before violence erupts and Charlotte, who refuses to use the ticket Grace holds for her, pins a flower on Grace's dress and dabs perfume on her wrists "like a child helping her mother dress for a party" (264). In keeping with the taut tone of this work, which is also the tone characteristic of Didion's work generally, the expression of love is tacit, but it is clear.

The times when Grace most cared about Charlotte were those times when Charlotte showed her vulnerability to being hurt or angered by political, publicly suffered events. Specifically, these were times when the ruling powers of Boca Grande, primarily Grace's brothers-in-law and her son, showed their callousness to the needs of the people by withholding and then destroying supplies of needed vaccines. In witnessing Charlotte's passion (the term, I believe, is merited) she also witnesses a different—that is, a relatively uninformed and seeming unalert but nevertheless engaged— mode of response to public events. In changing her mode of witnessing and witnessing-for Charlotte, coming to validate commitment and speaking-for more than detachment and speaking-about, Grace implicitly changes her vision of her own proper role as a witness of events in Boca Grande and a

witness for the people of that unhappy state. She has also not been the political witness or the political influence that she now wishes she had chosen
to be.

The fact that Grace departs to safety during the October coup while
Charlotte stays behind is centrally important, not necessarily in determining
the reader's estimate of Grace—which is probably rather detached in any
case, because of the nature of her voice as narrator, for much of the novel—
but in determining our final assessment of the puzzling Charlotte Douglas.
Grace's departure is reasonable—even if Didion did later refer to it dismissively as "running out."[45] There is no reason for her not to go to safety, since
there is nothing she could expect to accomplish by staying behind. Even if
there were, there would be no "points" to be gained (to adopt Leonard
Douglas's crass language) by disregarding personal safety. In leaving the
country she is merely being a "prudent traveler."

Charlotte, however, has never been a prudent traveler. At the point when
she decides to remain in Boca Grande, personal safety is not a motivator for
her. Of the two people she wanted to see again, one (Warren) is dead and
the other (Marin) is estranged from her. Charlotte has no particular reason
to want to live on. But she does have a compelling reason to rectify her own
view of herself before she dies. She has lived for years with a sense of guilt
for having left her first husband, Warren, without telling him she was going to do so, thereby failing to face up to her own actions. The fact that in
leaving him she was, for once, being prudent and following dictates of self-
preservation—he was both psychologically and physically abusive and
had once inadvertently struck Marin, still a small child, while hitting at
Charlotte—did not, in her own mind, absolve her of guilt. That it is a guilt
that Warren, ever the master manipulator, manages to use later in maneuvering her into a defensive and expiatory posture does not alter the fact that
she feels wrong for having run out. There is also the possibility, of course,
that Warren is not only a mad villain (as he indisputably is) but also the
voice of a higher morality; that is, there is also the possibility that for all his
shocking discourtesies and vices, and despite the fact that he says he took
her from Leonard because he "just wanted to fuck [her] again" (163), he actually does want Charlotte to achieve a level of moral transcendence. When
Leonard tries to persuade her not to go through the pain of seeing the hydrocephalic baby but simply to check out of the hospital and leave it there

for professional care, Warren insists that Leonard "wants you to walk away from here the same way you walked away from everything else in your life" (179). When the point of decision comes in Boca Grande, it is these words that define for Charlotte her vision of herself. Explaining to Leonard that she plans to stay, she says, "I walked away from places all my life and I'm not going to walk away from here" (262). The fact that it is not her country and that no practical purpose can possibly be served by remaining is irrelevant. All that matters to her is the gesture of not walking away. The moral vision of this novel is ultimately one of significant gesture.

A Book of Common Prayer is in this respect a singularly astringent text. It presents and implicitly advocates an act of virtue—a going beyond morality—undertaken for no instrumental reason but solely for its intrinsic meaning or value. "Behavior," Didion once told an interviewer, "is right or wrong. . . . In order to maintain a semblance of purposeful behavior on this earth you have to believe that things are right or wrong."[46] As readers, we are prepared by precedents of all sorts, including biblical narrative, to accept as a "happy" tragic ending the idea of self-sacrifice for a cause. We are probably not prepared to accept the idea of self-sacrifice (self-destruction?) for no cause. Yet that is precisely what Didion asks us not only to accept but to esteem.

In the days leading up to her final, calm walk to torture and death, Charlotte also demonstrates heroism in more customary, or practical, ways—that is, self-sacrifice for a cause. When the clinic where she does voluntary work in a birth control program is bombed by terrorists for reasons that Didion purposely leaves unclear, Charlotte (it is Leonard telling this) "goes charging in where . . . the ceiling's still falling, she gets three people out, she's a heroine, she's mad as hell, she's shouting '*Goddamn you all*' the whole time." Moreover, Leonard points out that it is "*they*" who tell him about it; "*Charlotte* doesn't" (255). That is, in the most purely heroic style, she seeks no glory or recognition for her bravery; she doesn't talk about it. In addition, she makes it clear to Grace and her son (Charlotte's lover) Gerardo—who, corrupt as he seems, is the only possible force for stability in the Boca Grande of the future—precisely what it is in the actions of the conspirators that offends her: their disregard of the needs of the people. Taking on something of the manner and the conversational éclat of Warren (an important indication that something like a redemptive heritage may actually be possible in the world of this novel), she demonstrates to Gerardo, by entrapping him in criticism of her own seeming inanity, the emptiness of his political rhetoric. When he replies "Bullshit" to her statement that if she could learn to use a diaphragm anyone could (meaning, the women who come to the clinic where she volunteers), she tells him, "Then don't you talk at me any more about what 'the people' can do." She has made her point, distinguishing her genuine belief in "what 'the people' can do" (a belief that Grace quickly labels "egalitarian") from his empty rhetoric (234). She leaves Gerardo something to think about, as she does again the last time she sees him, when she tells him in effect that their sexual relation has meant nothing to her and that he is not among the people she finds worth thinking about: "I've got two or three people in my mind but I don't quite have you" (274). It is a judgment on his ethical standing, and we know that he remembers it, because he tells his mother.

Unlike these words and actions that may serve some constructive purpose, however tenuous, Charlotte's decision to remain in Boca Grande and her subsequent torture and death can serve no purpose whatever unless as a symbolic act, a gesture. It is clear that she knows what is likely to happen. When she refuses to go out with Gerardo by helicopter, she tells him "I do realize," and as she walks to the restaurant on her final night, wearing clean clothes and tying a scarf carefully about her head, she mails Grace her ring and Marin's address—clearly, messages sent because she does not expect to survive the night. She faces her death, then, knowingly. She is taken away and interrogated and is shot in the back—precisely, Grace realizes, as she would not have wanted, because being shot in the back implies that one is running away. The coup ends and nothing seems to have changed. She has indeed died to no (evident) purpose.[47] Yet Charlotte seems to believe, and Didion to convey, that there is value in facing death resolutely when one chooses not to live, in going with dignity and courage, in providing one more piece of evidence of the evil of corrupt politics, merely for the sake of serving these values and realizing them in action. She dies to manifest the fact that she is willing to die, that she is unwilling to run away from public disorder. At minimum, she proves that to herself. In Didion's own biblically resonant words, she "finds her life by leaving it."[48] By staying in Boca Grande in the face of the trouble she knows is at the boiling point and by refusing to cower in her apartment or a hotel, she instigates a demonstration of the evil and the pointlessness of power struggles, of violence itself. She also, perhaps, dies in judgment on the disorder *to which* she would necessarily be running if she ran *from* the disorder in Boca Grande, since nothing else exists except insofar as variations of degree.

This is not merely a revelation of women's "victimization," nor is it the inevitable result of her "sexual adventurism."[49] Instead, her death is a passion—Victor Strandberg calls it a "martyrdom," "the Passion of Charlotte Douglas"[50]—whose meaning or purpose exists virtually in the realm of the mystical, a belief in the "existential" gesture for its own sake, a belief that it is better for an idea or a mode of resolution to exist in the world and be acted upon, even if no one knows it, than for it not to exist at all.

It is not quite true, however, that no one knows it. Gerardo knows it. As we have seen, he remembers Charlotte's words of judgment on him. And Grace knows it. The practical value of that knowledge can only be scant, since Grace, too, will die very soon. But she will die in the country where she has invested her life, despite the fact that it is a "place I have no business [no practical purpose] being" (266). In doing so, she follows Charlotte's example; she stays. Moreover, by way of Grace, Marin knows. Because Grace bothers to go to find Marin and to press on her, despite her own fury with the girl's self-righteousness, the fact of her mother's devotion, Marin "breaks"; the hard shell of her political certainty cracks, opening her to her mother's love and to a more compassionate realization of human imperfection. Grace has become, at the end of her life, not a prudent traveler at all, but a very imprudent one. She speaks the very words, "I will be her witness," that she labels not useful for prudent people.[51] The implication is that witnessing to virtue is or may be somehow redemptive in an ultimate sense, even if we can see no effect of doing so—just as refusing to flee a country not one's own, in revolution, when one is very likely to die, may be somehow redemptive in an ultimate sense. It is an implication of undeniably mystical import at best. Didion does not claim that we can see any tangible result of such witnessing in the world of events and public history.

Despite being a difficult and thorny book, *A Book of Common Prayer* was received with what Mark Royden Winchell calls "a general chorus of approval."[52] It has continued to attract positive criticism, though in dwindling volume. *Democracy,* on the other hand, published seven years later, has generally been seen as a falling off in Didion's novelistic powers. A review in the *American Spectator,* perhaps the most hostile that greeted it, labeled the book "a failure" and a disappointment and its style a virtual self-parody: "One can sit down with the same syntax too many times, just as one can bump into the same heroine once too often."[53] Why a narrative style hailed in one book should be slammed in the next, unless it is seen as being nonfunctional in that particular work, is not entirely clear. Certainly *Democracy* is similar in style to the earlier two novels, but that is essentially to say that it is recognizably in Didion's style. The tautness and repetitions of *A Book of Common Prayer* are sufficiently varied in *Democracy,* in my judgment, to accommodate the change in novelistic world. In theme—message, I would almost say—there are also continuities. The motif of redemptive connection between women that we see in *A Book of Common Prayer* appears again as a relationship of trust and partial understanding between central actor and narrating observer, in this case Inez Christian Victor and "Joan Didion." But that is a spacious motif, after all, and Inez is by no means merely Charlotte Douglas one more time. The motif of departure and journey, linked to women's independence and fulfillment, is also carried forward, with perhaps a larger measure of naturalness and plausibility added to its thematic power. *Democracy* is an at least equally impressive achievement.

Besides extending themes that are central to *A Book of Common Prayer,* the novel also extends elements of *Salvador,* which it followed by a year. Clearly, in that slight travel book that must have been, as Thomas Mallon comments in his review of *Democracy,* annoying to conservatives, Didion recognizes the corrupt imperialism of (primarily) the political Right in America. That is, she recognizes or perhaps "confirms" (since it seems to have been this very recognition that led her there) that the United States was supporting in El Salvador a repressive regime consisting of members of a ruthless oligarchy. This recognition, recorded in *Salvador* and continued in *Miami,* published three years after *Democracy,* is a profoundly reshaping one for Didion and is directly related to my earlier assertion that the term "conservative" is as inadequate to describing her stance toward public affairs as the term "liberal."[54] Katherine Usher Henderson is both astute and accurate in observing that *Democracy* "reflects the inner changes in Didion that both led to and resulted from her trip to Salvador" and that it was her "awareness of America's interventionist strategies in foreign countries" which "intruded" between herself and the novel of Hawaii that she avowedly meant to write.[55]

"Joan Didion" reports in *Democracy* that the intended novel was to have opened with Inez's memory of her mother dancing and was to have included such details as who wore what on certain occasions and from and to whom such family treasures as furniture and flat silver were passed down (social minutiae traditionally associated with women), as well as the hardships experienced by the American missionary-imperialists who came to Hawaii in the mid-nineteenth century.[56] If so, that indicates even in the discarded plan what I see as one of the two central points of the book as it finally shaped itself: that public affairs and private life impinge on each other and are, in fact, inseparable. (It is a point Didion makes again in *The Last Thing He Wanted*, where the effort of the central character, Elena, to atone to her father for her inadequacies as a daughter leads to her getting "caught" in the public tangle of U.S. relations with, once again, Central America—a tangle that produces "ten volumes, two thousand five hundred and seven pages" of "transcripts of the hearings before [a] select committee.")[57]

Democracy is indeed "the last look through more than one door" (15). If one of those doors is the story of Inez's failed marriage and the love she shared with another man, another is the notion that the United States can or should control events in places like El Salvador or Vietnam. Looking back through the door of the novel she meant to write, Didion/"Didion" sees what becomes, in Alan Nadel's perception of the finished work, a "subtext" in which Inez Victor "represents Americans facing the dissolution of their patriarchal, hegemonic conception of themselves."[58]

We see in *Democracy* and in the two books of political observation that preceded and followed it, *Salvador* and *Miami,* the culmination of Didion's long presentation of herself as a woman compelled, by whatever inner concern or fidelity, to redirect her attention from her personal life to the public issues in which that personal life is enmeshed. This self-fashioning becomes in itself a kind of fiction, in the sense of a representation in a narrative mode having epitomizing symbolic functions, hence a continuum with the overt development of a fictional character named Joan Didion. It is, then, another version of the story we have been reading of the heroine who walks out the door, after having looked if not escaped through the windows. Didion's nonfiction is a reporting of her social/cultural/political times and a reflection on her own role in these times. Hence the issue of genre that many critics have observed in relation to her nonfiction, that it is not precisely journalism and not precisely personal essay. Her interest is in the process of discovery and communication and the emotional effects of that process on the discoverer-communicator, as well as in the substance observed and conveyed. She "draws attention to the writing process itself by referring to where she is as she writes," thus telling "the story of the search for truth."[59] If that approach risks rejection as preciousness or self-indulgence,[60] it can also serve in a compelling way what is perhaps Didion's most recurrent theme, the involvement of the personal in the public. As Merritt Mosley comments, the author's location at the time of writing "is not one of the expected data an essay provides," but in Didion's work it is a purposeful inclusion.[61] Both her setting-intensive fiction and her nonfiction, which especially in *Salvador* and *Miami* tends to take the form of travel writing, are centrally concerned with "the accurate recreation of character meeting place"—or perhaps the impossibility of such accuracy.[62] Such meetings, which are actions at once personal and public, are also, especially in her later work, political.

If we see in *Democracy* a continuation of Didion's long dislike of shallow liberal cant or "radical chic," what Strandberg calls her "disdain for flash politics,"[63] we see, as well, her recoil from the political practices and interests that have for the past fifty years characterized the Right. She is disgusted at the machinations of macro-level business interests (not that the sway of such interests can be assigned exclusively to the Right) and at the human results of international political aggression, regardless what one calls its motivation. This deconstructive political vision, invalidating Right as well as Left, is continuous with her stance in both *Salvador* and *Miami*, where she makes it clear that she objects as strongly to the extralegal maneuverings of that conservative standard-bearer Ronald Reagan and the reactionary aggression of Cuban exiles in Miami, fomenting rightist revolution in Central America as an approach to getting at Fidel Castro, as she does to the long-ago side-steppings of liberal standard-bearer John F. Kennedy and the falsifying political rhetoric that glosses over political realities—a rhetoric employed as readily by the Left as by the Right. She is politically engaged, but not in any readily assignable partisan sense.

Didion's concern with falsifying political rhetoric and her yoking of corrupt public speech with corruption in private speech raise, once again, a parallel with Denise Levertov, whose similar concerns are evident in these lines from "Staying Alive":   ·

> A five-year-old boy addresses
> a four-year-old girl. "When I say,
> *Do you want some gum? say yes."*
> "Yes . . . " "Wait!—Now:
> Do you want some gum?"
> "Yes!" "Well, yes means no,
> so you can't have any."
> He chews. He pops a big delicate bubble at her.

> O language, virtue
> of man, touchstone
> worn down by what
> gross friction . . .

>   And
> " 'It became necessary
> to destroy the town to save it,'
> a United States major said today. . . . "

The kind of irony that Levertov pinpoints here in association with political as well as private life runs all through Didion's works. In her writings of the late 1970s and 1980s especially, from *A Book of Common Prayer* through *Miami,* she is intensely engaged with political morality and its symbiosis with what she sees as a spread of meretricious personal values.

As in *A Book of Common Prayer,* Didion's movement between the private and the public or the political in *Democracy* is centered in the story of a woman's act of departure from her marriage and her subsequent movement out into the world until she finds her "angle of repose" in what would appear to be a peripheral outpost of twentieth-century civilization. Here, the central act or pattern of action, departure, occurs in a succession of generations, so that with repetition it comes to seem, given the prevailing social structure, an essentially female, rather than merely individual, act. Women in this book necessarily, it seems, either leave or become mindless automata. Inez and her sister, Janet, are abandoned by their mother as children when she ends the "loneliness" of her marriage to their father (22) by taking ship for the mainland as soon as possible after the end of World War II. When Inez subsequently leaves her politician husband and when Janet, though only sporadically, also leaves hers, they are reenacting their mother's departure. The wife of Jack Lovett, the sometime military officer, sometime international operative Inez loves from the age of seventeen, also walks out the marital door, packing up and taking flight in what appears to be merely a departure, not (like Charlotte Douglas's and Inez's) a departure into some version of the politicized public sphere. Inez's daughter, Jessie, carries on the family pattern into the third generation when she also debouches, hopping a flight from Seattle to Vietnam on impulse during what may be thought of either as the Fall of Saigon or the Liberation of Saigon, depending on one's political perspective, but in any event is surely the Ordeal of Saigon.

Since Jessie's departure goes against the flow of American power into (and then out of) Vietnam, it might be seen as a political statement of demurral from national politics. But in fact it is not. It is only a statement of the emptiness of her entire life, her inability to find meaning or satisfaction in it. The family life of the Victors and the individual lives of each of the major characters mirror the "collapse" going on simultaneously in Southeast Asia.[64] Inez "walked out" of her aunt and uncle's house and out of her marriage (165); Jessie "walked out" of the clinic where she was in treatment for drug dependence (167). We would have "guessed" that Inez's experience as a wife would lead her to make such a departure, the narrator says (152), because we understand the nature of women's lives.

Like many of Didion's earlier characters, but more insistently so, the central figures of *Democracy* are inveterate travelers. Inez and her politician husband, Harry Victor, a U.S. senator who aspires or has aspired to be president, fly incessantly from place to place campaigning or going on "fact-finding visits" or transparently symbolic tours of solidarity with people in this or that country. They set up "homes" that are non-homes, merely sets for the image he wants to project. The recurrent code phrase that Harry's publicity manager uses for Inez's public self-presentation as politician's wife derives from airplane travel: "trot out the smile and move easily through the cabin." She has been trotting out that fixed smile and making those moves for so many years that it has all become a blur. But her most meaningful and authentic action on any airplane as Harry Victor's wife—because it is her only free, unscripted action—is an act of demurral from the expected role. Flying back to New York after the loss in the California primary that has derailed Harry's campaign for the presidential nomination, she dances in the aisle and sings "It's All Over Now, Baby Blue"—in the presence of reporters.

Jack Lovett, too, is an inveterate world traveler, constantly on planes or providing planes for unspecified political purposes, turning up in New York, in
Hawaii, in Jakarta, on various atoll islands in the Pacific, "shuttling between
Saigon and Hong Kong and Honolulu" (151). The Victors and Lovett and
their various hangers-on occupy a world in motion, a world lacking a fixed
center except insofar as Inez and Jack constitute a shared center in each
other. Fittingly, in this social world, deaths are associated with airplanes:
Inez and Janet's mother is "killed in the crash of a Piper Apache near Reno,"
that emblem of social transience (148); Inez, Harry, and their son fly in after
Janet is fatally shot; and within hours of Jack's death from a stroke in a swimming pool in Jakarta, Inez is on a chartered plane flying his body to Hawaii
for burial. Immediately after the interment, she boards a flight for Kuala
Lumpur.

Inez's flight to Kuala Lumpur, however, is not merely one more stage in
the constant shuttling. It is her withdrawal to make a stand. There, as she
had once said she wanted to do when pressed to name a public project she
could claim as her special interest for campaign purposes, she works with
refugees—involuntary transients. Her social work with refugees is comparable to Charlotte Douglas's volunteer efforts in cholera immunization and
birth control in Boca Grande. Both are evidence of an extension of their concern to public service in relief of suffering, and both can be seen as essentially futile or insignificant efforts, having little impact on the staggering extent of such suffering. Insofar as these efforts are nonprofessional and
caregiving, or quasi-maternal, in nature, they are also, of course, traditionally "feminine" kinds of social-conscience activities for upper-middle-class
white females. Didion does not allow us to suppose, however, that either is
merely pro forma. If the benevolent work performed by Charlotte and Inez
resembles the easily dismissible benevolences of society matrons who have
no notion of addressing systemic human problems in more thoroughgoing
ways, it is nevertheless, for them, real work, expressive of real impulses and
revealing, too, an intent to reject their previous social roles. It would be easy,
perhaps, to regard Inez's determination to stay at Kuala Lumpur as quixotic
or romantic, a gesture of personal grieving and estrangement—that is, a
backward-looking gesture and, like Charlotte's election of death, one lacking
in tangible purpose. But it is precisely here that the two novels are actually
quite different.

If *A Book of Common Prayer* narrates a woman's departure from her private, domestic life in order to achieve a broadening of awareness that ultimately embraces international political realities and entails a judgment on those realities, but an altogether emblematic judgment, *Democracy* narrates a departure from *both* private and public life in order to embrace a more honest private and public life and thereby make a judgment that entails commitment to effective action. Inez's withdrawal—or what might be conceived, by analogy with Charlotte's, as a "Passion" except that she lives rather than dies—possesses real content. Henderson is precisely correct, I believe, in seeing *Democracy* as representing, despite its many superficial similarities to the earlier novels, a major turn in Didion's career as novelist. For the first time she has "created characters capable of *successful* loyalties and of *purposeful* lives" (my emphasis). In the "two strong and autonomous women whose lives mesh in a pattern of order and purpose" in the course of the novel—that is, Inez and "Joan Didion"—she makes an "uneasy affirmation of the possibility of personal meaning in a world where society and politics are defined by artifice and self-seeking."[65] Inez is seen by "Joan Didion" in the act of performing needed if not necessarily glamorous tasks, and she is quoted as saying that she means to stay in Kuala Lumpur "until the last refugee [is] dispatched" (*Democracy*, 222).[66] That is equivalent to saying that she will be there for the rest of her life. After an adult life of "continual travel" producing a "deep anxiety," she commits herself, as Mark Muggli observes, to "a work that gives her her first permanence"[67]—but a permanence far removed from the home and the windows or "windows" through which she viewed the world in her earlier years.

The particular work in which Inez is engaged, assistance with the care and resettlement of refugees, is again one that merges the private and the public dimensions of her life. When asked, as Harry Victor's wife, to name a "special interest" for public relations purposes, she had seized on work with refugees with "considerable vehemence" because it expressed her own sense of displacement; she was herself "a kind of refugee" (54). The refugees she works with have been made such by public, political processes. But her own refugee status might well be seen as an indirect result of such processes as well. The entire position of the Christians in Hawaii, the difference in social class and family history that made Inez and Janet's mother, Carol, a permanent "outsider in the islands" (22), the assumptions about the acceptable degrees of latitude for men and for women that contribute to Carol's loneliness, the conditioning in thinking of her sexuality as her only effective currency that led her to write bitterly to Paul "Who do you f—— to get off this island?," which in turn led to her mother-in-law's telling the girls that their mother had deserted them so she could go to nightclubs (24–25)—all of these are examples of how public, social patterns impinge on private life. The family crisis that triggers Inez's departure, her father's murder of Janet and of a Nisei congressman who was apparently Janet's lover, is also, as a reviewer of the novel pointed out, a "violent mixing of domestic self-destruction and racial chauvinism" reflecting Didion's "impressive . . . political imagination."[68] As a result of this crisis, Inez is thrown once again into the company of the man she has loved since their brief (and scrupulously suspended) sexual affair before her marriage. Her departure with him from Hawaii, then, is the result of deeply held personal emotions, maintained over a long period of time with a mutual faithfulness that is reflected in her faithfulness to her undertaking in Kuala Lumpur.

Her departure from her marriage also reflects, of course, her weary disillusionment with the political image-making she has lived with for many years. She is weary and disillusioned, too, with the shallowness of her children, the shady business dealings of her family members, and the callousness she sees in public life at every level toward the human dimensions of international turmoil—the callousness she undertakes to counter with her personal commitment to refugee relief. When, shortly before her departure with Jack Lovett, she "look[s] out the window for a long time" before speaking to Harry of their marriage in the past tense (170), her vision is, in an image much like that we have seen in Willa Cather's work and elsewhere, expanded considerably beyond the walls of the room where they are conversing. Flying with Jack to Hong Kong on a flight that leaves Honolulu at 3:45 A.M. is an experience of "dawn all the way"—that is, the dawning of a new light, a new life.

If that new life is partly a life that brings her into acquaintance with the conduct of politics at a level of realpolitik she has never before known, because Jack is involved in the real and sometimes dirty facts while Harry was involved in pretenses and posturings, it is also a new life that brings her to a recognition of her own involvement in the larger processes of a historicized world: "The world that night was full of people flying from place to place and fading in and out and there was no reason why she or Harry or Jessie or Adlai, or for that matter Jack Lovett or B.J. or the woman in Vientiane on whose balcony the rain now fell, should be exempted from the general movement" (197). She turns her face toward that world even as she turns her face toward the hope for a life (what life remains) with Jack Lovett. In both, she undertakes to live with an honesty that has never before characterized her experience, private or public. Honesty in one, it appears, entails honesty in the other, just as corruption in the one eventuates in corruption in the other. This is very much the perspective of Levertov and Adrienne Rich and the position that Mary Austin took and tried to live by over a half a century earlier.

As fully as Toni Morrison, although in a very different manner and with reference to very different experiences, Joan Didion has been a writer both intellectually and emotionally impelled by a keen sense of history. Both writers, looking back, see a spectacle of displacement and suffering. If Morrison's is the longer perspective and the one more readily understood as a vision of sorrow, Didion's racially and economically privileged viewpoint is one that nevertheless takes in the hardships and failings of such groups as the Donner-Reed party, with whom she feels a powerful personal tie because of the presence of an ancestor among them. Didion's historical range, centered in the experience of westering and the (largely destructive) conquest of the harsh California environment, has lingered most obsessively over what she perceives as the loss of centering values, the resulting aimlessness of young Americans in the 1960s and afterward, and a national miring in the violence and dishonesty of imperialistic intrigue. She is a person "at home in the larger world."[69] Perhaps because the narrative she deals with locates its chief disasters in relatively recent years, she rarely achieves even a glint of the affirmation to which Morrison wins through at the end of *Beloved* or *Jazz*. Didion's voice is by far the more acerbic and the less tragic. The two are agreed, however, in seeing, as the answer to a spectacle of dispossession and dispersal, the achievement of a home, a place of centering that may, in fact, be actually only a metaphoric "place" of centering and must be, whether geographic or mental, a place of openness, of free choice, a place where women may remain because they choose to remain, not because social strictures compel them to.

Didion's main characters experience griefs that are specifically female in quality at the same time as they are also general, political. Morrison's share griefs that are specifically racial, but often female as well. Both create characters whose individual lives are viewed in relation to deep-seated social and cultural patterns, and both envision intensely personal resolutions that involve, in some way, an immersion in the generality of life. In Didion's work, the insistence of the person's involvement with generality, the polis, history, has strengthened in the course of her career. In *Miami* she espouses (in Sandra Hinchman's words) "repoliticization" of the "social fabric" of the United States in order to counter rents in that fabric caused by the increasing splintering of one group from another.[70] In *Democracy* and *A Book of Common Prayer,* she envisions the possibility that women may be able to move beyond their obsession with "sexual surrender and infant death" and the political vagueness into which their socialization has maneuvered them, in order to become the artisans of that mending.

POSTSCRIPT
Wandering Naked in the Cold

In months of snowy winter
When cozy houses hold,
She'd break down doors
To wander naked
In the cold.
> —Langston Hughes

Blithely travel-stained and worn,
Erect and sure,
All our travelers go forth,
Making down the roads of Earth
Endless detour
> —Josephine Miles

Only looking back is there a pattern.
> —Louise Erdrich

If Salman Rushdie is in fact the single most famous international and intranational migrant of our time, it is doubly significant that the tale he cites as his "very first literary influence" is the 1939 film *The Wizard of Oz*.[1] His statement is a peculiarly compelling one for me, not only because of its remarkable apparent candor (one might expect a writer of the stature of Rushdie to name *The Brothers Karamazov, Ulysses, Moby-Dick*) but because of my own particular feeling for the film. Probably half the adults of my generation—in this country at least, I wouldn't have known about India—would say the same: that *The Wizard of Oz* ranks as the all-time film experience of their childhood and also very possibly the all-time school library experience. So I can't claim that my response is either very unusual or anything like so literary as Rushdie's. For me it is the simple confluence of two factors: the memories of the film's magic that I share with millions of others, and the fact that we, film and I, share a birth year. That fact gives me a personal stake in it and thereby a personal stake in Rushdie's statement, as I also have—in being a woman who has gazed through many a window and gone out a few doors to wander naked in what have seemed like cold blasts indeed—a personal stake in the subject of this book.

Rushdie gives a spirited reading of the film as a rite of passage. Its "driving force," he says, is "the inadequacy of adults," which "forces children to take control of their own destinies, and so, ironically, grow up themselves." It is unfortunate, in his view, that a "sentimental moralizing" studio system forced this marvelous road narrative into the straitjacket of a precautionary tale preaching "east west, home's best." True, he concedes, against the "human dream of *leaving*" there exists an equally powerful "dream of roots"; but that countervailing dream doesn't stand a chance in this zestful tale of the road. "As the music swells and that big, clean voice flies into the anguished longings of the song, can anyone doubt which message is the stronger?" And so, he reasons, the "conservative little homily" stitched onto "this radical and enabling film" is a betrayal of its real message.[2] Fortunately, he believes, it is a betrayal no one need take very seriously, since in comparison with the power of Oz and Dorothy's emergence as a true heroine, the desirability of a return to the gray world of Kansas and her condescended-to role there is not very convincing.

Persuasively argued as Rushdie's reading of this important cultural artifact is, I find that my own childhood experience of the film was different. To what extent the difference is cultural, to what extent individual, and to what extent gendered is hard to say, but I suspect that any number of girls may have begun to think of escape and braving the perils of the road in order to gain independence and personal authority through the experience of having seen Judy Garland and then gone around humming "Somewhere Over the Rainbow" for days or weeks.

Rushdie remembers experiencing *The Wizard of Oz* as a liberating message. I remember experiencing it as a fantasy of liberation—a different matter altogether. He remembers Dorothy's decision to go up against the Wicked Witch of the West as a sign of her growth, her strength. I remember it as a fearful doom, an ordeal she was driven to undertake but one that I wished she hadn't had to. He remembers finding implausible her desire to go home to such a shabby place as a black-and-white Kansas farm. I believed every word of it. (I don't even remember thinking Kansas looked so terribly shabby—maybe just Kansas on a bad day). Most significantly, Rushdie seems to have been able to dismiss rather easily that specious cautionary message: however glamorous and exciting the escape, home is better; better not leave home. Not I. I took that message seriously. Not that I didn't experience some ambivalence about it. I liked Oz, but I liked home, too. Or at least I liked the *idea* of home. Whether I believed it in the film or not (that is, believed Dorothy thought home was so great, believed she really wanted to be there; certainly I remember resenting the fact that her aunt and the others didn't take seriously her reports of the wonderful place she had been to, and thinking yes, that's just how it always is), I knew for sure that I was *supposed* to believe the message of go home, stay home, home's best.

How could I think otherwise? Everything in my early conditioning was giving me the same message. If I went off without permission to my aunt's house two blocks away for so much as an hour or two, the household was disrupted; my mother cried and accused my dad of not caring how I wandered around. It was impressed upon me by every responsible adult I knew that it was dangerous to walk to the store or take the bus across town to my piano lesson or go to the swimming pool with a friend. We—we girls, that is—had to be very careful; we mustn't let a stranger in a car drive close enough to grab us when we were walking to school; we must ignore wolf whistles, act as though we just didn't hear them. In short, for our own good, we were to efface ourselves when we went out on the public streets. Looking back, I seem to have stumbled over my own feet and fallen down a lot. At the time I thought I was just a klutz. Now I wonder. Maybe I was acting out the message I had been taught, that girls are unable to navigate public spaces. When I sat on a neighbor's back porch, as a euphoric high school senior, and daydreamed out loud about getting a college degree and a teaching certificate and an apartment of my own, she was shocked that I would imagine living away from home unmarried and told me so in no uncertain terms.

Not all the messages were the negative ones of fear and disapproval and sexist language and separate conditioning of our aspirations. There were also, to persuade us with positive enticements, the magazines full of home decorating illustrations, the marvelous and intricate recipes, the suggested table settings for dinner parties, the ads that featured happy women in happy homes. I bought it all the way. Or *almost* all the way: a crucial difference. So did most of the girls of my generation. But there was still that ambivalence. I understood what was wrong when women described themselves as "just a housewife"; I saw the simpers when they made a point of saying, instead, "homemaker"; I despised it and vowed (inwardly, of course) never to describe myself either way. And yet I dreamed of making that home, keeping that house—while at the same time I dreamed of being a superb concert pianist or, more realistically, a paragon of a secretary. I never wondered how it all might fit together.

Oddly enough, all the while I was absorbing those cultural messages in glorification of home, I was hearing my mother and her weary friends describe the domestic life as drudgery, a life sentence either to hard physical labor or, if one shirked it, social and personal disgrace. (Unwaxed floors, unsorted laundry, untried recipes meant failure as a woman.) I saw my mother's and her friends' mental numbness and her determination that I would have a chance to do things she had only dreamed of, before I, too, settled—as was fully expected—into that drudgery, that numbness. What I am saying is, there were conflicting messages. There were messages that made one want to go out the door and not look back, to avoid at all cost, like Ruth and Sylvie, the doom of housekeeping—only not to the point of actually going, as they do, on the road of vagrancy. I was never brave enough even to imagine that. Going away and making my own home in what I thought (in my hopefulness, my ignorance) would be my own way was about my limit. I knew, without being told, that *Little House on the Prairie* was a backward-looking fantasy; but it was a fantasy I doted on. And the last book of the Laura Ingalls Wilder series that I read so voraciously, *Those Happy, Golden Years,* with its romance of leaving home and going *to a new home* with a man to love, was, at the threshold to adolescence, the most compelling dream I knew.

All this means that I wasn't able to experience *The Wizard of Oz* the way Salman Rushdie experienced it. Everything in my conditioning militated against it. That film, born the same year as I was, bespoke for me a more genuine, more thoroughgoing ambivalence than it ever did for him. And it is that ambivalence, I believe, which makes the film so significant a cultural icon. It came at a time when more women than ever before were wanting to go over some rainbow or other—were actually envisioning, in fact, in the brightest technicolor, the possibility of doing so—but a time when our older authority figures were for the most part doing everything they could to persuade us that we hadn't seen Oz, hadn't considered staying there if we had, had really wanted, all the time, to come home.

So I can relate to the ambivalence about leaving home that is so compelling in the novels of Mary Austin and Willa Cather and Anne Tyler. I can feel the strength of those contrary pulls shaping their novels. Austin and Cather and Tyler speak for a multigenerational epoch of women—white women, for the most part, since women of color have so often been denied even the dream—who glimpsed the open road as compellingly as Walt Whitman did half a century earlier and who determined, in some way, to take that road, yet who wanted the completeness of road and home, both. And why not? Why shouldn't women imagine being complete persons, as men seemed to be? Had we ever heard anyone ask a man which he wanted, a family or a career?

Now, freed of my secret and socially inculcated assumption in early life that women were simply less interesting creatures than men, I can relate, too, to Sarah Orne Jewett's quiet determination to demonstrate the adequacy, the radiance, of women's home-centered communities. And to Joan Didion's tortured determination to address, and have her women characters address, the public needs of a world that can't be reached by staying at home. But in my earlier years, the years when I was most subjected to the cultural messages being blared at a generation of (white) females, I couldn't have heard either Jewett's or Didion's voice of community. The assumptions drilled into me, or at any rate the assumptions I absorbed, were the individualistic ones of exceptionalism, the private world, private endeavor, private goals. I can remember how it irritated my mother when my grandmother used to complain that there wasn't an open, uncurtained front window at our house where she could sit and look out at the street, and their recurrent disagreements over that point strikes me now as having been all too emblematic. No, the curtains and blinds were kept shut; the street was screened off; we were to look to the inside.

The messages drilled into young black women then were, of course, far less hopeful even than these. A Toni Morrison, an Alice Walker, or, in a different ethnic community, a Sandra Cisneros could never have assumed all that I thought I could assume. It is nothing short of miraculous that such women are able to restore and reclaim pasts and futures that were taken away from them, suppressed, bludgeoned almost into nonexistence. And yet a Morrison or a Walker or a Cisneros is able to envision ways of reconciling the open window and the open door with the life of mutuality, and to do so with a complexity that awakens the imaginations of readers. They, too, have faced their ambivalence, and more than ambivalence, and if the balance in their works is different from that in the works of a Levertov or a Rich or a Tyler, it is no less an act of defiance and of reconciliation—but in multiple dimensions at once. That is what unifies the writings of the figures considered in this study: their refusal to give up defiance in order to achieve reconciliation, their refusal to give up on reconciliation while insisting on defiance, which means insisting on departure. Together, they illustrate a spectrum of possible negotiations of that tricky tightrope. Certainly they are not the only writers who have walked it. But they have done so, I believe, with particular éclat.

I have been emboldened to make such blatant use of first-person address here not only by the example of that noted migrant Salman Rushdie but by the extraordinarily personal and yet extraordinarily literary essays by women scholars collected in the volume *Private Voices, Public Lives.* Still, even with these powerful authorizations to speak in the first person, I have to ask myself, why should readers *care* that I was born the same year Judy Garland's *Wizard of Oz* was released or how I felt about it or about home or the imperative to look through the windows or go out the door? Only for this reason, and I am convinced it is true: that my experience of these things is widely representative, that it is an index to an important aspect of American culture in our time. And here the essays in *Private Voices, Public Lives*—by Susan Rosowski, Ann Romines, Ann Fisher-Wirth, Melody Graulich, and the others who contributed—and the thinking and honesty and openness of those essays become a resource in an additional way. They confirm that my own sense of being pulled two ways, toward home and toward venturing, is indeed a widely shared one. Leaf through the volume: on page after page, that same duality of impulse, that same need to go out the door but also to come back, to escape being pent in where the air is so stale but also to have and inhabit a home. Ann Putnam writes of "the inevitable conflict between human attachments and autonomy, this tension between love and work." Charlotte McClure describes "my early impersonation of my mother's ladyhood and my later rebellion against it." Ann Romines explains how her public work as teacher and scholar leads her back to private memories of her home and her grandmother. Susan Rosowski writes of moving between home spaces and university spaces and about "reclaiming love and family plots . . . to include our work."[3] All twenty-six of these essayists are women who have gone out the door of the house. Yet every one of them speaks of the necessity of staying, as well as going, and moreover of the necessity of connecting the going with the staying. Like Josephine Miles, in the second epigraph to this postscript, and like the novelists discussed in this book, these women scholars speak of making "endless detour" by, and back to, home, not as a stopping point, but as a place with windows and doors that one can go out of once again.

The authors I have examined at length here—Mary Austin, Willa Cather, Anne Tyler, Toni Morrison, and Joan Didion—have gone down a variety of roads, but have continued to detour, in their own ways, by home. All of them imagine necessary departures on journeys of selfhood and of reconciliation, in which the apparent detours turn out to be, after all, integral parts of the trip. Of the two contextualizing figures I invoked in the first chapter, Sarah Orne Jewett is an insistently detouring, looping-back journeyer, Marilynne Robinson more nearly a linear, outward-bound one. But even Robinson has her detours by home, when Sylvie and Ruth go back, in the imagination, to home, looking *in* the window and imagining the thoughts of the niece/sister who refused to go on the road.

Austin and Cather speak of the persistent appeal of the journey and also the appeal of looping back to home. Cather, especially, speaks of the appeal of staying inside and, like Isabel Archer in James's *Portrait of a Lady,* letting her imagination jump out the window—though not so much because the doors are closed as because she likes being there, so long as she can see out a long way.[4] Tyler speaks, somewhat differently, of the urge to get out and the necessity to come back. Morrison speaks—with perhaps the most complexly inflected voice of all—of the challenge to recapitulate and reclaim a departure and journey made long ago but misrepresented by the mapmakers, the roadmasters. Reclaiming the heritage of that historic journey, she incorporates it into her own, which is both a journey out and, at the same time, a journey back, reconciling male and female. Didion records the imperative to break out of stultifying, trivializing containment by entering into an active role in public history, but views with regret and anxiety the possibility that the journey may never reach its goal and that, in the process, the roots that hold society (and selves) together may have been severed. That is, the persistent pull both ways that is felt by Austin, Cather, and Tyler she also feels, but she experiences it less as a hope than as a gnawing fear of dual loss. Didion, of all the group examined here, has gone furthest along the road to the public, with the most pointed misgivings about doing so.

There may be, among the postmoderns who are not considered here, women writers who are all journey, who have never had to make a decisive departure because they were never really (imprisoned at) home. They speak a different language, to a different cultural world. It is not my world, but it is a new and, I suppose, exciting one. The writers I have considered, who speak to the experience of doubleness and looping, departing and returning, are rooted in the female culture of modernism, whether as participants or as heirs who have carried its liminality into the postmodern world, and they illustrate both the poignance and the power of that culture and its myths.

NOTES

PREFACE

Epigraph: Anne Sexton, "Rats Live on No Evil Star," in *The Death Notebooks* (Boston: Houghton Mifflin, 1974), 18.

1. Susan Rosowski, in her eloquent essay "Rewriting the Love Plot Our Way: Women and Work" (in *Private Voices, Public Lives: Women Speak on the Literary Life,* ed. Nancy Owen Nelson [Denton: University of North Texas Press, 1995], 32), speaks for me and for many other women of my generation who cannot recall encountering more than one or two women writers in their undergraduate and graduate degree programs. Rosowski notes, tellingly, that it was while she was teaching on a term appointment at the University of Nebraska that she first began to read Willa Cather, "never having heard her name mentioned in any of my classes."

2. Rainer Maria Rilke, *Selected Works,* vol. 2, *Poetry,* trans. J. B. Leishman (London: Hogarth Press, 1967), 243.

3. Janis P. Stout, "Breaking Out: The Journey of the American Woman Poet," *North Dakota Quarterly* 56, no. 1 (1988): 40–53. Annis Pratt makes a somewhat similar argument in "*Surfacing* and the Rebirth Journey" (in *The Art of Margaret Atwood,* ed. Arnold Davidson and Cathy N. Davidson [Toronto: Anansi, 1981], 145), seeing the uncompleted journey motif as being related to the difficulty of return for a woman transformed by quest: "She is met upon her ascent . . . with a forceful backlash, an attempt to dwarf her personality and re-accommodate her to secondary status. It is for this reason that so many women's rebirth novels are, at best, open-ended, the hero's precise place in society being left to guesswork on the part of the reader."

4. Annis Pratt, *Archetypal Patterns in Women's Fiction* (Bloomington: Indiana University Press, 1981), 169.

5. Carolyn Heilbrun, *Reinventing Womanhood* (New York: Norton, 1979), 185.

6. Eudora Welty, "The House of Willa Cather," in *The Eye of the Story: Selected Essays and Reviews* (New York: Random House, 1977), 53.

7. Karen R. Lawrence, *Penelope Voyages: Women and Travel in the British Literary Tradition* (Ithaca: Cornell University Press, 1994), 20.

8. Rachel Blau DuPlessis, *Writing Beyond the Ending: Narrative Strategies of Twentieth-Century Women Writers* (Bloomington: Indiana University Press, 1985), 142.

9. Michael Awkward summarizes Stephen Henderson's 1973 argument that "whites are experientially unsuited to offer competent readings of Afro-American literature" and the ensuing debate among black scholars in *Negotiating Difference: Race, Gender, and the Politics of Positionality* (Chicago: University of Chicago Press, 1995), 34ff. In the words of Houston A. Baker, Jr., "White women scholars . . . have been cautioned not to assume that their analytical canons . . . are adequate for the study of black women's creativity"; *Workings of the Spirit: The Poetics of Afro-American Women's Writing* (Chicago: University of Chicago Press, 1991), 11. Awkward joins Baker and Henry Louis Gates, Jr., in the belief that it is possible to learn to read "racial and gendered" texts across the "lines or boundaries" of group distinction just as, according to Clifford Geertz's theories, anthropologists are able to do "thick description" of cultures by learning to construe "symbol systems." The depressing history of relations between white and black women is summarized polemically by Barbara Omolade in "Black Women and Feminism," in *The Future of Difference,* ed. Hester Eisenstein and Alice Jardine (New Brunswick, N.J.: Rutgers University Press, 1985), 247–57.

10. Interview with Toni Morrison in *Black Women Writers at Work,* ed. Claudia Tate (Harpendon: Oldcastle Books, 1985), 121. On "negative socialization," see bell hooks, *Ain't I a Woman: Black Women and Feminism* (Boston: South End Press, 1981), 157.

11. Tey Diana Rebolledo, *Women Singing in the Snow: A Cultural Analysis of Chicana Literature* (Tucson: University of Arizona Press, 1995), 183, 80.

12. Joseph Urgo, *Willa Cather and the Myth of American Migration* (Urbana: University of Illinois Press, 1995), 40, 58, 62, 156.

13. Cf. Patricia Nelson Limerick, *The Legacy of Conquest: The Unbroken Past of the American West* (New York: Norton, 1987), on the West as "many complicated environments occupied by natives who considered their homelands to be the center, not the edge" (26).

14. Alice Walker, "For My Sister Molly Who in the Fifties," in *Revolutionary Petunias and Other Poems* (New York: Harcourt Brace Jovanovich, 1973), 19.

CHAPTER 1. THE IMAGINATION OF DEPARTURE

Epigraphs: Edna St. Vincent Millay, Sonnet, in *Collected Poems* (New York: Harper and Row, 1956), 591; Theodore Roethke, "The Waking," in *The Collected Poems* (Garden City, N.Y.: Doubleday Anchor Books, 1975), 104.

1. Muriel Rukeyser, "The Gates. XI," in *The Collected Poems* (New York: McGraw-Hill, 1978), 570.

2. Susanna Finnell, "Unwriting the Quest: Margaret Atwood's Fiction and *The Handmaid's Tale,*" in *Women and the Journey: The Female Travel Experience,* ed. Bonnie Frederick and Susan H. McLeod (Pullman: Washington State University Press, 1993), 212; Margaret Atwood, *The Handmaid's Tale* (Boston: Houghton Mifflin, 1986), 295.

3. Hélène Cixous, "The Laugh of the Medusa," trans. Keith and Paula Cohen, *Signs* 1 (1976): 875–93.

4. Lawrence, *Penelope Voyages,* 18. Lawrence's bibliography provides an excellent mapping of recent scholarship on Victorian women travelers and their writings, including texts long ignored but now again available.

5. Paula E. Geyh refers to the window's "double nature . . . apparent in the way that, closed or open, it might either divide or connect the inside and the outside"; "Burning Down the House? Domestic Space and Feminine Subjectivity in Marilynne Robinson's *Housekeeping,*" *Contemporary Literature* 34 (1993): 110–11. Even when open, the liminal space of the window is part of an enclosing structure.

6. The Enlightenment doctrine of separate spheres opposes "an ideal of women's virtuous domestic retirement to the scandal of women's visibility in public life." Margaret R. Higonnet, "New Cartographies: An Introduction," in *Reconfigured Spheres: Feminist Explorations of Literary Space,* ed. Higonnet and Joan Templeton (Amherst: University of Massachusetts Press, 1994), 3. This collection of essays illustrates the keen interest in literary space in recent decades, especially with increased attention to postcolonial literatures and approaches. Even so, we are only beginning to study the distinctiveness of women writers' and artists' spatial sensibilities.

7. My thanks to Lea Elaine Green, a student in my graduate seminar at Texas A&M University, for her grouping of these texts and her felicitous phrasing.

8. In *Writing Beyond the Ending,* DuPlessis presents a richly generative analysis of such narrative disruption and its social significance. For her argument as to the powerful social messages conveyed by narrative conventions (with acknowledged reliance on Raymond Williams's *Marxism and Literature,* 1977), see especially pp. ix–xi and 1–3.

9. Neo-Jungian Estella Lauter, in *Women as Mythmakers: Poetry and Visual Art by Twentieth-Century Women* (Bloomington: Indiana University Press, 1984), similarly argues that for visionary artist Remedios Varo and her "female protagonists" the quest "requires a rupture with the values that confine them within ordinary life situations" (95).

10. Dana A. Heller, *The Feminization of Quest-Romance: Radical Departures* (Austin: University of Texas Press, 1990), 7. Heller devastatingly quotes Frye to the effect that woman "achieves no quest herself, but she is clearly the kind of being who makes a quest possible," and Campbell that the monodrama of traditional quest myth pits

"the son against the father for the mastery of the universe, and the daughter against the mother to *be* the mastered universe" (4). My own study *The Journey Narrative in American Literature: Patterns and Departures* (Westport, Conn.: Greenwood, 1983) illustrates the prevailingly masculine cast of traditional journey narrative.

11. Teresa de Lauretis, *Alice Doesn't: Feminism, Semiotics, Cinema* (Bloomington: Indiana University Press, 1984), 160.

12. Roland Barthes, *A Lover's Discourse: Fragments,* trans. Richard Howard (New York: Hill and Wang, 1978), 13; quoted by Lawrence, *Penelope Voyages,* ix.

13. De Lauretis, *Alice Doesn't,* 121, 133, 140.

14. Julia Kristeva, "Women's Time," trans. Alice Jardine and Harry Blake, in *Feminist Theory: A Critique of Ideology,* ed. Nannerl O. Keohane, Michelle Z. Rosaldo, and Barbara C. Gelpi (Chicago: University of Chicago Press, 1982), 37. I am indebted to Thomas Foster's discussion of the Kristeva essay in "History, Critical Theory, and Women's Social Practices: 'Women's Time' and *Housekeeping,*" *Signs* 14 (1988): 73–99.

15. Lawrence, *Penelope Voyages,* xii, 19.

16. Melody Graulich, Afterword to Mary Austin, *Cactus Thorn* (Reno: University of Nevada Press, 1988), 111. It is well to remember Patricia Nelson Limerick's caution that "the creature known as 'the pioneer woman' is a generic concept imposed on a diverse reality" (*The Legacy of Conquest,* 50).

17. Nancy K. Miller, *The Heroine's Text: Readings in the French and English Novel, 1722–1782* (New York: Columbia University Press, 1980), 157. DuPlessis, who cites Miller's comment in her analysis of the romantic "script" of nineteenth-century novels, sees Jane Austen's *Emma* and *Pride and Prejudice* as "valorizing" the institution of marriage. One might, however, see them as books that valorize personal assertiveness by women and personal growth by men and women alike, by demonstrating that assertive women can find happiness within a social system that more commonly enforces very different behaviors. I persist in thinking of Austen as a more disruptive writer than DuPlessis does. To adopt DuPlessis's own mapping of the continuum, I join with Sandra M. Gilbert and Susan Gubar (in *The Madwoman in the Attic: The Woman Writer and the Nineteenth-Century Imagination* [New Haven: Yale University Press, 1979]) in emphasizing "the subversive" in these texts, whereas DuPlessis (*Writing Beyond the Ending,* 201) emphasizes "the dominant." The difference in twentieth-century novels of departure and journey is that the subversive has become a part of, and often the focus of, the dominant action.

18. Domna C. Stanton, "Difference on Trial: A Critique of the Maternal Metaphor in Cixous, Irigaray, and Kristeva," in *The Poetics of Gender,* ed. Nancy K. Miller (New York: Columbia University Press, 1986), 158–59.

19. Lawrence, *Penelope Voyages,* 17–20.

20. Ibid., 21.

21. Josephine Donovan terms *Pointed Firs* "structurally innovative" but "diffi-

cult to classify by genre" since it is "more unified than a collection of sketches, yet looser than the traditional novel"; *Sarah Orne Jewett* (New York: Frederick Ungar, 1980), 99.

22. Quoted by Elizabeth A. Meese, *Crossing the Double-Cross: The Practice of Feminist Criticism* (Chapel Hill: University of North Carolina Press, 1986), 12. Elizabeth Ammons provides a useful discussion of the "nuclear" structure of geographic motion in *The Country of the Pointed Firs,* which "ray[s] out from this central edifice/relationship in disparate and seemingly random directions" but "collects weight at the middle," in an "inclusive and accumulative" weblike pattern; "Going in Circles: The Female Geography of Jewett's *Country of the Pointed Firs,*" *Studies in the Literary Imagination* 16 (1983): 85; *Conflicting Stories: American Women Writers at the Turn into the Twentieth Century* (New York: Oxford University Press, 1992), 52.

23. Margaret Roman, *Sarah Orne Jewett: Reconstructing Gender* (Tuscaloosa: University of Alabama Press, 1992), 11–13.

24. The publication history of *The Country of the Pointed Firs* is summarized by Cynthia J. Goheen in a note to her article "Rebirth of the Seafarer: Sarah Orne Jewett's *The Country of the Pointed Firs,*" *Colby Library Quarterly* 23 (1987): 154–64, as follows: "*The Country of the Pointed Firs* appeared first in the *Atlantic Monthly* in four installments between January and September of 1896. Before Houghton, Mifflin and Company published the novel at the year's end, Jewett revised the manuscript. Among other changes she added two final chapters, 'Along Shore' and 'The Backward View,' and compressed 'The Bowden Reunion' into one, bringing the total to twenty-one chapters. When the novel was republished a year after Jewett's death, the editors tacked on two short stories and called them chapters twenty-two and twenty-three. In a 1919 reprinting yet another short story was added, and the order of the last four chapters was rearranged. Willa Cather's 1925 edition rearranged the last four yet again. The fact that Jewett neither added chapters to the text nor authorized others to do so indicates that for her, at least, *The Country of the Pointed Firs* comprised twenty-one chapters only" (154–55). Ammons comments that Cather, following the lead of Jewett's publishers, "ruin[ed] the book structurally" ("Going in Circles," 86); see also Ammons, *Conflicting Stories,* 55.

25. Jewett, *The Country of the Pointed Firs and Other Stories,* with an introduction by Mary Ellen Chase and an introduction to the Norton Edition by Marjorie Pryse (New York: Norton, 1981), 8.

26. The development of the closeness of the narrator and Mrs. Todd is initiated in the shift from third-person to first-person narration in the second chapter, a change that moves the reader closer to the narrator and thus, as their relationship develops, closer to Mrs. Todd as well.

27. Donovan (*Sarah Orne Jewett,* 108) accurately calls it "the central image of community in the work" but does not comment on the accompanying reiteration of female independence.

28. See Roman's chapter 11, "The Postponed Marriage," in *Sarah Orne Jewett,* 183–96.

29. Elaine Showalter designates "the kitchen, with its worn rocking chair" as the primary architectural image of women's domestic fiction in the early nineteenth century; *Sister's Choice: Tradition and Change in American Women's Writing* (Oxford: Oxford University Press, 1994), 14. Doorways and windows are, I believe, even more persistingly prevalent.

30. One needs to qualify the attribution of geographic freedom to male experience, however, since freedom of motion has rarely been available to men of lower class and deprived economic status. With few exceptions—among them, the important ones of American homesteaders and later hoboes (a few of whom, contrary to usual supposition, were women)—the men whose geographic freedom is sung and chronicled have been those of the upper classes.

31. Judith Fryer, *Felicitous Space: The Imaginative Structures of Edith Wharton and Willa Cather* (Chapel Hill: University of North Carolina Press, 1986), 49–50.

32. Meese, *Crossing the Double-Cross,* 122.

33. David Minter, *A Cultural History of the American Novel* (Cambridge: Cambridge University Press, 1994), 12. In characterizing that movement as one from Europe to the New World and the frontier, or from the frontier back to cities and to Europe, Minter omits the movement from Africa to the New World, the movement from Mexico up into what is now the southwestern United States, and the complex and largely compelled movements of American Indians as they were displaced by the advance of Euro-Americans.

34. Ibid.

35. Susan H. Armitage acknowledges that women's sense of being "uncomfortable and out of place on the frontier" was not "the whole story," since actual documents left by pioneer women "paint a much more varied portrait, representing an entire range of human experiences and emotions." Armitage demonstrates, nevertheless, the accuracy of the portrayal of "female reluctance" through an array of "letters, diaries, oral histories, and autobiographical novels"; "Reluctant Pioneers," in *Women and Western American Literature,* ed. Helen Winter Stauffer and Susan J. Rosowski (Troy, N.Y.: Whitston Publishing Company, 1982), 40–51. Annette Kolodny discusses social changes (including the constriction of their range of available achievement and importance) that contributed to middle-class white women's willingness to imagine happy, bucolic lives on the trans-Ohio frontier, and their dismay when the "dream of a domestic Eden" became a "nightmare of domestic captivity"; *The Land Before Her: Fantasy and Experience of the American Frontiers, 1630–1860* (Chapel Hill: University of North Carolina Press, 1984), 9, 166–69.

36. Robert Seidenberg and Karen DeCrow, *Women Who Marry Houses: Panic and Protest in Agoraphobia* (New York: McGraw Hill, 1983), 106, 209. Seidenberg and De-

Crow estimate (4) that of the five to twenty million people in the United States suffering from agoraphobia at the time, 88 percent were female, most of them married.

37. Gillian Brown, "The Empire of Agoraphobia," *Representations* 20 (1987): 136–37.

38. Ibid., 134–37, 152.

39. Charlotte Perkins Gilman, *The Living of Charlotte Perkins Gilman: An Autobiography* (New York: Appleton-Century, 1935), 97, 92–93.

40. Jacqueline Rose, "Where Does the Misery Come From?: Psychoanalysis, Feminism, and the Event," in *Feminism and Psychoanalysis,* ed. Richard Feldstein and Judith Roof (Ithaca: Cornell University Press, 1989), 32.

41. Cf. Kathleen M. Kirby, "Thinking through the Boundary: The Politics of Location, Subjects, and Space," *Boundary II* 20, no. 2 (1993): 173: "Spatial tropes underlie some of the most refreshing and influential of recent critical developments on subjectivity."

42. DuPlessis points out that "domesticity and withdrawal to [Dickinson's] family's house are viewed differently" in Rich's essay than they are in her poem "Diving into the Wreck" (*Writing Beyond the Ending,* 229).

43. Adrienne Rich, "Vesuvius at Home: The Power of Emily Dickinson," in *On Lies, Secrets, and Silence: Selected Prose, 1966–1978* (New York: Norton, 1979), 157–83; *The Complete Poems of Emily Dickinson,* ed. Thomas H. Johnson (Boston: Little, Brown, 1960). The numbers associated with Dickinson's poems here refer to their numbering in the Johnson edition.

44. Such departures, then, implicate the "ideal of an autonomous" self that has traditionally been a goal of American feminism, as distinct from the "subversion/dispersion of the core" that has characterized French feminism. Jane Gallop, "Introduction," and Carolyn Burke, "Rethinking the Maternal," in Eisenstein and Jardine, *The Future of Difference,* 106–9.

45. Fryer, *Felicitous Space,* 217.

46. Porter, *The Collected Stories* (New York: Harcourt, Brace and World, 1965), 221.

47. Cather, *Willa Cather on Writing* (New York: Knopf, 1949), 109. Porter's marginal annotations are found in her personal copy preserved in the Library of Katherine Anne Porter, Special Collections, University of Maryland at College Park Libraries; quoted by permission.

48. Porter, *The Collected Essays and Occasional Writings of Katherine Anne Porter* (Boston: Houghton Mifflin/Seymour Lawrence, 1970), 32.

49. Minter, *History of the American Novel,* 57, 60.

50. Mary Suzanne Schriber, "Edith Wharton and Travel Writing as Self-Discovery," *American Literature* 59 (1987): 258–59, 261, 264.

51. Minter, *History of the American Novel,* 70.

52. Elizabeth Ammons, *Edith Wharton's Argument with America* (Athens: University of Georgia Press, 1980), 121.

53. Blanche H. Gelfant, " 'Lives' of Women Writers: Cather, Austin, Porter / and Willa, Mary, Katherine Anne," in *Women Writing in America: Voices in Collage* (Hanover, N.H.: University Press of New England, 1984), 228–29.

54. Willa Cather to Dorothy Canfield Fisher, February 16, 1933, Dorothy Canfield Fisher Papers, University of Vermont. Cather's statement is biographically significant, due to the clear evidence that her fiction draws pervasively on her own experience.

55. See Shari Benstock's informative *Women of the Left Bank: Paris, 1900–1940* (Austin: University of Texas Press, 1986), esp. 8–20. The women Benstock writes about, she says, "appeared to share a common factor in expatriating: they wanted to escape America and to find in Europe the necessary cultural, sexual, and personal freedom to explore their creative intuitions" (10).

56. Annis Pratt, in *Archetypal Patterns,* 6, 169, and *passim,* sees women's experience in general as one in which the "drive towards growth as persons is thwarted" by the erection of culturally enforced "social enclosure." In her view, in order for a woman to achieve authenticity it is unavoidable that she will "turn away" from cultural forms that seek to encase her in conformity, and thus it is unavoidable that she will become in some way an oddity.

57. Geyh, "Burning Down the House," 104.

58. Marilynne Robinson, *Housekeeping* (New York: Farrar, Straus & Giroux, 1980), 3.

59. Gilbert and Gubar, *The Madwoman in the Attic,* 85; Geyh, "Burning Down the House," 109.

60. Meese, *Crossing the Double-Cross,* 60.

61. Martha Ravits, "Extending the American Range: Marilynne Robinson's *Housekeeping,*" *American Literature* 61 (1989): 659, 653–54.

62. Cf. the ending of Australian novelist Christina Stead's *The Man Who Loved Children* (1940), where the growing-up girl Louie, pondering her own act of running away from home, also recognizes the significance of the bridge by way of which she departs: "They would look everywhere and conclude that she had gone for a walk. 'So I have,' she thought, smiling secretly, 'I have gone for a walk round the world.' She pictured Ernie, Evie, the twins, darling Tommy, who loved the girls already and loved her, too; but as for going back towards Spa House, she never even thought of it. Spa House was on the other side of the bridge." Christina Stead, *The Man Who Loved Children,* with Introduction by Randall Jarrell (1940; New York: Holt, Rinehart and Winston, 1965), 526–27. The lingering, in this passage, over the names of those Louie is leaving behind conveys the possibility also raised in *House-*

keeping that one can depart from structures without abandoning relational feeling. I am indebted to DuPlessis's mention of this little-read novel (*Writing Beyond the Ending*, 99).

63. Ravits, "Extending the American Range," 645. Ravits astutely notes (645 and 661) that the invocation of *Moby-Dick* that opens the novel occurs within a "revision of Biblical patrilinear genealogies" and observes echoes of the Book of Ruth, not only in the narrator's name but in aspects of the story. The parallel with Ruth is also noted by, for example, Phyllis Lassner, in "Escaping the Mirror of Sameness: Marilynne Robinson's *Housekeeping*," in *Mother Puzzles: Daughters and Mothers in Contemporary American Literature*, ed. Mickey Pearlman (New York: Greenwood Press, 1989), 51, and is taken as the foundation of a reading by Anne-Marie Mallon, "Sojourning Women: Homelessness and Transcendence in *Housekeeping*," *Critique* 30 (1989): 95–105.

64. Lassner, "Escaping the Mirror of Sameness," 50.

65. Anne-Marie Mallon is incorrect, I believe, in her idea that "we applaud silently" when Lucille announces her irritation with the disorderliness of the household and judge that "it is she who shows the greater strength and wisdom" in her "realliance" with convention ("Sojourning Women," 96–97).

66. Geyh, "Burning Down the House," 119. Madelon Sprengnether's brief psychoanalytic reading of *Housekeeping* as a text that locates "the dream of presence" in "absence" and "deconstructs 'mother' " as it deconstructs housekeeping enlarges the application of the work's insistence on the complementarity of dual needs (such as for home and for freedom from home); *The Spectral Mother: Freud, Feminism, and Psychoanalysis* (Ithaca: Cornell University Press, 1990), 239–42.

67. Ann Romines sees the book as ending with "the transient's palpable and eloquent longing for her lost sister." Although she does not point out that it also ends with the the home sister's imagined longing for the transient, she observes soundly that "they are forever incomplete in their separation"; *The Home Plot: Women, Writing, and Domestic Ritual* (Amherst: University of Massachusetts Press, 1992), 295.

68. Geyh, "Burning Down the House," 119; Foster, "History, Critical Theory, and Women's Social Practices," 95.

69. Urgo, *Willa Cather,* 140.

CHAPTER 2. MARY AUSTIN

Epigraphs: Mary Austin, *Cactus Thorn* (Reno: University of Nevada Press, 1988), 35; Katherine Anne Porter to Robert Penn Warren, October 8, 1942, Robert Penn Warren Papers, the Yale Collection of American Literature, Beinecke Rare Book and Manuscript Library, Yale University.

1. Mary Austin to Witter Bynner, n.d. but by internal evidence 1928; bMS Am 1629 Houghton Library, Harvard University, quoted by permission.

2. Austin, *The Land of Little Rain* (1903; reprint, University of New Mexico Press, 1974), 17, 48, 116. Marjorie Pryse has seen the title as a verbal echo of Jewett's title *The Country of the Pointed Firs;* Introduction to Mary Austin, *Stories from the Country of Lost Borders* (New Brunswick: Rutgers University Press, 1987), xv–xvi. Jewett is, to be sure, a strong presence in the work, but the more direct echo in the title is of *Land of Poco Tiempo* ("poco tiempo" means "little time," or "in a little while"), 1893, by Charles Lummis. Lummis was an active mentor of Austin's in the years leading up to publication of this her first book.

3. This point was made by an early commentator, Dudley Wynn, in "Mary Austin, Woman Alone," *Virginia Quarterly Review* 13 (1937): 243–56.

4. Melody Graulich, Introduction to *Western Trails: A Collection of Short Stories by Mary Austin* (Reno: University of Nevada Press, 1987), 2; Graulich, Afterword to Mary Austin, *Earth Horizon* (1932; Albuquerque: University of New Mexico Press, 1991), 376.

5. T. M. Pearce, *Literary America, 1903–1934: The Mary Austin Letters* (Westport, Conn.: Greenwood Press, 1979), 251; Nancy Porter, Afterword to Austin, *A Woman of Genius* (Old Westbury, N.Y.: Feminist Press, 1985), 307; Vera Norwood, Introduction to Mary Austin, *Heath Anthology of American Literature,* 2nd ed. (Lexington, Mass.: D. C. Heath, 1994), 918. I will argue that traces of ambivalence or what might be called counter-feminism sometimes appear in the novels.

6. For a feminist interpretation of *The Land of Little Rain,* see Ammons, *Conflicting Stories,* 89–99.

7. Since Austin was nineteen and had finished college at the time, Gelfant's reference (" 'Lives' of Women Writers," 235) to her migration to California as a "childhood trip west" is somewhat distorting. My summary of factual information about Austin's life draws on the work of Augusta Fink (*I-Mary: A Biography of Mary Austin* [Tucson: University of Arizona Press, 1983]); Esther Lanigan Stineman (*Mary Austin: Song of a Maverick* [New Haven: Yale University Press, 1989]); and T. M. Pearce (*Mary Hunter Austin* [New York: Twayne Publishers, 1965]). Fink judges accurately enough that all of Austin's work is "in a sense autobiographical" (*I-Mary,* ix).

8. Austin, *A Woman of Genius* (1912; reprint, Old Westbury, N.Y.: Feminist Press, 1985), 7–8.

9. For accounts of an early spiritual experience in which Mary gained her sense of a deeper self by meeting God under a walnut tree, see *Earth Horizon,* 5; also, Fink, *I-Mary,* 15, and Stineman, *Mary Austin,* 18.

10. Fink, *I-Mary,* 39.

11. Graulich, Introduction to *Western Trails,* 1.

12. Larry Evers, Introduction to Austin, *The Land of Journeys' Ending* (1924; reprint, Tucson: University of Arizona Press, 1983), xi.

13. It is difficult to understand T. M. Pearce's statement that Austin "never joined in the attack upon the Middle West which grew from *Main Travelled Roads* into the Prairie School of Middle Western writers." Not in the same way, perhaps. Pearce, "Mary Austin and the Pattern of New Mexico," in *Southwesterners Write: The American Southwest in Stories and Articles by Thirty-Two Contributors,* ed. T. M. Pearce and A. P. Thomason (Albuquerque: University of New Mexico Press, 1946), 309; originally published in *Southwest Review* 22 (1937): 140–48.

14. Nancy Porter, in her Afterword to the Feminist Press edition of *A Woman of Genius,* states that townspeople where Austin and her husband lived in the Owens Valley considered her "an oddity" (299). Porter provides a fine summary of Austin's efforts to combine marriage with career.

15. Austin's stance vis-à-vis economic development of California's Central Valley was not simple, however. Even though she praised the area for its indigenous beauty and life-forms, she passionately supported the water rights of the small settlers who opposed the claims of Los Angeles, even while she scoffed at the boosterism of those like Wallace Austin who hoped to profit by providing irrigation to those settlers.

16. Austin, *Earth Horizon,* 96; Austin, "Regionalism in American Fiction," *English Journal* 21 (1932): 97–106.

17. Ammons, *Conflicting Stories,* 88–97.

18. Pryse, Introduction to *Lost Borders,* xxvii–xxviii; Melody Graulich, Afterword to *Cactus Thorn,* 107.

19. Jewett, *The Country of the Pointed Firs,* 239; Austin, *Little Rain,* 163.

20. Austin, *The Flock* (Boston: Houghton Mifflin, 1906), 12.

21. Faith Jaycox, "Regeneration through Liberation: Mary Austin's 'The Walking Woman' and Western Narrative Formula," *Legacy* 6 (1989): 8–9.

22. Cf. Janie's telling her story to Pheoby, who passes it on to other women, in Zora Neale Hurston's *Their Eyes Were Watching God* (1937; reprint, New York: Harper and Row Perennial Library, 1990).

23. Austin, *Western Trails,* 94.

24. Vera Norwood errs, in "The Photographer and the Naturalist: Laura Gilpin and Mary Austin in the Southwest," *Journal of American Culture* 5, no. 2 (1982): 24, in representing "The Walking Woman" as a story in which "the man must be deserted for the woman to continue her journey in the wilderness."

25. Karen S. Langlois regards that fact as evidence of disingenuousness in "Marketing the American Indian: Mary Austin and the Business of Writing," in *A Living of Words: American Women in Print Culture,* ed. Susan Albertine (Knoxville: University

of Tennessee Press, 1995), 151–68. The sentence from the lecture introduction is quoted in Stineman, *Mary Austin,* 193.

26. The date of the building of Austin's house is often given as 1924, for example, in Peggy Pond Church, *Wind's Trail: The Early Life of Mary Austin,* ed. Shelley Armitage (Santa Fe: Museum of New Mexico Press, 1990), 14. She bought the land in 1924, but apparently the house was not completed until late 1925.

27. Mabel Dodge Luhan, in *Mary Austin, A Memorial,* ed. Willard Hougland (Santa Fe: Laboratory of Anthropology, 1944), 22. Quoted by Shelley Armitage in her essay "Mary Austin: Writing Nature," in Church, *Wind's Trail,* 3, and by Pearce, *Mary Hunter Austin,* 51. Few people, however, would have agreed that the imperious and waspish Austin was one of the best companions in the world, in any setting.

28. Norwood, "The Photographer and the Naturalist," 24.

29. DuPlessis, *Writing Beyond the Ending,* 85.

30. Nancy Porter, Afterword to *A Woman of Genius,* 312.

31. Stineman, *Mary Austin,* 136.

32. Austin, *Isidro* (Boston: Houghton Mifflin, 1905), 353.

33. Stineman, *Mary Austin,* 100.

34. Austin, *Santa Lucia* (New York: Harper & Brothers, 1908), 346.

35. Stineman, *Mary Austin,* 102.

36. William's peculiar naming leads one to ask if she is in part a portrait of Willa Cather, since Cather called herself William during adolescence when she was trying to shape a personality free of limitations by gender. Not only is the character named William, but her name was chosen in memory of an uncle killed in the Civil War at Manassas. Cather adopted the middle name Sibert, which she used routinely in her signature for a number of years, in honor of her uncle William Seibert Boak, who died as a result of wounds received at Antietam. It is not an easy question to answer. The parallels seem too strong to be coincidental; yet biographers have consistently dated the beginnings of Austin's acquaintance with Cather at about 1910, two years after *Santa Lucia*'s publication. I have found no evidence of an earlier meeting. Moreover, Cather did not characteristically share such personal information with people she knew only casually. I would conjecture that by 1908 Austin knew someone who not only knew Cather but knew her well enough to have heard these details. The link could have occurred by way of the *Overland Monthly,* where both published stories in 1897 and 1898. See David Stouck, "Mary Austin and Willa Cather," *Willa Cather Pioneer Memorial Newsletter* 23, no. 2 (1979): n.p., on similarities between the two stories.

37. Austin, *No. 26 Jayne Street* (Boston: Houghton Mifflin, 1920), 353.

38. Shelley Armitage, Introduction to Church, *Wind's Trail,* xix.

39. Scholars have differed in their dating of Austin's entry into feminist causes. Pearce (*Literary America,* 63) states that she moved to New York and joined the asso-

ciation in 1912, but prints a letter dated October 9, 1911, showing her address as 456 Riverside Drive, New York City, in which Anna H. Shaw invites her to speak. The discrepancy, if there is one, may hinge on vagary in Pearce's phrase "moved to." Nancy Porter states that Austin became involved in social causes in 1911 (Afterword to *A Woman of Genius,* 304). Augusta Fink places the beginning of her activity in public causes in the late fall of 1914 (*I-Mary,* 172). On the Heterodoxy Club, see Dee Garrison, *Mary Heaton Vorse: The Life of an American Insurgent* (Philadelphia: Temple University Press, 1989), 67. Garrison numbers the Heterodoxy Club among the five organized groups that gave birth to the prewar Village spirit (the others being the staff of the *Masses,* the Liberal Club, the Provincetown Players, and participants in Mabel Dodge's salon—among whom Austin was one), and considers it a nursery of modern feminism (67). See also Judith Schwarz, *Radical Feminists of Heterodoxy: Greenwich Village, 1912–1940* (Lebanon, N.H.: Victoria Publishers, 1982). Schwarz does not mention Austin, however.

40. Austin, *The Lovely Lady* (Garden City, N.Y.: Doubleday, Page, 1913), 114–15.

41. That Kate Bixby's situation—i.e., working as a schoolteacher despite being married—does not sound radical today is owing to the efforts of women like Austin. In her day it was not generally possible to do so. If a note found among her papers was accurate, the radicalness of this idea contributed to the story's being "rejected by many editors" (Austin, *Western Trails,* 274, editor's note).

42. Pearce places Austin and Steffens's meeting in 1906 (*Literary America,* 41); Fink places it in 1907 (*I-Mary,* 154).

43. Karen S. Langlois, "Mary Austin and Lincoln Steffens," *Huntington Library Quarterly* 49 (1986): 364; Graulich refers to the relationship as a "painful affair" (Introduction to *Western Trails,* 13); Fink says more coyly that their relationship "deepened" in 1911 (*I-Mary,* 156).

44. Mabel Dodge Luhan, *Movers and Shakers* (New York: Harcourt, Brace, 1936), 67–68.

45. Ibid.; Fink (*I-Mary,* 166) also says Austin was "determined that their relationship must continue until she herself terminated it"; Langlois, drawing on a file of unpublished letters at Columbia University Library, presents the story as an insane attempt to gain control over a relationship that never existed ("Mary Austin and Lincoln Steffens").

46. Pearce calls her "a rebel to her religious and educational background" (*Literary America,* 102).

47. Fink, *I-Mary,* 127. It is possible that Austin and Sterling, too, had an affair, but more likely that their relationship was a rather fervent friendship. Stineman (*Mary Austin,* 88) describes Sterling as her "soul mate" and discounts the likelihood of a sexual relationship.

48. Austin, *Outland* (New York: Boni and Liveright, 1919), 11.

49. Mary Austin to F. A. Duneka, n.d. but apparently written between November 12, 1908, when Duneka asked to see the manuscript of *Outland,* and January 30, 1909, when Austin expressed disappointment that he had not liked the fantasy work; the Pierpont Morgan Library, New York, MA2347, quoted by permission.

50. Austin, "Going West," in *Bookman,* September 1922; quoted in Fink, *I-Mary,* 259.

51. Austin, *The Ford* (Boston: Houghton Mifflin, 1917), 48, 27.

52. Stineman, *Mary Austin,* 47. Actually, Anne is a real estate broker, though she does own the ranch that her father had earlier lost.

53. The book also refers to a wealthy woman in Taos who has fallen in love with and married an Indian—clearly a reference to Dodge and Tony Luhan. Austin may have inserted the reference to the woman in Taos as a diversionary measure to lead readers away from the main trail. Eudora, like Mabel Dodge, is a wealthy New York patron of the arts known as a catalyst for events, who comes to New Mexico because of a sense of life force there, buys an old estate, and has it renovated. In addition, she is portrayed as being, like Mabel, sexually voracious.

54. Mark Schlenz, "Rhetorics of Region in *Starry Adventure* and *Death Comes for the Archbishop,*" in *Regionalism Reconsidered: New Approaches to the Field,* ed. David Jordan (New York: Garland Publishing, 1994), 70, 76.

55. Austin, *Starry Adventure* (Boston: Houghton Mifflin, 1931), 390.

56. Lawrence, *Penelope Voyages,* 17.

CHAPTER 3. WILLA CATHER

Epigraphs: Sarah Orne Jewett, "The Confessions of a House-Breaker," in *The Mate of the Daylight, and Friends Ashore* (Boston: Houghton Mifflin, 1884), 234; statement by Gertrude Atherton found in Francis Whiting Halsey, ed., *Women Authors of Our Day in Their Homes: Personal Descriptions and Interviews* (New York: James Pott & Co., 1903), 251, and quoted by Ammons in *Conflicting Stories,* 123.

1. I use the term *Bildungsroman* despite Susan Fraiman's interrogation of it and her suggestion that we "jettison once and for all the notion of a 'female *Bildungsroman*' " because of its originary bent to "define development in emphatically masculine terms"; *Unbecoming Women: British Women Writers and the Novel of Development* (New York: Columbia University Press, 1993), 5–13. Despite the problems Fraiman points out with the term, when strictly construed, I believe that when loosely construed it conveys a meaning in conveniently brief form. Cather's participation in an individualistic national myth was recognized over half a century ago by Alfred Kazin, who praised her novels for instilling aspirations toward "the individual discovery of power, the joy of fulfilling oneself in the satisfaction of an appointed des-

tiny"; *On Native Grounds* (1942; New York: Harcourt Brace Jovanovich, 1970), 251. Deborah Carlin observes that that view has "staying power"; *Cather, Canon, and the Politics of Reading* (Amherst: University of Massachusetts Press, 1992), 7.

2. Nancy Porter, Afterword to Austin, *A Woman of Genius,* 295. Regarding the historical emergence of career women, see Carroll Smith-Rosenberg, "The New Woman Androgyne," in *Disorderly Conduct: Visions of Gender in Victorian America* (New York: Knopf, 1985), and Ammons, *Edith Wharton's Argument with America.* Both are cited by Porter. The earliest comparative study of Austin and Cather that I know of is David Stouck's "Mary Austin and Willa Cather," an influence study focused on two specific short stories. See also my own more general study, "Willa Cather and Mary Austin: Intersections and Influence," *Southwestern American Literature* 21, no. 2 (1996): 39–60. Since preparing that essay I have learned that Melody Graulich presented a paper at the 1987 meeting of the Western Literature Association entitled "Baskets and Pots: Mary Austin and Willa Cather." Gelfant has explored some of the parallels between Austin and Cather in relation to the intersection of gender with modernism and with literary professionalism; see " 'Lives' of Women Writers," 225–48. The essay interrogates assumptions that underlie biographies of women writers.

3. Ammons, *Conflicting Stories,* 87.

4. Willa Cather to Ferris Greenslet, February 11, [1919?], and December 8, [1919?], Houghton Library, Harvard University, bMS Am 1925.

5. Willa Cather to Mary Austin, June 26, 1926, Mary Hunter Austin Collection, The Huntington Library.

6. Willa Cather to Mabel Dodge Luhan, November 22, 1933, Yale Collection of American Literature, Beinecke Rare Book and Manuscript Library, Yale University. The inscription is quoted by Pearce, *Literary America,* 205, and by James Woodress, *Willa Cather: A Literary Life* (Lincoln: University of Nebraska Press, 1987), 395.

7. Austin, *Earth Horizon,* 359; Austin, "Regionalism in American Fiction," 97–106.

8. Ammons (*Conflicting Stories,* 192) comments that the "mercurial relationship" between Austin and Cather may have been "the result of keen competition, a sign of shared territory"; Stineman (*Mary Austin,* 128) also believes it possible that Cather "regarded Austin as a competitor for the same literary territory," since both had "come to the Southwest for literary inspiration at approximately the same time."

9. Cather, *Death Comes for the Archbishop* (1927; Random House Vintage Classics, 1990), 297. Toni Morrison refers to this duality as adventure and safety; see Gloria Naylor and Toni Morrison, "A Conversation," *Southern Review* 21 (1985): 577.

10. Cather, interview reported in the *Philadelphia Record,* August 9, 1913; reprinted in Bernice Slote, ed., *The Kingdom of Art: Willa Cather's First Principles and Critical Statements, 1893–1896* (Lincoln: University of Nebraska Press, 1966), 448. Cather

also described her shocked reaction to the Nebraska landscape and her early home-sickness there in a letter to Witter Bynner, June 7, 1905, Houghton Library, bMS Am 1629, Harvard.

11. Urgo, *Willa Cather,* 5.

12. Ammons (*Conflicting Stories,* 139) observes that Cather "implicitly names but in no way attends to" such dynamics of power and exclusion as those of race.

13. Gelfant comments that both Cather and Austin "wanted maternal approval while behaving unacceptably"; " 'Lives' of Women Writers," 234. She tersely summarizes, "Cather had enjoyed being in homes other than her own from the time she was a child"; " 'What Was It . . . ?': The Secret of Family Accord in *One of Ours,*" in Murphy, *Willa Cather: Family, Community, and History,* ed. John J. Murphy (Provo, Utah: Brigham Young University Humanities Publications Center, 1990), 96. James Woodress takes a more positive view in "A Dutiful Daughter and Her Parents," in *Willa Cather: Family, Community, and History,* 19–31.

The importance of pre-oedipal bonding to the mother is argued in object relations theory based on, and extending, the "fleeting and fragmentary observations" made by Freud late in his career; Sprengnether, *The Spectral Mother,* 186. Sprengnether critiques both the "drift toward essentialism" in the influential writings of Nancy Chodorow on maternal bonding (*The Reproduction of Mothering: Psychoanalysis and the Psychology of Gender* [Berkeley: University of California Press, 1978]) and misreadings of Chodorow by feminists who construe her as being more essentialist than she is. Both Chodorow and Adrienne Rich (*Of Woman Born: Motherhood as Experience and Institution* [New York: Norton, 1976]) are challenged by Domna Stanton as bearing "undeniable traces of essentialism" (see "Difference on Trial"). For a useful summary and bibliography of writings on the maternal relation see Elizabeth Abel, "Narrative Structure(s) and Female Development: The Case of *Mrs. Dalloway,*" in *The Voyage In: Fictions of Female Development,* ed. Abel, Marianne Hirsch, and Elizabeth Langland (Hanover, N.H.: University Press of New England, 1983), 161–85. Also, in the same volume, see Ellen Cronan Rose, "Through the Looking Glass: When Women Tell Fairy Tales" (209–27).

14. Woodress, "A Dutiful Daughter," 23, 21, 30. Something of the severity of that clash is conveyed in a letter from Cather to Dorothy Canfield Fisher, undated but apparently following an exchange of letters between Canfield Fisher and Cather's mother in May 1903; Dorothy Canfield Fisher Papers, Bailey-Howe Library, University of Vermont.

15. Marcus Klein, Introduction to Cather, *My Mortal Enemy* (1926; New York: Random House Vintage Classics, 1990), ix. See, however, Slote's argument that Cather "had a rather glittering life of it, both professionally and socially" during this year; "First Principles: Writer in Nebraska," in *The Kingdom of Art,* 22–23. Woodress gives a balanced summary of the frustrations of this period in Cather's life in *Willa*

Cather: A Literary Life, 89–111. His incisive comment that Red Cloud "both attracted and repelled her" (60) puts its finger on her dual impulse with a nice precision.

16. Willa Cather to Mariel Gere, May 2, 1896, Willa Cather Pioneer Memorial, Red Cloud, Nebraska.

17. Katherine Anne Porter, *The Collected Essays,* 32.

18. Cather, "Katherine Mansfield," in *Willa Cather on Writing* (1949; reprint, Lincoln: University of Nebraska Press, 1988), 108–9.

19. E. K. Brown, with Leon Edel, *Willa Cather: A Critical Biography* (1953; reprint, Lincoln: University of Nebraska Press, 1987), 140.

20. Welty, "The House of Willa Cather," 49. Charles L. Woodard suggests that the term *recognition* is often more appropriate than the term *influence* as a description of the relation between writers; *Ancestral Voice: Conversations with N. Scott Momaday* (Lincoln: University of Nebraska Press, 1989), 138. One reason for preferring it is that it gives the later or "influenced" writer an active rather than a passive role. Certainly *recognition* is, for this reason as well as for Welty's sense of the confirmation of something already apprehended though perhaps not acknowledged, a useful and accurate term with respect to Cather's reading of Jewett.

21. Roman, *Sarah Orne Jewett,* 5, 13–15.

22. Undated letter to Mrs. Flynn, extracted by E. K. Brown, Yale Collection of American Literature, Beinecke Rare Book and Manuscript Library, Yale University. Katherine Anne Porter, whose view of Cather was a curious mixture of admiration and defensive belittlement, marked in her personal copy of the Brown/Edel biography of Cather (ix) a statement about Sarah Orne Jewett's having counteracted in Cather, by her "example and her precepts," the "cult of Henry James." "Miss Jewett the carved cherrystone," Porter wrote in the margin, "trying to undermine Henry James the granite sea wall!!" On the next page she marked a passage about the abatement of Cather's reading of Jewett and wrote in, "Because probably she knew instinctively she was Miss Jewett's superior and could not be really changed by her—Whereas James. . . . .!" Henry James was always one of Porter's shining lights. Brown, with Edel, *Willa Cather: A Critical Biography* (1953), copy located in the Library of Katherine Anne Porter, Special Collections, University of Maryland at College Park Libraries.

23. Jewett, *The Country of the Pointed Firs,* 229. Cather, *A Lost Lady* (1923; New York: Random House Vintage Classics, 1990), 13–14. Cather told Jewett in a letter written on May 10, 1908, from Italy, that she kept a copy of "The White Heron" always with her; Houghton Library, Harvard, bMS Am 1743.1.

24. Merrill Skaggs, *After the World Broke in Two: The Later Novels of Willa Cather* (Charlottesville: University Press of Virginia, 1991); Romines, *The Home Plot,* 151.

25. Willa Cather to Louise Pound, June 28, 1912, Alderman Library, University of Virginia.

26. Cheryll Burgess, "Willa Cather's Homecomings: A Meeting of Selves," in Murphy, *Willa Cather: Family, Community, and History*, 49; citing Elizabeth Shepley Sergeant, *Willa Cather: A Memoir* (1953; Athens: Ohio University Press, 1992), 64.

27. Blanche Knopf to Willa Cather, July 24, 1933, Harry Ransom Humanities Research Center, University of Texas at Austin, Blanche W. Knopf–Willa Cather files, folder 689.1.

28. Willa Cather to Mary Hunter Austin, November 9, 1927, Huntington Library MS folder AU 1939.

29. Willa Cather to Mabel Dodge Luhan, November 22, [1932?], Yale Collection of American Literature, Beinecke Rare Book and Manuscript Library, Yale University.

30. Ann Keene pointed out the connection of Bunyan to Cather's central symbolism of the journey in a paper presented at the Sixth International Seminar on Willa Cather, in Quebec, on June 29, 1995. The title of Keene's paper was "Questions of Travel: The Journeys of Willa Cather." See also Slote, "First Principles: The Kingdom of Art," in *The Kingdom of Art*, 78.

31. Melody Graulich conjectures that Jewett's influence on Cather may have gone by way of Austin (Afterword to *Cactus Thorn*, 112). I believe it is more likely that both drew common elements from the same source.

32. Romines, *The Home Plot*, 151.

33. Cixous, "The Laugh of the Medusa," 887.

34. Cather, *My Mortal Enemy*, 51.

35. Cather, "On *The Professor's House*," *Willa Cather on Writing*, 31–32. St. Peter's household is "not only overfurnished but also fatally feminized," impelling his escape from "a voracious materialism" to the integrity represented by Tom, which proves, however, problematic; Sandra M. Gilbert and Susan Gubar, *No Man's Land: The Place of the Woman Writer in the Twentieth Century*, vol. 2, *Sexchanges* (New Haven: Yale University Press, 1989), 207.

36. Joseph Church, in "Transgressive Daughters in Sarah Orne Jewett's *Deephaven*," *Essays in Literature* 20 (1993): 232, points out Jewett's similar use of a large window to represent "means of perception." Paula Geyh discusses the "liminal space of the window" in "Burning Down the House" (105). Ann Romines, in referring to Thea's attraction in *The Song of the Lark* to "small, enclosed womblike spaces," slights the important presence in these enclosed spaces of windows that open their vistas (*The Home Plot*, 146).

37. Cynthia K. Briggs, "Insulated Isolation: Willa Cather's Room with a View," in *Cather Studies I*, ed. Susan J. Rosowski (Lincoln: University of Nebraska Press, 1990), 160.

38. Ammons reminds us (*Conflicting Stories*, 121) that *many* novels by women during this period took women artists as their protagonists. Austin was not Cather's

only exemplar. Ammons concludes, "Clearly, writing about the woman artist . . . compelled not only Willa Cather but almost all serious turn-of-the-century women writers." Nancy Porter asserts (Afterword to *A Woman of Genius,* 296) that Cather's novel was "directly influenced" by Austin's. Sally Allen McNall, who finds it "similar," examines parallels of both novels to Mary Wilkins Freeman's *The Butterfly House* (1912), but does not suggest influence; McNall, "The American Woman Writer in Transition: Freeman, Austin, and Cather," in *Seeing Female: Social Roles and Personal Lives,* ed. Sharon S. Brehm (New York: Greenwood Press, 1988), 43–52. Gelfant briefly compares the two novels but also does not assert influence (" 'Lives' of Women Writers," 246). Cather may have found the echoing of the two names Olivia and Olive (Fremstad) suggestive.

39. Cather, *The Song of the Lark,* "New edition containing revisions made by the author" (Boston: Houghton Mifflin, 1937), vii.

40. Cather, *The Song of the Lark* (1915; reprint, New York: Bantam Classic, 1991), 214.

41. Cather called *O Pioneers!* her second "first novel" and said it very nearly wrote itself "spontaneously," so perfectly did it emerge from her own essence; "My First Novels [There Were Two]," *Willa Cather on Writing,* 92, 95. Despite her assertion of near-spontaneousness in the writing of *O Pioneers!,* an assertion taken up by Katherine Anne Porter in her "Reflections on Willa Cather," her work was not characteristically easy or random at all, but highly deliberate and self-critical.

42. Sergeant, *Willa Cather,* 95. Tom Quirk has a very different explanation for *O Pioneers!:* her reading of Henri Bergson; see Quirk, *Bergson and American Culture: The Worlds of Willa Cather and Wallace Stevens* (Chapel Hill: University of North Carolina Press, 1990), 135–39.

43. David Stouck summarizes the composition process in his "Historical Essay" in the Scholarly Edition of *O Pioneers!,* ed. Susan J. Rosowski and Charles W. Mignon (Lincoln: University of Nebraska Press, 1992), 284–86.

44. Cather to Ferris Greenslet, September 13, [1914?], and June 30, [1916]; Ferris Greenslet to Willa Cather, July 5, 1916; Houghton Mifflin Collection, Houghton Library, Harvard University, bMS Am 1925 (335).

45. The female quality of the landscape throughout the Panther Canyon sequence—even though it is traditionally, because of being rugged, a masculine landscape—was first pointed out by Ellen Moers in *Literary Women* (Garden City, N.Y.: Doubleday, 1976), 258–59. Ammons (*Conflicting Stories,* 93) astutely links the "erotic iconography" of Panther Canyon's "life-giving cavity in the earth" to Austin's hidden springs and Jewett's hollow pennyroyal plot in *The Country of the Pointed Firs.*

46. Cather, *Lucy Gayheart* (1935; New York: Random House, 1976), 134.

47. Merrill M. Skaggs, "Death in C Major: Willa Cather's Perilous Journey Toward the Ordinary in *Lucy Gayheart,*" *Literature and Belief* 8 (1988): 82; Gelfant,

"What Was It," 100. Cf. Susan J. Rosowski, *The Voyage Perilous: Willa Cather's Romanticism* (Lincoln: University of Nebraska Press, 1986), 240, and Woodress, *Willa Cather: A Literary Life,* 460. Urgo (*Willa Cather,* 115) reads Lucy Gayheart's character more positively yet, emphasizing her redemptive role as an "Idea or an image" for her hometown: "Cather remythologizes the spiritual dimension of American existence through the story of a young woman whose death inspires the townspeople to recall her in terms of moving images. In particular Lucy's biography transforms the life of a distinctly mundane and linear-minded businessman."

48. Elaine Sargent Apthorp, "Re-Visioning Creativity: Cather, Chopin, Jewett," *Legacy* 9 (1992): 15, 10–11.

49. Willa Cather to Dorothy Canfield Fisher, n.d. except Wednesday, probably March 8, 1922, Dorothy Canfield Fisher Papers, Bailey-Howe Library, University of Vermont. Regarding Cather's letters to Fisher about *One of Ours* and their significance in relation to the long but interrupted friendship between the two, see Mark Madigan, "Willa Cather and Dorothy Canfield Fisher: Rift, Reconciliation, and *One of Ours*," in Rosowski, *Cather Studies I,* 115–29.

50. Rosowski, "Willa Cather's Subverted Endings and Gendered Time," in Rosowski, *Cather Studies I,* 76.

51. Gelfant ("What Was It," 100) writes that Claude "shares the desire for 'something splendid' " that leads Thea to leave home in *The Song of the Lark,* but "unlike her, he lacks both genius and support (financial and moral)." Sally Peltier Harvey notes that "images of imprisonment abound" in *One of Ours,* and calls the book an emotional expatriation; *Redefining the American Dream: The Novels of Willa Cather* (Rutherford, N.J.: Fairleigh Dickinson University Press, 1995), 64–66.

52. Maureen Ryan states that Cather's "refusal to make Enid sympathetic demonstrates her rejection of the romantic attitudes that Claude and his circle share" and observes that the novel "demonstrates over and over that not all soldiers, or heroes, are men"; "No Woman's Land: Gender in Willa Cather's *One of Ours*," *Studies in American Fiction* 18 (1990–91): 70, 74.

53. Woodress, *Willa Cather: A Literary Life,* 282. The letter Woodress paraphrases and in part quotes is at the Houghton Library, Harvard.

54. Austin, *Outland,* 11.

55. Cather, *The Professor's House* (1925; Random House Vintage Classics, 1990), 179.

56. Alexander's movements may also project Cather's own uncertain impulses at the time toward British refinement and back toward American identity for the pursuit of a writing career. Moreover, *Alexander's Bridge* was not rooted in a sense of place or places so fully and personally known as to realize themselves readily and tangibly on the page. Cather had made trips to England during her years with *McClure's,* but inevitably she knew the country only as an outsider.

57. Carlin, *Cather, Canon, and the Politics of Reading,* 6–7.

58. Doris P. Grumbach, in "A Study of the Small Room in *The Professor's House,*" *Women's Studies* 11 (1984): 331, writes that "the narrative progress of the novel depends in part upon movement among places."

59. In her noted essay "The Novel Démeublé," in the same volume as "On *The Professor's House,*" Cather also used a window metaphor to express, through the well-known disfurnishing metaphor, her own urge to "escape the confinement of traditional realism and find her own fictional forms"; Susan Rushing Adams, unpublished paper "Reenvisioning Cather's Spaces: Dualities of Landscape and Meaning," 41.

60. Rosowski, *The Voyage Perilous,* 131. Briggs states that at the end of the novel St. Peter is "ready to return to the world" ("Insulated Isolation," 168).

61. See especially Sharon O'Brien, *Willa Cather: The Emerging Voice* (New York: Oxford University Press, 1987); and Judith Fetterley, "*My Ántonia,* Jim Burden, and the Dilemma of the Lesbian Writer," in *Gender Studies: New Directions in Feminist Criticism,* ed. Judith Spector (Bowling Green, Ohio: Bowling Green State University Popular Press, 1986), 43–59. Gelfant discussed sexuality not with regard to lesbianism but as an area of regressive anxiety in her groundbreaking article "The Forgotten Reaping Hook: Sex in *My Ántonia,*" *American Literature* 43 (1971): 60–82.

62. O'Brien, *Willa Cather,* 431.

63. See Sandra Cisneros, *My Wicked, Wicked Ways* (New York: Turtle Bay, 1993). At the beginning of the section by that title, Cisneros quotes from Maxine Hong Kingston to the effect that a bad girl is "almost like a boy" (21). Tey Diana Rebolledo comments, "This insight into bad girls does not mean that they want to be boys but is rather an acknowledgment that bad girls transgress the realm of propriety for females by acting outside the rules and by desiring completion and freedom for themselves. For Cisneros, the transgression is represented by the girl who moved away from the protection of her family, the girl who lived alone, the girl who writes" (*Women Singing in the Snow,* 192–93).

64. Mary Austin may have played a role in Cather's anxiety about the sexually alluring woman, evident in the story of Marie Shabata, as well as in her linkage of westward movement with writing. Well acquainted as she was with Lincoln Steffens, who preceded her as editor at *McClure's,* and with members of Steffens's circle, including Ida Tarbell and Mabel Dodge Luhan, she would surely have known about Austin's vexed relationship with Steffens. Austin's pursuit of Steffens in New York seems to have been a common topic of discussion, and one in which Austin was generally held up to ridicule. If she was aware of such gossip, Cather would have seen in the incident an example of a capable, creative woman's throwing herself to destruction, of a kind, for the sake of passion. Austin, well known at the time, primarily on the basis of *The Land of Little Rain* and her bruited knowledge of American

Indians, would also have served her, of course, as an example of a woman who went west and developed as a writer as a result of that journey.

65. Woodress, *Willa Cather: A Literary Life,* 245. Rosowski (*The Voyage Perilous,* 49–52) sees Alexandra not so much as androgynous but as a goddess able to accomplish what men could not. David Stouck astutely reads the split in the novel between Alexandra and Marie as a doubling of the Eve figure in a story of Eden and the Fall. Alexandra's is the "story of creation," Marie's the story of the sinning Eve cast out of the garden; *Willa Cather's Imagination* (Lincoln: University of Nebraska Press, 1975), 31.

66. As chapter 2 of this study demonstrates, movement west assumed the same linkage for Mary Austin. Judith Bryant Wittenburg points out that Jewett, too, linked the impulse toward exploration with the expansion of the imagination and thus with writing, through the "imaginative forays" of Kate and Helen in *Deephaven,* which, "as they respond to what they see, or attempt to project themselves" into the experiences of others, are linked to "physical wanderings"; "*Deephaven:* Sarah Orne Jewett's Exploratory Metafiction," *Studies in American Fiction* 19 (1991): 156, 160. I would add that in *The Country of the Pointed Firs,* the opening of the narrator's awareness of the stories of others is also developed in the course of her forays.

67. Cather, *My Ántonia* (1918; Random House Vintage Classics, 1994), 5. Patrick W. Shaw plausibly observes that in *My Ántonia* Cather solves "the dilemma of how to fulfill the feminine 'obligations' and yet remain creatively unfettered" by splitting herself into the "dual personae" of Ántonia and Jim; *Willa Cather and the Art of Conflict: Re-Visioning Her Creative Imagination* (Troy, N.Y.: Whitston Publishing Co., 1992), 53. In cautioning that the "potential irony inherent" in her investing herself in a "toothless, ugly slattern" and a male of such "quaint romanticism" as Jim should cause us to question "positivist . . . eulogi[stic]" readings of the novel (54–55), Shaw is excessively severe on Ántonia, though not on Jim.

68. That the "I" of the introduction is indeed a professional writer, i.e., Cather herself transmogrified into a fictional character, is implied in Jim's question as to why she has "never written anything about Ántonia." Cather more than once effaced the distinction between fact and fiction.

69. Cather, *The Troll Garden* (1905; reprint, Lincoln: University of Nebraska Press, 1983).

70. Willa Cather to Ferris Greenslet, March 28, 1915, Houghton-Mifflin Papers, Houghton Library, Harvard University, bMS Am 1925 (341).

71. Cather's love for the immigrant communities and languages she encountered near Red Cloud, represented here in the Shimerda family, may have contributed to her ambivalence toward the United States's role in World War I, since nativist backlash accompanying entry into the war brought such measures as repression of for-

eign-language instruction. In *One of Ours,* for instance, an evasiveness in narrative language (persistent use of free indirect discourse) allows her to be both ironic and complicit at the same time. These important connections between historicist and stylistic reading are pointed out by Guy Reynolds in *Willa Cather in Context: Progress, Race, Empire* (New York: St. Martin's Press, 1996), 104.

72. Ann Fisher-Wirth, "Out of the Mother: Loss in *My Ántonia,*" in *Cather Studies II,* ed. Susan J. Rosowski (Lincoln: University of Nebraska Press, 1993), 66–67. Fisher-Wirth contrasts Ántonia's becoming "increasingly immobile" with Jim's being "increasingly mobile" and points out that she "comes to represent . . . the function of space."

73. Lawrence, *Penelope Voyages,* 1–20. Romines (*The Home Plot,* 148) calls Ántonia, in this aspect of her characterization by Jim, the "mother lode," or "raw material."

74. Janet Giltrow and David Stouck, "Willa Cather and a Grammar for Things 'Not Named,' " *Style* 26 (1992): 109. Urgo believes that "it is not until his life crosses Ántonia's and those of the other first-generation European immigrants that he realizes the fact . . . of his own restlessness" (*Willa Cather,* 55). But his life crosses theirs when he is a child, and his childhood journey to the plains was not impelled by restlessness, but by the loss of his parents. Indeed, his undeniable restlessness as an adult is also impelled, at least in part, by loss—of marital love.

75. Jim Burden's *locus amoenus* is distinctly more plausible than that found by Claude in the immediate vicinity of the battlefield in *One of Ours,* but represents a similar urge toward a home purified of the shabby sameness of one's real home and serving as a retreat from conflict.

76. Romines, *The Home Plot,* 149. Regarding Jim's sleeping in the barn, see p. 142.

77. Cather to Ferris Greenslet, February 15, 1926, bMS Am 1925 Houghton Library, Harvard University. Merrill Skaggs demonstrates the importance of Cather's pairing and sequencing of novels in *After the World Broke in Two.*

78. James Woodress, *Willa Cather: Her Life and Art* (New York: Pegasus, 1970), 203.

79. Cf. my similar reading in *Strategies of Reticence: Silence and Meaning in the Works of Jane Austen, Willa Cather, Katherine Anne Porter, and Joan Didion* (Charlottesville: University Press of Virginia, 1990), 79–81, 99–100: Mrs. Forrester "should have the choice of other ways to win."

80. *A Lost Lady,* then, might also be linked with Cather's early short story "A Wagner Matinee," which, in Romines's words, is "marked by fear of heterosexual marriage and of the domestic routine in which marriage is likely to involve a woman" (*The Home Plot,* 133).

81. Especially in *Shadows on the Rock*, but also in such works as *A Lost Lady* and *My Mortal Enemy*, Cather shows that for women in general there are few options in life. In *Shadows on the Rock* these are marriage, the church, and prostitution.

82. What or who is meant by the phrase "my mortal enemy" has been much debated. Cather stated unambiguously in a letter to Pendleton Hogan dated February 5, 1940, that Myra had come to regard Oswald as her mortal enemy; Alderman Library, University of Virginia. Ann Fisher-Wirth, reading Myra as a "true Romantic," emphasizes in the death scene the fact that Myra has succeeded in becoming "a runaway once again" by leaving her apartment to die "into infinitude and openness" on a "wild headland overlooking the Pacific"; "Dispossession and Redemption in the Novels of Willa Cather," in Rosowski, *Cather Studies I,* 41, 52. Although I find Fisher-Wirth's reading powerful, I feel that it envisions, more than locates, a victorious note in Cather's text.

83. Cather, *Obscure Destinies* (1932; reprint, New York: Random House Vintage Books, 1974), 190.

84. I am indebted to Richard Millington, in private conversation, for this point as well as for his observation that Cather's stated uncertainty about her endorsement of the society she depicted in *Shadows on the Rock* indicates her modernity, expressing as it does the modernist's divided consciousness and self-monitoring. By seeing in *Archbishop* and the later works a turn toward caution or defensiveness, I am espousing, in essence, a view that Fisher-Wirth ("Dispossession and Redemption," 52 n. 10) labels "dated."

85. Cather to Luhan, n.d. but datable 1925, August 7, [1925], May 25, [1926], and "Saturday" [1926]; all in the Yale Collection of American Literature, Beinecke Rare Book and Manuscript Library, Yale University. In her turn to Indian materials in *Death Comes for the Archbishop,* Cather was almost certainly responding once again, in part, to her awareness of the writings of Mary Austin and Austin's role as public figure. Various of her letters make it clear that she not only was interested in the Indians of the Southwest herself but was keenly aware of the phenomenon of widespread popular interest in Indian life at the time. Certainly she knew of Austin's particular identification with Indian materials, if for no other reason than the publication of three of Austin's Indian-adaptation poems in *McClure's* in late 1911 and early 1912, while she was still active as managing editor: Mary Austin, "Medicine Song," *McClure's* 37 (1911): 504; "The Song of the Hills," *McClure's* 37 (1911): 615; and "The Song of the Friend," *McClure's* 38 (1911–12): 351. The first and third of these bear the note "From the Paiute Indian Dialect, Done into English by Mary Austin." The second has a similar note, "From the Yokut Indian Dialect, Done into English by Mary Austin."

86. Edward H. Spicer, *Cycles of Conquest: The Impact of Spain, Mexico, and the United*

States on the Indians of the Southwest, 1533–1960 (Tucson: University of Arizona Press, 1962), 248. Elizabeth Ammons points out (*Conflicting Stories,* 133) that the Indians in *The Song of the Lark* and *The Professor's House* are all dead, "the favorite white version of Indians, of course, while their descendants in *Death Comes for the Archbishop* appear as romanticized decorative details." Cather indeed participated in a surge of romanticizing interest in the Southwest in the 1920s and 1930s represented, for example, in Oliver La Farge's 1927 novel of the Navajo, *Laughing Boy,* which she heartily admired. David Stouck's view that she had a "great affinity" for the cultures of the Indians in the Southwest ("Willa Cather and the Indian Heritage," *Twentieth-Century Literature* 22 [1976]: 433) needs to be balanced by reassessments such as Ammons's. See also Mike Fischer's historicist reassessment (but with respect to the Plains Indians of Nebraska) in "Pastoralism and Its Discontents: Willa Cather and the Burden of Imperialism," *Mosaic* 23, no. 1 (1990): 31–44.

87. Fryer, *Felicitous Space,* 313; Woodress, *Willa Cather: Her Life and Art,* 233. Cather's conception of frontiering in terms of journey (but also her discomfort in contemplating roads that "led out, but never back again") is evident in her article "Nebraska: The End of the First Cycle," *Nation* 117 (1923): 236–38.

88. Gaston Bachelard, *The Poetics of Space,* trans. Maria Jolas (Boston: Orion Press, 1964), 183–210. The work was first published in French in 1958.

89. Fryer, *Felicitous Space,* 316.

90. Austin commented that she was "very much distressed to find that [Cather] had given her allegiance to the French blood of the Archbishop; she had sympathized with his desire to build a French cathedral in a Spanish town. It was a calamity to the local culture. We have never got over it. It dropped the local mystery plays almost out of use, and many other far-derived Spanish customs" (*Earth Horizon,* 359). Cather complained to Mabel Dodge Luhan (November 22, 1933, Beinecke Rare Book and Manuscript Library) that it wasn't her fault the archbishop was French.

91. Willa Cather to Burgess Johnson, 1928, extracted by E. K. Brown, Yale Collection of American Literature, Beinecke Rare Book and Manuscript Library, Yale University.

92. Rosowski, *The Voyage Perilous,* 162. Fryer calls the structure of the late novels "separate moments, with increasingly greater spaces between them" (*Felicitous Space,* 226).

93. The terms I quoted are used by Rosowski, *The Voyage Perilous,* 176, and Woodress, *Willa Cather: Her Life and Art,* 233. Woodress calls *Shadows* a "static" book.

94. Cather, *Shadows on the Rock* (1931; Random House Vintage Books, 1971), 228, 258.

95. Skaggs, *After the World Broke in Two,* 140.

96. Regarding the association in the minds of French Canadians of the North and Northwest with "the widest possible idea of departure" and freedom, see Jack Warwick, *The Long Journey: Literary Themes of French Canada* (Toronto: University of Toronto Press, 1968), 34–47.

97. Fisher-Wirth, "Dispossession and Redemption," 49–50.

98. After her mother's death, Cather wrote Blanche Knopf that she would probably go to Jaffrey or possibly, instead, to Virginia; Willa Cather to Blanche Knopf, September 20, [1931], Knopf Papers, Blanche Knopf–Cather files, folder 689.1, Harry Ransom Humanities Research Center, University of Texas at Austin.

99. The exile state in which the story begins is elucidated by Richard Giannone in "Willa Cather and the Unfinished Drama of Deliverance," *Prairie Schooner* 52 (1978): 25–46, and by Jenny Hale Pulsipher in "Expatriation and Reconciliation: The Pilgrimage Tradition in *Sapphira and the Slave Girl*," *Literature and Belief* 8 (1988): 89–100. Pulsipher's commitment to the pilgrimage tradition leads her to underplay the darkness of the novel as well as its escape motives in favor of viewing it as an allegorical journey to the heavenly city, to the point that she can seemingly accept without demurral the funeral preacher's depiction of the slave Jezebel, kidnapped from her home, as one who "*fled* the 'City of Destruction' " in order to join the other characters in "traveling toward a better land" (93, emphasis added).

100. One wonders if Cather may have felt beset by young men (either real or hypothetical) at the instigation of a mother who wanted her to marry.

101. Fryer, *Felicitous Space,* 336; Cather to Fisher, February 17, 1933, Fisher Papers, Bailey-Howe Library, University of Vermont.

102. At the end of *The Song of the Lark,* however, she does generalize the sense of escape in showing the effect of Thea's life on her sister Tillie and, by way of Tillie's stories of Thea, with others. The generalizing of Thea's self-realization entails a generalizing of the language of the open window. Tillie's stories of Thea are like a window thrown open onto the "restless currents of the world" for others (*Lark,* 367–68).

103. Romines, *The Home Plot,* 182.

104. Denise Levertov, "Today," in *To Stay Alive* (New York: New Directions, 1971), 55.

105. Susan Rosowski, "Willa Cather and the Intimacy of Art, Or: In Defense of Privacy," *Willa Cather Pioneer Memorial Newsletter* 36 (1992–93): 49.

106. Sarah Orne Jewett to Annie Fields, July 5, 1889, in Jewett, *The Letters of Sarah Orne Jewett,* ed. Annie Fields (Boston: Houghton Mifflin, 1911), 47.

107. I do not understand Judith Fryer's statement (*Felicitous Space,* 262) that Carl Lindstrum, Alexandra's husband, is "clearly a companion only." They *are* shown as being companionable, but that does not mean their relationship is not erotic as well. Her marriage to Carl, at an age of full adulthood, might be likened to the mar-

riage of the shepherdess in Jewett's "William's Wedding" (which Cather certainly knew), in that both have proven their independence before entering into adult sexuality.

CHAPTER 4. ANNE TYLER

Epigraphs: Willa Cather, "Katherine Mansfield," in *Willa Cather on Writing*, 108–9; Katherine Anne Porter, "Pale Horse, Pale Rider," in *The Collected Stories of Katherine Anne Porter* (New York: Harcourt, Brace, 1965), 269.

1. Annis Pratt, *Archetypal Patterns,* 135–36. Pratt is following a distinction made by Carol Christ.

2. John Updike, "Loosened Roots," in *Critical Essays on Anne Tyler,* ed. Alice Hall Petry (New York: G. K. Hall, 1992), 89. Repetitiveness is evident in the language of Anne Goodwin Jones's description of Tyler's fictional theme of "staying at home or running away or coming back home or making a new home or failing to"; "Home at Last, and Homesick Again: The Ten Novels of Anne Tyler," *Hollins Critic* 23, no. 2 (1986): 2. See also Doris Betts, "The Fiction of Anne Tyler," *Southern Quarterly* 21, no. 4 (1983): 28, on "leaving and returning."

3. Tyler's novels, in chronological order, are *If Morning Ever Comes* (1964; reprint, New York: Berkley, 1983); *The Tin Can Tree* (1965; reprint, New York: Ballantine, 1992); *A Slipping-Down Life* (1970; reprint, New York: Berkley, 1983); *The Clock Winder* (1972; reprint, New York: Ballantine, 1992); *Celestial Navigation* (1974; reprint, New York: Ballantine, 1993); *Searching for Caleb* (1975; reprint, New York: Ballantine, 1993); *Earthly Possessions* (1977; reprint, New York: Berkley, 1984); *Morgan's Passing* (1980; reprint, New York: Ballantine, 1992); *Dinner at the Homesick Restaurant* (1982; reprint, New York: Ballantine, 1992); *The Accidental Tourist* (1985; reprint, New York: Berkley, 1986); *Breathing Lessons* (New York: Knopf, 1988); *Saint Maybe* (1991; reprint, New York: Ballantine, 1992); *Ladder of Years* (New York: Knopf, 1995).

4. Carol S. Manning, "Welty, Tyler, and Traveling Salesmen: The Wandering Hero Unhorsed," in *The Fiction of Anne Tyler,* ed. C. Ralph Stephens (Jackson: University Press of Mississippi, 1990), 110; Geyh, "Burning Down the House," 104.

5. Joseph C. Voelker, *Art and the Accidental in Anne Tyler* (Columbia: University of Missouri Press, 1989). See also Mary Ellis Gibson, "Family as Fate: The Novels of Anne Tyler," *Southern Literary Journal* 15, no. 3 (1983): 47–58 (especially p. 55), and Frances H. Bachelder, "Manacles of Fear: Emotional Affliction in Tyler's Works," in *Anne Tyler as Novelist,* ed. Dale Salwak (Iowa City: University of Iowa Press, 1994), 49. Bachelder comments accurately enough that Tyler views "humankind as essentially menaced by fear and trauma."

6. Tyler, "Why I Still Treasure 'The Little House,' " *New York Times Book Review,* November 9, 1986, 56. See Elizabeth Evans, "Early Years and Influences," in Salwak, *Anne Tyler as Novelist,* 4.

7. Virginia Lee Burton, *The Little House* (Boston: Houghton Mifflin, 1942).

8. Barbara Harrell Carson, "Complicate, Complicate: Anne Tyler's Moral Imperative," *Southern Quarterly* 31, no. 1 (1992): 29.

9. Theresa Kanoza, "Mentors and Maternal Role Models: The Healthy Mean between Extremes in Anne Tyler's Fiction," in Stephens, *The Fiction of Anne Tyler,* 31. Kanoza notes several examples of resistance to such enclosure. In the same volume, Frank W. Shelton observes that it is "difficult to derive a consistent stance" in Tyler's fiction toward "spatial enclosure and escape" ("Anne Tyler's Houses," 45).

10. Mary F. Robertson, "Anne Tyler: Medusa Points and Contact Points," in *Contemporary American Women Writers: Narrative Strategies* (1985); reprinted in Petry, *Critical Essays on Anne Tyler,* 201, 199.

11. Here I explicitly disagree with Barbara Harrell Carson ("Complicate, Complicate," 31), who argues that Tyler's "rejection of the ideal of radical independence" entails rejection of the urge to simplify the trappings of life. To be sure, one can find instances in Tyler's work when such an urge reaches an extreme and becomes dehumanized, a sign of isolation. But more often it represents a sensible and person-centered prioritization.

12. Frank W. Shelton, "The Necessary Balance: Distance and Sympathy in the Novels of Anne Tyler," *Southern Review* 20 (1984): 855.

13. See, for example, Tyler's "The Fine, Full World of Welty," *Washington Star,* October 26, 1980, D1, D7; and her "Still Just Writing," in *The Writer on Her Work: Contemporary Women Writers Reflect on Their Art and Situation,* ed. Janet Sternberg (New York: Norton, 1980), 3–16. Welty has also expressed her admiration of Tyler. See Evans, "Early Years and Influences," 11.

14. Romines, *The Home Plot,* 192–93.

15. Susan Gilbert's assertion that Tyler's characters are always impelled into flight by "failures of vision" seems to me excessively negative; "Anne Tyler," in *Southern Women Writers: The New Generation,* ed. Tonette Bond Inge (Tuscaloosa: University of Alabama Press, 1990), 263.

16. Evans, "Early Years and Influences," 2–3.

17. Shelton, "The Necessary Balance," 857.

18. Romines, *The Home Plot,* 193, 270, 243, 273.

19. Ibid., 243–49, 266–71.

20. Cather is sometimes ambivalent about both elements of the home-departure polarity as well. Romines has pointed out cogently that Clara, in "The Bohemian Girl," is caught in a "complex and vulnerable situation" in that, even though she has the negative motivation of her husband's exploitativeness and disregard and the posi-

tive motivation of her love for Nils, the decision to leave with him is difficult because "she must leave the prairie, to which she has powerful ties," as if, in the words of the story, "her soul had built itself a nest there on that horizon." Romines also comments that "The Bohemian Girl" offers "one of the few successful heterosexual marriages in Cather's fiction" and "seems to propose a new marital plot of shared mobility and nonrestrictive housekeeping" (*The Home Plot,* 138–39). Without arguing direct influence, one might see in this story by Cather an anticipation of the "marital plot" envisioned by Tyler in *Searching for Caleb.* Tyler expressed her admiration of Cather (specifically, of *The Professor's House*) in a letter to the author, March 9, 1995.

21. At the Quaker commune outside Raleigh, North Carolina, where she grew up until the age of eleven, Tyler was mostly educated at home, worked at the co-op store, read aloud and was read to, and had never used a telephone until the family moved into town. The family kept goats produced from a breeding stock from the farm of Mrs. Carl Sandburg. See Evans, "Early Years and Influences," 2–4, and Voelker, *Art and the Accidental,* 2–3 and *passim.*

22. Stella Nesanovich ("The Early Novels: A Reconsideration," in Salwak, *Anne Tyler as Novelist,* 16) comments on the motif of isolation within the family. Voelker notes the recurrence of the "absconded father," observing that the father's abandonment is often established as having occurred "prior to the opening events of the novel" (*Art and the Accidental,* 25). Tyler's emphasis is on the effects on those left behind.

23. Tyler's scanting views of black characters are always rather reductive, perhaps indicating one of the admitted limitations of her fictive realm. It is well to remember, however, that she attributes to a black character in *The Tin Can Tree* one of the most resonant aphorisms in all her work: "Bravest thing about people, Miss Joan, is how they go on loving mortal beings after finding out there's such a thing as dying" (96).

24. Voelker calls Joanne "a sexually empowered character—a relative rarity in Tyler's fiction" (*Art and the Accidental,* 21).

25. Nesanovich, "The Early Novels," 19.

26. Ibid.

27. Alice Hall Petry, "Tyler and Feminism," in Salwak, *Anne Tyler as Novelist,* 36.

28. Voelker (*Art and the Accidental,* 32) attributes Ansel's withholding from the others his knowledge of Joan's departure to an intention to save the information for future "moral blackmail." That reading seems to me unnecessarily harsh. Ansel *is* maddeningly selfish, an emotional cripple. But Tyler is always amazingly tolerant even of emotional cripples.

29. Betts, "The Fiction of Anne Tyler," 28.

30. Nesanovich, "The Early Novels," 31.

31. The label "committed recluse" fixed on Mrs. Emerson by Voelker (*Art and*

the Accidental, 57) strikes me as inaccurate. She is, to be sure, strongly identified with her house and directs her attention inward, toward her children, but she plays bridge, serves on unnamed "committees," and goes out in the car on errands without anxiety. I do not see her as an agoraphobe.

32. Susan Gilbert, who observes Tyler's linkage of downward mobility with the "happiest changes," seems both to deplore critics' failure to perceive that pattern as having political implications and, at the same time, to deplore Tyler's failure to entertain political dimensions of life; "Private Lives and Public Issues: Anne Tyler's Prize-Winning Novels," in Stephens, *The Fiction of Anne Tyler,* 139.

33. Tyler, "Because I Want More Than One Life," *Washington Post* August 15, 1976; reprinted in Petry, *Critical Essays on Anne Tyler,* 45–49.

34. Katha Pollitt, Review of *Searching for Caleb, New York Times Book Review,* January 18, 1976; reprinted in Petry, *Critical Essays on Anne Tyler,* 83.

35. Susan Gilbert, "Anne Tyler," 265. Gilbert also applies the term to Emily and Leon Meredith in *Morgan's Passing.* It could be applied to others of Tyler's characters as well.

36. Anne Ricketson Zahlan, "Traveling Towards the Self: The Psychic Drama of Anne Tyler's *The Accidental Tourist,*" in Stephens, *The Fiction of Anne Tyler,* 84–85. In the same volume, Doris Betts notes (in "Tyler's Marriage of Opposites," 13) her "emphasis on life-as-journey" and her "stead[y]" aim toward "reconciliation."

37. Petry, "Tyler and Feminism," 39, 41, 33.

38. A related issue is that of whether feminism should join or resist the postmodern evacuation of identity and agency; see Betsy Erkkila, "Ethnicity, Literary Theory, and the Grounds of Resistance," *American Quarterly* 47 (1995): 563–95.

39. I find it surprising that Frank Shelton, who generally examines Tyler's theme of detachment versus involvement with considerable sensitivity, dismisses *Earthly Possessions* as adding "nothing substantial to the theme" of the "runaway housewife" ("The Necessary Balance," 857).

40. Alberta Emory, with her gypsy-like attire and her stock of theatrical costumes, is another of Tyler's characters seeking freedom through trying on alternative identities.

41. Petry, "Tyler and Feminism," 38.

42. Linda Wagner-Martin, "*Breathing Lessons:* A Domestic Success Story," in Salwak, *Anne Tyler as Novelist,* 166–68. Kanoza agrees that at the end she is "home from her long-awaited journey and at-home with her life" ("Mentors and Maternal Role Models," 35).

43. This echo of *Earthly Possessions* evinces a growing inter-referentiality among Tyler's novels. Luke's mother, Ruth, in *Homesick Restaurant,* is at one point seen living at the Pauling boardinghouse from *Celestial Navigations.* The three drivers who give Luke rides when he hitchhikes to Ezra's restaurant are also in the process of escape

or endless motion. Voelker (*Art and the Accidental,* 133) says that they thus serve to "demonstrate that the Tulls' troubles are virtually everybody's."

44. Margaret Morganroth Gullette states that Beck Tull "can be shown as no worse than a negligible guest" because he was "adequately punished by his self-made exclusion from his children's lives"; *Safe at Last in the Middle Years: The Invention of the Midlife Progress Novel: Saul Bellow, Margaret Drabble, Anne Tyler, and John Updike* (Berkeley: University of California Press, 1988), 115.

45. Mary Ellis Gibson ("Family as Fate," 57) sees in the novel's patterns of fatedness, the concluding sequence, and especially the title of *Homesick Restaurant,* an indication that "fatalism and despair are balanced by attempted human sympathy and nourishment" and that "homesickness may make possible human efforts to connect." Such a reading is sustained by the fact that Ezra, a chapter earlier, with characteristic goodwill, imagines a circle of mutual help that is more inclusive than the family circle of pain.

46. Charlotte Templin ("Tyler's Literary Reputation," in Salwak, *Anne Tyler as Novelist,* 185) cites a *Publisher's Weekly* report that "paperback and book club deals netted $1.3 million before the novel was released."

47. Susan Gilbert, "Private Lives and Public Issues," 139. Templin, observing the frequent objections to Tyler's novels as "painting a rosy picture of reality," recognizes that this judgment will lead to her placement "in a lower rank" ("Tyler's Literary Reputation," 190, 196). John Updike, a major voice in the assessment of Tyler's work and in general a promoter of her reputation, praised the darkening of her vision in his review of *Dinner at the Homesick Restaurant,* "More Substance, Complexity of Family Relationships—Buried Horrors of Family Life," *New Yorker,* April 5, 1982, 193–97.

48. Robert Towers ("Roughing It," *New York Review of Books* November 10, 1988; reprinted in Petry, *Critical Essays on Anne Tyler,* 146) comments that Tyler "captures the flavor of car travel in America today" with unfailing success. Tyler has also both frequently and successfully depicted travel by train and by bus. She less often sends her characters out by plane, and seems not to find the experience of flying very interesting.

49. Zahlan, "Traveling Towards the Self," 87. As Zahlan notes, however, it is also Grandfather Leary, who had himself "longed to travel" when it was too late to do so, who in a dream urges Macon not to "sit in this old house and rot" (*Accidental Tourist,* 148)

50. Rose Quiello, "Breakdowns and Breakthroughs: The Hysterical Use of Language," in Salwak, *Anne Tyler as Novelist,* 60.

51. As Lin T. Humphrey notes, *The Accidental Tourist* is "a tightly crafted, balanced novel"; "Exploration of a Not-So-Accidental Novel," in Salwak, *Anne Tyler as Novelist,* 153. The balancing of their declarations is evidence of that structural craft.

52. William K. Freiert, in "Anne Tyler's Accidental Ulysses," *Classical and Modern Literature* 10 (1989): 71–79, reads Macon as a modern Odysseus. Sarah English, in *"The Accidental Tourist* and *The Odyssey,"* in Salwak, *Anne Tyler as Novelist,* 157, finds that the novel "ironically inverts" the *Odyssey.* Gullette, in *Safe at Last,* 106, advises us to work free of the *Odyssey* parallel. Carol Manning views Beck Tull of *Dinner at the Homesick Restaurant* as an Odysseus figure as well; "Welty, Tyler, and Traveling Salesmen," 117.

53. Jones, "Home at Last, and Homesick Again," 13; Humphrey, "Exploration of a Not-So-Accidental Novel," 153.

54. Karen L. Levenback, "Functions of (Picturing) Memory," in Salwak, *Anne Tyler as Novelist,* 82; Wagner-Martin, *"Breathing Lessons:* A Domestic Success Story," 171.

55. Voelker, *Art and the Accidental,* 8–9.

56. Wagner-Martin (*"Breathing Lessons:* A Domestic Success Story," 164) calls the opening situation a brilliant stroke.

57. Joseph Voelker (*Art and the Accidental,* 170) is on sounder ground than many readers of *Breathing Lessons* when he observes that in the central section of the novel "the initial coolness of Ira's observation breaks up like an ice floe, and the buried *Menschlichkeit* of this disappointed solitaire addict carries all before it." It is unfortunate that a study with such rich insights is so often marred by errors of factual detail. In describing Maggie's regret over her role in helping put a friend's mother into a nursing home, Voelker says that the woman was "restrained in her wheelchair with a posy" (170). He seems to take this oddly utilitarian flower as an accessory of the absurd clown suit she is wearing. But Tyler did not write "posy"; she wrote "Posey." A Posey belt is a standard piece of equipment in a nursing home, mainly used for providing unsteady patients a convenient handhold on their nurses and nurses a handhold on patients. This is only one example of many.

58. Gullette, *Safe at Last,* 107.

59. Shelton, "Anne Tyler's Houses," 45.

60. Linda Wagner-Martin is overly severe, I think, in calling him (in *"Breathing Lessons:* A Domestic Success Story," 171) an "interfering, jealous younger brother who tells tales that turn out to be false." Although the specific tale he told seems not to have been literally true, he was right in the main. Also, it seems to me that Tyler does not so much show in Ian that "human nature can be changed" as she lets some elements in his character emerge in response to need.

61. Tyler's depictions of "motherly" men, especially Ian Bedloe, may have sprung in part from Welty's Jack Renfro in *Losing Battles* (1970), of whom it is said, "Jack's going to make a wonderful little mother."

62. Lawrence, *Penelope Voyages,* x–xiii.

63. Its counterpointing use of fairy tales, a motif related to Emily's profession of

puppeteering, is perhaps the most interesting technical development in *Morgan's Passing*. Aileen Chris Shafer demonstrates that fairy tales serve both as patterns for and as counterpoints to reality in the novel; see Shafer, "Beauty and the Transformed Beast: Fairy Tales and Myths in *Morgan's Passing*," in Salwak, *Anne Tyler as Novelist*, 125–37.

64. Betts, "The Fiction of Anne Tyler," 29; Tyler quoted in Marguerite Michaels, "Anne Tyler, Writer 8:05 to 3:30," *New York Times Book Review* May 8, 1977; reprinted in Petry, *Critical Essays on Anne Tyler*, 40. On Tyler's self-identification with Jeremy, see "Olives Out of a Bottle," in Petry, *Critical Essays on Anne Tyler*, 31. In her introduction, Petry points out that "there are enough parallels . . . to suggest that she was in large measure writing about her own situation as a creative individual" (9).

65. Catherine Peters, "Opting Out," *London Times Literary Supplement* August 27, 1976; reprinted in Petry, *Critical Essays on Anne Tyler*, 80–81; Jones, "Home at Last, and Homesick Again," 2.

66. Even Justine's name, the same as her great-grandfather's plus one letter, demonstrates continuity *cum* change.

67. Showalter, *Sister's Choice*, 130; Lawrence, *Penelope Voyages*, 20. On transgressiveness in narrative structure, see also Nancy K. Miller, *Subject to Change: Reading Feminist Writing* (New York: Columbia University Press, 1988), 8, defining a "*feminist* act in a *feminist* poetics" as a "process of resistance, revision, and emancipation" in women's writings that revise conventional plot patterns.

68. De Lauretis, *Alice Doesn't*, 134.

69. Priscilla Paton's phrase in private communication to the author, January 10, 1995, referring to Robert Frost and Elizabeth Bishop. Periodization of Tyler's work is difficult, both in its social dimensions and in its strictly literary aspects. In her seeming immersion in the flow of experience, her embrace of bizarre oddities within everyday realism, and her avoidance of conspicuous aestheticism, with its implications of order and coherence, Tyler shows affinities with postmodernism. But the formal structure of her novels (often more structured than they at first appear) and their anxious reach for stability show an affinity with modernism.

70. Wagner-Martin, "*Breathing Lessons*: A Domestic Success Story," 170.

CHAPTER 5. TONI MORRISON

Epigraph: Alice Walker, "Women," in *Revolutionary Petunias and Other Poems*, 19.

1. Langston Hughes, "West Texas," in *Selected Poems of Langston Hughes* (New York: Random House Vintage Books, 1959), 164.

2. Grace A. Epstein, "Out of Blue Water: Dream Flight and Narrative Construction in the Novels of Toni Morrison," in *State of the Fantastic: Studies in the Theory and Practice of Fantastic Literature and Film*, ed. Nicholas Ruddick (Westport, Conn.:

Greenwood Press, 1992), 141; DuPlessis writes of the "double marginalization" of being both female and racially (or by economic class or sexual preference) othered (*Writing Beyond the Ending*, 33).

3. Morrison is quoted by Paul Gilroy as having said in an interview that her own and other African-American novelists' "turn to history" is a manifestation of their being "responsible." She avows her conscious resistance to a cultural bent toward erasure of the past that has made possible the maintenance of a myth of America as a place where people can "start over, where the slate is clean." Gilroy, *Modernity and Double Consciousness* (Cambridge: Harvard University Press, 1993), 222.

4. Caroline Rody, commenting on the surprising frequency with which post–civil rights movement writers turn back to the matter of slavery, writes that "history" functions as a "trope for the problem of reimagining one's heritage"; "Toni Morrison's *Beloved*: History, 'Rememory,' and a 'Clamor for a Kiss,' " *American Literary History* 7 (1995): 102. Such reimagining necessarily disrupts the historiography of those who have imagined from a self-reassuring white perspective.

5. Farah Jasmine Griffin, *"Who Set You Flowin'?": The African-American Migration Narrative* (New York: Oxford University Press, 1995), 184.

6. Eve Lennox Birch, *Black American Women's Writing: A Quilt of Many Colours* (New York: Harvester/Wheatsheaf, 1994), 193; Sally Keenan, " 'Four Hundred Years of Silence': Myth, History, and Motherhood in Toni Morrison's *Beloved*," in *Recasting the World: Writing after Colonialism,* ed. Jonathan White (Baltimore: Johns Hopkins University Press, 1993), 48.

7. Interview quoted by Barbara Offutt Mathieson in "Memory and Mother Love: Toni Morrison's Dyad," in *Memory, Narrative, and Identity: New Essays in Ethnic American Literatures,* ed. Amrithit Singh, Joseph T. Skerrett, Jr., and Robert E. Hogan (Boston: Northeastern University Press, 1994), 217. Regarding her earlier "preoccupation," see Christina Davis, "An Interview with Toni Morrison," *Presence Africaine* 1988; reprinted in *Conversations with Toni Morrison,* ed. Danielle Taylor-Guthrie (Jackson: University Press of Mississippi, 1994), 231.

8. DuPlessis, *Writing Beyond the Ending,* 142. In DuPlessis's view, the hero of a narrative of the "multiple individual" also breaks out of "individual consciousness" in her "rupture from gender-based ends." One of the novels she sees as exemplifying such a narrative is Alice Walker's *Meridian,* which she describes as a "collective biography of a multiple individual, who articulates social and spiritual questions" (158).

9. Marshal Darling, "In the Realm of Responsibility: A Conversation with Toni Morrison," *Women's Review of Books,* March 1978; reprinted in Taylor-Guthrie, *Conversations with Toni Morrison,* 247–8.

10. Morrison said in 1988 that she had moved into greater concern with "the relationships of black men and black women and the axes on which these relation-

ships frequently turn, and how they complement each other"; Davis, "An Interview with Toni Morrison," 232.

11. Nellie McKay, "An Interview with Toni Morrison," *Contemporary Literature* 24 (1983): 417.

12. Robert Stepto, " 'Intimate Things in Place': A Conversation with Toni Morrison," *Massachusetts Review* 18 (1977): 487; quoted by Marianne Hirsch, *The Mother/Daughter Plot: Narrative Psychoanalysis, Feminism* (Bloomington: Indiana University Press, 1989). Hirsch sees Sethe and Beloved as enacting a version of the myth of Persephone and Demeter, which, of course, centers on journey and return.

13. McKay, "An Interview with Toni Morrison," 413.

14. Langston Hughes, "One-Way Ticket," in *Selected Poems,* 177.

15. Baker, *Workings of the Spirit,* 19. Baker uses the topos of "the daughter's departure" to discuss black women's writing at the turn of the century, which he sees (e.g., in the fiction of Anna Julia Cooper and Frances Harper) as a "white-faced minstrelsy" designed to cultivate white approval. The Harlem Renaissance generation of Nella Larsen and Jessie Faucet, Baker argues, transforms this "minstrelsy" into a "novel of 'passing' " from which "Black southern vernacular energies remain an absence." In his discussion, Toni Morrison and Ntozake Shange draw on that vernacular energy to create a black female narrative of authentic and self-affirming power (26–35).

16. Much of the criticism on *Song of Solomon* has focused on folk motifs, particularly of the flying African-born slave. See, for example, Susan L. Blake, "Folklore and Community in *Song of Solomon*," *MELUS* 7, no. 3 (1980): 77–82. Blake calls attention to Morrison's use of the Georgia Writers' Project collection of folklore from coastal groups *Drums and Shadows: Survival Studies among the Georgia Coastal Negroes,* by the Savannah Unit of the Georgia Writers' Project of the Work Projects Administration, with foreword by Guy B. Johnson (Athens: University of Georgia Press, 1940). Numerous stories of enslaved Africans able to fly back to Africa are reported in this volume. In each retelling the motive to fly is dislike of the New World or unhappiness with the harshness of the imposed life.

17. Morrison, *Playing in the Dark* (Cambridge: Harvard University Press, 1992), 50.

18. Melvin Dixon, *Ride Out the Wilderness: Geography and Identity in Afro-American Literature* (Urbana: University of Illinois Press, 1987), 11. Birch, in *Black American Women's Writing,* 13–14.

19. Dixon, *Ride Out the Wilderness,* 14–19.

20. Hurston, *Their Eyes Were Watching God,* 17.

21. Henry Louis Gates, Jr., develops a linguistically, historically, and culturally informed definition of signifying as a complex practice of troping constituted of "figurative substitutions" and deferred meaning in black vernacular that "tend to be

humorous, or function to name a person or a situation in a telling manner"; see Gates, *The Signifying Monkey: A Theory of Afro-American Literary Criticism* (New York: Oxford University Press, 1988), 49; see all of chapter 2, pp. 44–88.

22. Morrison, *Playing in the Dark*, 23; Ammons, *Conflicting Stories*, 139. Rachel Blake's arrangements for Nancy's escape evince racial privileging in that her access to communication with other abolitionists is made possible by her race and education. Thus it participates in what Ammons sees as the link between racial privilege and the freedom of movement enjoyed by many of Cather's female characters, such as Thea Kronborg ("one very particular, highly privileged woman artist, the elite white woman artist"). Mrs. Blake's ability to play this role is, like the "very freedom of travel" available to Thea, in Ammons's reading, "open to her because she is white" (139).

23. Morrison, *Playing in the Dark*, 19–21, 27–28. No less a literary figure than Langston Hughes would, it seems, have disagreed with the general tenor of Morrison's comments. Cather acknowledged a letter of approval that he had sent; Willa Cather to Langston Hughes, April 15, 1941, Langston Hughes Papers, Box 40, Yale Collection of American Literature, Beinecke Rare Book and Manuscript Library, Yale University. That Hughes was pleased at receiving the acknowledgment is evident in his writing to Arna Bontemps on May 12 of that year that he had "had a nice note from Willa Cather to whom I wrote about her book"; Charles H. Nichols, ed., *Arna Bontemps, Langston Hughes: Letters, 1925–1967* (1980; New York: Paragon House, 1990), 81.

24. Morrison, *Playing in the Dark*, 18–19.

25. Mary Helen Washington, ed., *Invented Lives: Narratives of Black Women, 1860–1960* (New York, Doubleday, 1987), 7. Washington takes as emblematic the story of Harriet Jacobs (*Incidents in the Life of a Slave Girl*, 1861), who "was subjected to many kinds of imprisonment. She deliberately confined herself to a cramped attic space for many years in order to achieve freedom; she was confined by a slave narrative tradition that took the male's experiences as representative and marginalized the female's experience; and she was rendered nearly invisible by a fictional tradition that made white skin a requirement for womanhood" (12). Stepto merely mentions the names of Sojourner Truth and Harriet Tubman and gives only two and a half pages to *Their Eyes Were Watching God*; Stepto, *From Behind the Veil: A Study of Afro-American Narrative*, 2nd ed. (Urbana: University of Illinois Press, 1991).

26. A nationalist rhetoric in which westering is the vehicle for the (presumed) innately American urge toward freedom and expansive encounter with nature is—I repeat—less national than it has sometimes been supposed. For African Americans, the direction of freedom has been north. For Mexican Americans it has sometimes been north, but ambiguously so. For American Indians the historical pattern of westering on the part of Euro-American pioneers meant invasion, dislocation, and

oppression. The direction of freedom for native peoples was in some cases south and north; the Plains Indians, for example, migrated in a generally north-south route for hunting and raiding purposes. But for most Native Americans the directionality of freedom was (and to some extent still is) simply *here,* the center; they were free and fulfilled their lives by being where they were and, in their authenticating mythology, were meant to be. For Asian Americans the east-west directionality of movement has been, of course, highly complex and ambiguous.

27. Griffin, *"Who Set You Flowin',"* 13–47. Griffin (37) cites Darlene Clark Hine's "Black Migration to the Urban Midwest: The Gender Dimension, 1915–1945," in *The Great Migration in Historical Perspective: New Dimensions of Race, Class, and Gender,* ed. Joe William Trotter, Jr. (Bloomington: Indiana University Press, 1991), 127–46: "Many black women quit the South out of a desire to achieve personal autonomy and to escape from sexual abuse at the hands of southern white men as well as black men. The combined influence of domestic violence and economic oppression is key to understanding the hidden motivation informing major social protest and migratory movements in Afro-American history."

28. The hope for freedom in the North is, of course, often disappointed. James Baldwin writes, "And in exactly the same way that the South imagines that it 'knows' the Negro, the North imagines that it has set him free. Both camps are deluded." Baldwin, "A Letter from the South," in *Nobody Knows My Name: More Notes of a Native Son* (New York: Dial Press, 1961), 116.

29. Nella Larsen, *Quicksand and Passing,* ed. Deborah E. McDowell (New Brunswick, N.J.: Rutgers University Press, 1986), 22.

30. Griffin, *"Who Set You Flowin',"* 187; Morrison, *Jazz* (1992; reprint, New York: Penguin Books, 1993), 33.

31. Sterling A. Brown, "Slim in Hell," in *Folk-Say, IV,* ed. Benjamin A. Botkin (Norman: Oklahoma Folklore Society, 1932), 255–56.

32. Hurston's difficulty imagining a black female quester is analogous, in Washington's argument, to the difficulty experienced by reviewers of Gwendolyn Brooks's novel *Maud Martha* (1953) who "refus[ed]" to see the work as "part of any tradition in Afro-American or mainstream literature." They were unable to picture the questing figure as "a plain, dark-skinned housewife." Washington, *Invented Lives,* 249, xvii.

33. Hurston, *Dust Tracks on a Road* (1942; reprint, New York: HarperCollins Perennial Library, 1991), 2–6.

34. DuPlessis, *Writing Beyond the Ending,* 156; Mary Helen Washington, Foreword to *Their Eyes Were Watching God* (New York: Harper and Row Perennial Library, 1990), ix; Jerome E. Thornton, " 'Goin' on de Muck': The Paradoxical Journey of the Black American Hero," *CLA Journal* 31 (1988): 261–69.

35. Stepto, *From Behind the Veil,* 67.

272 Notes to Pages 157–166

36. Dixon, *Ride Out the Wilderness,* 89.

37. Ibid., 103. Dixon points out (107) that "return to self and to landscape is a constant theme in Alice Walker's fiction and essays." Rody notes the irony that the "aura of ascent" in historical novels by black writers, relating to the idea of "sociopolitical rise" and rise to writerly "authority," is linked to "psychological descent" ("Toni Morrison's *Beloved*," 96).

38. Griffin, *"Who Set You Flowin',"* 177.

39. Meese, *Crossing the Double-Cross,* 44–51.

40. Morrison, *Playing in the Dark,* 51–53.

41. Craig Hansen Werner, *Playing the Changes: From Afro-Modernism to the Jazz Impulse* (Urbana: University of Illinois Press, 1994), 67.

42. Adrienne Rich, *The Fact of a Doorframe: Poems Selected and New, 1950–1984* (New York: Norton, 1984), 164.

43. Morrison, *The Bluest Eye* (1970; New York: Pocket Books, 1972), 158. Another way to look at the deterioration of the text from the primer is to see it as representing what happens to the sensibleness—the rationality, in another sense—of a falsifying version of history itself, when its falsity becomes evident—when people begin to escape its spell. The official, sanctioned "history" falls apart.

44. Dixon, *Ride Out the Wilderness,* 142.

45. Morrison, *Sula* (1973; New York: Bantam Books, 1975), 15, 24–25.

46. This link between the robins and Sula's yearning for flight is made by Dixon in *Ride Out the Wilderness,* 151.

47. Bill Moyers, "A Conversation with Toni Morrison," in the "World of Ideas" series, Films for the Humanities and Sciences; text reprinted in Taylor-Guthrie, *Conversations with Toni Morrison,* 269.

48. Morrison has discussed her strong sense of place, especially her emphasis on the gendered nature of interior spaces, in an interview with Robert Stepto, "Intimate Things in Place," first published in 1977 and reprinted in *Chant of Saints,* ed. Michael S. Harper and Robert B. Stepto (Urbana: University of Illinois Press, 1979), 213–29.

49. Baker (*Workings of the Spirit,* 37) calls the African American's return to the South "the most difficult moment to activate."

50. A. Leslie Harris, "Myth as Structure in Toni Morrison's *Song of Solomon*," *MELUS* 7, no. 3 (1980): 73.

51. Morrison, *Song of Solomon* (1977; New York: NAL, 1978), 179.

52. Awkward, *Negotiating Difference,* 150–52.

53. Keenan, "Four Hundred Years of Silence," 46. Keenan astutely argues that the "ambiguities of connection and separation between the slave mother and child" are a correlative of the similar ambiguities of "the relationship of African Americans to their history" (47).

54. Morrison, *Beloved* (New York: Knopf, 1987; NAL Penguin Plume, 1988), 36.

55. Mary Helen Washington, " 'I Love the Way Janie Crawford Left Her Husbands': Zora Neale Hurston's Emergent Female Hero," in *Invented Lives,* 249.

56. The intersection of race and gender is evocatively contemplated by Quandra Prettyman in a notable though brief essay, "Visibility and Difference: Black Women in History and Literature—Pieces of a Paper and Some Ruminations," in Eisenstein and Jardine, *The Future of Difference,* 239–46. More recently that intersection is confronted and interrogated (occasionally with devastating insistence) by Awkward in *Negotiating Difference;* see especially 85–91. Awkward cautions that close reading of Morrison's corpus "discourages a reading of her work as radically feminist" but insists that her novels have "a consistently female-centered perspective" (141).

57. See Gerda Lerner, *Black Women in White America: A Documentary History* (New York: Pantheon, 1972), 60–63, and Gilroy, *Modernity and Double Consciousness,* 65–68.

58. Contrary to Beloved's memory of bodies packed around her below decks, Deborah Gray Williams insists that "women did not generally travel the middle passage in the holds of slave ships but . . . on the quarter deck. . . . [T]he female passage was further distinguished from that of males in that women and girls were not shackled." Williams, *Ar'n't I a Woman? Female Slaves in the Plantation South* (New York: Norton, 1985), 63; quoted by Baker, *Workings of the Spirit,* 124.

59. Trudier Harris, "Escaping Slavery But Not Its Images," in *Toni Morrison: Critical Perspectives, Past and Present,* ed. Henry Louis Gates, Jr., and K. A. Appiah (New York: Amistad, 1993), 340.

60. Lori Askeland, "Remodeling the Model Home in *Uncle Tom's Cabin* and *Beloved,*" in *Subjects and Citizens: Nation, Race, and Gender from Oroonoko to Anita Hill,* ed. Michael Moon and Cathy N. Davidson (Durham: Duke University Press, 1995), 402.

61. The bit was a commonly used implement of domination. Morrison has cited memoir evidence that even an "enlightened slave owner" had recourse to the bit to control recalcitrant slaves; Bonnie Angelo, "The Pain of Being Black: An Interview with Toni Morrison," *Time,* May 22, 1989; reprinted in Taylor-Guthrie, *Conversations with Toni Morrison,* 257.

62. Stepto, *From Behind the Veil,* 62.

63. The terrible ambiguity of Sethe's act of loving murder is the most compelling instance of Morrison's engagement with the duality of good mother/bad mother, a theme that at least in part accounts for her attention to Cather's *Sapphira and the Slave Girl* in *Playing in the Dark.*

64. The scene in which Denver ventures out is sometimes experienced by white readers as harrowing since it shows so compellingly her fear of whites, any whites. Because of the powerful sympathy that Morrison has developed for Denver by this

point, such readers are forced to experience, momentarily at least, the justice of their labeling as beings to be feared.

65. Betty Fussell, "All That Jazz," *Lear's,* October 1, 1992; reprinted in Taylor-Guthrie, *Conversations with Toni Morrison,* 284.

66. Although *Jazz* has not elicited the lyrical celebration among reviewers that *Beloved* did, it has generally been received with admiration. A notable exception is the conspicuously hostile attack on the novel by Bruce Bawer in the conservative journal *New Criterion* 10, no. 9 (1992): 10–17. Bawer's essay, "All That Jazz," is replete with distortion, reductiveness, mockery, and name-calling (e.g., "hysterical"), with gratuitous swipes at *Playing in the Dark* and others of Morrison's works.

67. Houston A. Baker, Jr., *Blues, Ideology, and Afro-American Literature: A Vernacular Theory* (Chicago: University of Chicago Press, 1984), 7.

68. Steven C. Tracy, *Langston Hughes and the Blues* (Urbana: University of Illinois Press, 1988), 81 and, quoting Stanley Edgar Hyman, 86. See Joanne V. Gabbin's discussion of the "idea of liberation" in work songs, blues, jazz, and other traditional forms; *Sterling A. Brown: Building the Black Aesthetic Tradition* (Charlottesville: University Press of Virginia, 1994), 109–10.

69. Dana Micucci, "An Inspired Life: Toni Morrison Writes and a Generation Listens," *Chicago Tribune,* May 31, 1992; reprinted in Taylor-Guthrie, *Conversations with Toni Morrison,* 275.

70. Werner, *Playing the Changes,* xvii.

71. Baker, *Blues, Ideology, and Afro-American Literature,* 7; Micucci, "An Inspired Life," 275.

72. The Great Migration was in progress before World War I, but was accelerated as American industry began supplying matériel to the belligerents. According to Waldo Martin, over a million and a half African Americans left the South between 1910 and 1930, many of them between 1916 and 1919, which he designates "the years of the Great Migration"; Martin, "The Making of Black America," in *Making America: The Society and Culture of the United States,* ed. Luther S. Luedtke (Chapel Hill: University of North Carolina Press, 1992), 354. The phrase "Great Migration" is also customarily used with reference to mass movement northward by southern blacks during the first decade of the century.

73. Jacob Lawrence's *Migration of the Negro* series also includes panels on the fact of lynching as an impetus to migration out of the South and on the race riots in East St. Louis, the riots in which Morrison's character Dorcas is orphaned. The series of sixty 12 × 18 paintings in tempura on hardboard is divided between the Phillips Gallery in Washington, D.C., and the Museum of Modern Art in New York. See *Jacob Lawrence: The Migration Series,* ed. Elizabeth Hutton Turner, with introductory essay by Henry Louis Gates, Jr. (Washington, D.C.: Rappahannock Press, in association with the Phillips Collection, 1993).

74. Carolyn Jones, of Louisiana State University, called attention to Murray's work and to Toni Morrison's engagement with it in "Race and Intimacy in Murray's *South to a Very Old Place*," a paper delivered at the American Literature Association meeting in Baltimore in May 1995.

75. Albert Murray, *South to a Very Old Place* (New York: McGraw-Hill, 1971), 137.

76. Ibid., 4–5.

77. Ibid., 219, 223. Ralph Ellison similarly defined the blues as "an impulse to keep the painful details and episodes of a brutal experience alive in one's aching consciousness, to finger its jagged grain, and to transcend it, not by the consolation of philosophy but by squeezing from it a near-tragic, near-comic lyricism"; cited by Werner in *Playing the Changes*, xxi.

78. Murray, *South to a Very Old Place*, 222.

79. *Harper's* December 22, 1900, quoted in Jervis Anderson, *This Was Harlem: A Cultural Portrait, 1900–1950* (New York: Farrar, Straus & Giroux, 1981), 10–11.

80. Anderson, *This Was Harlem*, 6.

81. Donald A. Petesch, *A Spy in the Enemy's Country: The Emergence of Modern Black Literature* (Iowa City: University of Iowa Press, 1989), 178–79; Anderson, *This Was Harlem*, 137. Petesch comments, in a phrase that might have been intended to describe Joe and Violet Trace, that "the newly arrived migrant to the city could not but react with surprise, and pleasure."

82. Langston Hughes, *Black Magic: A Pictorial History of the Negro in American Entertainment* (Englewood Cliffs, N.J.: Prentice-Hall, 1967), 80. Scholarship on the origins and evolution of jazz is extensive and by no means undisputed. Charles O. Hartman writes in his challenging and theoretically informed *Jazz Text: Voice and Improvisation in Poetry, Jazz, and Song* (Princeton: Princeton University Press, 1991), 9, that "everyone realizes" jazz combines "essential elements of West African music and European concert music." But not everyone does, in fact, agree that European traditions contributed to jazz. Interestingly, W. E. B. DuBois, in *The Negro* (1913), accepted the idea that spirituals, blues, and ragtime were of mingled African and European origins, constituting a "new and original music to the western world," but "found it difficult to accept African-American folk music like blues, jazz, and popular gospel," preferring spirituals and "black artists who embraced white Western traditions and the professionally trained arrangers of folk music, who could make the music more 'respectable,' rather than the untutored people who created the music"; Tracy, *Langston Hughes and the Blues*, 19–21. Tracy's second chapter, "Defining the Blues" (79–140), provides a substantive account of the scholarly literature on blues, as well as Hughes's pronouncements.

83. Baker, *Blues, Ideology, and Afro-American Literature*, 122.

84. This feature of the blues tradition is argued by Maria V. Johnson in " 'You

Just Can't Keep a Good Woman Down'": Alice Walker Sings the Blues," *African American Review* 30 (1995): 226.

85. Dixon, *Ride Out the Wilderness,* 148.

86. Morrison, *Playing in the Dark,* 49.

CHAPTER 6. JOAN DIDION

Epigraphs: Salman Rushdie, *Imaginary Homelands: Essays and Criticism, 1981–1991* (London: Granta Books, 1991), 12; Denise Levertov, "Staying Alive. Entr'acte," in *To Stay Alive* (New York: New Directions, 1971), 49; Levertov, "A Traveler," in *A Door in the Hive* (New York: New Directions, 1989), 6.

1. Didion, "On Keeping a Notebook," in *Slouching Towards Bethlehem* (New York: Simon and Schuster, 1968), 133.

2. Thomas Mallon, Review of *Democracy, American Spectator* 17 (August 1984); John Lownsbrough, "Didion Moves East But Remains at Home in the Essay," *Toronto Globe and Mail,* August 22, 1992; both reprinted in *The Critical Response to Joan Didion,* ed. Sharon Felton (Westport, Conn.: Greenwood Press, 1994), 196, 242. Didion is reported to have voted for Barry Goldwater in 1964; Michiko Kakutani, "Joan Didion: Staking Out California," *New York Times Magazine,* June 10, 1979; reprinted in *Joan Didion: Essays and Conversations,* ed. Ellen G. Friedman (Princeton, N.J.: Ontario Review Press, 1984), 35. The traces of elitism Lownsbrough mentions are found in Didion's *After Henry* (Simon and Schuster, 1992). In an earlier essay, "In the Islands," after describing icily the retrograde elitism of certain guests at the Royal Hawaiian Hotel who are "the natural inheritors of a style later seized upon by Patricia Nixon and her daughters," she indulges a wish that she and her daughter might maintain such a style of living themselves; *The White Album* (New York: Simon and Schuster, 1979), 140.

3. Rushdie, *Imaginary Homelands,* 15. After the imposition of the radical Muslim fatwa following publication of *Satanic Verses,* Rushdie gave up having a fixed place of residence, instead moving continually among hotels, registering under assumed names.

4. Jennifer L. Randisi, "The Journey Nowhere in Didion's *Run River,*" *Markham Review* 11 (1982): 41. Lynne T. Hanley observes accurately that Didion's first two novels "feature neurotic, well-heeled west coast women, whose brushes with the nuclear peril or the wars around the world are rare, accidental and unexamined"; "To El Salvador," *Massachusetts Review* 24 (1983): 16.

5. Sara Davidson, "A Visit with Joan Didion," *New York Times Book Review,* April 3, 1977; reprinted in Friedman, *Joan Didion,* 14.

6. Susan Stamberg, "Cautionary Tales," interview aired on National Public Radio on April 4, 1977; reprinted in Friedman, *Joan Didion,* 24.

7. Kakutani, "Joan Didion: Staking Out California," 29; Louis Simpson, "Lines Written Near San Francisco," in *Collected Poems* (New York: Paragon House, 1988), 166. Simpson writes, "How sad it is, the end of America!"

8. Gelfant, "What Was It," 86. Such a view has been questioned recently by Joseph Urgo and Sally Peltier.

9. Cather once wrote to Sinclair Lewis, for instance, that she hoped he and his wife would come to visit her so that they could discuss the current problems of the country. Undated letter, Lewis Papers, Beinecke Rare Book and Manuscript Library.

10. O'Brien, *Willa Cather,* 434.

11. Mary Austin to R. L. Scaife, June 11, 1920, Houghton Mifflin Collection, bMS Am 1925, Houghton Library, Harvard University; quoted by permission.

12. De Lauretis, *Alice Doesn't,* 184, citing Catharine MacKinnon, "Feminism, Marxism, Method, and the State: An Agenda for Theory," *Signs* 7 (1982): 535.

13. Adrienne Rich, "Translations," in *The Fact of a Doorframe,* 170. All parenthetical references to Rich's poetry are to this volume.

14. Mikhail Bakhtin, *The Dialogic Imagination: Four Essays,* trans. Caryl Emerson and Michael Holquist (Austin: University of Texas Press, 1981), 217. The widespread recognition of the task Bakhtin enunciates is not unrelated to an increase in critical attention to the writing of women at various levels of aestheticizing and in various genres. Genaro M. Padilla has importantly observed, in examining women's personal narratives as a distinct subset of Mexican-American autobiographical writing, that women "refused to distinguish the domestic space of the 'woman's sphere' in a way that makes private/public a strict binary opposition; rather, domestic space provides the vantage point from which history is witnessed as well as the strategic space from which women act upon history." *My History, Not Yours: The Formation of Mexican American Autobiography* (Madison: University of Wisconsin Press, 1993), 118.

15. De Lauretis, *Alice Doesn't,* 123–29.

16. Marianna Hirsch pointedly adopts a journey metaphor in speaking of Rich's presentation of herself, in "When We Dead Awaken: Writing as Re-Vision," as "someone attempting to chart new territory"; *The Mother/Daughter Plot,* 125.

17. De Lauretis, *Alice Doesn't,* 133.

18. "In the Wake of Home" includes a reference to Margaret Garner's killing of her children, the incident Morrison would use in *Beloved,* published four years after the poem.

19. Lorrie Smith, "Songs of Experience: Denise Levertov's Political Poetry," *Contemporary Literature* 1986; reprinted in *Denise Levertov: Selected Criticism,* ed. Albert Gelpi (Ann Arbor: University of Michigan Press, 1993), 178. This volume offers several valuable essays relating to Levertov's political thematics, including an excerpt from Rachel Blau DuPlessis's *Writing Beyond the Ending* (1985), here entitled "The Cri-

tique of Consciousness and Myth in Levertov, Rich, and Rukeyser." Smith points out that Levertov's political poetry of the 1960s was anticipated by her participation in antinuclear protests in the 1950s and by the poem "During the Eichmann Trial" in the 1958 volume *The Jacob's Ladder.*

20. Sandra M. Gilbert, "Revolutionary Love: Denise Levertov and the Poetics of Politics," *Parnassus* 1985; reprinted in Gelpi, *Denise Levertov,* 201.

21. Levertov, "Brass Tacks," *Footprints* (New York: New Directions, 1972), 39.

22. Levertov, "On the Edge of Darkness: What Is Political Poetry?" in *Light Up the Cave* (New York: New Directions, 1981), 129.

23. Levertov, "Poetry and Revolution: Neruda Is Dead—Neruda Lives" and "On Muriel Rukeyser," in *Light Up the Cave,* 130, 189.

24. Levertov, "Embrasure," *Breathing the Water* (New York: New Directions, 1987), 15; "From Afar," *Life in the Forest* (New York: New Directions, 1978), 87.

25. For the events of the decade, I have drawn on Allen J. Matusow, *The Unraveling of America: A History of Liberalism in the 1960s* (New York: Harper and Row, 1984).

26. Albert Gelpi, Introduction to *Denise Levertov,* 4.

27. Ironically, perhaps, 60 percent of voters surveyed early in 1969 said that their biggest worry was the high cost of living; Matusow, *The Unraveling of America,* 175.

28. Michelle Carbone Loris, "Innocence, Loss, and Recovery in the Art of Joan Didion," *Dissertation Abstracts International* A46 (1985): 162.

29. Leonard Wilcox, "Narrative Technique and the Theme of Historical Continuity in the Novels of Joan Didion," in Friedman, *Joan Didion,* 68.

30. Stout, *The Journey Narrative,* 114.

31. Thomas Mallon, "The Limits of History in the Novels of Joan Didion," *Critique* 21 (1980); reprinted in Friedman, *Joan Didion,* 62.

32. Chris Anderson, "The Cat in the Shimmer," in *Style as Argument: Contemporary American Nonfiction,* ed. Anderson (Carbondale: Southern Illinois University Press, 1987); reprinted in Felton, *The Critical Response to Joan Didion,* 58–59.

33. Didion, *A Book of Common Prayer* (New York: Simon and Schuster, 1977), 262.

34. Didion, *Miami* (New York: Simon and Schuster, 1987), 23.

35. Evan Carton, "Joan Didion's Dreampolitics of the Self," *Western Humanities Review* 1986; reprinted in Felton, *The Critical Response to Joan Didion,* 41.

36. Didion variously implies that the traditional roles might in themselves be appealing if they had not been—in ways she does not specify—debased and abused.

37. Hanley, "To El Salvador," 16.

38. Ibid., 18–19.

39. Didion, *Salvador* (New York: Simon and Schuster, 1983), 13; cf. *Common Prayer,* 22.

40. Felton, Introduction to *The Critical Response to Joan Didion,* 6. Felton notes that *Salvador* is the work for which Didion has "received the most negative criticism." The book has also been called, however, Didion's "most successful piece of writing, both as rhetorical criticism and as rhetorical performance" (Anderson, "The Cat in the Shimmer," 60). For Levertov's exposure of atrocities in El Salvador, see "Unresolved," in *Candles in Babylon* (New York: New Directions, 1982), 104.

41. Mary Louise Pratt, *Imperial Eyes: Travel Writing and Transculturation* (New York: Routledge, 1992), 225–26. Didion's longtime hostility toward Ronald and Nancy Reagan, dating from the years of their political rise in California, should give one pause about labeling her a political "conservative," since a personal devotion to Reagan and to whatever policies are customarily intended by the term "Reaganism" have come to be taken as touchstones of conservatism. Didion is a prime illustration of the fact that one may be temperamentally or in theory conservative without automatically being an adherent to a "conservative" agenda. She also criticizes Reagan sharply in *Miami,* 158–59.

42. Jennifer Brady, "Points West, Then and Now: The Fiction of Joan Didion," *Contemporary Literature* 20 (1979); reprinted in Friedman, *Joan Didion,* 56.

43. Ibid., 43.

44. Patricia Merivale is overly ingenious, I believe, in conjecturing that the power adding "outside hardware" to the action is Grace herself ("Through Greeneland in Drag: Joan Didion's *A Book of Common Prayer,*" *Pacific Coast Philology* 15 (1980); reprinted in Felton, *The Critical Response to Joan Didion,* 103). Although Grace learns that she is not only a limited but an unreliable narrator, I find no evidence that she is constituted as a lying narrator. I take at face value her speculations on that score on page 272:

> The *guerrilleros* appeared to have more of everything than anyone except Leonard Douglas had supposed they had. Some say Kasindorf and Riley supplied the excess, some say other agencies. Some say Victor.
>
> I think not Victor but have no empirical proof.
>
> I also think (still) that Leonard Douglas was not involved but again this conclusion is not empirical.
>
> In any case.

The phrase "in any case" seems to me less cryptic, in the sense of a clue, than weary. In any case, that is all she can say, that is all she knows; or in any case it doesn't matter, what is important is what happened to Charlotte.

45. Davidson, "A Visit with Joan Didion," 20.

46. Ibid., 18.

47. Mark Royden Winchell terms Charlotte's death a "gratuitous act of courage" that "accomplishes nothing tangible"; *Joan Didion,* rev. ed. (Boston: Twayne, 1989),

107. Merivale ("Through Greene-land in Drag," 104) reads Charlotte's final act of sending her emerald ring to Marin as the transmission of resources to pay for more arms for another revolution. In this reading, her death is not entirely without practical result. Again, however, I find this reading over-ingenious and inconsistent with Charlotte's violent revulsion against wanton violence, seen most clearly in her reaction to the destruction of vaccine and the bombing of the clinic.

48. Davidson, "A Visit with Joan Didion," 21.

49. Samuel Chase Coale finds that "victimization becomes a woman's vision" not only in *A Book of Common Prayer* but in much of Didion's other work as well; "Joan Didion: Witnessing the Abyss," in *Hawthorne's Shadow: American Romance from Melville to Mailer* (Lexington: University Press of Kentucky, 1985); reprinted in Felton, *The Critical Response to Joan Didion*, 108. Victor Strandberg's reading that Charlotte's murder was "ordained within hours of her first night with Victor" because her "sexual passions lead inescapably to a messy, emotionally chaotic life, surrounded by embattled males," curiously reverses blame; "Passion and Delusion in *A Book of Common Prayer*," *Modern Fiction Studies* 27 (1981); reprinted in Friedman, *Joan Didion*, 149.

50. Strandberg, "Passion and Delusion," 158.

51. The structure of the novel, then, is the ouroboros, the serpent with its tail in its mouth; the beginning (the opening words) is the point at which it arrives at the end.

52. Winchell, *Joan Didion*, 101.

53. Mallon, Review of *Democracy*, 195–98.

54. Winchell (*Joan Didion*, 126) believes that "the brunt of Didion's satire" in *Democracy* is "borne by fatuous New Age liberals." That may be true, but the brunt of her direct aversion is borne by fomenters of war and self-enrichers whom she and most readers would, I believe, associate with conservatives. Winchell points out accurately that Inez's decision to persevere in refugee work "reflects neither liberal sentimentality nor conservative obligation so much as Christian charity" (131)—although there is no suggestion in the book that Christianity or any other organized religion plays a part in her decision.

55. Katherine Usher Henderson, "The Bond between Narrator and Heroine in *Democracy*," in *American Women Writing Fiction: Memory, Identity, Family, Space*, ed. Mickey Pearlman (Lexington: University Press of Kentucky, 1989), 71, 73.

56. Didion, *Democracy* (New York: Simon and Schuster, 1984), 19–21.

57. Didion, *The Last Thing He Wanted* (New York: Knopf, 1996), 10. Besides its attention to corruptions in America's foreign policy in Central America, Didion's latest novel connects with her earlier work in a number of important ways: stylistic features such as reliance on emphatic fragmentation at the level of the sentence, deconstruction of generic lines between fiction and reportage, a mother's desperate attempt to protect her daughter (as in *A Book of Common Prayer*), and the insistent presence of air travel that whisks her character away from any secure sense of emplacement but

ultimately leaves her stranded in a site of expatriated death. Readers of *Democracy* will recognize such freighted terms as "dropping cargo" and the "jettisoning" of assumptions (*Last Thing He Wanted,* 3 and 5).

58. Alan Nadel, "Failed Cultural Narratives: America in the Postwar Era and the Story of *Democracy,*" *Boundary II* 19, no. 1 (1992): 96.

59. Carolyn Goffman, "Beyond Reportage in *Salvador,*" *Connecticut Review* 13, no. 2 (1991): 18.

60. See, for example, George Russell's review "Mooning over Miami," *Commentary* 85, no. 1 (1988): 69–72.

61. Merritt Mosley, "Joan Didion's Symbolic Landscapes," *South Carolina Review* 1989; reprinted in Felton, *The Critical Response to Joan Didion,* 133. Mosley singles out for comment the peculiar locution at the start of "On Morality," in *Slouching Towards Bethlehem:* "As it happens I am in Death Valley." A similar phrase appears in the later essay "Shooters Inc.," where she "happened to be in Amman" (*After Henry,* 88).

62. Mark Z. Muggli, *Temperamental Journeys: Essays on the Modern Literature of Travel* (Athens: University of Georgia Press, 1992), 176. Mary Louise Pratt (*Imperial Eyes,* 225) observes that in *Salvador* Didion seems to attempt to "dismantle the genre" of travel writing.

63. Strandberg, "Passion and Delusion," 41. Nadel observes that Harry Victor is "a sort of Kennedy Democrat" ("Failed Cultural Narratives," 95).

64. Stuart Ching, " 'A Hard Story to Tell': The Vietnam War in Joan Didion's *Democracy,*" in *Fourteen Landing Zones: Approaches to Vietnam War Literature,* ed. Philip K. Jason (Iowa City: University of Iowa Press, 1991), 183.

65. Henderson, "The Bond between Narrator and Heroine in *Democracy,*" 70.

66. The insertion of the fictionalized author in her own narrative is only one of the ways in which fact and fiction merge in this book. Ching presents some of the ways in which events or details in the novel refer accurately to actual events ("A Hard Story to Tell," 184–85).

67. Muggli, *Temperamental Journeys,* 178.

68. Thomas R. Edwards, "An American Education," *New York Review of Books* 1984; reprinted in Felton, *The Critical Response to Joan Didion,* 193.

69. H. Wayne Schow, "*Out of Africa, The White Album,* and the Possibility of Tragic Affirmation," *English Studies* 67 (1986): 35.

70. Sandra K. Hinchman, "Didion's Political Tropics: *Miami* and the Basis for Community," in Felton, *The Critical Response to Joan Didion,* 238.

POSTSCRIPT

Epigraphs: Langston Hughes, "Strange Hurt," in *Selected Poems,* 84; Josephine Miles, "On Inhabiting an Orange," in *Collected Poems, 1930–83* (Urbana: University of Illinois Press, 1983), 7; Louise Erdrich, *Tracks* (New York: Henry Holt, 1988), 33.

1. Salman Rushdie, *The Wizard of Oz* (London: BFI Publishing, 1992), 9. I am indebted to Joseph Urgo's *Willa Cather and the Myth of American Migration* for bringing Rushdie's essay to my attention.

2. Ibid., 23.

3. Ann Putnam, " 'Tangled Together Like Badly Cast Fishing Line': The Reader and the Text in Katherine Anne Porter's 'Pale Horse, Pale Rider' "; Charlotte McClure, "From Impersonators to Persons: Breaking Patterns, Finding Voices"; Ann Romines, "The Voices from the Little House"; Susan Rosowski, "Rewriting the Love Plot Our Way: Women and Work"; all in Nelson, *Private Voices, Public Lives,* 4, 227, 27, 37.

4. Henry James, *The Portrait of a Lady* (1881; New York: New American Library, 1964), 30. It was David McWhirter who reminded me of this moment in a text that Cather, an early Jamesian, knew quite well.

BIBLIOGRAPHY

Abel, Elizabeth. "Narrative Structure(s) and Female Development: The Case of *Mrs. Dalloway*." In Abel, Hirsch, and Langland, *The Voyage In,* 161–85.

Abel, Elizabeth, Marianne Hirsch, and Elizabeth Langland, eds. *The Voyage In: Fictions of Female Development.* Hanover, N.H.: University Press of New England, 1983.

Adams, Susan Rushing. "Reenvisioning Cather's Spaces: Dualities of Landscape and Meaning." Unpublished Senior Honors Thesis, Texas A&M University, 1994.

Ammons, Elizabeth. *Conflicting Stories: American Women Writers at the Turn into the Twentieth Century.* New York: Oxford University Press, 1992.

———. *Edith Wharton's Argument with America.* Athens: University of Georgia Press, 1980.

———. "Going in Circles: The Female Geography of Jewett's *Country of the Pointed Firs.*" *Studies in the Literary Imagination* 16 (1983): 83–92.

Anderson, Chris. "The Cat in the Shimmer." In *Style as Argument: Contemporary American Nonfiction,* ed. Anderson. Carbondale: Southern Illinois University Press, 1987. Reprinted in Felton, *The Critical Response to Joan Didion,* 51–64.

Anderson, Jervis. *This Was Harlem: A Cultural Portrait, 1900–1950.* New York: Farrar, Straus & Giroux, 1981.

Angelo, Bonnie. "The Pain of Being Black: An Interview with Toni Morrison." *Time,* May 22, 1989; reprinted in Taylor-Guthrie, *Conversations with Toni Morrison,* 255–61.

Anzaldúa, Gloria. *Borderlands/La frontera: The New Mestiza.* San Francisco: Aunt Lute Books, 1987.

Apthorp, Elaine Sargent. "Re-Visioning Creativity: Cather, Chopin, Jewett." *Legacy* 9 (1992): 1–22.

Armitage, Shelley. "Introduction." In Church, *Wind's Trail,* ix–xxi.

Armitage, Susan H. "Reluctant Pioneers." In *Women and Western American Literature,* ed. Helen Winter Stauffer and Susan J. Rosowski, 40–51. Troy, N.Y.: Whitston Publishing Company, 1982.

Askeland, Lori. "Remodeling the Model Home in *Uncle Tom's Cabin* and *Beloved.*" In Moon and Davidson, *Subjects and Citizens,* 395–416.

Atwood, Margaret. *The Handmaid's Tale.* Boston: Houghton Mifflin, 1986.

Austin, Mary. *Cactus Thorn.* Reno: University of Nevada Press, 1988.

——. *Earth Horizon.* 1932. Albuquerque: University of New Mexico Press, 1991.

——. *The Flock.* Boston: Houghton Mifflin, 1906.

——. *The Ford.* Boston: Houghton Mifflin, 1917.

——. *Isidro.* Boston: Houghton Mifflin, 1905.

——. *The Land of Journeys' Ending.* 1924. Reprint, Tucson: University of Arizona Press, 1983.

——. *The Land of Little Rain.* 1903. Reprint, Albuquerque: University of New Mexico Press, 1974.

——. *The Lovely Lady.* Garden City, N.Y.: Doubleday, Page, 1913.

——. "Medicine Song (From the Paiute Indian Dialect, Done into English by Mary Austin)." *McClure's* 37 (1911): 504.

——. *No. 26 Jayne Street.* Boston: Houghton Mifflin, 1920.

——. *Outland.* New York: Boni and Liveright, 1919.

——. Papers located in the Houghton Library, Harvard University; the Huntington Library, San Marino, California; and The Pierpont Morgan Library, New York.

——. "Regionalism in American Fiction." *English Journal* 21 (1932): 97–106.

——. *Santa Lucia.* New York: Harper & Brothers, 1908.

——. "The Song of the Friend (From the Paiute Indian Dialect, Done into English by Mary Austin)." *McClure's* 38 (1911–12): 351.

——. "The Song of the Hills (From the Yokut Indian Dialect, Done into English by Mary Austin)." *McClure's* 37 (1911): 615.

——. *Starry Adventure.* Boston: Houghton Mifflin, 1931.

——. "Walking Woman." In *Stories from the Country of Lost Borders.* Edited by Marjorie Pryse. New Brunswick: Rutgers University Press, 1987.

——. *Western Trails: A Collection of Short Stories by Mary Austin.* Reno: University of Nevada Press, 1987.

——. *A Woman of Genius.* 1912. Old Westbury, N.Y.: Feminist Press, 1985.

Awkward, Michael. *Negotiating Difference: Race, Gender, and the Politics of Positionality.* Chicago: University of Chicago Press, 1995.

Bachelard, Gaston. *The Poetics of Space.* Translated by Maria Jolas. Boston: Orion Press, 1964.

Bachelder, Frances H. "Manacles of Fear: Emotional Affliction in Tyler's Works." In Salwak, *Anne Tyler as Novelist*, 43–49.

Baker, Houston A., Jr. *Blues, Ideology, and Afro-American Literature: A Vernacular Theory.* Chicago: University of Chicago Press, 1984.

———. *Workings of the Spirit: The Poetics of Afro-American Women's Writing.* Chicago: University of Chicago Press, 1991.

Bakhtin, Mikhail. *The Dialogic Imagination: Four Essays.* Translated by Caryl Emerson and Michael Holquist. Austin: University of Texas Press, 1981.

Baldwin, James. "A Letter from the South." In *Nobody Knows My Name: More Notes of a Native Son,* 98–116. New York: Dial Press, 1961.

Barthes, Roland. *A Lover's Discourse: Fragments.* Translated by Richard Howard. New York: Hill and Wang, 1978.

Bawer, Bruce. "All That Jazz." *New Criterion* 10, no. 9 (1992): 10–17.

Benstock, Shari. *Women of the Left Bank: Paris, 1900–1940.* Austin: University of Texas Press, 1986.

Betts, Doris. "The Fiction of Anne Tyler." *Southern Quarterly* 21, no. 4 (1983): 23–37.

———. "Tyler's Marriage of Opposites." In Stephens, *The Fiction of Anne Tyler,* 1–15.

Birch, Eve Lennox. *Black American Women's Writing: A Quilt of Many Colours.* New York: Harvester/Wheatsheaf, 1994.

Blake, Susan L. "Folklore and Community in *Song of Solomon.*" *MELUS* 7, no. 3 (1980): 77–82.

Brady, Jennifer. "Points West, Then and Now: The Fiction of Joan Didion," *Contemporary Literature* 20 (1979); reprinted in Friedman, *Joan Didion,* 43–59.

Briggs, Cynthia K. "Insulated Isolation: Willa Cather's Room with a View." In Rosowski, *Cather Studies I,* 159–71.

Brown, E. K., with Leon Edel. *Willa Cather: A Critical Biography.* 1953. Reprint, Lincoln: University of Nebraska Press, 1987.

Brown, Gillian. "The Empire of Agoraphobia." *Representations* 20 (1987): 134–57.

Brown, Sterling A. "Slim in Hell." In *Folk-Say, IV.* Edited by Benjamin A. Botkin. Norman: Oklahoma Folklore Society, 1932.

Burgess, Cheryll. "Willa Cather's Homecomings: A Meeting of Selves." In Murphy, *Willa Cather,* 49–56.

Burke, Carolyn. "Rethinking the Maternal." In Eisenstein and Jardine, *The Future of Difference,* 107–14.

Burton, Virginia Lee. *The Little House.* Boston: Houghton Mifflin, 1942.

Carlin, Deborah. *Cather, Canon, and the Politics of Reading.* Amherst: University of Massachusetts Press, 1992.

Carson, Barbara Harrell. "Complicate, Complicate: Anne Tyler's Moral Imperative." *Southern Quarterly* 31, no. 1 (1992): 24–34.

Carton, Evan. "Joan Didion's Dreampolitics of the Self." *Western Humanities Review* 1986; reprinted in Felton, *The Critical Response to Joan Didion,* 34–51.

Cather, Willa. *Death Comes for the Archbishop.* 1927. New York: Random House Vintage Classics, 1990.

———. *A Lost Lady.* 1923. New York: Random House Vintage Classics, 1990.

———. *Lucy Gayheart.* 1935. New York: Random House, 1976.

———. *My Ántonia.* 1918. New York: Random House Vintage Classics, 1994.

———. *My Mortal Enemy.* 1926. New York: Random House Vintage Classics, 1990.

———. "Nebraska: The End of the First Cycle." *Nation* 117 (1923): 236–38.

———. *Obscure Destinies.* 1932. Reprint, New York: Random House Vintage Books, 1974.

———. *O Pioneers!* The Scholarly Edition. Edited by Susan J. Rosowski and Charles W. Mignon. Lincoln: University of Nebraska Press, 1992.

———. Papers located at the Alderman Library, the University of Virginia; the Yale Collection of American Literature, Beinecke Rare Book and Manuscript Library, Yale University; the Harry Ransom Humanities Research Center, the University of Texas at Austin; Houghton Library, Harvard University, the Houghton-Mifflin Collection; the Huntington Library, San Marino, California; the Bailey-Howe Library, University of Vermont.

———. *The Professor's House.* 1925. New York: Random House Vintage Classics, 1990.

———. *Shadows on the Rock.* 1931. New York: Random House Vintage Books, 1971.

———. *The Song of the Lark.* 1915. Reprint, New York: Bantam Classics, 1991.

———. *The Song of the Lark.* "New edition containing revisions made by the author." Boston: Houghton Mifflin, 1937.

———. *The Troll Garden.* 1905. Reprint, Lincoln: University of Nebraska Press, 1983.

———. *Willa Cather on Writing.* 1949. Reprint, Lincoln: University of Nebraska Press, 1987.

Ching, Stuart. " 'A Hard Story to Tell': The Vietnam War in Joan Didion's *Democracy.*" In *Fourteen Landing Zones: Approaches to Vietnam War Literature,* ed. Philip K. Jason, 180–88. Iowa City: University of Iowa Press, 1991.

Chodorow, Nancy. *The Reproduction of Mothering: Psychoanalysis and the Psychology of Gender.* Berkeley: University of California Press, 1978.

Church, Joseph. "Transgressive Daughters in Sarah Orne Jewett's *Deephaven.*" *Essays in Literature* 20 (1993): 231–250.

Church, Peggy Pond. *Wind's Trail: The Early Life of Mary Austin.* Edited by Shelley Armitage. Santa Fe: Museum of New Mexico Press, 1990.

Cisneros, Sandra. *My Wicked, Wicked Ways.* New York: Turtle Bay, 1993.

Cixous, Hélène. "The Laugh of the Medusa." Translated by Keith and Paula Cohen. *Signs* 1 (1976): 875–93.

Coale, Samuel Chase. "Joan Didion: Witnessing the Abyss." In *Hawthorne's Shadow:*

American Romance from Melville to Mailer. Lexington: University Press of Kentucky, 1985. Reprinted in Felton, *The Critical Response to Joan Didion,* 106–25.

Darling, Marshal. "In the Realm of Responsibility: A Conversation with Toni Morrison." *Women's Review of Books,* March 1978; reprinted in Taylor-Guthrie, *Conversations with Toni Morrison,* 246–54.

Davidson, Sara. "A Visit with Joan Didion." *New York Times Book Review,* April 3, 1977; reprinted in Friedman, *Joan Didion,* 13–21.

Davis, Christina. "An Interview with Toni Morrison." *Presence Africaine* 1988; reprinted in Taylor-Guthrie, *Conversations with Toni Morrison,* 223–33.

de Lauretis, Teresa. *Alice Doesn't: Feminism, Semiotics, Cinema.* Bloomington: Indiana University Press, 1984.

Dickinson, Emily. *The Complete Poems of Emily Dickinson.* Edited by Thomas H. Johnson. Boston: Little, Brown, 1960.

Didion, Joan. *After Henry.* New York: Simon and Schuster, 1992.

———. *A Book of Common Prayer.* New York: Simon and Schuster, 1977.

———. *Democracy.* New York: Simon and Schuster, 1984.

———. *The Last Thing He Wanted.* New York: Knopf, 1996.

———. *Miami.* New York: Simon and Schuster, 1987.

———. *Play It As It Lays.* New York: Simon and Schuster, 1970.

———. *Salvador.* New York: Simon and Schuster, 1983.

———. *Slouching Towards Bethlehem.* New York: Simon and Schuster, 1968.

———. *The White Album.* New York: Simon and Schuster, 1979.

Dixon, Melvin. *Ride Out the Wilderness: Geography and Identity in Afro-American Literature.* Urbana: University of Illinois Press, 1987.

Donovan, Josephine. *Sarah Orne Jewett.* New York: Frederick Ungar, 1980.

DuPlessis, Rachel Blau. *Writing Beyond the Ending: Narrative Strategies of Twentieth-Century Women Writers.* Bloomington: Indiana University Press, 1985.

Edwards, Thomas R. "An American Education." *New York Review of Books* 1984; reprinted in Felton, *The Critical Response to Joan Didion,* 190–95.

Eisenstein, Hester, and Alice Jardine, eds. *The Future of Difference.* New Brunswick, N.J.: Rutgers University Press, 1985.

English, Sarah. "*The Accidental Tourist* and *The Odyssey.*" In Salwak, *Anne Tyler as Novelist,* 155–61.

Epstein, Grace A. "Out of Blue Water: Dream Flight and Narrative Construction in the Novels of Toni Morrison." In *State of the Fantastic: Studies in the Theory and Practice of Fantastic Literature and Film,* ed. Nicholas Ruddick, 141–47. Westport, Conn.: Greenwood Press, 1992.

Erdrich, Louise. *Tracks.* New York: Henry Holt, 1988.

Erkkila, Betsy. "Ethnicity, Literary Theory, and the Grounds of Resistance." *American Quarterly* 47 (1995): 563–95.

Evans, Elizabeth. "Early Years and Influences." In Salwak, *Anne Tyler as Novelist,* 1–14.

Evers, Larry. Introduction to Mary Austin, *The Land of Journeys' Ending.* 1924. Reprint, Tucson: University of Arizona Press, 1983.

Felton, Sharon. "Introduction." In Felton, *The Critical Response to Joan Didion,* 1–11.

———, ed. *The Critical Response to Joan Didion.* Westport, Conn.: Greenwood Press, 1994.

Fetterley, Judith. "*My Ántonia,* Jim Burden, and the Dilemma of the Lesbian Writer." In Spector, *Gender Studies,* 43–59.

Fink, Augusta. *I-Mary: A Biography of Mary Austin.* Tucson: University of Arizona Press, 1983.

Finnell, Susanna. "Unwriting the Quest: Margaret Atwood's Fiction and *The Handmaid's Tale.*" In *Women and the Journey: The Female Travel Experience,* ed. Bonnie Frederick and Susan H. McLeod, 199–215. Pullman: Washington State University Press, 1993.

Fischer, Mike. "Pastoralism and Its Discontents: Willa Cather and the Burden of Imperialism." *Mosaic* 23, no. 1 (1990): 31–44.

Fisher-Wirth, Ann. "Dispossession and Redemption in the Novels of Willa Cather." In Rosowski, *Cather Studies I,* 36–54.

———. "Love, Work, and Willa Cather." In Nelson, *Private Voices, Public Lives,* 11–18.

———. "Out of the Mother: Loss in *My Ántonia.*" In Rosowski, *Cather Studies II,* 41–71.

Foster, Thomas. "History, Critical Theory, and Women's Social Practices: 'Women's Time' and *Housekeeping.*" *Signs* 14 (1988): 73–99.

Fraiman, Susan. *Unbecoming Women: British Women Writers and the Novel of Development.* New York: Columbia University Press, 1993.

Freiert, William F. "Anne Tyler's Accidental Ulysses." *Classical and Modern Literature* 10 (1989): 71–79.

Friedman, Ellen G., ed. *Joan Didion: Essays and Conversations.* Princeton, N.J.: Ontario Review Press, 1984.

Fryer, Judith. *Felicitous Space: The Imaginative Structures of Edith Wharton and Willa Cather.* Chapel Hill: University of North Carolina Press, 1986.

Fussell, Betty. "All That Jazz." *Lear's,* October 1, 1992; reprinted in Taylor-Guthrie, *Conversations with Toni Morrison,* 280–87.

Gabbin, Joanne V. *Sterling A. Brown: Building the Black Aesthetic Tradition.* Charlottesville: University Press of Virginia, 1994.

Gallop, Jane. Introduction to "Psychoanalysis and Feminism in France." In Eisenstein and Jardine, *The Future of Difference,* 106–7.

Garrison, Dee. *Mary Heaton Vorse: The Life of an American Insurgent.* Philadelphia: Temple University Press, 1989.

Gates, Henry Louis, Jr. *The Signifying Monkey: A Theory of Afro-American Literary Criticism.* New York: Oxford University Press, 1988.

Gelfant, Blanche H. "The Forgotten Reaping Hook: Sex in *My Ántonia.*" *American Literature* 43 (1971): 60–82.

———. *Women Writing in America: Voices in Collage.* Hanover, N.H.: University Press of New England, 1984.

———. " 'What Was It . . . ?': The Secret of Family Accord in *One of Ours.*" In Murphy, *Willa Cather,* 85–102.

Gelpi, Albert. "Introduction." In Gelpi, *Denise Levertov: Selected Criticism,* 1–8.

———, ed. *Denise Levertov: Selected Criticism.* Ann Arbor: University of Michigan Press, 1993.

Geyh, Paula E. "Burning Down the House? Domestic Space and Feminine Subjectivity in Marilynne Robinson's *Housekeeping.*" *Contemporary Literature* 34 (1993): 103–22.

Giannone, Richard. "Willa Cather and the Unfinished Drama of Deliverance." *Prairie Schooner* 52 (1978): 25–46.

Gibson, Mary Ellis. "Family as Fate: The Novels of Anne Tyler." *Southern Literary Journal* 15, no. 3 (1983): 47–58.

Gilbert, Sandra M. "Revolutionary Love: Denise Levertov and the Poetics of Politics." *Parnassus* 1985; reprinted in Gelpi, *Denise Levertov,* 201–17.

Gilbert, Sandra M., and Susan Gubar. *The Madwoman in the Attic: The Woman Writer and the Nineteenth-Century Imagination.* New Haven: Yale University Press, 1979.

———. *No Man's Land: The Place of the Woman Writer in the Twentieth Century.* Vol. 2, *Sexchanges.* New Haven: Yale University Press, 1989.

Gilbert, Susan. "Anne Tyler." In *Southern Women Writers: The New Generation,* ed. Tonette Bond Inge, 251–78. Tuscaloosa: University of Alabama Press, 1990.

———. "Private Lives and Public Issues: Anne Tyler's Prize-Winning Novels." In Stephens, *The Fiction of Anne Tyler,* 136–45.

Gilman, Charlotte Perkins. *The Living of Charlotte Perkins Gilman: An Autobiography.* New York: Appleton-Century, 1935.

Gilroy, Paul. *Modernity and Double Consciousness.* Cambridge: Harvard University Press, 1993.

Giltrow, Janet, and David Stouck. "Willa Cather and a Grammar for Things 'Not Named.' " *Style* 26 (1992): 91–113.

Goffman, Carolyn. "Beyond Reportage in *Salvador.*" *Connecticut Review* 13, no. 2 (1991): 15–22.

Goheen, Cynthia J. "Rebirth of the Seafarer: Sarah Orne Jewett's *The Country of the Pointed Firs.*" *Colby Library Quarterly* 23 (1987): 154–64.

Graulich, Melody. Afterword to Mary Austin, *Cactus Thorn.* Reno: University of Nevada Press, 1988.

———. Afterword to Mary Austin, *Earth Horizon.* 1932. Albuquerque: University of New Mexico Press, 1991.

———. Introduction to *Western Trails: A Collection of Short Stories by Mary Austin.* Reno: University of Nevada Press, 1987.

———. "Speaking Across Boundaries and Sharing the Loss of a Child." In Nelson, *Private Voices, Public Lives,* 163–82.

Griffin, Farah Jasmine. *"Who Set You Flowin'?": The African-American Migration Narrative.* New York: Oxford University Press, 1995.

Grumbach, Doris P. "A Study of the Small Room in *The Professor's House.*" *Women's Studies* 11 (1984): 327–45.

Gullette, Margaret Morganroth. *Safe at Last in the Middle Years; The Invention of the Midlife Progress Novel: Saul Bellow, Margaret Drabble, Anne Tyler, and John Updike.* Berkeley: University of California Press, 1988.

Hanley, Lynne T. "To El Salvador." *Massachusetts Review* 24 (1983): 13–29.

Harris, A. Leslie. "Myth as Structure in Toni Morrison's *Song of Solomon.*" *MELUS* 7, no. 3 (1980): 69–82.

Harris, Trudier. "Escaping Slavery But Not Its Images." In *Toni Morrison: Critical Perspectives, Past and Present,* ed. Henry Louis Gates, Jr., and K. A. Appiah, 330–41. New York: Amistad, 1993.

Hartman, Charles O. *Jazz Text: Voice and Improvisation in Poetry, Jazz, and Song.* Princeton: Princeton University Press, 1991.

Harvey, Sally Peltier. *Redefining the American Dream: The Novels of Willa Cather.* Rutherford, N.J.: Fairleigh Dickinson University Press, 1995.

Heilbrun, Carolyn. *Reinventing Womanhood.* New York: Norton, 1979.

Heller, Dana A. *The Feminization of Quest-Romance: Radical Departures.* Austin: University of Texas Press, 1990.

Henderson, Katherine Usher. "The Bond between Narrator and Heroine in *Democracy.*" In *American Women Writing Fiction: Memory, Identity, Family, Space,* ed. Mickey Pearlman, 69–93. Lexington: University Press of Kentucky, 1989.

Higonnet, Margaret R. "New Cartographies, an Introduction." In *Reconfigured Spheres: Feminist Explorations of Literary Space,* ed. Higonnet and Joan Templeton, 1–19. Amherst: University of Massachusetts Press, 1994.

Hinchman, Sandra K. "Didion's Political Tropics: *Miami* and the Basis for Community." In Felton, *The Critical Response to Joan Didion,* 233–39.

Hine, Darlene Clark. "Black Migration to the Urban Midwest: The Gender Dimension, 1915–1945." In *The Great Migration in Historical Perspective: New Dimensions of Race, Class, and Gender,* ed. Joe William Trotter, Jr., 127–46. Bloomington: Indiana University Press, 1991.

Hirsch, Marianne. *The Mother/Daughter Plot: Narrative, Psychoanalysis, Feminism.* Bloomington: Indiana University Press, 1989.

hooks, bell. *Ain't I a Woman: Black Women and Feminism.* Boston: South End Press, 1981.

Hughes, Langston. *Black Magic: A Pictorial History of the Negro in American Entertainment*. Englewood Cliffs, N.J.: Prentice-Hall, 1967.

———. *Selected Poems of Langston Hughes*. New York: Random House Vintage Books, 1959.

Humphrey, Lin T. "Exploration of a Not-So-Accidental Novel." In Salwak, *Anne Tyler as Novelist,* 147–54.

Hurston, Zora Neale. *Dust Tracks on a Road*. 1942. Reprint, New York: HarperCollins Perennial Library, 1991.

———. *Their Eyes Were Watching God*. 1937. Reprint, New York: Harper and Row Perennial Library, 1990.

Jaycox, Faith. "Regeneration through Liberation: Mary Austin's 'The Walking Woman' and Western Narrative Formula." *Legacy* 6 (1989): 5–12.

Jewett, Sarah Orne. "The Confessions of a Housebreaker." In *The Mate of the Daylight, and Friends Ashore*. Boston: Houghton Mifflin, 1884.

———. *The Country of the Pointed Firs and Other Stories*. With an introduction by Mary Ellen Chase and an introduction to the Norton Edition by Marjorie Pryse. New York: Norton, 1981.

———. *The Letters of Sarah Orne Jewett*. Edited by Annie Fields. Boston: Houghton Mifflin, 1911.

Johnson, Maria V. " 'You *Just* Can't Keep a Good Woman Down': Alice Walker Sings the Blues." *African American Review* 30 (1995): 221–36.

Jones, Anne Goodwin. "Home at Last, and Homesick Again: The Ten Novels of Anne Tyler." *Hollins Critic* 23, no. 2 (1986): 1–13.

Jones, Carolyn. "Race and Intimacy in Murray's *South to a Very Old Place*." Paper delivered at the American Literature Association, Baltimore, May 1995.

Kakutani, Michiko. "Joan Didion: Staking Out California." *The New York Times Magazine,* June 10, 1979; reprinted in Friedman, *Joan Didion,* 29–42.

Kanoza, Theresa. "Mentors and Maternal Role Models: The Healthy Mean between Extremes in Anne Tyler's Fiction." In Stephens, *The Fiction of Anne Tyler,* 28–39.

Kazin, Alfred. *On Native Grounds*. 1942. New York: Harcourt Brace Jovanovich, 1970.

Keenan, Sally. " 'Four Hundred Years of Silence': Myth, History, and Motherhood in Toni Morrison's *Beloved*." In *Recasting the World: Writing after Colonialism,* ed. Jonathan White, 45–81. Baltimore: Johns Hopkins University Press, 1993.

Keene, Ann. "Questions of Travel: The Journeys of Willa Cather." Paper delivered at the Sixth International Seminar on Willa Cather, in Quebec, on June 29, 1995.

Kirby, Kathleen M. "Thinking through the Boundary: The Politics of Location, Subjects, and Space." *Boundary II* 20, no. 2 (1993): 173–89.

Klein, Marcus. Introduction to Willa Cather, *My Mortal Enemy*. 1926. New York: Random House Vintage Classics, 1990.

Kolodny, Annette. *The Land Before Her: Fantasy and Experience of the American Frontiers, 1630–1860.* Chapel Hill: University of North Carolina Press, 1984.

Kristeva, Julia. "Women's Time." Translated by Alice Jardine and Harry Blake. In *Feminist Theory: A Critique of Ideology,* ed. Nannerl O. Keohane, Michelle Z. Rosaldo, and Barbara C. Gelpi, 31–53. Chicago: University of Chicago Press, 1982.

Langlois, Karen S. "Marketing the American Indian: Mary Austin and the Business of Writing." In *A Living of Words: American Women in Print Culture,* ed. Susan Albertine, 151–68. Knoxville: University of Tennessee Press, 1995.

————. "Mary Austin and Lincoln Steffens." *Huntington Library Quarterly* 49 (1986): 357–84.

Larsen, Nella. *Quicksand and Passing.* Edited by Deborah E. McDowell. New Brunswick, N.J.: Rutgers University Press, 1986.

Lassner, Phyllis. "Escaping the Mirror of Sameness: Marilynne Robinson's *Housekeeping.*" In *Mother Puzzles: Daughters and Mothers in Contemporary American Literature,* ed. Mickey Pearlman, 49–58. New York: Greenwood Press, 1989.

Lauter, Estella. *Women as Mythmakers: Poetry and Visual Art by Twentieth-Century Women.* Bloomington: Indiana University Press, 1984.

Lawrence, Karen R. *Penelope Voyages: Women and Travel in the British Literary Tradition.* Ithaca: Cornell University Press, 1994.

Lerner, Gerda. *Black Women in White America: A Documentary History.* New York: Pantheon, 1972.

Levenback, Karen L. "Functions of (Picturing) Memory." In Salwak, *Anne Tyler as Novelist,* 77–85.

Levertov, Denise. *Breathing the Water.* New York: New Directions, 1987.

————. *Candles in Babylon.* New York: New Directions, 1982.

————. *A Door in the Hive.* New York: New Directions, 1989.

————. *Footprints.* New York: New Directions, 1972.

————. *Life in the Forest.* New York: New Directions, 1978.

————. *Light Up the Cave.* New York: New Directions, 1981.

————. *To Stay Alive.* New York: New Directions, 1971.

Limerick, Patricia Nelson. *The Legacy of Conquest: The Unbroken Past of the American West.* New York: Norton, 1987.

Loris, Michelle Carbone. "Innocence, Loss, and Recovery in the Art of Joan Didion." *Dissertation Abstracts International* A46 (1985): 162.

Lownsbrough, John. "Didion Moves East But Remains at Home in the Essay." *Toronto Globe and Mail,* August 22, 1992; reprinted in Felton, *The Critical Response to Joan Didion,* 241–43.

Luhan, Mabel Dodge. *Mary Austin, A Memorial.* Edited by Willard Hougland. Santa Fe: Laboratory of Anthropology, 1944.

———. *Movers and Shakers*. New York: Harcourt, Brace, 1936.

Madigan, Mark. "Willa Cather and Dorothy Canfield Fisher: Rift, Reconciliation, and *One of Ours*." In Rosowski, *Cather Studies I*, 115–29.

Mallon, Anne-Marie. "Sojourning Women: Homelessness and Transcendence in *Housekeeping*." *Critique* 30 (1989): 95–105.

Mallon, Thomas. "The Limits of History in the Novels of Joan Didion." *Critique* 21 (1980); reprinted in Friedman, *Joan Didion*, 60–67.

———. Review of *Democracy*. *American Spectator* 17 (August 1984); reprinted in Felton, *The Critical Response to Joan Didion*, 195–98.

Manning, Carol S. "Welty, Tyler, and Traveling Salesmen: The Wandering Hero Unhorsed." In Stephens, *The Fiction of Anne Tyler*, 110–18.

Martin, Waldo. "The Making of Black America." In *Making America: The Society and Culture of the United States*, ed. Luther S. Luedtke, 341–61. Chapel Hill: University of North Carolina Press, 1992.

Mathieson, Barbara Offutt. "Memory and Mother Love: Toni Morrison's Dyad." In *Memory, Narrative, and Identity: New Essays in Ethnic American Literatures*, ed. Amrithit Singh, Joseph T. Skerrett, Jr., and Robert E. Hogan, 212–32. Boston: Northeastern University Press, 1994.

Matusow, Allen J. *The Unraveling of America: A History of Liberalism in the 1960s*. New York: Harper and Row, 1984.

McClure, Charlotte. "From Impersonators to Persons: Breaking Patterns, Finding Voices." In Nelson, *Private Voices, Public Lives*, 225–37.

McKay, Nellie. "An Interview with Toni Morrison." *Contemporary Literature* 24 (1983): 413–29.

McNall, Sally Allen. "The American Woman Writer in Transition: Freeman, Austin, and Cather." In *Seeing Female: Social Roles and Personal Lives*, ed. Sharon S. Brehm, 43–52. New York: Greenwood Press, 1988.

Meese, Elizabeth A. *Crossing the Double-Cross: The Practice of Feminist Criticism*. Chapel Hill: University of North Carolina Press, 1986.

Merivale, Patricia. "Through Greene-land in Drag: Joan Didion's *A Book of Common Prayer*." *Pacific Coast Philology* 15 (1980); revised and reprinted as "The Search for the Other Woman: Joan Didion and the Female Artist Parable," in Spector, *Gender Studies*, 133–47; also in Felton, *The Critical Response to Joan Didion*, 99–105.

Michaels, Marguerite. "Anne Tyler, Writer 8:05 to 3:30." *New York Times Book Review*, May 8, 1977; reprinted in Petry, *Critical Essays on Anne Tyler*, 40–44.

Micucci, Dana. "An Inspired Life: Toni Morrison Writes and a Generation Listens." *Chicago Tribune*, May 31, 1992; reprinted in Taylor-Guthrie, *Conversations with Toni Morrison*, 275–79.

Miles, Josephine. *Collected Poems, 1930–83*. Urbana: University of Illinois Press, 1983.

Millay, Edna St. Vincent. *Collected Poems*. New York: Harper and Row, 1956.

Miller, Nancy K. *The Heroine's Text: Readings in the French and English Novel, 1722–1782*. New York: Columbia University Press, 1980.

———. *Subject to Change: Reading Feminist Writing*. New York: Columbia University Press, 1988.

Minter, David. *A Cultural History of the American Novel*. Cambridge: Cambridge University Press, 1994.

Moers, Ellen. *Literary Women*. Garden City, N.Y.: Doubleday, 1976.

Moon, Michael, and Cathy N. Davidson, eds. *Subjects and Citizens: Nation, Race, and Gender from* Oroonoko *to* Anita Hill. Durham: Duke University Press, 1995.

Morrison, Toni. *Beloved*. New York: Knopf, 1987; NAL Penguin Plume, 1988.

———. *The Bluest Eye*. 1970. New York: Pocket Books, 1972.

———. *Jazz*. 1992. Reprint, New York: Penguin Books, 1993.

———. *Playing in the Dark*. Cambridge: Harvard University Press, 1992.

———. *Song of Solomon*. 1977. New York: NAL, 1978.

———. *Sula*. 1973. New York: Bantam Books, 1975.

Mosley, Merritt. "Joan Didion's Symbolic Landscapes." *South Carolina Review* 1989; reprinted in Felton, *The Critical Response to Joan Didion*, 133–43.

Moyers, Bill. "A Conversation with Toni Morrison." The "World of Ideas" series, Films for the Humanities and Sciences; reprinted in Taylor-Guthrie, *Conversations with Toni Morrison*, 262–74.

Muggli, Mark Z. *Temperamental Journeys: Essays on the Modern Literature of Travel*. Athens: University of Georgia Press, 1992.

Murphy, John J., ed. *Willa Cather: Family, Community, and History*. Provo, Utah: Brigham Young University Humanities Publications Center, 1990.

Murray, Albert. *South to a Very Old Place*. New York: McGraw-Hill, 1971.

Nadel, Alan. "Failed Cultural Narratives: America in the Postwar Era and the Story of *Democracy*." *Boundary II* 19, no. 1 (1992): 95–120.

Naylor, Gloria, and Toni Morrison. "A Conversation." *Southern Review* 21 (1985): 567–93.

Nelson, Nancy Owen, ed. *Private Voices, Public Lives: Women Speak on the Literary Life*. Denton: University of North Texas Press, 1995.

Nesanovich, Stella. "The Early Novels: A Reconsideration." In Salwak, *Anne Tyler as Novelist*, 15–32.

Nichols, Charles H., ed. *Arna Bontemps, Langston Hughes: Letters, 1925–1967*. 1980. New York: Paragon House, 1990.

Norwood, Vera. Introduction to Mary Austin, *Heath Anthology of American Literature*. 2nd ed. Lexington, Mass.: D. C. Heath, 1994.

———. "The Photographer and the Naturalist: Laura Gilpin and Mary Austin in the Southwest." *Journal of American Culture* 5, no. 2 (1982): 1–28.

O'Brien, Sharon. *Willa Cather: The Emerging Voice.* New York: Oxford University Press, 1987.

Omolade, Barbara. "Black Women and Feminism." In Eisenstein and Jardine, *The Future of Difference,* 247–57.

Padilla, Genaro M. *My History, Not Yours: The Formation of Mexican American Autobiography.* Madison: University of Wisconsin Press, 1993.

Paton, Priscilla. Letter to Janis P. Stout, January 10, 1995. Author's private collection.

Pearce, T. M. *Literary America, 1903–1934: The Mary Austin Letters.* Westport, Conn.: Greenwood Press, 1979.

———. "Mary Austin and the Pattern of New Mexico." *Southwest Review* 22 (1937): 140–48; reprinted in *Southwesterners Write: The American Southwest in Stories and Articles by Thirty-Two Contributors,* ed. T. M. Pearce and A. P. Thomason, 305–14. Albuquerque: University of New Mexico Press, 1946.

———. *Mary Hunter Austin.* New York: Twayne Publishers, 1965.

Peltier, Sally. *Redefining the American Dream: The Novels of Willa Cather.* Rutherford, N.J.: Fairleigh Dickinson University Press, 1995.

Peters, Catherine. "Opting Out." *London Times Literary Supplement* August 27, 1976; reprinted in Petry, *Critical Essays on Anne Tyler,* 80–81.

Petesch, Donald A. *A Spy in the Enemy's Country: The Emergence of Modern Black Literature.* Iowa City: University of Iowa Press, 1989.

Petry, Alice Hall. "Tyler and Feminism." In Salwak, *Anne Tyler as Novelist,* 33–42.

———, ed. *Critical Essays on Anne Tyler.* New York: G. K. Hall, 1992.

Pollitt, Katha. Review of *Searching for Caleb. New York Times Book Review,* January 18, 1976; reprinted in Petry, *Critical Essays on Anne Tyler,* 82–83.

Porter, Katherine Anne. *The Collected Essays and Occasional Writings of Katherine Anne Porter.* Boston: Houghton Mifflin/Seymour Lawrence, 1970.

———. *The Collected Stories.* New York: Harcourt, Brace and World, 1965.

———. Letter to Robert Penn Warren, October 8, 1942. The Robert Penn Warren Papers, Yale Collection of American Literature, Beinecke Rare Book and Manuscript Library, Yale University.

———. Marginalia, Porter Collection, McKeldin Library, The University of Maryland.

Porter, Nancy. Afterword to Mary Austin, *A Woman of Genius.* 1912. Old Westbury, N.Y.: Feminist Press, 1985.

Pratt, Annis. *Archetypal Patterns in Women's Fiction.* Bloomington: Indiana University Press, 1981.

———. "*Surfacing* and the Rebirth Journey." In *The Art of Margaret Atwood,* ed. Arnold Davidson and Cathy N. Davidson, 139–57. Toronto: Anansi, 1981.

Pratt, Mary Louise. *Imperial Eyes: Travel Writing and Transculturation.* New York: Routledge, 1992.

Prettyman, Quandra. "Visibility and Difference: Black Women in History and Literature—Pieces of a Paper and Some Ruminations." In Eisenstein and Jardine, *The Future of Difference,* 239–46.

Pryse, Marjorie. Introduction to Mary Austin, *Stories from the Country of Lost Borders.* New Brunswick: Rutgers University Press, 1987.

Pulsipher, Jenny Hale. "Expatriation and Reconciliation: The Pilgrimage Tradition in *Sapphira and the Slave Girl.*" *Literature and Belief* 8 (1988): 89–100.

Putnam, Ann. " 'Tangled Together Like Badly Cast Fishing Line': The Reader and the Text in Katherine Anne Porter's 'Pale Horse, Pale Rider.' " In Nelson, *Private Voices, Public Lives,* 3–10.

Quiello, Rose. "Breakdowns and Breakthroughs: The Hysterical Use of Language." In Salwak, *Anne Tyler as Novelist,* 50–64.

Quirk, Tom. *Bergson and American Culture: The Worlds of Willa Cather and Wallace Stevens.* Chapel Hill: University of North Carolina Press, 1990.

Randisi, Jennifer L. "The Journey Nowhere in Didion's *Run River.*" *Markham Review* 11 (1982): 41–43.

Ravits, Martha. "Extending the American Range: Marilynne Robinson's *Housekeeping.*" *American Literature* 61 (1989): 644–66.

Rebolledo, Tey Diana. *Women Singing in the Snow: A Cultural Analysis of Chicana Literature.* Tucson: University of Arizona Press, 1995.

Reynolds, Guy. *Willa Cather in Context: Progress, Race, Empire.* New York: St. Martin's Press, 1996.

Rich, Adrienne. *The Fact of a Doorframe: Poems Selected and New, 1950–1984.* New York: Norton, 1984.

———. *Of Woman Born: Motherhood as Experience and Institution.* New York: Norton, 1976.

———. "Vesuvius at Home: The Power of Emily Dickinson." In *On Lies, Secrets, and Silence: Selected Prose, 1966–1978,* 157–83. New York: Norton, 1979.

Rilke, Rainer Maria. *Selected Works.* Vol. 2, *Poetry,* Translated by J. B. Leishman. London: Hogarth Press, 1967.

Robertson, Mary F. "Anne Tyler: Medusa Points and Contact Points." In *Contemporary American Women Writers: Narrative Strategies* (1985); reprinted in Petry, *Critical Essays on Anne Tyler,* 184–204.

Robinson, Marilynne. *Housekeeping.* New York: Farrar, Straus & Giroux, 1980.

Rody, Caroline. "Toni Morrison's *Beloved:* History, 'Rememory,' and a 'Clamor for a Kiss.' " *American Literary History* 7 (1995): 92–119.

Roethke, Theodore. *The Collected Poems.* Garden City, N.Y.: Doubleday Anchor Books, 1975.

Roman, Margaret. *Sarah Orne Jewett: Reconstructing Gender.* Tuscaloosa: University of Alabama Press, 1992.

Romines, Ann. *The Home Plot: Women, Writing, and Domestic Ritual.* Amherst: University of Massachusetts Press, 1992.

———. "The Voices from the Little House." In Nelson, *Private Voices, Public Lives,* 19–28.

Rose, Ellen Cronan. "Through the Looking Glass: When Women Tell Fairy Tales." In Abel, Hirsch, and Langland, *The Voyage In,* 209–27.

Rose, Jacqueline. "Where Does the Misery Come From?: Psychoanalysis, Feminism, and the Event." In *Feminism and Psychoanalysis,* ed. Richard Feldstein and Judith Roof, 25–39. Ithaca: Cornell University Press, 1989.

Rosowski, Susan J. "Rewriting the Love Plot Our Way: Women and Work." In Nelson, *Private Voices, Public Lives,* 29–38.

———. *The Voyage Perilous: Willa Cather's Romanticism.* Lincoln: University of Nebraska Press, 1986.

———. "Willa Cather and the Intimacy of Art, Or: In Defense of Privacy." *Willa Cather Pioneer Memorial Newsletter* 36 (1992–93): 47–53.

———. "Willa Cather's Subverted Endings and Gendered Time." In Rosowski, *Cather Studies I,* 68–88.

———, ed. *Cather Studies I.* Lincoln: University of Nebraska Press, 1990.

———, ed. *Cather Studies II.* Lincoln: University of Nebraska Press, 1993.

Rukeyser, Muriel. *The Collected Poems.* New York: McGraw Hill, 1978.

Rushdie, Salman. *Imaginary Homelands: Essays and Criticism, 1981–1991.* London: Granta Books, 1991.

———. *The Wizard of Oz.* London: BFI Publishing, 1992.

Russell, George. "Mooning over Miami." *Commentary* 85, no. 1 (1988): 69–72.

Ryan, Maureen. "No Woman's Land: Gender in Willa Cather's *One of Ours.*" *Studies in American Fiction* 18 (1990–91): 65–75.

Salwak, Dale, ed. *Anne Tyler as Novelist.* Iowa City: University of Iowa Press, 1994.

Savannah Unit of the Georgia Writers' Project of the Work Projects Administration. *Drums and Shadows: Survival Studies among the Georgia Coastal Negroes.* Foreword by Guy B. Johnson. Athens: University of Georgia Press, 1940.

Schlenz, Mark. "Rhetorics of Region in *Starry Adventure* and *Death Comes for the Archbishop.*" In *Regionalism Reconsidered: New Approaches to the Field,* ed. David Jordan, 65–85. New York: Garland Publishing, 1994.

Schow, H. Wayne. "*Out of Africa, The White Album,* and the Possibility of Tragic Affirmation." *English Studies* 67 (1986): 35–50.

Schriber, Mary Suzanne. "Edith Wharton and Travel Writing as Self-Discovery." *American Literature* 59 (1987): 257–67.

Schwarz, Judith. *Radical Feminists of Heterodoxy: Greenwich Village, 1912–1940.* Lebanon, N.H.: Victoria Publishers, 1982.

Seidenberg, Robert, and Karen DeCrow. *Women Who Marry Houses: Panic and Protest in Agoraphobia.* New York: McGraw Hill, 1983.

Sergeant, Elizabeth Shepley. *Willa Cather: A Memoir.* 1953. Athens: Ohio University Press, 1992.

Sexton, Anne. *The Death Notebooks.* Boston: Houghton Mifflin, 1974.

Shafer, Aileen Chris. "Beauty and the Transformed Beast: Fairy Tales and Myths in *Morgan's Passing.*" In Salwak, *Anne Tyler as Novelist,* 125–37.

Shaw, Patrick W. *Willa Cather and the Art of Conflict: Re-Visioning Her Creative Imagination.* Troy, N.Y.: Whitston Publishing Co., 1992.

Shelton, Frank W. "Anne Tyler's Houses." In Stephens, *The Fiction of Anne Tyler,* 40–46.

———. "The Necessary Balance: Distance and Sympathy in the Novels of Anne Tyler." *Southern Review* 20 (1984): 851–60.

Showalter, Elaine. *Sister's Choice: Tradition and Change in American Women's Writing.* Oxford: Oxford University Press, 1994.

Simpson, Louis. *Collected Poems.* New York: Paragon House, 1988.

Skaggs, Merrill. *After the World Broke in Two: The Later Novels of Willa Cather.* Charlottesville: University Press of Virginia, 1991.

———. "Death in C Major: Willa Cather's Perilous Journey Toward the Ordinary in *Lucy Gayheart.*" *Literature and Belief* 8 (1988): 76–88.

Slote, Bernice, ed. *The Kingdom of Art: Willa Cather's First Principles and Critical Statements, 1893–1896.* Lincoln: University of Nebraska Press, 1966.

Smith, Lorrie. "Songs of Experience: Denise Levertov's Political Poetry." In *Contemporary Literature* 1986; reprinted in Gelpi, *Denise Levertov,* 177–197.

Smith-Rosenberg, Carroll. *Disorderly Conduct: Visions of Gender in Victorian America.* New York: Knopf, 1985.

Spector, Judith, ed. *Gender Studies: New Directions in Feminist Criticism.* Bowling Green, Ohio: Bowling Green University Popular Press, 1986.

Spicer, Edward H. *Cycles of Conquest: The Impact of Spain, Mexico, and the United States on the Indians of the Southwest, 1533–1960.* Tucson: University of Arizona Press, 1962.

Sprengnether, Madelon. *The Spectral Mother: Freud, Feminism, and Psychoanalysis.* Ithaca: Cornell University Press, 1990.

Stamberg, Susan. "Cautionary Tales." Interview aired on National Public Radio, April 4, 1977; reprinted in Friedman, *Joan Didion,* 22–28.

Stanton, Domna C. "Difference on Trial: A Critique of the Maternal Metaphor in Cixous, Irigaray, and Kristeva." In *The Poetics of Gender,* ed. Nancy K. Miller, 157–82. New York: Columbia University Press, 1986.

Stead, Christina. *The Man Who Loved Children.* Introduction by Randall Jarrell. 1940. New York: Holt, Rinehart and Winston, 1965.

Stephens, C. Ralph, ed. *The Fiction of Anne Tyler.* Jackson: University Press of Mississippi, 1990.

Stepto, Robert. *From Behind the Veil: A Study of Afro-American Narrative.* 2nd ed. Urbana: University of Illinois Press, 1991.

———. " 'Intimate Things in Place': A Conversation with Toni Morrison." *Massachusetts Review* 18 (1977): 473–89; reprinted in *Chant of Saints,* ed. Michael S. Harper and Robert B. Stepto, 213–29. Urbana: University of Illinois Press, 1979.

Stineman, Esther Lanigan. *Mary Austin: Song of a Maverick.* New Haven: Yale University Press, 1989.

Stouck, David. "Historical Essay." In Willa Cather, *O Pioneers!,* The Scholarly Edition, ed. Susan J. Rosowski and Charles W. Mignon, 283–303. Lincoln: University of Nebraska Press, 1992.

———. "Mary Austin and Willa Cather." *Willa Cather Pioneer Memorial Newsletter* 23, no. 2 (1979): n.p.

———. "Willa Cather and the Indian Heritage." *Twentieth-Century Literature* 22 (1976): 433–43.

———. *Willa Cather's Imagination.* Lincoln: University of Nebraska Press, 1975.

Stout, Janis P. "Breaking Out: The Journey of the American Woman Poet." *North Dakota Quarterly* 56, no. 1 (1988): 40–53.

———. *The Journey Narrative in American Literature: Patterns and Departures.* Westport, Conn.: Greenwood Press, 1983.

———. *Strategies of Reticence: Silence and Meaning in the Works of Jane Austen, Willa Cather, Katherine Anne Porter, and Joan Didion.* Charlottesville: University Press of Virginia, 1990.

———. "Willa Cather and Mary Austin: Intersections and Influence." *Southwestern American Literature* 21, no. 2 (1996): 39–60.

Strandberg, Victor. "Passion and Delusion in *A Book of Common Prayer.*" *Modern Fiction Studies* 27 (1981); reprinted in Friedman, *Joan Didion,* 147–63.

Tate, Claudia. "Toni Morrison." In *Black Women Writers at Work,* ed. Tate, 117–31. New York: Continuum, 1983.

Taylor-Guthrie, Danielle, ed. *Conversations with Toni Morrison.* Jackson: University Press of Mississippi, 1994.

Templin, Charlotte. "Tyler's Literary Reputation." In Salwak, *Anne Tyler as Novelist,* 175–96.

Thornton, Jerome E. " 'Goin' on de Muck': The Paradoxical Journey of the Black American Hero." *CLA Journal* 31 (1988): 261–80.

Towers, Robert. "Roughing It." *New York Review of Books,* November 10, 1988; reprinted in Petry, *Critical Essays on Anne Tyler,* 145–47.

Tracy, Steven C. *Langston Hughes and the Blues.* Urbana: University of Illinois Press, 1988.

Turner, Elizabeth Hutton, ed. *Jacob Lawrence: The Migration Series.* Introduction by

Henry Louis Gates, Jr. Washington, D.C.: Rappahannock Press, in association with the Phillips Collection, 1993.

Tyler, Anne. *The Accidental Tourist.* 1985. Reprint, New York: Berkley, 1986.

———. "Because I Want More Than One Life." *Washington Post,* August 15, 1976; reprinted in Petry, *Critical Essays on Anne Tyler,* 45–49.

———. *Breathing Lessons.* New York: Knopf, 1988.

———. *Celestial Navigation.* 1974. Reprint, New York: Ballantine, 1993.

———. *The Clock Winder.* 1972. Reprint, New York: Ballantine, 1992.

———. *Dinner at the Homesick Restaurant.* 1982. Reprint, New York: Ballantine, 1992.

———. *Earthly Possessions.* 1977. Reprint, New York: Berkley, 1984.

———. "The Fine, Full World of Welty." *Washington Star,* October 26, 1980, D1, D7.

———. *If Morning Ever Comes.* 1964. Reprint, New York: Berkley, 1983.

———. *Ladder of Years.* New York: Knopf, 1995.

———. *Morgan's Passing.* 1980. Reprint, New York: Ballantine, 1992.

———. *Saint Maybe.* 1991. Reprint, New York: Ballantine, 1992.

———. *Searching for Caleb.* 1975. Reprint, New York: Ballantine, 1993.

———. *A Slipping-Down Life.* 1970. Reprint, New York: Berkley, 1983.

———. "Still Just Writing." In *The Writer on Her Work: Contemporary Women Writers Reflect on Their Art and Situation,* ed. Janet Sternberg, 3–16. New York: Norton, 1980.

———. *The Tin Can Tree.* 1965. Reprint, New York: Ballantine, 1992.

———. "Why I Still Treasure 'The Little House.' " *New York Times Book Review,* November 9, 1986, 56.

Updike, John. "Loosened Roots." In Petry, *Critical Essays on Anne Tyler,* 88–91.

———. "More Substance, Complexity of Family Relationships—Buried Horrors of Family Life." *New Yorker,* April 5, 1982, 193–97.

Urgo, Joseph. *Willa Cather and the Myth of American Migration.* Urbana: University of Illinois Press, 1995.

Voelker, Joseph C. *Art and the Accidental in Anne Tyler.* Columbia: University of Missouri Press, 1989.

Wagner-Martin, Linda. "*Breathing Lessons:* A Domestic Success Story." In Salwak, *Anne Tyler as Novelist,* 162–74.

Walker, Alice. *Revolutionary Petunias and Other Poems.* New York: Harcourt Brace Jovanovich, 1973.

Warwick, Jack. *The Long Journey: Literary Themes of French Canada.* Toronto: University of Toronto Press, 1968.

Washington, Mary Helen. Foreword to Zora Neale Hurston, *Their Eyes Were Watching God.* New York: Harper & Row Perennial Library, 1990.

———. " 'I Love the Way Janie Crawford Left Her Husbands': Zora Neale Hurston's

Emergent Female Hero." In *Invented Lives: Narratives of Black Women, 1860–1960,* ed. Washington, 237–54. New York: Doubleday, 1987.

Welty, Eudora. *The Bride of Innisfallen and Other Stories.* New York: Harcourt, Brace, 1955.

———. *The Golden Apples.* New York: Harcourt, Brace, 1949.

———. "The House of Willa Cather." In *The Eye of the Story: Selected Essays and Reviews,* 41–60. New York: Random House, 1977.

———. *Losing Battles.* New York: Random House, 1970.

———. *The Optimist's Daughter.* New York: Random House, 1972.

Werner, Craig Hansen. *Playing the Changes: From Afro-Modernism to the Jazz Impulse.* Urbana: University of Illinois Press, 1994.

Wilcox, Leonard. "Narrative Technique and the Theme of Historical Continuity in the Novels of Joan Didion." In Friedman, *Joan Didion,* 68–80.

Williams, Deborah Gray. *Ar'n't I a Woman? Female Slaves in the Plantation South.* New York: Norton, 1985.

Winchell, Mark Royden. *Joan Didion.* Rev. ed. Boston: Twayne, 1989.

Wittenburg, Judith Bryant. "*Deephaven:* Sarah Orne Jewett's Exploratory Metafiction." *Studies in American Fiction* 19 (1991): 153–64.

Woodard, Charles L. *Ancestral Voice: Conversations with N. Scott Momaday.* Lincoln: University of Nebraska Press, 1989.

Woodress, James. "A Dutiful Daughter and Her Parents." In Murphy, *Willa Cather,* 19–31.

———. *Willa Cather: A Literary Life.* Lincoln: University of Nebraska Press, 1987.

———. *Willa Cather: Her Life and Art.* New York: Pegasus, 1970.

Wynn, Dudley. "Mary Austin, Woman Alone." *Virginia Quarterly Review* 13 (1937): 243–56.

Zahlan, Anne Ricketson. "Traveling Towards the Self: The Psychic Drama of Anne Tyler's *The Accidental Tourist.*" In Stephens, *The Fiction of Anne Tyler,* 84–96.

INDEX

adventure, masculine, 59, 86

African-American history, 161, 162, 165–66, 272 (nn. 43, 53); African-American novelists and, 148, 151, 156, 157, 161, 268 (n. 3), 268 (n. 4), 272 (n. 37); Toni Morrison and, 148, 149, 160–61, 165, 232

African-American literature, geography in, 150, 154, 156–57, 187; theme of confinement in, 160

African-Americans, and the South, 180

African diaspora, 147, 166, 170

Africans, flying, 150, 154, 163, 164, 165, 269 (n. 16)

agoraphobia, 13–14, 98, 106, 110, 120, 138, 144, 241 (n. 36)

Alexander's Bridge. See Cather, Willa

America, myth of, xvi, 148, 187, 198, 240 (n. 33), 248 (n. 1), 270 (n. 26)

Ammons, Elizabeth, 35, 64, 152, 270 (n. 22); on feminized landscape, 253 (n. 45)

Anderson, Chris, 200

androgyny, 44, 57, 59, 61, 107, 120, 122–23, 140–41, 143, 165, 186

Anzaldúa, Gloria, xv, 172

Apthorp, Elaine, 76

architectural images, 70, 240 (n. 29); walls, 15, 71, 92, 94–98, 102; windows and doors, 7, 12, 42, 95, 97–98, 194, 217,

223, 232, 237 (n. 5), 252 (n. 36), 255 (n. 5)

architecture, gendered, 12, 17

Armitage, Shelley, 46

Armitage, Susan H., 240 (n. 35)

artists, female, in fiction, 252–53 (n. 38)

Asian-American literature, xv

Atherton, Gertrude, 62

Atwood, Margaret, 1, 7

Austen, Jane, 238 (n. 17)

Austin, Mary, xiii, xiv, 7, 15, 19–20, 22, 29, 31, 39, 42, 43, 46, 57–58, 60, 62, 69, 74, 93, 102, 155, 190, 191, 193, 224, 230, 232; and American Indians, 29, 35, 40; and androgyny, 44, 57, 59, 61; career of, 31–32, 35, 37; and Cather, Willa, 62–65, 77, 93, 246 (n. 36), 249 (n. 2), 249 (n. 8), 259 (n. 90); and desert landscape, 31–32, 34, 35, 38, 253 (n. 45); and domesticity, 41, 47, 53, 192; and economic development, 245 (n. 15); feminism of, 30, 37, 40, 46, 47, 54, 244 (n. 6), 246–47 (n. 39); heterosexuality of, 103; and home, idea of, 28–29, 33–34, 38, 39, 46, 47, 57–59, 60, 191; home-centered journeys of, 28, 70, 103; home of (Casa Querida), 37–38, 56, 62, 63, 246 (n. 26); and Jewett, 28, 35, 104, 191; and liberation of women,

About the Author

JANIS P. STOUT is Professor of English at Texas A&M University. Her other books include *Sodoms in Eden: The City in American Fiction before 1860* (1976), *The Journey Narrative in American Literature: Patterns and Departures* (1983), *Strategies of Reticence: Silence and Meaning in the Works of Jane Austen, Willa Cather, Katherine Anne Porter, and Joan Didion* (1990), and *Katherine Anne Porter: A Sense of the Times* (1995), winner of the 1996 C. Hugh Holman Award of the Society for the Study of Southern Literature. She has also published three novels: *A Family Likeness* (1982), *Eighteen Holes* (1994), and *Home Truth* (1992).

Ⓧ 08/3/8

3995

25⁰⁰

10254/6 LICRT